REALIZING GOD

Lectures on Vedanta
by
SWAMI PRABHAVANANDA

Edited by
Edith Dickinson Tipple

Advaita Ashrama
(PUBLICATION DEPARTMENT)
5 DEHI ENTALLY ROAD · KOLKATA 700 014

Published by
Swami Bodhasarananda
Adhyaksha, Advaita Ashrama
Mayavati, Champawat, Uttarakhand
from its Publication Department, Kolkata
Email: mail@advaitaashrama.org
Website: www.advaitaashrama.org

First Edition, September 2010
3M3C

ISBN 978-81-7505-337-3

Printed in India at
Trio Process
Kolkata · 700 014

FOREWORD

This book has been edited from transcripts of Swami Prabhavananda's lectures and talks contained in the Archives of the Vedanta Society of Southern California. They span the years 1935-1976. I had intended to combine lectures of similar titles into a single chapter, but from year to year, even from month to month, the swami changed content when speaking on the same topic. Feeling that the lectures of the 1960s represent him at his prime, I began with those and afterward added valuable material from other decades. With a view to documenting his thought clearly, I have left material from each lecture as a separate item, with its original source in the Archives cited at the end. There are some unavoidable repetitions in such a presentation, but they serve to illustrate the swami's multi-faceted thinking on any given subject.

Swami Prabhavananda's only aim was to point the student toward realization of God – as he used to say, "by hook or by crook", meaning in any way that appealed. His use of the expression was typical of his understanding of the culture in which he spoke, in this instance referring to the crooked staff of the shepherd of lost souls, Lord Jesus Christ, reining in his wayward lambs. It also referred to a Bengali saying, "Adopt any means whatsoever, but keep your mind fixed on Krishna."

The task of presenting Swami Prabhavananda's legacy has been approached with a great sense of responsibility. I have tried not to intrude between him and the reader, but have striven to let his personality shine through on the printed page.[1] I am deeply indebted to Swami Krishnananda, who transcribed these lectures, to the VSSC Archives for making them available, and to David Nelson for editorial advice.

Edith Dickinson Tipple

1 August 2010

---

1. For biographical information see the Afterword.

CONTENTS

CONTENTS

RENAISSANCE OF VEDANTA

TODAY IS ROOTED in yesterday; today's religion is rooted in the religion of the past. For this reason we must try to understand Vedanta in its original form before we discuss its recent development.

The oldest scriptures of India and the most important to Hindus of all schools of Indian thought past and present (except Buddhism and Jainism) are the Vedas, the origin of their faith and their highest written authority. The term *Vedas* as used by orthodox Hindus not only refers to a large body of texts composed in infinitely remote times and handed down generation after generation, but in another sense stands for nothing less than divine truth itself. Of this inexpressible truth, the Vedic texts are necessarily but a pale reflection, but regarded in the second context, they are infinite and eternal, the perfect knowledge which is God.

"As clouds of smoke arise from a lighted fire kindled with damp fuel, so has issued the breath of the Vedas from the bosom of God." From this can be understood the Hindu claim that the religion of Vedanta is *Sanatana Dharma*, the Eternal Religion. No teacher, no prophet, can be regarded as its founder. Just as physical laws operating in the universe neither Newton nor Einstein can be said to have founded or discovered, similarly there are spiritual truths eternally existing. These truths have been discovered by seers, known as *rishis*. In the words of the ancient Vedic commentator Sayanacharya, "God created the whole universe out of the knowledge of the

Vedas." That is to say, Vedic knowledge is coeval with God. The authority of the Vedas does not depend upon anything external: they themselves are authority, being the knowledge of God. Why they are accepted as such we shall see later, but their truth is verifiable in transcendental consciousness by any spiritual aspirant.

It is the Vedas in the concrete sense of scriptures with which we are henceforth concerned. As such, they are divided into two major parts, *karmakanda*, the work portion, and *jnanakanda*, the knowledge portion. The knowledge portion consists of the Upanishads, and they came to be spoken of as the Vedanta – the *anta* or "end" of the Vedas, that is, the latter portion of the Vedas. The word *anta*, in addition to its literal meaning, has the figurative meaning of goal or purpose.

A modern Hindu, speaking of the Vedanta, may have both meanings more or less in mind. The scriptures refer to the last part of the Vedas, their highest wisdom, the wisdom of God.

The teaching of the Upanishads is summed up in several sacred sayings known as *mahavakyas*. They are: *Tat tvam Asi*, "That thou art"; *Aham Brahmasmi*, "I am Brahman"; *Prajnanam Brahma,* "Pure Consciousness is Brahman"; *Ayam Atma Brahma,* "This Self is Brahman." They are to be found strewn throughout the pages of the Upanishads. They are concise utterances, given by the teacher to the disciple, to be meditated upon. It is interesting to note that the ten orders of monks of the school of Shankara are differentiated to this day by the particular mahavakya upon which they meditate.

This, then, is the fundamental truth of the philosophy of Vedanta, the identity between Brahman and Atman. To a superficial reader who fails to penetrate deeply into the mystery of the human soul, this doctrine of identity may easily become the ground for misconception and misinterpretation.

But the Upanishads give us a profound analysis of essential human nature, an analysis which upholds the identity of the spirit within with the Godhead. According to this account, the human being is called *jiva*, one who breathes, denoting the biological and physiological aspects of life. His individual self is further indicated by the word *bhokta*, the enjoyer, and *karta*, the doer.

This individual self is not meant to be the Atman that is one with Brahman. To show the distinction between the individual soul and the Atman, let me quote to you some of the teachings of the Upanishads: "Both the individual self and the Universal Self have entered the cave of the heart, the abode of the most high, but the knowers of Brahman ... see the difference between them as between sunshine and shadow." [Katha Upanishad]

In the Mundaka Upanishad we read: "Like two birds of golden plumage, inseparable companions, the individual self and the Immortal Self are perched on the branches of the selfsame tree. The former tastes of the sweet and bitter fruits of the tree; the latter tasting of neither, calmly observes. The individual self, deluded by forgetfulness of his identity with the divine Self, bewildered by his ego, grieves and is sad. But when he recognizes the worshipful Lord as his own true Self, and beholds His glory, he grieves no more ... The Lord is the one life shining forth from every creature. Seeing him present in all, the wise man is humble, puts not himself forward. His delight is in the Self, his joy is in the Self, he serves the Lord in all. Such as he, indeed, are the true knowers of Brahman."

What is the nature of Brahman that is identical to the Atman? Brahman in this connection is described as beyond all expression: "Brahman is he whom speech cannot express and from whom the mind, unable to reach, comes away baffled." [Taittiriya Upanishad] "That which cannot be expressed in words but by which the tongue speaks — know that to be Brahman. Brahman is not the being who is worshiped of men. That which is not comprehended by the mind but by which the mind comprehends — know that to be Brahman. Brahman is not the being who is worshiped of men." [Kena Upanishad]

In another passage we read: "He, the self-luminous, subtler than the subtlest, in whom exist all the worlds and all those that live therein - he is the imperishable Brahman. He is the principle of life. He is real. He is immortal. Attain him, my friend, the one goal to be attained!" [Mundaka Upanishad]

So though he is beyond mind and speech, beyond human comprehension, he can be attained. One realizes this identity of Atman and Brahman in what is known as *samadhi* or transcendental consciousness. We shall presently come to explain that point, but before we come to that, we must mention that Brahman is described also as the cause of the universe. Viewed as such, Brahman is known as *saguna*, that is, the personal God with divine attributes. To quote the Upanishads: "The one absolute, impersonal Existence, together with his inscrutable Maya, appears as the divine Lord, the personal God, endowed with manifold glories. With his divine power he holds dominion over all the worlds. At the periods of creation and dissolution of the universe, he alone exists. [Svetasvatara Upanishad]

To the Hindus, creation is beginningless and endless. That it is beginningless is proved by a simple process of logic. If creation had a beginning, then the Creator must also have had a beginning, because until there is creation there can be no Creator. But to admit that the Creator had a beginning would be to admit that God had a beginning, since God is not God until he creates. To think of God as having had a beginning would be a manifest absurdity. God, who contains within himself the seed, the material cause of the universe, first brings forth this universe out of his own being, and then in due time takes it back again into himself. This process of creation and dissolution goes on forever, for it is as endless as it is beginningless: eternity is witness not of one universe only — for instance, that of which we are now a part — but of an infinite succession of universes. The birth, life, and destruction of a universe constitutes one cycle. To say that there was neither a first cause and will never be a last is to say that there was never such a cycle. And to say it will never be the last is only a way of asserting that the creative function of God is, like himself, eternal.

The phenomenon of creation is described in the Mundaka Upanishad as follows: "As the web comes out of the spider and is withdrawn, as plants grow from the soil and hair from the body of man, so springs the universe from the eternal Brahman."

What is our fate? Do we, like the universe, continue to undergo birth, death, and rebirth endlessly from a beginningless time? To quote the Svetasvatara Upanishad: "This vast universe is a wheel. Upon it are all creatures that are subject to birth, death, and rebirth. Round and round it turns and never stops. It is the wheel of Brahman. As long as the individual self thinks it is separate from Brahman, it revolves upon the wheel in bondage to the laws of birth, death, and rebirth. But when, through the grace of Brahman, it realizes its identity with him, it revolves upon the wheel no longer. It achieves immortality."

Herein we get the idea of what is known in Indian thought as reincarnation, and also the idea of liberation achieved through union with Brahman. There is divinity in each soul — Atman is Brahman — but as long as the Atman is identified with the sheaths of the body — vital principle, mind, intellect, and ego — it appears as an individual being separate from the Godhead. It is through ignorance, which is universal, that this identification continues. We remain subject to reincarnation — to birth, death, and rebirth — until we awaken spiritually and realize the truth of God. Then we achieve immortality.

According to Vedanta, continuity of existence is not in time. The soul reincarnates again and again, but that is not immortal life. Immortality is achieved when the individual self realizes its true nature as one with the Godhead. Ultimately every soul will experience this union. Reincarnation merely gives it repeated opportunities to do so.

The supreme goal of life, therefore, is to achieve *moksha*, liberation from the bondages of birth, death, and rebirth, which is attained by realizing the Godhead within, by realizing the Atman as Brahman. And Vedanta emphasizes that this state can be attained here and now. No one needs to wait till after the death of the body. For one who has achieved liberation during life on earth, the vision of the world becomes transformed into the vision of Brahman. Such a person is then called *jivanmukta*, free while living. Forever free from delusion, free from all selfish desires, free from all sense of want. Every desire is extinguished by the ineffable experience of the Self. For one who has not achieved liberation in life, there is the possibility of obtaining it at the moment of death, provided that preparation for this experience has been the sole aim of life.

It must be admitted that the Vedantic conception of immortality which is found in the Upanishads runs counter to a common human desire. Most of us cling fondly to what we call our individuality or personality and we long to retain it through what we think of as an infinite extension of earthly time. Against this proposition there lies implicit in the Upanishads the following argument: This so vaunted individuality of ours, what is it after all? Born as it is of the false identification of the Self with the non-Self, it is but the illusory product of a radical misunderstanding. It has no genuinely real, no ultimate, existence. Further, if only we will but observe and reflect, we shall realize that everything which pertains to this particularized self — whether of body or mind — is in a state of incessant change. To cherish our finite individuality is, therefore, to expend our affections on what moment by moment we are losing forever. On the other hand, beside this elusive, ever-vanishing self, there is another Self, the Atman, motionless behind the flux. In that, and only in that, lies our higher and truer individuality which, so long as we continue in our blindness, we can never know. It is only when we have achieved *moksha* that we come to know of it, and then we realize it in its fullness.

What is meant by the knowledge of Atman-Brahman which leads to liberation is not what we ordinarily understand by that word. In the Mundaka Upanishad we find that a sharp distinction is made: "There are two kinds of knowledge, the higher and the lower. The lower is knowledge of the Vedas and also of phonetics, ceremonials, grammar, etymology, metre, and astronomy. The higher is knowledge of that by which one knows the changeless reality. By this is fully revealed to the wise that which transcends the senses, which is uncaused, which is indefinable; and which has neither eyes nor ears, neither hands nor feet, which is all-pervading, subtler than the subtlest — the ever-lasting, the source of all."

The lower knowledge, being of the intellect and the senses, is limited to the objective, finite world, with Brahman or Atman unseen but seeing, unheard but hearing, unperceived but perceiving. Knowledge of the Atman or Brahman is, of course, the higher knowledge. It is known as *Turiya*, the Fourth. *Turiya* is beyond the three states of ordinary consciousness: the states of waking, dreaming, and dreamless sleep. It is thus defined in the Mandukya Upanishad: "The Fourth, say the wise, is not subjective experience nor objective experience, nor experience intermediate between these two, nor is it a negative condition which is neither consciousness nor unconsciousness. It is not the knowledge of the senses, nor is it relative knowledge, nor yet inferential knowledge. Beyond the senses, beyond the understanding, beyond all expression is The Fourth. It is pure unitary consciousness, wherein awareness of the world and of multiplicity is completely obliterated. It is ineffable peace. It is the supreme good. Know it alone!"

As already stated, to experience *Turiya* is to become a knower of Brahman, to be liberated from every finite bond. Such is the all-important purpose of life. But how is this purpose to be achieved? Through two main types of spiritual discipline, say the Upanishads: self-control or inner-check, and the practice of meditation. Just what is meant by self-control, the first discipline, is explained in a famous passage from the Katha Upanishad: "Know that the Self is the rider and the body the chariot; that the intellect is the charioteer, and the mind the reins. The senses, say the wise, are the horses; the roads they travel are the mazes of desire. The wise call the Self the enjoyer when he is united with the body, the senses, and the mind. When a man lacks discrimination and his mind is uncontrolled, his senses are unmanageable, like the restive horses of a charioteer. But when a man has discrimination and his mind is controlled, his senses, like the well-broken horses of the charioteer, lightly obey the rein. He who lacks discrimination, whose mind is unsteady, and whose heart is impure, never reaches the goal, but is born again and again. But he who has discrimination, whose mind is steady, and whose heart is pure, reaches the goal and, having reached it, is born no more. The man who has a sound understanding for a charioteer, a controlled mind for reins, he it is who reaches the end of the journey, the supreme abode of Vishnu, the All-pervading. ... This Brahman, the Self deep-hidden in all beings, is not revealed to all; but to the seers, pure in heart, concentrated in mind — to them is he revealed."

The importance of the second type of spiritual discipline, meditation, is emphasized in the following passages from the Svetasvatara Upanishad: "Like oil in sesame seeds, butter in cream, water in the riverbed, fire in tinder, the Self dwells within the soul. Realize Him through truthfulness and meditation. Like butter in cream is the Self in everything. Knowledge of the Self is gained through meditation. The Self is Brahman. By Brahman is all ignorance destroyed. ... Be devoted to the eternal Brahman. Unite the light within you with the light of Brahman."

And in the Katha Upanishad we read: "None beholds him with the eyes, for he is without visible form. Yet in the heart is he revealed, through self-control and meditation. When all the senses are stilled, when the mind is at rest, when the intellect wavers not — that, say the wise, is the highest state. This calm of the senses and the mind has been defined as yoga. He who attains it is freed from delusion."

There are four yogas or paths of union with Brahman. Raja Yoga is the path of self-control and meditation. Jnana Yoga is the path of discriminative knowledge, which consists of hearing the truth of Brahman, reasoning upon it, and meditating upon it. Bhakti Yoga is the path of love or devotion to God. Karma Yoga is the path of selfless work. The four paths are mentioned in the Upanishads in rudimentary form. They are discussed in greater detail in the auxiliary scriptures, especially in the Bhagavad Gita, and also in the Puranas and Tantras. The auxiliary scriptures, which are more recent than the Upanishads, are also accepted as authority by the Hindus

2

inasmuch as they explain and popularize the Upanishadic teachings.

In addition to the auxiliary scriptures, there are *sutras* or aphorisms which constitute the basic Indian philosophical literature. Western scholars regard the second century A.D. as the *sutra* period. The six schools of Indian Philosophy — Nyaya, Vaisheshika, Samkhya, Yoga, Purva Mimamsa, and Vedanta — are based upon *sutras*.

The most important aphorisms are the Yoga Sutras of Patanjali and the Vedanta Sutras of Vyasa.[1] The Yoga Sutras explain in detail how *samadhi* or God-consciousness is attained by following the path of concentration and meditation. The Vedanta Sutras are important to all Vedantic schools of thought inasmuch as every philosopher has commented upon them in order to establish his particular doctrine. For a Vedantist, the Upanishads, the Bhagavad Gita, and the Vedanta Sutras are considered the most authoritative and fundamental of all the scriptures.

Based upon these, three main schools of Vedantic thought developed in India. First, Advaita Vedanta. It was Shankara in the seventh century A.D. who expounded Advaita Vedanta in a comprehensive and clear manner. He accomplished this by writing commentaries on the basic Vedantic texts mentioned above. None of the many commentaries written before Shankara are extant. Shankara propounded the philosophy of nondualism — that Brahman alone is real and that the appearance of the universe as we know it is a superimposition upon Brahman.

The second school of thought developed approximately two centuries after Shankara. Is is known as the Vishishtadvaita or

---

1. The actual author was Badarayana of the 5th century B.C Vyasa is a generic name meaning compiler. He is a legendary character, since all works attributed to him took shape over many centuries.

qualified monism of Ramanuja. Ramanuja rejected Shankara's theory of superimposition and propounded his own theory of transformation. According to Ramanuja, Brahman is related to the world of the living and the non-living as the soul is related to the body: all living creatures and non-living matter constitute the qualifications of Brahman; individual souls are parts of Brahman, the whole. Brahman is *saguna*, personal, with blessed attributes.

The third school of thought is the Dvaita or dualism of Madhva. Madhva, who was born toward the end of the twelfth century, interpreted Vedanta as radical pluralism. According to him, God, matter, and souls are absolutely different from one another.

During the following six centuries, many other saints, too numerous to mention, left their mark of spirituality on the course of Indian philosophy and religion. In the nineteenth century, through English rule and the spread of English education in India, the materialism of the age touched Her shores. Lord MacCauley said that if Indians were given an English education, they would come to understand that their religion was superstition. And that is exactly what happened. Young Hindus neglected study of their own scriptures; Sanskrit learning was at its lowest ebb. Western scholars, on the other hand, translated the Vedas, the Upanishads, and the Bhagavad Gita, thus bringing to the attention of English-educated Hindus the greatness of their own spiritual heritage. In the life of Sri Ramakrishna, about whom I shall presently speak, an incident is mentioned which bears out the general lack of the Hindus' regard for their scriptures at that time. One of Sri Ramakrishna's young disciples told his Master what a wonderful book the Bhagavad Gita was. Sri Ramakrishna smiled and said, "Some Englishmen must have said so."

Vedanta was given a new impetus with the advent of Sri Ramakrishna, who was born in 1836. In his teens he was engaged as a priest in a temple at Dakshineswar, not far from Calcutta. Unbeknown to the people of the world, he practiced spiritual disciplines so intensively that the state of *Turiya*, which we mentioned while dealing with the Upanishads, almost became his natural state of awareness. In other words, he lived in God-consciousness practically all of his life.

The most characteristic aspect of the Vedanta as taught by Sri Ramakrishna can be summed up in the words—tolerance, reconciliation, and harmony. The ideas these words represent are not, of course, new to Indian religion, which from its remote beginning has seldom been morally exclusive or dogmatic. But in the Vedanta of Sri Ramakrishna they find a comprehensive and definitive embodiment. He not only brought into agreement the diverse views of Vedanta, but also managed to include in his native faith all the faiths of the outside world. The idea of the unity and universality of the religious sentiment could hardly be carried further. In the ultimate reaches of Vedanta there were, to be sure, no diverse views to be reconciled. When the aspirant attained the ultimate goal, views of whatever kind ceased to exist. An aspirant, absorbed in *Turiya*, the transcendental consciousness, had become one with God. But at lower levels, where the mind tried to determine the nature of God and the universe, differences arose early. Some said that God was personal, some that he was impersonal. Some said he was with form, some that he was without form. Sri Ramakrishna, bringing to bear his own mystic experiences, dissolved in his simple way all such oppositions. He said: "Infinite is God, and infinite are his expressions. He who lives continuously in the consciousness of God and in this alone, knows him in his true being. He knows his infinite expressions, his various aspects. He knows him as impersonal, no less than as personal. He indeed has attained the supreme illumination who not only realizes the presence of God, but knows him as both personal and impersonal, who loves him intensely, talks to him, and partakes of his bliss. Such an illumined soul realizes the bliss of God while he is absorbed in meditation, attaining oneness with the indivisible impersonal being, and he realizes the same bliss as he comes back to normal consciousness and sees this universe as a manifestation of that being and as a divine play. To reason out the truth of God is one thing and to meditate on God is another, but when illumination comes through the grace of God, then only is the truth of God known and experienced. Just as a dark room is lighted when you strike a match, so is the heart lighted up by the grace of God. Then alone are all doubts dissolved away."

As we have seen, the three main schools of thought in Vedanta are dualism, qualified monism, and nondualism. Sri Ramakrishna reconciled these in the following manner. Quoting an ancient verse from the Hindu scriptures, he told how Rama, who was worshiped as a divine incarnation, asked his faithful devotee, Hanuman, how he looked upon him. Hanuman replied: "When I consider myself as a physical being, Thou art the master, I am thy servant. When I consider myself as an individual being, Thou art the whole, I am one of Thy parts. And when I realize myself as the Atman, I am one with Thee." Thus, Sri Ramakrishna pointed out that dualism, qualified monism, and nondualism are not mutually exclusive and contradictory concepts, but successive steps in realization, the third and last being attained when the aspirant loses all consciousness of self in union with God. Thus, in a way more or less peculiar to himself, through attention mainly to the mystic experience, Sri Ramakrishna harmonized conflicting notions of God and religion.

But this was not his only way. Another, still more peculiar to him, might in current terms be called pragmatic. According to him, any idea of God, any mode of worshiping him that worked, that led the aspirant to the ultimate goal, must be valid and true. But how could one be sure that an idea or a method is really effective? Clearly, only by trying it oneself. That, in all simplicity and sincerity, is what Sri Ramakrishna did. First he practiced the teachings of many divergent denominations within Hinduism. Then he practiced the teachings of other faiths, including Islam and Christianity. Through each religious path, he attained the realization of God. In the end Sri Ramakrishna arrived at the grand conclusion with which the ancient *rishis* of the Vedas began: "Truth is One; sages call it by various names." In Sri Ramakrishna's words: "So many religions, so many paths to reach one and the same goal."

In defining this goal Sri Ramakrishna was, of course, at one with all his spiritual ancestors — simply to realize God within one's own soul. Sri Ramakrishna emphasized the importance of means: "Adopt adequate means for the end you seek to attain. You cannot get butter by crying yourself hoarse saying that there is butter in the milk. If you wish to make butter, you must turn the milk into curd and churn it well. Then alone you can get butter. So if you long to see God, practice spiritual disciplines. What is the use of merely crying, "Lord, Lord!"

In the course of its long history, reaching far back into an unrecorded past, Indian religion has had its share of denominations and doctrines, of reformations and revivals. It has nevertheless preserved unchanged, at its core, four fundamental ideas. These may be simply expressed: God is. He can be realized. To realize him is the supreme goal of human existence. He can be realized in many ways.

God is. This tremendous proposition, though variously interpreted, is, of course, common, not only to the religions of India, but to all religions of the world. In every age god-men have proclaimed it, each according to his own spiritual vision. And in every age people have asked for proof that it is true. Many plausible demonstrations have been devised by philosophers, establishing God as a logical necessity. However, there is not a single argument substantiating God's actuality on the basis of reason which has not been contradicted by equally plausible arguments of opposing philosophers. The only real proof that God is must be sought elsewhere.

God can be realized. That is to say, he can be known, felt, experienced immediately, in the depths of one's own soul. Upon this all-inspiring fact, the religions and philosophies of India, without exception, have been founded. From the dim ages of the Vedic seers, down through the many centuries to our own day, it has been consistently declared that the ultimate reality of the universe can be directly perceived, though never in normal consciousness. To the unique transcendent state, in which the miracle happens, various names have been given: *Turiya, samadhi, nirvana.*

To realize God is the supreme goal of human existence. On this, all Indian religions and philosophies have at all times been agreed: "Arise! Awake! Approach the feet of the Master and know That!" says the *rishi* of the Katha Upanishad. "Study of the scriptures is fruitless," says the great Shankara, "so long as Brahman has not been experienced." "He is born to no purpose," says Sri Ramakrishna, "who, having the rare privilege of being born a man, is unable to realize God."

It will be observed that the call for tolerance, harmony, and universal consent applies only to the paths, not to the goal. The Upanishads say: "Neti, neti." The Atman, or Brahman within, is not this, not that. In that ecstatic realization, says

Sri Ramakrishna, speaking out of his own abundant experience, all thoughts cease, no power of speech is left by which to express Brahman.

If this were all, there would, of course, be no religious doctrines, no religious philosophies — but it is not all. The mystics sooner or later emerge from transcendental consciousness, and then it sometimes happens that they talk, not for their own sake, but for the good of their fellow human beings. In talking, they may express variously the same ultimately inexpressible truth. The seers and philosophers of India, as elsewhere, have defined God in many ways, often apparently contradictory. Hence, divergent denominations have arisen. But what is to be noted is that seldom, if ever, do the differences in doctrine lead to intolerance, let alone to persecution. On the rare occasion when a system of philosophy or religion tried to prove and establish its own truth at the expense of others, it could not get very far; it could never dominate the minds of the people of India as a whole, as, thoroughly ingrained in their hearts was the spirit of understanding and sympathy. After all, they felt, it was the saintly life that counted. Saints and sages have been produced by following the order of Shankara, but also by following the order of Ramanuja, of Madhva, and of others. And they are recognized as such, not only by their particular followers, but by the whole of India. Moreover, by natural extension of their liberal attitude, Hindus revere the saints and sages of religions other than their own.

The first systematic attempt to harmonize the many doctrines of Hinduism is to be found in the teachings of the Bhagavad Gita, the Bible of the Hindus. By the fifth century B.C. many schools of thought with varied ideas of God and the Godhead, as well as varied paths, had come into existence. These were all incorporated in the teachings of the Gita. Sri

Krishna says: "Whatever path men travel is my path. No matter where they walk, it leads to me."

After many centuries, when Hinduism came for the first time into contact with a foreign religion, attempts were made by two great teachers, Guru Nanak and Kabir, to harmonize the newly arrived Islam with the native faith. And more recently when confronted by Christianity, Hinduism has once more, especially by the precepts and practices of Sri Ramakrishna, continued its role of peacemaker among the creeds.

It is perhaps natural, in conclusion, to emphasize strongly the age-old effort of India to reconcile differing faiths. For it is probably by continuing this effort on an international scale that She is doing most for the spiritual welfare of humanity. To bring together against rampant evil the great religions of the world is no doubt a gigantic task. But it is one for which India has a special qualification. She strives for unity, not by calling for a common doctrine, but only by pointing to a common goal, and by exhorting men and women to its attainment. The path, She assures us, matters little. It is the goal that is supreme. What is the goal? It is only, once again, to realize God. (1)[2]

---

2. For date and title of lecture, see Sources.

CONCEPTS

RELIGION

As you all know, there is a ferment today in the religions of the world. Not merely a ferment, that is to say agitation, in the minds and hearts of people, but a rebellion, especially among the younger generation. Where all this will lead is anybody's guess, but I firmly believe that ultimately it will lead to true spirituality and mysticism as exemplified in the lives of the great teachers of the world, and in our present age in the life of Sri Ramakrishna and his disciples.

You are well aware of how drugs have become widespread among the younger generation. What is the motive behind it? They are dissatisfied with present conditions, with their present consciousness, and they think, mistakenly, that drugs will lead them to some transcendental experience. But I can tell you with personal authority that drugs may give people some visions, but they are not spiritual visions and have nothing to do with ecstasy or *samadhi*. Furthermore, they do harm to the brain, sometimes permanently, whereas ecstasy and mysticism in their true sense and value transform the lives of those who have them.

I must point out to you the gradual changes that have come in the West from a historical standpoint. The predominating characteristic of modern Western civilization can be summed up as the scientific spirit, rationalism, secular humanism, which can be traced back to Classical antiquity. It was the Greek mind that laid the foundation of natural science: everything must be tested and experimented and reasoned. This is fundamental to Greek civilization, and it is the principal of the modern West.

The Greek mind concerned itself with natural man as he is known to himself — his bodily desires and mental powers. Of course in Greece we also find Pythagoras and Plato, who were great mystics, but they did not and could not exert much influence on the Greek mind.

Later we come to the two great religions of the world, Judaism and Christianity. They made fine contributions to Western thought, the chief one being the insufficiency of reason or intellect. They insisted upon historic revelation. Both religions stand on revelation: God reveals his will and his law to his prophets and lawgivers. All religions, of course, are based on revelation. Reason is insufficient; it cannot reach high enough. Religion is not against reason and scientific observations — but religion transcends them.

Then again, when righteousness is practiced on authority without experimentation and experience of the truth of God, what happens? Fanaticism, narrowness. "Fanaticism," in the words of Vivekananda, "is a sort of disease in the brain." As you all know, in the name of religion there have been great wars — killing, murder, all kinds of diabolical acts.

With the coming of the Renaissance, there came intellectual and scientific advancement, but traditional religion was thrown aside and morality declined. Today, in whatever remnants we have of Christianity as existing Catholicism and Protestantism is a rebellion against creeds and dogmas and doctrines. On the one side are conservatives, on the other liberals, and they are coming to a point when they again reassert the scientific spirit and rationalism, secular humanism.

The present chaos of the world has brought us to a period of re-thinking. In every country thinkers are beginning to look with suspicion on the past and present way of life and are asking, "Are we traveling the right path? How can we live in peace and harmony?" That is the predominant thought in the minds of the present young generation who have reached the point where, with only darkness, destruction, annihilation, we must reconsider and readjust.

Now let us consider the East. From a beginningless past the religions of India have also been based upon revelation, but not upon the authority of the revelations. In the words of the great seer philosopher, Shankara, "In matters relating to Brahman, the scriptures are not the only authority. There must be personal experience."

It is not enough to believe in God. Practically, there is no proof for the existence of God — but God is. He can be known and experienced. You find so many definitions of God, and they all quarrel about the nature of God. Sri Ramakrishna used to say, "Go to the neighborhood of God, realize God, then you will realize that his name is Silence." Nobody can express that experience in the sense in which we compare experience. You may have had a wonderful blissful experience and live in that joy — but what kind of joy? What kind of bliss? We try to compare it with sense experiences, but there is no comparison, because it is not a relative experience: it is the experience of the Absolute Reality.

Then again Sri Ramakrishna pointed out that before the bee sits on the flower and begins to suck the honey, it makes a big noise. But as soon as the bee begins to suck, it becomes silent. Then, having drunk, and becoming intoxicated, it makes a sweet humming sound. So we find that these great prophets, great mystics, great teachers of the world who have come face to face with God try to express God. They experience the same Reality, but their expressions differ.

Mathew Arnold defined religion as ethical life with a touch of emotionalism. But if righteousness is practiced on authority because such-and-such prophets ask us to behave and live in such-and-such a way, it does not work. When we realize what the purpose of life is — to realize God — then we shall know that the good or righteous is that which leads us to him, and evil is that which leads us away from him. We have to reach a stage when, like the jasmine flower giving fragrance without knowing that it is giving fragrance, we become so holy that we do not think what is right or what is wrong — but what we do is right.

As civilization moves in cycles, up and down, religion moves up and down. At times people have tried to read the scriptures without trying to experience or realize the truth of God, but whenever religion declines, when truth becomes forgotten, a great teacher comes, not to give anything new, but to reinstate what we call *Sanatana Dharma*, the Eternal Religion.

Nobody founded the truth. When you say Christ is the founder of Christianity or Buddha is the founder of Buddhism, you are wrong. Christ discovered the eternal truth; Buddha discovered the eternal truth. Just as there are laws of science, does the scientist invent, or discover? There are eternal verities of life. The great ones discover them. They want us to discover those truths for ourselves.

In the present age, when India came in contact with Western civilization, the idea of Western civilization was to drink wine and eat beef. Religion degenerated. So Ramakrishna and his disciples came. I had the blessed opportunity to meet his disciples. You could not call them Hindus or Christians or Buddhists or Muslims: they were men of God. Sri Ramakrishna was a Hindu, he was a Christian, he was a Muslim. His chief apostle, Vivekananda, pointed out that he was the embodiment of the truth of all religions.

Thomas Carlyle once observed that a man's religion is the chief thing about him, but Carlyle did not equate religion with the joining of churches and recitation of creeds. Religion is the ultimate concern of human life; otherwise there is no meaning to life. Religion gives you the experience — the realization — of God, the truth, ultimate Reality. This is not only the idea of the Indian sages and seers, nor is it only a new idea with Ramakrishna and his disciples. If you go to the source of any religion, you will find all the great teachers have pointed out that you have to know the truth for yourself. Jesus said, "Ye shall know the truth, and the truth shall make you free." And Buddha said, "If there were not an unconditioned, an uncaused something, how could there be any escape from the caused and conditioned?" Mohammed said about the people who only study and quote scriptures, "They are like asses carrying a burden of books." And Shankara, the seer-philosopher of India, gave almost the same comparison, "An ass carrying a load of sandalwood does not get the fragrance."

Let us hear some of Sri Ramakrishna's teachings on the essential identity of the great religions. He said, "So many religions, so many paths to reach the same goal. I have practiced Hinduism, Islam, Christianity, and in Hinduism again the ways of the different sects. I find that it is the same God towards whom all are directing their steps, though along different paths. The tank has several *ghats* or approaches. At one Hindus draw water and call it *jal*. At another Muslims draw water and call it *pani*. At a third Christians draw the same liquid and call it water. The substance is one, the names differ, and everyone is seeking the same truth. Every religion of the world is one such *ghat* or approach. Go with a sincere and earnest heart by any of these *ghats*, you will reach the water of eternal bliss, but do not say that your religion is better than that of another."

Abraham Lincoln once said, "I cannot without mental reservation assent to long and complicated creeds and catechisms. If the church would ask simply for assent to the Savior's statement of the substance of the Law: 'Thou shalt love the Lord thy God with all thy heart, with all thy strength, with all thy mind. And thou shalt love thy neighbor as thyself.'"

Swami Vivekananda summed it up with these words: "Do not care for doctrines, do not care for dogmas, or sects, or churches or temples; they count for little compared with the essence of existence in each man, which is spirituality; and the more that this is developed in a man, the more powerful is he for good. Earn that first, acquire that, and criticize no one, for all doctrines and creeds have some good in them. Show by your lives that religion does not mean words, or names, or sects, but that it means spiritual realization. Only those can understand who have felt. Only those that have attained to spirituality can communicate it to others, can be great teachers of mankind. They alone are the powers of light."

The question arises, what about humanism? Repeating the words of another great teacher, "Compassion for all beings," Sri Ramakrishna pointed out, "Compassion. Compassion. Isn't God dwelling in every being? Serve God, worship God in all beings!" And Swami Vivekananda happened to listen to that conversation. He came out of the room and said, "If I live, I'll give this truth to the world: service to humanity in the spirit of worshiping God." In other words, secular humanism is transformed into spiritual humanism. Scientific temper and rationalistic spirit are not opposed to religion and revelation if by religion we understand experiment and experience. Intellect and revelation become harmonized. Humanism becomes spiritualized. (2)

The proof of the Reality is not in the vision of the seers and prophets and sons of God. The proof of the Reality is not in the scriptures of the world. They are only guideposts.

The proof lies in the fact that each individual can discover this very same truth. Philosophy or religion is experimental. My master often used to say that until you have reached that realization, you are still on the outskirts of religion.

Religion begins with spiritual vision. You are a philosopher. You become truly religious only when you have the direct vision, direct experience, for yourself. You cannot understand the beauty of the moon by looking at it through others' eyes; you have to see the moon for yourself. That Reality — God, Brahman, Allah, whatever name you may call it — who is known as the source of knowledge, of happiness, remains a mere concept, a mere theory, until you have come face to face with that Reality, until you have the direct vision of God. In other words, to be a philosopher, to be a spiritual person, is to be a *rishi*, a seer.

Now we must understand that this experience is not of the senses, nor is it merely intellectual understanding, nor an emotional experience. It is transcending the senses, it is transcending this impure mind. My master often used to say that that vision is achieved only when the mind becomes purified and subtle — not with the gross mind.

Sri Ramakrishna used to say that this world is an illusion, and it remains an illusion until you see the Reality. When you see the Reality, this world also becomes real. The appearance has no meaning; it is all in a flux — but you find meaning to this flux when you see that unchanging, absolute Reality underlying it.

If we sum up the whole principle of religion, at the core we find a few fundamental principles. First is that behind this appearance of a universe of name and fame, the universe of mind and matter, there is an underlying Reality, which Meister Eckhart called the Divine Ground, and which the Upanishads call Brahman. Without, or apart, from that Reality, the universe is non-existent — it is maya.

Another principle is that the individual has a double nature, just as the universe has a double nature: the appearance, and the Reality. When you see the Reality, you see the meaning of the appearance. The double nature of a human being we call the phenomenal ego and the divine Self, the Atman. This Atman is one with Brahman, one with the Reality. In other words, in each of us the infinite God is dwelling, and this phenomenal ego is only an appearance covering that divine ground, Brahman, the Reality.

The next point is that we are capable of directly experiencing this Reality. It is possible for every individual to experience. And the purpose and end of everyone's life is to attain this knowledge.

The conditions or the methods and means by which this attainment is possible will be understood simply if we can understand what the obstruction to that vision is. The power is of transcendental consciousness, which is inherent in every one of us. It is not a special gift of a few individuals, but is innate in every one — only it lies in a dormant state. What causes the dormant state is the phenomenal ego that we accept as real. The moment we accept it as real, we are thrown into the appearance of a universe, and the Reality remains hidden and unknown.

If you study the disciplines as taught by all the great teachers of the world, you will find that the purpose behind all discipline is to free oneself from the phenomenal ego. That is the one aim. To a Christian mystic or a Buddhist mystic or a Hindu mystic — whatever religion one may follow — the principle of discipline is to free oneself from all selfishness, all sense of ego. There are people who might not believe in religion, but there is none in this world who does not believe in being unselfish. And the very principle of spiritual life is to become completely unselfish. In the words of our great poet

Kalidas, "to own the whole world, by disowning your own self." That is the fundamental principle.

What causes all troubles and sufferings and miseries in this world is selfishness, ego! It is the root cause of all our sufferings — individual, national, collective, or universal. There is a universal ignorance that exists — the phenomenal ego — and there is the attempt to enrich this ego.

Sri Ramakrishna used to say in a very simple way: "As long as the servant is in the house and managing the house, the master remains away." It is the same with us. The servant ego has mastered this whole being, and so the master is away and we do not realize God. Let the servant ego be the servant, realize its own position, and then the master begins to rule. That is the principle. (3)

If you go to the source of every religion, you will find the same teaching, and that is: love the Lord. When that love comes, the love for mankind becomes normal and natural; there is no distinction felt between man and woman, between race and race.

The world will not be saved either by Hinduizing everyone or Christianizing everyone. But we must all join hands together and try to spiritualize all people. Every religion has dreamed of an ideal of universality. Let me point out in this connection what kind of universality the Hindu dreams of. Swami Vivekananda, an apostle of Sri Ramakrishna, said, "If there is to be a universal religion, it must be one which will have no location in place or time, which will be infinite like the God it will preach, and whose sun will shine upon the followers of Krishna and of Christ, on saints and sinners alike, which will not be Brahmanical or Buddhistic, Christian or Muslim, but the sum-total of all these, and still have infinite space for development; which, in its catholicity, will embrace in its infinite arms and find a place for every human being. ... It will be a religion which will have no place for persecution or intolerance in its polity, which will recognize divinity in every man and woman, and whose only scope or form will be centered in aiding humanity to realize its own true divine nature."

Vivekananda, and all the apostles of Sri Ramakrishna, saw in him the embodiment of such an ideal of universality. This does not mean that all people will have to accept the personality of Sri Ramakrishna, but the principle, the ideal, for which he stood. That ideal is to be realized. For instance, Sri Ramakrishna said once that he did not belong to India. Another time he said, "I have my children in far off lands, whose language I do not know."

From a commonsense viewpoint we find that all religions have a tremendous life power in them, for not one of these great religions has died: they are still living, because each of them has the truth. Vedanta and Buddhism, the most ancient religions of the world, have both recognized always, from a beginningless time as it were, the liberty of all humanity in regard to religion. Swami Vivekananda says in this connection, "It has been proved to the world that holiness, purity, and chastity are not exclusive possessions of any church in the world, and that every system has produced men and women of the most exalted character. In the face of this evidence, if anybody dreams of the exclusive survival of his own religion and the destruction of others, I pity him from the bottom of my heart, and point out to him that upon the banner of every religion will soon be written in spite of their resistance, 'Help and not fight,' 'Assimilation and not destruction,' 'Harmony and peace and not dissension.'" Do you not see what is happening today? I'd say that either every existing church will have to recognize this truth, or it will die out, it cannot live.

Sri Krishna, centuries back, in the Bhagavad Gita pointed out, "I am the thread that runs through all these pearls." Each pearl is, as it were, a religion, and the Lord God is the thread that unites them.

Before we consider the concept of unity, and wherein lies the unity, let us also note the differences that exist. Thus we shall be able to determine where the unity lies. Every religion is divided into three parts: philosophy or theology, which presents its hopes and sets forth basic principles; mythology, philosophy by legends and lives of saints; then ritualism or symbology. Now let us consider these one by one.

First, every religion has a different conception of theology and philosophy. There are divergent opinions. Because they are only opinions, only one theology, one doctrine, would be a death to religion itself. Without freedom of thought, no growth is possible in any department of life. For instance, motion is possible only where there is friction. Opposing thoughts create thoughts. It's a good thing that there are many philosophies, many theologies. But in this connection let me point out a teaching of Sri Ramakrishna. He made a pun on the Bengali word *dahl*, which has two meaning: one is "sect," the other "scum." So he said, "*Dahl* grows on a stagnant pond." Let there be sects. But if there is sectarianism — that is, "my *ism* is the only *ism*" — then it has stunted growth. And what happens? It dies out.

Now let us take mythology. Of course a Christian would say, "My mythology is history, not legend," and a Hindu would say. "My mythology is history, not legend." Let me give two examples from these two religions. Jonah was swallowed by a great fish, and he stayed in its stomach for three days. Then the whale spat him out, and Jonah carried on his mission. This is history! Now in Hindu legend Shukadeva is a well-known saint and the narrator of the Srimad Bhagavatam. In the mythology you read that this Shukadeva was in his mother's womb for sixteen years, and when he was born, he was a young man of sixteen. This is history!

Now let us consider ritualism. The Hindus worship a symbol called *shivalinga*, the symbol of the impersonal Brahman united with Shakti, or the Mother power. Non-Hindus, especially Christian missionaries, preach that Hindus worship the phallic symbol. Now you take the Christian ritualism of what you call the sacrament, communion. You take bread and wine; the bread is the flesh of Christ and the wine is the blood of Christ. To Christians it is wonderful, because they consider that they are having Christ within themselves so they can commune with him. Wonderful! But to a non-Christian, do you know how it appears? Cannibalism.

So is there no common ground for the religions of the world? Most Christians believe we can all meet in the holy personality of Christ. And there are Hindu Vaishnavas who believe that without worshiping Krishna, you can never be saved. What are we to do? Let Krishna and Christ fight it out? Let me quote what this same Krishna taught in the Bhagavad Gita: "When goodness grows weak, when evil increases, I make myself a body. In every age I come back to deliver the holy, to destroy the sin of the sinner, to establish righteousness." From this we can understand the Hindu ideal that it is the same God, the same being, who is born in different ages under different names and forms. And if we take the words of all these great ones superficially, we shall misunderstand. For instance, what did Jesus say? "I am the way, the truth, and the life. Come unto me, all ye that labor and are heavy-laden, and I will give you rest." Superficially he is the only one. Now again, Sri Krishna before him said, "Give me your whole heart. Love and adore me. Worship me always. Bow to me only, and you shall find me. Lay down all duties in me, your refuge. Fear no longer, for I will save you from sin and bondage." Same words, identical words. And in this present age, what does Sri Ramakrishna say? "I am the sanctuary. If a man gathers his whole mind and fixes it on me, then indeed he achieves everything."

We Vedantists firmly believe that each one of these great ones is right. If you follow Christ, you will reach the same goal as if you follow Krishna or Ramakrishna. All roads lead to Rome, but Rome must be your destination. The ideal, the goal, must be fixed in your mind, and that goal is to realize that which is eternal amongst the noneternals of life. To that end, the harmony of all religions, or the ideal of universality, is not in philosophy or theology, not in mythology, not in ritualism, but in our search for God, the ultimate Reality, and realizing it. (4)

None of us today can properly maintain that we live within the boundaries of one religion, one culture, or one nation. Through the progress of modern science, time, space, and geographical limitations have become completely revolutionized. In a way this has forced us to become intensely aware of the cultural habits of other people. And it has opened our eyes to the fact that there are other religions, other faiths, other ways to approach the same Godhead. Unfortunately, there are still some who believe that theirs is the only true religion, and nations where nationalism is very strong.

Today many churches emphasize loving one's neighbor and doing good to others. But does that work? They cannot live together in a family peacefully. And why can't they? Because they do not love the Lord. Unless you learn to love the Lord, unless that becomes your ideal, it is not possible to love. When there comes that love for the Lord within your heart, love will overflow for all mankind, because you will learn to see that one God, one Brahman, one Self, in every being. If I hurt you, I hurt myself and I hurt God. If I hate you, I hate God and I hate myself. That is the understanding we have to come to. In order to come to that understanding, we have to devote ourselves completely to realizing, to experiencing, God. This does not mean that you give up everything, but that in every action you learn to see the presence of Brahman, the presence of God. Always keep that ideal. Love your wife, love your husband, love your children, love your neighbor, knowing that it is the one God that is dwelling in every being. Then is it that love will really come to you.

I will quote one passage from the Upanishads: "Brahman may be realized while yet living in the ephemeral body. To fail to realize Him is to live in ignorance and, therefore, subject to birth and death. The knowers of Brahman are immortal. Others, knowing Him not, continue in bonds of grief." [Brihadaranyaka Upanishad] (5)

Buddha pointed out that the practicality of religion is to go beyond all suffering and misery — which you can only do by experiencing the ultimate truth. In this particular age, Sri Ramakrishna came to experiment and experience that same truth of God. We find his disciple, Vivekananda, when he was a young boy, had one question: "Sir, have you seen God?" Sri Ramakrishna said: "Yes, I have seen him, and I see him more clearly and definitely than I see you." And that is religion.

Religion needs just two hypotheses. One is: God is. The other is: what is the proof? Chaos and confusion arise when religion is based on faith, on what somebody said. As Swami Vivekananda told a disciple, "Give me what you know. What matters what Christ said or Shankara said? Tell me what you know." That is the point in religion: God is. And the proof is that he can be known and experienced. Until and unless

God reveals himself to you, there is nobody who can know and talk about God. Yes, he can be known, he can be seen, you can experience the truth of God!

Sri Ramakrishna used to say, "That God that you are seeking is your very Self." It is possible for everyone to see him, to know him, to realize him. No human being can enjoy the pleasures of the senses as intensely as a pig or a dog. Humans are born for something else – and that is to know the Reality.

What is Reality? That which is and never is not. Everything else today is, tomorrow is not. It is only when we have the vision of God, the experience of God, that there is fulfillment. Then we are satisfied forever. You have to reach that here and now.

When one realizes God, one can understand the scriptures, because there are many teachers in many scriptures who have known God. They speak differently sometimes, there seem to be contradictions. For instance, you will find God is defined as personal, as impersonal, as having attributes, again as attributeless; as having forms, and again as formless. When Sri Ramakrishna was asked, his answer was: "Go to the neighborhood of God and you will find that all contradictions meet there." In other words, as long as we are trying to understand God outside of religion, as philosophers sitting in chairs philosophizing about God, we will never come to any understanding. We have to be inside of religion and practice spiritual disciplines, to struggle. We have to come to the neighborhood of God. (6)

GOD, SOUL AND THE UNIVERSE

Opinions differ, because whatever you express in the relative world is relatively true. All difficulty arises when we consider our opinion to be the only opinion, and that what we say is the absolute truth. Nobody can express in words any truth that is absolute, and relative truths are apparently contradictory. But we find a harmony, a conciliation, if we go to the heart of religion, to the heart of truth; then apparent contradictions melt away. To quote Vivekananda, "We never move from falsehood or from error to truth, but from lower to higher truth."

All opinions, all doctrines and theological ideas, can be reduced to three schools of thought: dualism, qualified monism, and non-dualism.

Dualism is the idea that God and insentient matter, together with sentient beings, are separate and distinct, that God is independent and insentient matter and sentient creatures are dependent upon God. In other words, the material of the universe and God are separate, but they both exist eternally. And the material cause of the universe, *prakriti* (made up of the gunas, the three energies) and God are separate. However, God takes hold of *prakriti* and creates the universe of mind and matter. Of course, in Christianity God creates the universe out of nothing.

In the Upanishads we read: "In the beginning was God, was Brahman. He willed to be many, and out of himself he issued forth this whole universe." [Chandogya Upanishad] But nowhere in Indian philosophy is to be found any beginning to the universe: it is eternal, beginningless and endless. There is a beginning to a cycle, there is evolution, and there is involution, but creation is infinite; there can be no exhaustion.

According to dualism, because of ignorance people do not feel they are dependent on God but think they are independent. Accordingly, they become mixed up with sowing and reaping and birth, death, and rebirth, until they learn to depend upon the Creator, God. Those who surrender themselves to God attain liberation.

Qualified monism points out that God, matter, and soul are not separate, but distinct. To quote the Upanishads: "As the web comes out of the spider and is withdrawn, as plants grow from the soil and hair from the body of man, so springs the universe from the eternal Brahman." [Mundaka Upanishad] In other words, he is the efficient cause as well as the material cause of the universe. He has become the universe, has transformed into the universe, and the relation between the universe of mind and matter, of sentient and insentient, is that they are the same. There is the ocean and there are waves: waves are not the ocean; waves are part of the ocean but they are not separate from it.

Similarly, human souls and all creatures are parts of that infinite Being. God is defined as *sat* (truth, existence), *chit* (knowledge or consciousness), and *ananda* (bliss and love): *Sat-chit-ananda*. Qualified monists consider these to be attributes of God, but non-dualists consider them one with God: existence itself, not an attribute.

According to nondualism, creation has no absolute reality: it is the superimposition of something upon God. Brahman alone is real. You are Brahman, I am Brahman. One, not parts — the infinite cannot be divided into parts — so if God is dwelling within you, he is dwelling infinitely within you. There are not many souls, many Atmans, but one appearing as many. You see nothing but Brahman all the time. You live, move, and have your being in Brahman all the time. You are one with Brahman all the time, but through ignorance you see yourself separate and different: this is forgetfulness of God.

This is not, however, a complete illusion. Shankara does not deny any experience, but he says there are degrees of reality. For instance, a mirage has reality as long as you are seeing it; but when you go near, it disappears. Therefore, it has no absolute Reality. Then again, dreams are real as long as you are dreaming; when you wake up, the dream breaks and you realize it was only a dream, that it had no reality. What we experience in our waking state has an empirical reality, but this again disappears when we experience or realize God.

So what is the reconciliation between the three (dualism, qualified monism, and nondualism)? Religion is an experience, not an opinion. It is not speculation, not theory. What guarantee is there that the conception of the God of the theologian tallies with the reality of God? None. Except, as the seer says: "I have seen him. I know him. I have become one with him." If he says, "Now believe me," be careful. "I have known the truth, but you also can know" — that is the one proof for the existence of God, and it cannot be refuted. Mere authority is not enough. You have to have a personal experience. Then is it that you have known the truth. A real spiritual aspirant is one who is seeking to know, not intellectually, but by coming face to face with the reality.

You see, the heart of religion is to see God, to know God. Where is that God? Where can we find him? That is the one problem. Study the scriptures; that is very important. Study theology or doctrines and try to understand intellectually. But whether you accept or do not accept makes no difference. Only when you want to find God for yourself have you begun your spiritual life. Believing in God will not give you freedom from suffering and misery. You have to wake up. You have to live in that blissful consciousness. Where is that consciousness to be found? Within your own soul. When you see God, realize God, you find him within your own being. The fact is that God dwells within each one of us, but we are not all dwelling in God. (7)

The difference between what you call pantheism and the teachings of Vedanta — either qualified monism or nondualism — is that when Vedanta points out that God is everywhere, in everything, it does not identify God with nature, and God does not exhaust himself in nature. He is immanent as well as transcendent. In other words, you are a part of that whole, you cannot be separated from God, ever. But you are not aware of it, because of ignorance.

Nondualistic philosophy is very simple: it has few doctrines. It is said, "What has been spoken in hundreds of scriptures, I shall give in one sentence: "Brahman alone is real: this universe is only an appearance, it has no reality, and the *jiva*, the individual soul, is none other than Brahman." In other words, there is one vast existence, and the nature of that is pure knowledge or consciousness, and pure love and joy. There are no attributes: knowledge itself, love itself, joy itself, truth itself.

Buddha said, "Brahman I know: I dwell in that." The sage of the Upanishad says, "I have known that truth which is beyond darkness." Not speculation, but a fact. Religion means to realize that truth. Sri Ramakrishna said, "You cannot even say one, because when you say one, there is the idea of two."

Christ taught the three schools of thought recognized by Vedanta. When he taught us to pray to the Father in Heaven, Father is separate from us. That is dualism. When he said, "I am the vine, ye are the branches," that is qualified monism. Then again when he said, "I and my Father are One," that is nondualism. Please understand that this is not only an experience of Christ — "I and my Father are One." It has been experienced by saints and sages in different countries, belonging to different religions and sects. It is a universal experience. (8)

These three schools of thought (dualism, qualified monism and nondualism) are not contradictory. There is a harmony: they can be reconciled. But such harmony can be established or explained only through mysticism, in a laboratory in our own mind. A scientist's discoveries come through the power of the mind, through concentration, the focusing of ideas and thoughts; thus comes an intuitive knowledge. That same power of mind focused towards the Reality within reveals the truth in its totality. All of us have to demonstrate this truth for ourselves. It is not believing, not accepting — but of course there has to be a working faith. If you study physics or chemistry, you have to have faith in the science itself. Similarly, there must be a working faith in the words of the scriptures or revealed truths as experienced by the great sages and seers of the past and present.

Swami Vivekananda said the scriptures are not finished yet, the revelation is not finished. It is beginningless and endless, and we must be ready to accept the revelations of the past and the present, and welcome those that will come in the future. From that standpoint we shall find that there is a harmony between the different ideas, that they are not contradictory.

To a dualist God is a personal being. This personal being may be considered as with form or without form. You see, the definition of a personal being is one with attributes or qualities. He is good, he is generous, he is gracious, he is merciful. The ideal is first to establish a relationship with God, as in this world there are different relationships: servant-master, friend-friend, parent-child, child-parent, lover-beloved. These relationships are in every religion. Just offhand I am thinking of what Jesus said to his disciples: "Ye are not my servants anymore, ye are my friends." If you read the Song of Solomon, you find the sweet relationship of lover and beloved.

When the vision opens up, we see Brahman, God, behind everything. And God has attributes such as truth, pure consciousness, infinitude. According to nondualists, these are not attributes but are one substance. In qualified nondualistic philosophy, the universe of name and form is a transformation of God. But according to nondualists, it is not transformation but a superimposition on divine Reality.

From a theological standpoint, there is no harmony or reconciliation of these schools of thought; they remain contradictory. But when you understand religion as realization, there is reconciliation. In this connection I will mention that when we were in Madras we asked our brother disciple who was the abbot, a disciple of Maharaj but senior to me, what exactly the experience was. When it comes, is it *advaita* (nondualism) or qualified non-dualism, or what? We wrote a letter to Swami Turiyananda, a disciple of Ramakrishna, and the substance of his answer was this: God or Brahman is the source of all religions, but nothing that comes out from that source can totally explain the source itself. No philosophy or religion can explain the supreme truth. Nondualists reach that which is inexpressible, but that, again, is not the total reality. So we wrote Swami Turiyananda back and said, "But they all say that nondualism is the highest." He answered, "What do I care about that? I see that beyond nondualism there is a state." It is said that you have to reach a state where Vedas become no Vedas. Sri Ramakrishna used to say, "Here, (he could never utter the word 'I') what has been experienced is beyond all scriptures." My master said to us one time, "After *nirvikalpa samadhi* — that is, after you reach the highest *samadhi* where you reach your oneness — after that, religion begins." So we are playing in the kindergarten, you know.

God is not mere speculation, not a mere theory, but a matter of experience. In the Katha Upanishad we read: "None beholds him with the eyes, for he is without visible form. Yet in the heart is he revealed, through self-control and meditation. When all the senses are stilled, when the mind is at rest, when the intellect wavers not — that, say the wise, is the highest state. This calm of the senses and the mind has been defined as yoga. He who attains it is freed from delusion. ... To him who sees the Self revealed in his own heart belongs eternal bliss, to none else, to none else." (9)

OM

From the very earliest Vedic times until the present day, the syllable OM has been considered an aid to meditation and to realizing our oneness with the divine. In the Atharva Veda we read: "This word is the eternal word and the word OM is the seed of all knowledge and power." In the Katha Upanishad we read: "Of that goal which all the Vedas declare, which is implicit in all penances, and in pursuit of which men lead lives of continence and service, of that will I briefly speak. It is — OM. This syllable is indeed supreme ... It is the strongest support ... He who knows it is revered as a knower of Brahman."

We read in the Mundaka Upanishad the method of meditaton: "Affix to the Upanishad, the bow incomparable, the sharp arrow of devotional worship; then, with mind absorbed and heart melted in love, draw the arrow and hit the mark — the imperishable Brahman." What is the bow? "OM is the bow, the arrow is the individual being, and Brahman is the target. With a tranquil heart, take aim. Lose thyself in him, even as the arrow is lost in the target."

But the question arises, "How may one find devotion to God? How can we worship him and meditate on him? In spite of the fact that there are many definitions of God, it remains an abstraction. We need something concrete to hold onto, as we hold onto a pillar. The great psychologist of India, Patanjali, realizing this fact, offers a concrete and definite way of understanding God which the mind can grasp and meditate upon: "The word which expresses him is OM. This word must be repeated with meditation on its meaning. Hence come knowledge of the *purusha* (or Brahman) and destruction of all obstacles to that knowledge."

The entire history of the syllable is in the revelations we find in the Vedas and Upanishads. Later, in the hands of philosophers, it became what is known as *sphotavada*, the philosophy of the Word or Logos. A similar doctrine of Logos was evolved many centuries after the Vedas and the Upanishads by the Greek philosophers. The Hindu mind depended upon revelation, whereas the Greek mind, through the reasoning process, tried to breach the gulf, as it were, that existed between man and God.

In the earliest Greek philosophers, the conception of the Logos was crude and identified with one or another of the elements which they considered the substance of the universe — air, water, ether, and fire. Heraclitus, in the 6th century B.C., was the first to break away from purely physical elements. He substituted the material First Cause of the universe as a principle which he called intelligence or reason. Then again, he somewhat equivocally identified intelligence with a physical element, fire.

Then came Plato, and the idea of Logos was completely transformed. To Plato the idea (or word) and thought are identical, and this idea or thought is in the mind of God. The whole universe is a shadow of those ideas and thoughts, which are an archetype in the mind of God.

Then the Stoics denied completely the validity of Plato and his ideas. They fell back upon Heraclitus's element of reason or intelligence — minus the physical element of fire. Reason, according to the Stoics, is within each individual, immanent; and with this reason properly used, one can reach the ultimate Reality.

Somewhat later an Alexandrian Jewish philosopher, Philo (who was a contemporary of Jesus) harmonized the Platonic and Stoic ideas. He accepted what the Stoics pointed out as reason or intelligence being immanent in all beings and things. But he, being a Jew, accepted the Platonic idea of a transcendental God. Thus, his description of the Logos as mediator between God and man and the world reflects two sources: the Greek and the Jewish. It speaks of an infinite variety of forces, through which an active relation between God and humanity is effected.

In this connection let me point out that it was Philo who said the Logos is the "first-begotten Son of God." And it was accepted by St. John, the writer of the fourth Gospel, with little addition to fit into the theology of Christianity. We read in the first verse of the Gospel according to St. John: "In the beginning was the Word, and the Word was with God, and the Word was God." This verse is almost identical to a verse we find in the Vedas: "In the beginning was God, with whom was the Word, and the Word was verily the Supreme Brahman."

The Christian Logos, as we read in the fourth Gospel, "was made flesh and dwelt among us (and we behold his glory, the glory as of the only begotten of the Father), full of grace and truth." The Christian Logos thus was incarnate once in the person of Jesus, whereas the *sphota* of the Hindus was, is, and will incarnate itself, not in person only, but in all things and all beings throughout the universe, each of whom may directly realize God through the power of *sphota*, or the word OM. In the Mandukya Upanishad, for instance, we read: "The syllable OM, which is the imperishable Brahman, is the universe. Whatsoever has existed, whatsoever exists, whatsoever shall exist hereafter, is OM. And whatsoever transcends past, present, and future, that also is OM."

4

You cannot have the idea of God without the word which expresses God. Languages may be different, but the word must express the same. Why should this word necessarily be OM? The Hindus reply that God is a basic fact of the universe which must be represented by the most basic, the most natural, the most comprehensive of all words. They claim this sound is OM. It contains three letters: Aah, ooh, mmm. To quote Swami Vivekananda: "The first letter is A, the root sound, pronounced without touching any part of the tongue or palate. M represents the last sound of the series, being produced by closed lips. And the U, or ooh rolls from the very root to the end of the sounding board of the mouth. Thus AUM represents the whole phenomena of sound-producing."

OM is not a particular language, it is not a Sanskrit word, or a Greek word, but it is universal, the mother of all words, all sounds. The mystic, whether Christian or Muslim or Buddhist or Hindu, can hear this cosmic sound OM vibrating in the universe. When your mind becomes tranquil, when it becomes concentrated, there are different sounds that can be heard. Ultimately you hear the sound OM vibrating.

What matters most is the appreciation of the power of the word. According to Hindus, God is infinite, and infinite are his expressions. As such, the same God, the same Reality, has many names. But when a Hindu receives a mantra, the sacred word, whatever the chosen ideal, the word OM is added to it to show that this chosen ideal represents the eternal Reality, the unchangeable, imperishable Brahman. But again, Hindus do not insist that you cannot realize God without the help of the word OM. "Various are thy names, O Lord. In each and every name Thy power resides."[3] We must remember that the name and

---

3. Prayer of Chaitanya.

the chosen ideal, are identical. In other words, the moment you chant the name of the Lord, the presence of the Lord is there.

My master said: "*Sahaja* yoga is to keep your mind constantly on God — while you are sitting, while you are walking, while you are doing something." Once he was asked, "Then how can we do our work? Our mind needs to be concentrated in the work!" He replied, "Do you know what percentage of the mind people use to concentrate upon any work?" Generally the mind is restless, no matter what you are engaged in. You may think you are concentrated on the work, but instead you are thinking that you will vote for this man or that one. Then you begin to think Republican or Democrat. All kinds of thoughts arise in the mind, all kinds of words. Or even no thoughts arise, but you begin to utter some word mentally. Human nature is like that. So my master pointed that if you practice meditation and concentration, you will find that applying twenty percent of your mind to work is enough, and you can give eighty percent to God. No matter what you may be doing, no matter in what situation you may be, you can chant the name of the Lord. It makes no difference: even if it is mechanical, it sinks into your subconscious mind. And then you will find that when you are in trouble, suddenly that name comes to you and you begin to think of God.

Think of that! If you make a practice of it, it will happen. The appeal is couched in these terms in Christianity: "Lord Jesus Christ, have mercy on me. One who accustoms himself to this appeal experiences as a result so deep a consolation and so great a need to offer the prayer always that he can no longer live without it. And it will continue to voice itself within him of its own accord."[4] "Many so-called enlightened people regard this frequent offering of one and the same prayer as

---

4. "The Way of a Pilgrim."

useless and even trifling, calling it mechanical and a thought-less conception of simple people. But unfortunately they do not know the secret which is revealed as a result of this mech-anical exercise; they do not know how this frequent service of the lips imperceptibly becomes a genuine appeal of the heart, sinks down into the inward life, becomes a delight, becomes, as it were, natural to the soul, bringing it light and nourish-ment and leading it on to union with God."[5] (10)

BRAHMAN/SHAKTI

Although there are different stages of unfoldment, in the highest experience, Sri Ramakrishna used to say, there is no difference: "All jackals in their highest pitch have the same cry." Hindu, Christian, Buddhist, Muslim, or Jew — anyone who reaches that ultimate truth is no longer Hindu or Chris-tian or anything other than one who is established in God. Sri Ramakrishna used to say that everything, even the scriptures — the Vedas, the Bible, the Koran — have been defiled because they have been uttered by the lips of man, but that there is one truth, the truth of God, that has never been defiled because it has never been uttered. It is like a dumb man trying to express the taste of some delicious food; he can only say "aah."

Then again, Sri Ramakrishna said that in one ocean of ex-istence, knowledge, and bliss, there is a stick which divides it. The stick is the sense of ego: you enjoy the bliss of God, you love to talk about God with his devotees. And then God be-comes known, not only as impersonal but as personal. There is this creation, and God is the Creator. But then again, where there is no creation, God is the impersonal. When, coming back to your consciousness, you see this universe, then you

---

5. "The Pilgrim Continues His Way."

see God as a personal being; he is the creator. It is not that the impersonal being is one thing and the personal being another: it is the same Reality. When there is no movement, no creation, that is impersonal. When there is movement, when there is creation, that is personal. Shakti, or power, is one with Brahman. When it becomes active, then there is creation; when that power is inactive, one with Brahman, it is the Absolute, the impersonal Reality.

Sri Ramakrishna said: "The primordial power (Shakti) is ever at play creating, preserving, and destroying. This power is called Kali. Kali is verily Brahman, and Brahman is verily Kali. It is one and the same Reality. When we think of it as inactive, that is to say, not engaged in the act of creation, preservation, and destruction, then we call it Brahman. But when it engages in these activities, then we call it Kali or Shakti. The Reality is one and the same; the difference is in name and form. It is like water, called in different languages by different names, such as *jal*, *pani*, water, and so forth ... In the same way, some address the Reality as 'Allah,' some as 'God,' some as 'Brahman,' some as 'Kali,' and others by such names as 'Rama,' 'Jesus,' 'Durga,' 'Hari.'"

From a philosophical standpoint Brahman and Shakti, the Mother Power, are inseparable. When there is no stir, no movement, no creation, then it is called *nirguna* Brahman, Brahman without attributes. You cannot say that he is good, or he is love – he has so many qualities, and yet he is attributeless.

Then again, this universe is an emanation from the Mother power. Then he/she/God becomes *saguna* Brahman — God with attributes. God with attributes is known philosophically as the personal God, and that also is known as Mother. All forms, the many forms of gods and goddesses, emanate from that Mother. The divine incarnation — a Christ or Krishna, a Ramakrishna — are all emanations of the Divine Mother.

And those forms are also eternal. Today the Christ form is existing: you can see him. Ramakrishna is living: you can see him. Krishna is living: you can see him. And if you see him, it is the same as seeing Brahman.

The eternal Mother is described in the scripture this way: In the beginning of a cycle of creation, when there is neither moon nor sun nor planets nor earth, but only darkness enveloped in darkness, there is Mother alone, formless, the eternal consort of the Absolute Brahman. This Mother is the Shakti power composed of three gunas, bundles of energy. When they are at rest, in harmony, there is no creation. When there is disharmony, then the universe emerges — the universe of mind and matter composed of these three gunas, Mother. An individual remains subject to them, and that is bondage. So we have to propitiate Mother, as it were, to free us from the bondage of the gunas; we have to transcend them.

Sri Ramakrishna used to give the illustration: "Mother gives dolls to children, and the children get busy playing with the dolls. But when any one of these children gives up the dolls and cries for Mother, Mother comes immediately and takes the child on her lap. Similarly, this whole creation is all the playthings of life, and we are busy playing with the dolls. When you become tired – you have to go through experience, then get tired – when you see the vanity of everything and come to this understanding that we read in the Bible, "Vanity of vanities, all is vanity, except to love God," then we cry for Mother, then we cry for God. (11)

I will tell you this: none of us can have any conception of God. We conceive of God personal and God impersonal and speak philosophically: Brahman associated with the universal maya is known as the personal God; that is, he who creates, who preserves, and in whom this universe is dissolved. And when we consider Brahman as Brahman itself, then it is impersonal. These are mere words. It is only when we realize, when we experience God that we know that he is personal, he is impersonal, he is with attributes, he is without attributes, and he is beyond. His name is Silence. A person who has experienced God will never describe him as this and not that. But what can we do in our ignorance? It does not matter. Your conception is true to you, it is the reading of that Reality with your limited concept, but you are reading the Reality! (12)

It is said that Mother is composed of three gunas or bundles of energy; at the same time, she transcends the gunas. You cannot define them, but you can tell them by their expressions. When the expression is of calmness, purity, tranquility, that is *sattva*. When there is passion, restlessness, activity, that is *rajas*. When there is lethargy and dullness, that is *tamas*. These three bundles of energy make up this universe of mind and matter. The mystic sees this energy as consciousness; Mother has become everything.

There are two aspects of Mother: one that leads you to freedom and another that leads you to bondage, to ignorance. The individual who identifies with these gunas, does not see Mother, does not know Mother. But the moment when Mother is known, there is the realization that She also is God, who leads to freedom.

Sri Krishna points out in the Gita how difficult it is: "How hard to break through is this my maya, made of the gunas." You see, it is God's maya, Brahman's maya. Mother and Brahman are inseparable, and it is this maya, this Mother, which has deluded us. Christ, in the Lord's Prayer, points out: "Lead us not into temptation." It is very difficult for a Christian mind, which has the Devil to account for evil, to understand how Christ prays to God not to lead us into temptation. Yes,

God is leading us into the temptations of this universe, his creation. Mother is tempting us. Sri Ramakrishna used to say that people are busy with God's creation, forgetting the Creator. That is the delusion, the bondage.

Now again, if we can surrender ourselves, take refuge in Mother, take refuge in God, then we come out of this maya, this ignorance, easily. As Sri Krishna says: "He who takes refuge in me only shall pass beyond maya, he and no other." (13)

One of Sri Ramakrishna's gurus, from whom he learned the truth of nondualistic Vedanta, was Totapuri. When Totapuri saw Sri Ramakrishna chanting the name of Mother and clapping his hands, he said, "Oh, you are preparing chapattis." He used to make fun of Sri Ramakrishna. But then one time he had colic pain and could not control it. Other times he could take his mind away from his body, but this time he couldn't, so he said to himself: "Ah, this body is a great obstacle." He went to drown himself in the river Ganges, but as he walked from one side of the river to the other, the water was not deep enough to drown him. He said, "What is this maya?" Then he saw the Divine Mother's play and realized that without her power, no one can move even a finger. He came back a completely changed man. He went to Sri Ramakrishna and said, "Now I have recognized your Mother."

When Swami Vivekananda went to the temple of Mother Kali, he would call Sri Ramakrishna superstitious for bowing down to the image. Then Vivekananda's father, who had earned plenty of money but had been so charitable that he gave it all away, died and there was nothing left. Vivekananda was a young man and wanted to earn a living to support his mother and two brothers, but he couldn't find a job. At long last he came to Sri Ramakrishna and said, "Please do something. Pray to Mother." Sri Ramakrishna said, "Why don't you go and ask Mother yourself? Go to the temple, and, I tell you, whatever you ask of her, she will grant you." So he proceeded to the temple of Mother. As soon as he saw the image, it became living – conscious, full of bliss – and he was in ecstasy. All he prayed for was: "Mother, grant me love, grant me knowledge, grant me dispassion." When he came back, Sri Ramakrishna said, "Did you ask?" "I forgot." "Go again, but remember." Again he went, and the same thing happened. You know, when you have that experience, everything seems so trivial; you cannot think of triviality. Then the third time Sri Ramakrishna said, "All right, I grant you that your people, your family, will never starve." Then he pointed out the truth that Brahman and Mother power are just like fire and heat; they cannot be separated. (14)

THE KUNDALINI

What I am going to speak about this morning is not theory or metaphysics, but simply a report of the experience of great illumined souls. Just as, through the telescope of the astronomer, things invisible to the naked eye become visible, spiritual truths unknown to ordinary individuals become visible when the divine sight opens.

Religion is fundamentally the knowledge of the truth of God. In order that we can be really spiritual, we must participate in spiritual visions and experiences. Spiritual knowledge is knowledge that cannot be arrived at by argument or reason, by intellect, but is to be experienced by the purified heart. Religion remains mere talk, has no sense or meaning, until we begin to have religious experiences. The gloom of darkness covering our vision does not lift by argument or reason. As we read in the Gita, what is night to ordinary individuals is day to illumined souls. What remains hidden from sight becomes revealed to the illumined soul. To be spiritual is to have that gloom of darkness and ignorance lifted so that we come face to face with the spiritual verities of life.

Too much preaching about theories and beliefs and dogmas and doctrines has been done in the name of religion. These cannot help us until the ignorance that covers our sight is removed. Religion is knowledge, but not the knowledge that the intellect can give us. All spiritual illumination, all spiritual knowledge, comes from within.

Modern science tells us that infinite power exists in the minutest atom. It is not that there exists only a limited and finite power, but infinite power. A scientist who examines a drop of water will find the whole of the solar system existing in this minute object. What is in the universe outside of ourselves is also inside.

Great illumined souls say that the seat of consciousness, which is contentless consciousness and which is one with the infinite Brahman, is seated in the center of the brain. There has come forgetfulness of that consciousness, but they point out that there is a divine energy in every one of us which remains dormant. They call that the *kundalini*, which literally means "coiled up, sleeping." When that becomes awakened and that energy becomes released, spiritual unfoldment follows.

This coiled up energy is located at the base of the spine, and when it becomes unfolded, it passes through different spiritual realms, as it were, giving different visions and experiences. When it becomes united with Brahman, seated in the brain, there comes full illumination.

For you to understand this, I have to explain the spiritual nerves and spiritual centers, which we technically call lotuses. We must remember that these nerves and centers,

these lotuses, are not physical, but they have correspond-
ing physical regions where they are located. They are vital
centers of consciousness only visible to the yogi's eye: when
the divine sight opens, one can see them. If you dissect a
human body, you will never find these nerves and centers,
just as by dissecting a human body you will never find its
soul. And yet they exist as tangible spiritual centers.

To explain fully: there is the spinal column, where all the
centers are located. In the spinal column is a central canal
and there are channels on either side, the left called *ida*, the
right called *pingala*. The center is called *sushumna*. There is
no function in the central channel of the spine; our life energy ordinarily flows through the channels on the right and
left. Now, the life energy has to be made to flow through
the central channel, through the *sushumna*. It is technically
known as the doorway to Brahman. The moment any spiritual
energy flows through that central channel, a new consciousness evolves, just as one who is blind might get physical sight
and so begin to experience the world in a new way.

At the base of the spine is a triple knot of spiritual nerves
forming a triangle, and within that triangle is the *kundalini*,
the coiled-up energy. It looks like a serpent, as thin as the
thread of a lotus stalk. This center at the base of the spine,
the *muladhara*, is the seat of the subconscious mind.

The next center is technically called *svadhisthana*. It is
situated at the root of the genitals and is said to be the seat
of lust and greed. The lotus bud there has six petals. If the
energy rises to this center, there comes, to a degree, the conquest of lust and greed.

The next center, the *manipura*, is situated at the root of the
navel and has ten petals. It is the seat of psychic power. As
the energy rises to that center through the *sushumna*, psychic
visions and experiences and occult powers manifest.

The next center is the center of the heart, which is technically called *anahata*. But before I come to that, let me point out how most people's minds are within these three lower centers: worldliness, lust, physical enjoyment, and experience. Their minds are downward, and until there is an attempt to make the mind move upward, there can be no spiritual growth. You may go to church, you may read, you may do good work; they may help you, but until there is an awakening of the higher centers, there can be no spiritual growth.

All kinds of impulses are in us. If we say we have to satisfy these impulses because they are there, we remain in the animal, beastly, plane. It is only by overcoming these impulses that there is any possibility of spiritual growth. We cannot even think of God as long as the mind remains within the lower centers of consciousness. If we think of God at all, God is accepted as a means to realize our selfish and personal ends and to attain our personal satisfaction in the physical plane.

So the *anahata* is located in the heart. When the *kundalini* rises to this spiritual center – this is really the first *spiritual* center – one has the vision of spiritual life. There comes an illumination. *Anahata* literally means "unstruck sound." Sound is produced by striking two objects, but as the mind is lifted up to this spiritual center, one can hear the spiritual sound, which is produced without striking two bodies. While one is in that spiritual center, there is the experience of a spiritual life, and one hears the Cosmic Word, the Cosmic Sound, OM.

Here again, let me explain that this whole creation comes out of the thought of God. Thought and word are identical. If you study any philosophy, you will find this truth brought out – that the whole universe came out of the thought of God and that thought and word are identical. Hindus claim that this word OM is the first word that arose after creation, that the whole creation proceeds from the word. Creation, then, is a kind of degeneration, and to rise above creation is to become regenerated. The creation is outgoing, it is degeneration; and regeneration is to go back to God. Now in the process of going back to God we retrace, as it were, the same process by which there is creation. Creation proceeded from the sound OM, and regeneration begins with the sound OM.

The next higher center, at the throat, is called the *vishuddha*, which literally means purity. When the mind with the *kundalini* comes to this center of spiritual consciousness, there is a complete regeneration, complete transformation. It is said that one, through spiritual struggles, may rise to the center in the heart, but there is always the possibility of being dragged down to the lower centers. But if the mind rises to this center called the *vishuddha*, one becomes established in purity: nothing, no worldliness, can drag the aspirant down again. The outward sign is that the individual cannot think of anything but God, cannot speak of anything but God, cannot hear of anything but God. If somebody talks about worldly things, there comes a real, physical pain.

The next higher center, called *ajna*, is between the eyebrows. *Ajna* literally means command. Here one attains what we technically call *savikalpa samadhi*. Through absorption there comes the direct experience of God in his personal aspect, but there still remains a separation from God. Here one hears the voice of God with the command to give blessings to others. In other words, one really becomes a spiritual teacher. In the life of Sri Ramakrishna we read how he would approach spiritual teachers and ask, "Have you yet the command of God?" They didn't even understand what he meant. Some would say they have heard the voice of God asking them to go and teach, but whether it was the voice of God or ego, they did not know. But this is a direct command, a direct vision and communion.

At one time my master said he did not do anything without the will of God. I asked him, "What do you mean by the will of God? The same way I or anybody can think and do something and then impute that to the will of God?" One can very sincerely feel that he is doing something by the will of God. Most spiritual souls try to do that and try to wipe out their ego. But when I asked my master if that is what he meant, he said, "No." I said, "Do you mean to say that you see him and he talks to you?" He said, "Yes." A direct communion – to see God, to talk to God – is possible. When the mind comes to that spiritual center within the eyebrows, you have a direct communion with God.

Sri Ramakrishna used to say that when the mind comes there, there is still the separation, still the ego left: *I* hear the will of God, *I* see him. But one feels like a moth before a fire. The fire is protected by a glass, and the moth beats and beats against that glass to jump into the fire. The same desire arises to beat against that separation and to attain to the highest center, called "the thousand-petalled," the *sahasrara*, in the brain.

There the *kundalini* becomes united with Shiva, with Paramatman, the higher Universal Self. And there is complete union. That is *nirvikalpa samadhi*, the Absolute. When the mind rises to that highest center in the brain, there is no longer any vision or experience: There is the knowledge of union.

To those who ask, "Do we lose our individuality?" I ask, "What do you think your individuality is?" There is no answer to that: they simply say, "What I am." But don't you lose what you are? Aren't you losing your self with every growth that comes in you? In fact, we do not know our true individuality. When we reach that attainment, then is it that we know our individuality, and we know that it is in the Infinite. (15)

THE PRACTICE OF RELIGION

Religion has to be made living. We must live the ideal that Christ lived. It is not only possible for a Christ to achieve that end, it is just as possible for every human being on earth. One time I asked an illumined soul,[6] "What is religion?" He answered, "To make the lips and the mind one and the same."

We achieve things, we work tremendously, we devote our whole lives to attaining something, and then what happens? We close our eyes for good. Then what do our achievements amount to? Nothing. If we do not strive to reach union with the Godhead in this very life, our existence is wasted away in the vanities of life. Vain is everything! But then, everything takes on a new life, as it were, if we understand the goal and if we strive to reach that goal.

What is good and what is evil? If any action makes you forget God, that action has no value. But if your activity helps you to unite with God, then that action is good. You see, the whole of life takes a new form; there comes an actual transformation. As Sri Ramakrishna used to say, add zeroes one after another and they are valueless; put *one* first and the value increases. Life is empty and zero without that *one*. If you forget that *one*, if you forget that God, all your achievements and activities in life amount to nothing. People try to forget by getting intoxicated, but that forgetfulness does not last long.

There is a beautiful aphorism in Patanjali: "Nature is for the soul, not the soul for nature."[7] Swami Vivekananda said, "The bee came to suck the honey, but its feet got stuck in the

---

6. Swami Turiyananda
7. This is a quote from Swami Vivekananda's lecture titled "The Secret of Work": "Remember that great saying of the Sankhya, 'The whole of nature is for the soul, not the soul for nature.'"

honey." Instead of enjoying this world, we are enjoyed by the world. My master used to say, "They talk about enjoyment, but who can really enjoy this world? Can the brute enjoy the world? It is only a God that can enjoy life. Be a God! Then only can you enjoy the world."

An illumined soul does not run away from the world, but lives in the world and works for the good of all. Though living in the world, such a person is not of it. There is the illustration of a lotus leaf. You pour water on it, but the water cannot make that leaf wet; the lotus stays in water, but the water does not attach itself to the leaf. It is the same with the illumined soul. (16)

The Divine Mother Durga, the mother of the universe, has two children, Karttika and Ganesha. Karttika is outgoing and is the god of worldly success and prosperity. He is also the god of warriors. Ganesha is contemplative. His mind is inward, devoted to the Divine Mother. One day the Mother held a treasure, a necklace, before them and announced, "Whoever goes around the universe speedily and comes back to me first will receive this treasure of a necklace." Karttika immediately flew around the universe. Of course he was confident that he was the one who would get the treasure. Ganesha took his time, slowly going around the Mother and bowing down to her. Mother gave him that treasure of a necklace and when Karttika came back, he saw Ganesha wearing the necklace. This legend is symbolic. Please remember that both of them are children of the Divine Mother. I'd say that Karttika represents time and technology and Ganesha represents religion or spiritual life. Karttika probes into the outer universe, Ganesha probes into the inner universe.

Exemplars who probe the inner universe are not wanting. There have been great spiritual giants in every religion. They have cleared a path for us; we have only to follow it. Now, of course, in order to follow we must know what the goal of life actually is. Is it the acceptance of certain dogmas, beliefs, and doctrines? Is it to go out and do something? Can we do good to the world only with our hands and feet? These are things to consider.

Spiritual life or spiritual pursuit is not blind and purposeless. It is not something to achieve in the next life. It has a specific end and definite goal to be attained here and now, not after the death of the body. So the spiritual aspirant must think clearly and definitely and understand that goal, for only then will the pursuit of spiritual life be serious and meaningful as the fulfillment of one's life. And fulfillment comes when we realize the eternal, the unchangeable Reality amongst the noneternals of life, when we attain that highest abiding joy in the midst of the fleeting pleasures of life. Where is it? It is all within ourselves.

As the seers of the Upanishads point out: "I have known that Truth" [Svetasvatara Upanishad]. They also tell us: "Ye also shall know the Truth. Then only can you attain freedom and immortality." In the Upanishads again we read: "Brahman may be realized while yet living in this ephemeral body. To fail to realize him is to live in ignorance, and therefore to be subject to birth and death. The knowers of Brahman are immortal; others, knowing him not, continue in the bonds of grief." [Brihadaranyaka Upanishad]

Those who claim to have known God, seen God, had the direct experience of God, are very few in any age. How can we convince ourselves that they are not deluded? Maybe Christ was deluded, Ramakrishna was deluded; they were insane perhaps. But look at their lives, their character! Pure! Look at the power behind them! A majority does not prove the truth. Though a majority can elect a president, a majority cannot elect God.

The fact is that they are in the minority because very few want that. My master one time said, "People's minds are busy with trivial things. Who wants the real treasure?" He also said, "We have the treasure to offer, but people come to get potatoes and onions and eggplants. They can manage to do all kinds of worldly works, but when it comes to spiritual effort, they say, 'Where is the time for it?'" Buddha called this laziness and the greatest sin.

You have to have what we call *viveka*, or discrimination. You have to consider that no matter how your mind runs after worldly things (and that is natural), God is the only treasure, which no moth can eat, as Jesus says. He is the one treasure. And at the same time you have to convince yourself, in spite of your tendencies for worldly things, that "flat, tame and unprofitable are the uses of the world," as Shakespeare writes in *Hamlet*. You have to come to that understanding. (17)

Before we can understand what is meant by the practice of religion, we must try to understand what the purpose of living is, what the meaning of this human life is. The answer is difficult to find independently of one who has had the illumined knowledge of the truth of God. If you analyze, you find that today you seek for this, another day for that. You are not sure. You seek for pleasures – happiness and things like that – but how to find it and what the goal is, we do not know.

If we go to the scriptures or to the words of those who are illumined, who have known the meaning of life, it is pointed out to us that there are four pursuits of life: *dharma*, *artha*, *kama*, and *moksha*. The meaning of *dharma* is the formation of character. We have within us both good and bad tendencies, and we have to live in such a way that a greater emphasis is given to the good tendencies. You see, every person is born with a character. A child has a character, and there are both good and bad tendencies. The child must be taught to live and act in such a way that the good tendencies develop. The character is to be formed by good deeds and pure thoughts, and that means selfless action. One time Swami Vivekananda said to his brother disciples: "Whatever you do for yourself is not religion; whatever you do for others is religion."

So that is the first thing you have to understand – that you have to form a character that is selfless. Then again, you can't live on character, so there is the pursuit of economic freedom, *artha*. But the pursuit is not for the sake of economic freedom in itself, but for something very great. The selfless character you try to form is not the end, but is a means to something higher. The first stage is known as *brahmacharya*, student life, in which the individual learns to acquire *dharma*, a character with good tendencies, along with knowledge, learning. Next, comes married life and the pursuit of economic freedom and the satisfaction of legitimate desires. The third stage of life is retirement. And in the last stage of life one renounces everything and is completely dedicated to God.

As a general rule, one has to pass through all these stages and ultimately renounce everything. The ultimate ideal is complete detachment and renunciation. But in order to achieve that, you have to learn such detachment and devotion to God beginning with life as a student. Gradually those virtues grow and culminate when you are completely absorbed in God. Now generally there are these four stages of life, but it is said that no matter in what stage you may be – student or householder or retiree – any moment that great dispassion possesses you, you take to the last stage of life. You can renounce at any moment in life. The highest goal, therefore, is what we call *moksha*, which is liberation from the bondages of birth, death, and rebirth.

The Hindu and Buddhist idea of the law of karma and reincarnation is that one passes through birth, death, and rebirth many times over. According to what one sows, one reaps. This law of karma is working in everyone's life. And liberation means to be freed from that and to attain immortality. Generally the idea is that immortality means continuity of existence – even what you call matter continues to exist in some form or other; because nothing in this world is destroyed or lost. But immortality does not mean that.

In every religion immortality is something you have to attain. In the Svetasvatara Upanishad there is a verse which says that this vast universe is a wheel going round and round, and all creatures are within this wheel of birth, death, and rebirth. As long as you consider yourself separate from the Atman, from God, so long do you go round this wheel. But the moment you realize and experience that you are the Atman, one with Brahman, the moment you unite yourself with God, you are free and attain immortality.

Swamiji said, "Each soul is potentially divine." Mind you, he says "potentially." It has to be manifested. And, "The goal is to manifest this divinity within by controlling nature, external and internal. Do this either by work, or worship, or psychic control (meaning meditation), or philosophy – by one, or more, or all of these – and be free. This is the whole of religion. Doctrines, or dogmas, or rituals, or books, or temples, or forms, are but secondary details." This is the substance of what religion means.

So what is meant by controlling nature? We identify ourselves with nature. For instance, I begin to feel this desk is mine, that I have a right to it. This house is mine, it belongs to me, I possess it. I identify myself with external nature or inner nature in the mind, which is subject to the gunas. One time it is calm, another time restless or passionate. Again it is lethargic. I identify myself with the moods of the mind, whereas my true nature is Atman, divine. So we have to control external and internal nature by realizing our true being.

Sri Ramakrishna and Swami Vivekananda and all the disciples of Ramakrishna placed before us an ideal which is not one-sided, but which combines all four yogas in one life. In other words, you have to be active as well as meditative, to be devotional as well as philosophical.

People think they have to work out their karma, but you can never work out your karma. You see, every time you work, you are acting and creating new karmas. It is a chain of cause and effect: the effect becomes the cause, and again there is the effect, and so it goes on; there is no end. But when you attain to the knowledge of Brahman, then the law of karma can no longer attach itself to you. If you have done awful deeds, and suddenly illumination comes, you are freed from all that; the effects will not hurt you.

But understanding the ideal is not enough. There are three things necessary for liberation. The first two are human birth and the desire for liberation – for the knowledge of Brahman, for attaining union with God. You have to have longing for it. When Sri Ramakrishna was asked how to know God, his answer was, "Intensely long for him." If you do that, the path becomes clear. That longing does not come all at once, but even a slight desire can be intensified.

The third condition is the association with a holy personality. In the Gita we read: "These illumined souls who have realized the truth will instruct you in the knowledge of Brahman if you prostrate yourself before them, question them, and serve them as a disciple." To prostrate means to listen to the truth taught by the teacher eagerly. To question means to reason upon the teaching and ask about it; otherwise, you won't understand. And to serve the guru means to follow the teachings and to meditate.

What is the practice really? There are two aspects; one is called negative, the other positive. They are both important: purification of the heart; and meditation upon God, love for God, devotion to God. St. Augustine said, "You must have steadfast self-discipline and cleansing of the soul." You have to discipline yourself. You see, I make a rule that you must go to the shrine and meditate for so many hours, but how shall I know what you are doing? You have to discipline yourself.

And what does purification of the heart mean? Thinking of God without any distractions, without desires, cravings, or ambitions. There is a prayer we chant every morning: "Ah, how I long for the day when an instant's separation from Thee, O Govinda, will be as a thousand years; when my heart burns away with its desire and the world without Thee is a heartless void." We have to pray earnestly that the heart may be cleansed and fixed in the Lord; we have to feel that anything without him has no sense or meaning.

Practice, practice, practice! We forget, then again remember. Whatever we hear, every sound, is Brahman. Deify everything.

Now again, there has to be philosophy. We must learn to discriminate between the eternal and the noneternal. We have to realize, to feel, that God alone is real. There is the world, there are duties, and friends, and relatives, but they all have meaning only because of God. And all passes away except God. In him again, you find everything, everybody.

Be devoted to God and meditate upon God. It doesn't matter if you believe in God with form or without form; have some ideal – whatever appeals to you! There are different ways to meditate according to any aspect or ideal, but here is my point. No matter how you worship God – it does not make any difference what your conception of God is – meditate upon that. God sees your heart. Whatever you may be conceiving, he reveals himself to you as he is in reality. That is your only way of knowing God. We cannot conceive exactly of what is beyond thought, beyond comprehension – but *try* to comprehend, *try* to think of him in your own childish way. He will reveal himself to you as he is. (18)

ACTIVE AND CONTEMPLATIVE LIFE

The degree to which you enjoy the bliss of God in this life will determine the degree to which you will enjoy the bliss of God after death. There is a very false idea prevalent amongst many followers of many religions that heaven is to be attained, that we shall find God, after we die. But if we study the source of any religion, we shall find that the truth has been brought out that heaven is within ourselves, and that it has to be attained here and now. If in this life we have not been able to overcome hatred, jealousy, and passions, when we die the death of the body, we shall not be able to overcome them. Wherever we go after death, we carry the same mind, the same consciousness, with us.

I shall try to explain to you, in short, the Hindu theory of evolution, which brings out the ultimate end and goal of every being on earth. You see a huge tree. That tree comes from a very tiny seed. Our theory is that the whole of that tree is in the seed. What we find in the effect is in the cause. In the process of evolution, there is no extraneous substance that gathers, but what is already in the cause unfolds in course of time.

At one extreme we find in this universe dull, dead, inert matter; at the other extreme we find a Christ, a Buddha, an illumined seer. There is no difference whatsoever between a Christ and God; there is no difference between an illumined seer who has attained unitive knowledge and God. Not the least bit of difference. In the Upanishads we read: "A

knower of Brahman becomes Brahman." [Mundaka Upani-
shad] Knowledge of God means unity with God, becoming
God. Therefore it stands to reason that God, which we find
unfolded in a Christ or a Buddha, exists completely in the
minutest dull, dead, inert matter.

In the vegetable kingdom and in the mineral kingdom,
there is that infinite God. By that is meant eternal life, infinite consciousness, abiding happiness. That is God. It exists
in a potential form everywhere, but remains covered with
darkness. In the mineral kingdom there is just darkness, but
when we come to the vegetable kingdom, we find that, though
matter or darkness predominates, there is a certain release of
consciousness: the plant can react. When we come to the animal kingdom, we find that consciousness predominates, but
there is no self-consciousness, no intelligence. When we come
to human beings, we find self-consciousness evolved; but the
human is a slave to matter, to darkness. In the illumined seer
or a Christ or Buddha, we see that infinite consciousness infinitely released. Along with that is attained eternal life and
infinite bliss. The illumined seer transcends the self-consciousness, or ego, which limits infinite consciousness. The sense of
ego is wiped out, and infinite consciousness becomes released
or unfolded.

Now, the condition for this unitive knowledge of God, to
release this God from within us – the "birth in spirit" as Jesus
calls it, or the "awakening" as Buddha says – is to unite our
mind with the spirit. In other words, contemplative life, the
life of union with God, is the end. But we find that the natural
tendency is to unite our thoughts with the objective universe,
because the senses are outgoing. That is how they have been
created. The mind is attached to the senses and so, as the
senses go out, the mind also goes outward into the external
world, forgetting the kingdom of God which is within.

Further, the natural tendency is to seek fulfillment through activities and life in the world. If we understand that the goal is to unfold the Godhead within – and about that our religions are in complete agreement – then we can easily understand that activity or active life is not the end, but that contemplative life in union with God is the end.

Why, then, does the mind become attached to the objective world? Because, through ignorance, it accepts the shadow of life, the appearance of life, as real. Through ignorance that infinite God within remains covered: the mind gets a reflection of that consciousness, of that happiness, of that eternal life, and wants to realize it. But the mind does not know that it is already within, and so it tries to find it in the objective world through the senses. This is life on the plane of the ego, which arises when there is forgetfulness of God within. It obstructs our vision of the Reality.

Try to understand what the objective world is. It is an appearance. Appearance cannot exist without something behind it. As you understand what there is behind the appearance, you will find that God alone exists. You see, you cannot blind your eyes or numb your senses and sense organs. That would not be religion; that would not be growth. Try to find out how God is the ground of all this appearance and how God is the reality within you. When you understand that, go into the external world and work. Be active, use your senses and sense organs, but all the time remember that, under all circumstances, at all times, in all places, in every thing, you must see God and God alone. (19)

THE SELF

Our whole life in this world is centered around "I," the self. I want this, I want to know that, I seek such-and-such things, I am happy or unhappy, and so forth. Yet very few of us inquire into what this "I" is, what this self is, what it is that desires for this, that seeks for that.

At one time Albert Einstein made this wonderful remark: "If you ask me to explain the nature of this universe, I can do it; but if you ask me what is here, I do not know." In the teachings of the Upanishads we find this truth brought out: "Know the Self alone. Give up all other vain talk." [Mundaka Upanishad]

In every religion and philosophy we find the discussion of the nature of the self and its relation to God. Generally speaking, I might say that there are three main schools of thought: dualism, qualified monism, and nondualism. If we go to any religion in the world, we shall find that it falls into one or the other of these three schools of thought. Let me point out that they are not contradictory, but are different stages of spiritual unfoldment. The supreme Reality, the supreme Truth, is realized as the experience of nondualism, no matter to what religion one may belong and no matter whether one begins as a dualist, qualified monist, or nondualist.

But concerning these schools of thought not being contradictory, Sri Ramakrishna quoted an old verse: "As long as I consider myself a physical being, Thou art the master, I am Thy servant. When I consider myself an individual being, Thou art the whole, I am Thy part. When I consider myself as Atman, I am one with Thee."

There are some common points between the three schools of thought. The first is that they all believe in a personal God, the creator, preserver, and destroyer of the universe. And there is the common belief in what we call divine incarnation, that God incarnates as a human being. As we read in the Gita, which is the authority for all schools of thought, "When goodness grows weak, when evil increases, I make myself a body.

In every age I come back to deliver the holy, to destroy the sin of the sinner, and to establish righteousness." When we say that God incarnates, it is not once, but in many different incarnations. It is the same God who incarnates in different forms to suit the needs of different ages.

Nondualism, however, does not limit itself to the ideal of a personal God but also accepts an impersonal, attributeless Brahman. Of course there are not two Gods, one personal, the other impersonal. As long as we see this universe, as long as we think of God as endowed with the power to create and manifest his power, then he is a personal being. But when he withdraws this power unto himself and there is no creation, that is known as the impersonal Brahman. It is the same God that appears as personal and impersonal. Then again, Sri Ramakrishna pointed out that he is beyond, that no one can define him: he is inexpressible, he is indefinable. You see, when you say impersonal, you are also limiting him.

When you realize God, you go beyond all scriptures. It is said in the Vedas that we have to reach a state where the scriptures become no scriptures. Sri Ramakrishna used to say that everything has been defiled through the lips of man, but there is one truth, the truth of God, that has never been defiled, because it has not been expressed in words. His name is Silence.

The Vedas say: "Thou art That." What is the true meaning of *thou*, and what is the true meaning of *That*?

If we take them in their literal, superficial meaning, Brahman, That, and Atman, thou, have opposite attributes, like the sun and a glowworm, a king and his servant, the ocean and the waves. Their identity is established only when they are understood in their proper significance, not in a superficial sense. Atman referred to as the individual soul associated with maya is not one with the personal God. The difference between personal God and the individual is that personal God is associated with his maya – that power to create, preserve, and destroy – and he is the master of His maya; whereas, the individual soul is also Brahman associated with a part of that maya, but is subject to that maya. The individual soul cannot be identified with personal God. Take away maya from Brahman, take away maya from the individual soul, then Brahman and Atman become one.

Now let us try to understand what this individual self or ego is, and how there is Brahman, the true Atman, within us. The individual self is nothing but Brahman identified with what is known technically as sheaths. When this identification arises, then there is the sense of ego, "I" as a separate being. Now of course how this identification has come about is a matter of deep philosophical discussion. In short, I shall try to explain by saying that it is only a statement of fact which is experienced by everybody. It is a universal experience, this ignorance and identification. One may have encyclopedic knowledge and have studied all the scriptures of the world, yet this identification continues to remain.

Let me point out the big difference between light and darkness. You cannot mistake light for darkness, and darkness for light. Similarly, there is the distinction between "I" and "this." There is no mistake about that, but through some inscrutable power we identify "I" with "this." For instance, you are not the body, you are changing. The actions of the body are objects of your experience, and yet there is the identification with the body: I am sick or I am healthy, I am fat or I am thin. It is a statement of fact, this ignorance.

Buddha was very pragmatic. He said, "Why bother about how this ignorance came about? It is just like a man struck by a poisoned arrow; someone comes to take it out and heal him, but he says, 'I will not let you take it out unless you tell me who shot the arrow, what kind of man he was. Was he dark, was he fair, was he tall, was he short?'" You see, it is useless. You are suffering, you are in ignorance, and there is a way out of this ignorance. It cannot be explained, because, as long as we are in ignorance, it is only hearsay to us that we are in ignorance. We do not really comprehend that we are in ignorance. As long as we are in ignorance, there is no explanation. If you find yourself pure, free, and divine – one with Brahman – that question does not arise.

Now let us try to analyze what this true Self is. As mentioned before, the Self, according to the Upanishads, is encased by five sheathes: the sheath of a body, the sheath of what is known as vital energy, the sheath of mind, the sheath of intellect, and the sheath of ego. According to Western psychology, mind, intellect, and ego are all called mind, but in Indian psychology, they differ because of their different functions. I'll not enter into that, but I must point out the difference between Western and Eastern psychology.

According to Western psychology, mind is intelligent. Intelligence is its inherent nature, and mind is identified with the soul or Self. In the East, mind is nonintelligent; only the pure consciousness of the Atman reflected upon the mind makes it appear to be intelligent. You see, I can move my body, not because of the power of the body itself, but because of that pure consciousness behind it, because of Brahman, God.

In the West we find philosophers at a loss to explain how the mind becomes unconscious. If consciousness is its inherent nature, it will always remain conscious. The inherent nature of fire is heat, so if it loses heat, it is no longer fire. According to Indian psychology, the mind is just like iron placed in fire. It is hot. But take the iron away from the heat, and it is no longer hot – because heat is not its inherent nature. Berkeley said, "In sleep and trance, the mind exists not. There is no time, no succession of ideas; to say that mind exists without thinking is a contradiction."

The explanation in Indian psychology is that John, after a good sleep, continues to be John, since experiences unite themselves to the system which existed at the time he went to sleep. They leave themselves in his thoughts, they do not fly to any other being. This continuity of experience requires us to admit a permanent Self underlying all contents of consciousness. In the Katha Upanishad we read this truth: "He through whom man experiences the sleeping or waking state is the all-pervading Self; knowing him, one grieves no more."

To simplify, we can classify these five coverings in three headings: physical, subtle, and causal. When we are awake, we are in these three states and conscious of all three: physical, subtle, and causal. When we dream, we are not conscious of the physical, but we still have the covering of the mind, of the subtle body. And when we are in dreamless sleep, there is still the covering of what we call the causal sheath. This sheath is blissful, because it is nearmost to the Atman, the nature of which is bliss. That is why, when we wake up, we feel, "What a rest I had! How happily I slept!"

Within these three states of consciousness, the Atman cannot be known, Brahman cannot be known. You have to go beyond them and reach what we call the Fourth, *Turiya*, the transcendental, to realize that the Atman is Brahman.

This idea that the Atman is Brahman is not unique to Vedanta. If we study the many religions of the world, we shall find they also say the same thing. Sri Ramakrishna used to say in fun, "All jackals in their highest pitch have the same cry, you can't distinguish them." In Romans we read: "The Spirit itself beareth witness with our spirit that we are the children of God, and if children, then heirs of God, and joint heirs with Christ." But it is a matter of experience. However you understand and study the scriptures, your ignorance is direct and immediate. And only direct and immediate experience can take it away. In the Mahabharata we read: "He who has no personal knowledge but has heard many things cannot understand the scriptures, even as a spoon has no idea of the taste of the soup."

Now, how to realize this truth. There are two kinds of truth. That which is perceived by the five ordinary senses, or inferred from the data provided by them is one kind of truth. Another is that which is perceived by the subtle, super-sensuous power of yoga.

Swami Vivekananda gives the example of a mirror covered with dust; there is no reflection. Take away the dust and you see a perfect reflection. The mind or intelligence must be cleaned to attain the purity in which the truth becomes revealed immediately. In the Upanishads we read: "By the purified mind alone Brahman is to be achieved." [Katha Upanishad] I would say that you have purity of heart when your mind spontaneously moves toward God, when it is thinking of God all the time.

And I would say, to achieve this purity of heart, there are two practices: self-control (or following ethical life), and meditation. In the Upanishads we read: "This Self, who understands all, who knows all, and whose glory is manifest in the universe, lives within the lotus of the heart, the bright throne of Brahman ... With mind illumined by the power of meditation, the wise know him, the blissful, the immortal." [Mundaka Upanishad] Of course, meditation does not mean that we close our eyes and give up our duties and actions, but our actions must be dedicated to God. That also must be a process of meditation.

In the Gita, discussing meditation, we read: "A man can be said to have achieved union with Brahman when his mind is under perfect control and freed from all desires so that he becomes absorbed in the Atman and nothing else. The light of a lamp does not flicker in a windless place." That is the simile used for the one-pointed mind of a yogi who meditates upon the Atman. "When, through the practice of yoga, the mind ceases its restless movements and becomes still, he realizes the Atman. Then he knows that infinite happiness which can be realized by the purified heart, but is beyond the grasp of the senses."

The ego is completely wiped out only in the highest *samadhi*, when one is completely absorbed in meditation. When one comes back from that, the ego comes back – but it is a harmless ego, just like a burnt rope. Then again, there is the experience called *savikalpa samadhi* when one has the vision of God and at the same time the sense of ego. You may call that qualified nondualism. After that, when you come to normal consciousness, as Sri Ramakrishna said, it is just like an ocean divided by a line – the line of that ego: you are here, God is there. So you think of God, you mediate upon God, you pray to God. (20)

THE IMPERSONAL LIFE

Before we can understand what an *im*personal life means, we have to understand what personal life means, and what individuality means.

According to Vedanta, man is fundamentally spirit and is encased in three sheathes, physical, subtle, and causal. The spirit is spirit because it is an unchangeable Reality, the nature of God. In all human beings there is a sense of that presence. We all know how we change – our body, mind, senses, sense-organs, everything changing every moment – but at the same time there is a consciousness in everyone, in the ignorant as well as the wise, that "I am I." You are what you are in spite of all the changes. But in our ignorance none of us know exactly what this "I am" is. The search for God, for Reality, ends ultimately in what I may call realizing the true nature of the Self, the Atman, as Brahman: "I and my Father are one."

Why is it that none of us knows this Atman? Because of an ignorance which is universal, from the highest intellectual man to the most ignorant and barbaric. For instance, every one of you can understand that you are not this body, but in your practical behavior, in all your experience in life, you identify yourself with the body. If somebody pinches you, you feel it.

Then again, ignorance creates something which has no reality: the ego, I as an individual being, separate from everybody and separate from God. The identification of the spirit, or Atman, with the body, mind, senses, and sense-organs has created the sense of ego. And upon this false self, the ego, is centered all our world. Each one of us, as it were, lives in our own world.

Sri Ramakrishna gave the illustration of an onion. You pull off one layer after another to find out what is inside, and there is nothing inside. Am I this body? Am I the character that I have? Am I the mind? They also change. What is your individuality? You are living under an illusion all the time that you have an individuality; it has no reality. Your whole life is centered upon that. As a result, you experience pleasure, pain, birth, death, heat, cold, all the dualities of life – in other words, this relative experience. And with this experience, we become attached to things that give us pleasure, we are averse to things and objects and persons that give us pain. In order to gain happiness or pleasure, we do this, good or bad, and we become subject to the law of karma: what we sow, we reap.

Let us see where the karma attaches itself. Who is doing the good or bad deeds? The Atman? No. You, I, everybody has the sense "I do this." Who is this "I?" That ego, that big fat ego! Now, as long as there is the identification of the Atman with the body, mind, senses, and so on, there is ego arising out of it, and we remain subject to the law of karma – to birth, death, and rebirth.

So what is the nature of Brahman or God or this Atman? *Sat-chit-ananda* – existence-consciousness-bliss. *Ananda* means bliss, the peace that passeth understanding. Now, these are not distinct, not different. *Sat* is *chit* and *ananda*. Where there is existence, there is life, there is consciousness, and there is happiness. To feel I am, or to know I am conscious, or I am happy—these are only the reflection of that Brahman, of *Sat-chit-ananda*. And when there is the urge to overcome this, we transcend this ego and reach the Reality, what we are truly.

The question arises in everyone, what about our individuality? Is it lost? As I just pointed out, you are not yet individuals. Where is your individuality? You are an ocean of existence, knowledge, and bliss. That is the background of every one of us. We are all the time united with that. Huge waves are a Christ or Buddha, and a little ripple is you or me, but our background is that one vast ocean of existence, knowledge, and bliss absolute.

There are two ways to transcend the ego. As G.C. Ghosh said about Swami Vivekananda, "Maya or ignorance tried to bind Vivekananda, but he got so big there was not enough rope to tie him down. And Nag Mahashay became so lean and thin that maya could not put a knot around him." These are the two paths: the path of knowledge and the path of devotion. Jnana, the path of knowledge, is very difficult. It is a direct path that denies the ego completely; it denies the universe of name and form and holds on to that Reality as Brahman: I am Brahman. No ego at all. But as Sri Ramakrishna said, "Is it possible to live like that? If you say there is no thorn and put your hand on a thorn, will it not prick you?" The path of devotion is to surrender your ego to God. But where is that God? Within yourself. The Atman is your chosen ideal. If you worship Christ, he is the Atman within you, dwelling within the shrine of your own heart.

Now again, I must tell you, there are main principles. The first is what we call *shraddha* or faith. You cannot just jump into transcendental consciousness, you have to struggle – through the grace of God. But in order to feel that grace, you have to set your sail. So there has to be struggle, and the first step is faith – in the words of the guru and in the words of the scriptures. The guru and the scriptures point out that God is within each one and that others have realized God, that you must have the faith in yourself that you too can realize God. You have to have this faith.

Then you have to have enthusiasm, you must have interest for the truth of God. For that, you have to meditate, you have to concentrate and think of God. Then interest grows. Enthusiasm comes, and you begin to think of God more and more. From that enthusiasm comes a current of thought, what St. Paul taught as praying unceasingly or what Hindu philosophers call constant recollectedness. As that comes to you, you attain to the knowledge of the Atman or Brahman, which means nothing but self-realization. You realize your own soul as one with God. (21)

Mahavakyas have power behind them. The guru, during initiation into the monastic life, utters one of these *mahavakyas*, according to the particular sect to which that monk belongs. There are four such *mahavakyas* and they have the same meaning, though the words are different. They convey the one supreme truth that the Atman, the Self, is one with Brahman.

This truth is very hard to grasp. It is to be realized and experienced within our own consciousness. Sri Ramakrishna, in this present age, emphasized this one truth of religion, the substance of all religions, that you have to experience the truth of God. Not by learning or by subtle arguments and not by the study of the scriptures, because this truth goes beyond the scriptures or any expression. He pointed out again and again, "You can see God, you can talk to God, you can see him more intimately than I see you before me." You can converse with him, you become one with him. He is your very Self. And to reach that union with Him, to realize that "I am Brahman," is the supreme realization and the experience of total reality.

When we say that Vedanta believes in oneness with God, and then we say, "I am God," there is this misunderstanding: How can I claim to be God who is the creator of this universe? I may realize the Atman, but can that be one with the God who creates and sustains this universe and unto whom this universe goes back? It is not possible. I may realize the Atman as Brahman, but I won't be one with God in that sense: I won't be able to create the universe. When I realize the Atman as Brahman, the universe disappears. Do not misunderstand that this is the same as "I am one with God." God as a personal being and I as an individual being are separate.

When we experience Brahman as the Absolute, the impersonal, then there is no creation, no universe. We can only spell these words, but nobody has the ability to conceive or think of that. But it can be experienced. And when it is experienced, you become dumb, though you may try to express it. It's just like a dumb man trying to express how ice cream tastes.

So how did this universe come into existence? Brahman, when associated with his power – *prakriti*, maya, shakti – manifests creation. Brahman associated with his shakti we call Ishvara or personal God. I cannot be one with that personal God, who is the creator. Then what am I? I am a *jiva*, an individual being, which is Brahman associated with part of that power. In other words, you are also Brahman, but associated and identified with part of this maya, part of this power.

Brahman associated with the universal power, as Ishvara, has control over his shakti, his maya. You and I, as *jivas*, with that little part of maya, are under the control of this maya; we are ignorant, we are deluded. To realize the supreme truth, we have to rise above and beyond the part of maya with which we are identified. We shall come to that. But as long as you have physical consciousness and consider yourself as weighing so many pounds or feeling not so well, so long are you separate from God. In fun Swami Vivekananda used to say, "When I am feeling very well, I am Brahman; and when I have a stomach ache, I say, 'Oh, Mother!'"

With qualified nondualism we feel, "I am an individual being, a part of the universal being, a part of Ishvara, not Brahman." Brahman, the Absolute, cannot have parts; the infinite cannot be divided into parts. But as regards the personal God – God as the creator and preserver – I am his creation, I am a part of him. And then again, when the supreme experience comes and I transcend the body and mind and senses, there is purified mind, and I realize my oneness.

Now of course this is a matter of experience, but what kind of experience? In any kind of knowledge you have the duality of subject and object, and also there is a separate process of knowledge. I see this. I know this. I and this are separate. As long as we have this separateness, the thing in itself is not known. Whatever sensation is brought to the mind by external objects, that sensation is read as that object. The wife considers her husband wonderful at one time, and then again says, "Oh, what a nasty fellow he is!" The same way the husband with the wife. It depends upon the mood. It is not that there is anything wrong with the wife or husband; it is the reading.

If you read properly, there is Brahman in the husband, in the wife, and in yourself. That is the truth that we have to realize. This experience is not, therefore, subject-object, but what Shankara points out as the untying of the three knots of knowledge. The subject, the object, and the process of knowledge become unified: this is in English called unitary consciousness. You see, there is no way to express this. Whether a Christian, a Buddhist, a Muslim, a Jew, or a Hindu, one who attains that supreme truth realizes identity with Brahman. This Atman is Brahman.

Why do we have to realize and experience God? Why not simply believe in God, be good, do good, and, when we die, go and live with the saints of God in heaven? That's a very comfortable religion, but that's not Christianity or Hinduism or Buddhism or anything; it's no religion at all. Matthew Arnold defined religion as ethical life with a tinge of emotionalism. But the truth has to be experienced, and true religion is experiencing God. Throw away all dogmas, doctrines, and theology and establish a relationship with God. Think of God, love God, worship God, meditate upon God, be united with God. That is the whole of religion.

You may consider yourselves weaklings and sinners, but if you go to any scripture, what does it say? In the Psalms you read: "Ye are Gods." In Romans you read: "The Spirit itself beareth witness with our Spirit that we are the children of God. And if children, then heirs, heirs of God, and joint-heirs with Christ." If Christ realized "I and my Father are one," that's the experience you and I must also have.

In the Mundaka Upanishad a beautiful picture is given: "Like two birds of golden plumage, inseparable companions, the individual self and the immortal Self are perched on the branches of the selfsame tree. The former tastes of the sweet and bitter fruits of the tree; the latter, tasting of neither, calmly observes. The individual self, deluded by forgetfulness of his identity with the divine Self, bewildered by his ego, grieves and is sad." You see, it is the individual who by tasting the sweet and bitter fruits of the tree of life is grieved and is sad. "But when he recognizes the worshipful Lord as his own true Self, and beholds His glory, he grieves no more."

There is an analysis in the Upanishads. The Atman, which is one with Brahman, is covered in five sheathes. One, the physical body, is made up of food. It is called the *annamaya-kosha*. Then the *pranamayakosha*, the vital sheath, gives us the power to breathe and live. The *manomayakosha*, the sheath of mind, receives the impressions from the outer world. Then the *vijnanamayakosha* is the sheath of discrimination. And the *anandamayakosha*, the blissful sheath, is the sheath of ego.

In our three states of consciousness – waking, dreaming, and dreamless sleep – we identify with one or the other of the sheathes, or with all the sheathes. When you are awake, you identify yourself with all the sheathes. When you are dreaming, you identify yourself with some of the sheathes. When you are in deep sleep, you identify yourself with the sheath of ego – or causal, or blissful, sheath. It is blissful because it is very near to the Atman, which is blissful. In that state there remains just one sheath of ignorance, which is the cause of all delusion.

Within the three states of waking, dreaming, and dreamless sleep, nobody can see God. But when you have attained the supreme truth beyond the three states of consciousness and you come back, your vision has changed: it is not only in *samadhi* that you can see God. *Samadhi*, or *nirvana*, is beyond these three states. When you come back, you have the eye of the spirit, as it were. Then, even in the so-called dreaming and waking states, you see God. I have seen my master absorbed inwardly, but externally he would be teaching or talking to us.

At one time I was having a discussion with another brother disciple. I said that one can only see God in *samadhi*, and I tried to explain away the experiences of some of the direct disciples of Sri Ramakrishna or his own experience by saying that they were in *bhava-mukha*.[8] My master happened to hear me from his room. Coming out and standing by the door, he said, "So you have become omniscient." I asked him, "But sir, do you mean to say that with these physical eyes one can see God, and can talk to him?" Then he said, in English, "Show me the line of demarcation where matter ends and spirit begins." You see? As long as we do not have the eye of knowledge, as long as we are in ignorance, we may talk about spirit and God and all that, but we only see matter. But when the divine sight opens up and our eyes change, then we see no matter. Then nothing is matter: spirit alone is. God alone is.

But in order to have this experience, we have to practice spiritual disciplines. Sri Ramakrishna gave the illustration: There is fire in the fuel and you may say fire is here, but it doesn't come out. You have to light that fire. Then only can you cook and satisfy your hunger.

Shankara points out, "A buried treasure is not uncovered by merely uttering the words, 'Come forth.' You must follow

---

8. A high state of spiritual awareness between the relative and the Absolute, the mind moving between the *ajna* and *sahasrara chakras*.

the right directions, dig, remove the stones and earth from above it, and then make it your own. In the same way, the pure truth of the Atman, which is buried under maya and the effects of maya can be reached by meditation, contemplation and by the spiritual disciplines such as a knower of Brahman may prescribe – but never by subtle arguments."

The main principle in spiritual discipline is meditation, contemplation. You have to learn to go within. The senses are going outward; the mind is traveling outward. The senses have to be controlled; the mind has to be turned inward. You can't find God gazing into the sky. You have to find him within yourself first – then you find him everywhere. I have often repeated the truth that I learned from my master. "He who has it here (pointing to his own heart), has it everywhere. If he has it not here, he has it nowhere."

So the kingdom of heaven is within, and our outgoing mind has to be turned inward. With the help of that consciousness which is one with God, we are living and moving and having our being in God all the time, every moment of our life – because a living being is a conscious being, and consciousness is of the Atman, the Self, that is one with Brahman. With the help of that consciousness, I see you, and I can do good or bad deeds.

In the Mundaka Upanishad we read: "The sage knows Brahman, the support of all, the pure effulgent being, in whom is contained the universe. They who worship the sage, and do so without thought of self, cross the boundary of birth and death." The sage or *avatara* is like a pure mirror upon which is reflected the Atman, the Self. When they say: "I am the life, the way, the truth, the sanctuary, be devoted to me," that "me" is not any individual. That is Brahman. (22)

Hearing one of the four *Mahavakyas*, a disciple has to reason upon it – not to accept it at face value, but to reason it out and try to get an intellectual understanding of what this Atman is and what Brahman is.

It is not possible to prove the existence of God. So what is the proof? Go to a Christ and ask him and he will say: "I have seen him, I have known him." And he doesn't stop there. He also says, "You also can know him." That is religion.

Belief in God makes no difference. An atheist is much better, because an atheist is thinking. This may sound blasphemous, but it is the fact. You see, there is no atheist. One can be an agnostic, but atheism is not sincere. How can one know there is no God? An agnostic will experiment and experience the truth.

In the matter of inquiry into Brahman or God, the only proof is your personal experience. Until you have realized that, there is no difference between you and an agnostic or an atheist.

All the great teachers of the world from ancient times to the present have ultimately experienced "I and my Father are one." "I am Brahman." You may begin as a dualist and pray to God somewhere above, but you will begin to feel that God within. Ultimately that experience comes to every sincere seeker.

What we are all seeking is freedom, happiness, pure knowledge, pure love – and the nature of the Atman or God within us is such. There is the struggle in every one of us to unfold that divinity, but the struggle begins only when we realize that in the infinite alone are happiness and fulfillment. Then spiritual life has begun. Of course when you learn this truth, "Thou art That" or "That art thou," you do not identify *thou* with your empirical ego or self. That would be blasphemous. Man as he knows himself to be is not Brahman, is not God; he is a *jiva*, an individual being. (23)

The guru sees God in the disciple and points out, "That thou art. Meditate upon That." It is said that a disciple who learns to see Brahman in the guru becomes the guru. Sri Ramakrishna was seated with his disciples and said, "Do you know what I see? I see Brahman, I see Rama." My master one time said to me, "I see God playing in so many forms. Just masks." God has put on different masks – the mask of a sinner and the mask of a saint. But a holy man or woman sees no sinner – only Brahman, only God. That is the supreme experience. *And it is a matter of experience.*

Those who become interested in spiritual life may begin as dualists, worshiping God as a separate being, and they learn to love God. But when this love becomes intense, then the lover, the beloved, and love become one. So whether you begin as a dualist on the path of devotion, or a nondualist on the path of knowledge, ultimately you are led to that one nondual experience. If you go to the source of any religion, you will find that most theological ideas are dualistic, but the great mystics in every religion, in every age, in every country, have attained to the same experience of nondualism. When Christ says, "Be ye perfect, even as the Father which is in heaven is perfect," that perfection is achieved when this ideal, this goal, is attained.

One Christian mystic, Meister Eckhart, from the depths of his own experience, said, "Some there are so simple as to think of God as if he dwelt there, and of themselves as being here. It is not so. God and I are one." This experience is not merely an intellectual experience or understanding. You see, our ignorance, our limitations that we find in ourselves, are direct and immediate experience. We have to have another direct experience, just as the guru has had, and see that we are Brahman. Know it! Realize it! Until then, there will be no freedom from ignorance and limitation and the bondages of life.

The ultimate truth cannot be comprehended intellectually, because our intellect works within certain limitations – time, space, and relativity – and this experience is beyond time, space, and relativity. You have to hear about the truth, reason upon it, intellectually try to grasp it – though you cannot – and then meditate and meditate and meditate until it becomes revealed to you.

The Zen Buddhist authority, D. T. Suzuki, says: "Since ultimate truth cannot be comprehended intellectually, philosophers are not necessarily wise men." Only the person who has known the real Self, can know what he is talking about. Make every effort to realize the Self. For there can be no joy in the universe for one who is restricted to the empirical ego.

You see, we are restricted, we are confined, to this empirical ego, which I know as myself. Swami and John and Jill are not Brahman. This ego has no reality; it is a shadow, but we hold onto that shadow as real.

Please try to convince yourself that when you are worshiping, what you want to realize is within yourself, is your true Self, but covered by the physical sheath, the vital sheath, the sheath of mind, sheath of intellect, and the sheath of ego. None of these is Atman, the true Self. I consider myself as an individual being because I have a body and a mind separate from yours. I have an ego, and this is what separates each individual from God and each individual from others and from the universe. In reality, there is only unity, oneness. Ignorance is nothing but identifying the Atman, the true Self, with the sheathes.

You can easily understand through analysis that you are not the body, which is changing all the time; in a few years it will be a completely different body. And yet in every behavior, in every empirical experience, we identify ourselves with the body. If you pinch me, I say, "Ow!" It hurts because there is this identification. But when I have the knowledge of the Atman and am completely detached, you can hurt the body and I won't be hurt.

The mind is subject to pleasure and pain, and I identify myself with the mind. As such, sometimes I am happy, sometimes unhappy, sometimes in a good mood, other times in a bad mood. I identify myself with all the moods and changes of the mind. But in reality my true nature, the Atman, is blissful, and when that blissful nature is experienced, I remain in bliss.

When we say that God can be known, it is not within the three states of waking, dreaming and dreamless sleep. You have to transcend these three states, and this power to attain *samadhi* or *nirvana* is within every one of us potentially. Plato pointed that out in these words: "The object will not be to generate in the person the power of seeing. On the contrary, it assumes that he possesses it, though he is turned in a wrong direction and does not look to the right quarter. Its aim is to remedy this defect."

There is one ether, but there are walls, so there is ether within the walls and ether outside the walls. Take away the walls and there is one ether. Take away ignorance, there is one Atman, one God, one Brahman. (24)

I must try summarily to explain to you what is really meant by superconscious or transcendental revelation. In our relative knowledge or experience, I am the knower, and there is an object of knowledge. There is a subject, and there is an object. I know this; and this that I know is something separate from me. Now again, what I know and experience is only a relative truth, because when I see and experience it, what the object is in reality, I do not know. Only a sensation is produced by my perception of the object, which I interpret in my own way.

As the great German philosopher, Immanuel Kant, pointed out, the thing in itself remains unknown and, he said, unknowable. Our great Indian philosophers also pointed out that as long as there is the least demarcation between the subject and the object, the reality does not become known. But there is such a thing as untying the three knots of the knower, the object of knowledge, and the process of knowledge. There is such an experience of unified consciousness, and only when we reach that unified consciousness do we know the Reality. But of course you can't say, "I know it," because it is being and becoming. Some try to express the inexpressible by saying there is "thou and That" or "I and Brahman," but no, it is oneness: absolute existence, absolute knowledge, and absolute bliss. That is what is meant by the supreme ideal of life.

The Upanishads teach uncompromisingly the supreme truth of unity – of identity – between the Self and Brahman. They point out that one who realizes this Truth overcomes death, goes beyond sorrow, and reaches the ultimate goal. Of course, it is to be realized, to be experienced. We do not know what the Self is, nor do we know what Brahman is. We do not know what *thou* means, nor do we know what *That* means. So it is pointed out that you have to hear about this truth, then to reason upon it, and then to meditate upon it. Through meditation, the door opens up.

The individual self is what you may call the experiencer of happiness and misery, the one who tastes the sweet and bitter fruits of the tree of life. One who thinks, I am the doer, is bound by the law of karma, or cause and effect. What you sow, that you reap. But when you come to the absolute Reality, this individual self 'round which our whole world is centered becomes a shadow, a reflection without reality. Upon that shadow we build everything. (25)

Neti neti Atma. Not this, not that. Whatever you can think, can conceive, can sense, can perceive – that is not the Atman, that is not God. The Atman is something beyond, and the revelation of something beyond comes in a transcendental state of consciousness. First, you see, it is a denial of everything that we sense and perceive. There is one Reality, Brahman; everything else is unreal. All is Brahman. When you realize "I am He, I am That, or thou art That", you see That everywhere; it is a new vision.

Most of us have vision for only a few feet. If I am in misery, I try to find the cause of that misery and to overcome it, but then again I'm in misery. There is one problem and one worry after another. And there are also pleasures. Whether what we are seeking is spiritual life or not, we are all seeking to avoid suffering and misery completely. So we have to go to the root of the ignorance and get rid of it. What can get rid of ignorance? Knowledge. Wisdom. Ignorance is direct and immediate, and it can be removed by something that is immediate: light, knowledge, wisdom. Not the intellect! You may know intellectually that you are not the body, you can analyze and believe that, but if I give you a little pinch, you feel it. So you need a direct experience. You have to come to that knowledge where you are not identified, where at any moment you can detach yourself. Then you are free from all limitations, and your heaviest sorrow is turned into joy. (26)

As I was trying to think what the impersonal life means, I was reminded of a young boy, Sharat, who approached his master, Sri Ramakrishna. Ramakrishna asked him, "What is it that you want to attain in life?" His answer was: "I want to see Brahman, to see God, everywhere and in all, because I have heard this truth: 'All verily is Brahman.' I want to realize that." Sri Ramakrishna said, "That is the last word of religion. But my boy, you will attain that."

This Sharat became known as Swami Saradananda. He was one of the first apostles of Sri Ramakrishna. I'll tell you my experience with him. In a way he was instrumental in sending me to this country to represent the Order. As we were walking together – I was behind him – he suddenly turned toward me and said, "Well, you're going to cross seven rivers and seven oceans." I said, "Yes, Holy Sir, but I don't know what I can do." His reply was something that should go down in history. He turned toward me and said in English, "That's none of your business. We shall see to that." Now as I stand here and tell this story, it seems to me that if I can live that life and preach with that attitude, that would be the impersonal life.

To come to the point, Brahman is all. That is the last word of religion. When we attain that experience – it is not an emotional experience, not an intellectual understanding, but one that transcends emotion and intellect – we come face to face with Reality. When that Truth is experienced and you see Brahman in the face of everybody and within yourself, have you any separate identity? Have you any separate individuality? Aren't you living in all? That is the impersonal life.

From an intellectual standpoint, how can Brahman be all? Consider the physical universe. There seems to be a gap between your body and my body, but is there? Isn't there one mass of existence? Aren't the cells of your body, my body and all bodies revolving and touching one another?

Then consider the mind. I can communicate with you, and you with me. How is that possible? If you and I are completely separate, no communication is possible. In the mental world also there is one cosmic mind. Your mind and my mind and everybody's mind are so many waves in that cosmic mind. If we just analyze a little, we can see the truth of this.

Then when we consider the Spirit or God, there is but one. You and I and every being in the universe are just one Spirit: I am That, one with Brahman. To translate the phraseology of our Sanskrit, "From Brahma, the Creator, down to the blade of grass and the pillar, there is just one Spirit, one God pervading."

I made the distinction between the physical universe, the mind, and the spirit. That is how it appears from our intellectual standpoint, from this level of consciousness. But when you come to a higher level of consciousness and experience knowledge from the standpoint of total Reality, then there is neither body nor mind; there is just one unity: God, Spirit, nothing else.

What has modern science to say about it? The science of today, I would say, can be said to be metaphysics. What was the definition of matter and spirit in olden days? That consciousness is the property of the spirit, which distinguishes it from matter. But modern science points out that there is no matter; matter is dematerialized. Consciousness is present everywhere. The mineral kingdom seems like dull, dead matter, but the vision of an illumined soul is this: I went walking one day with a holy man and he pointed to a rock and said, "Look at that rock. That is God sleeping."

A great Hindu scientist, Dr. J.C. Bose, a contemporary of Vivekananda, came to Europe and America to prove that Brahman is everywhere. He had some delicate instruments which record reaction. That is how we know one has feeling and consciousness: by reaction. Dr. Bose proved that metal also reacts to feelings and thoughts. Not only is there feeling in plants and vegetables and flowers, but also in metals. The West has since proved that the vegetable kingdom responds to our feelings and thoughts – it is an established fact that plants respond to affection, kindness, and love.

There is a great objection to mysticism, that you are no longer an individual being if you are absorbed in God. Really, when we lose ourselves in God and see nothing but God, then is it that we have supreme happiness. The illustration given in the Upanishads is of a husband and wife in each other's embrace. There comes a moment when they feel an intense bliss: they have forgotten themselves. But this bliss we see in the world is a shadow. If you can lose yourself in the source of all bliss, it becomes abiding, permanent. To quote Sri Ramakrishna: "Then one experiences the bliss of sexual union through every pore of the body, that bliss of union with God." (27)

THE PROBLEM OF EVIL

The problem of evil is central to every religion and philosophy and to every individual. To quote the philosopher, Kapila, the supreme purpose of life is the complete cessation of suffering and misery. Mark the words "complete cessation." Yes, suffering comes, misery comes, and we overcome them. But they arise again. So the supreme purpose is not just a temporary overcoming, but a complete cessation of suffering and misery. It can be pointed out that the great teachers – a Kapila or a Christ – include so-called happiness in the category of suffering.

Let me give you an example. The other day I received a letter from a young Hindu girl who is happily married. Both husband and wife are graduates of American universities and they both have good jobs. They have no lack or want in the worldly sense, and they have a little baby. But she writes, "Swami, I have everything that makes for happiness in the world, but I am not happy. How can I find peace? How can I find happiness?"

There is the illustration of the great Buddha. He had everything that the world could offer, but he found suffering and misery in the three woes of mankind: old age, disease, and death. I may point out that every religion, every great teacher, shows the way to overcome suffering and misery. You may say the Oriental religions are pessimistic, seeing everything as suffering, but the word in our language means ever-changing, constant flux. This is also the attitude of Christ: "Ye shall have tribulations in the world, but I have overcome the world."

From a practical standpoint, how can we remove this suffering and overcome all tribulations? What is the way to peace? Every religion has given us the means, by which we can realize that infinite bliss in this very life. That is, if by religion we mean realization – experiencing the reality, the truth, of God. But theoretical doctrines and dogmas or philosophical speculations are confusing.

Why does God permit such suffering? I have no answer. This reminds me of an interesting incident. Two disciples of Ramakrishna – Swami Turiyananda, who was a great scholar; and Swami Adbhutananda, who was completely unlettered – were having a discussion. Swami Turiyananda was explaining the law of karma. Swami Adbhutananda listened with great interest, then asked his brother disciple, "Brother Hari, did the Lord appoint you as his lawyer that you have to justify the Lord's conduct?" And both of them had a hearty laugh.

You know, if you come to a holy man with your suffering, with a restless mind, not knowing where to find peace, does he give you a discourse? No. You sit in his presence and you find peace. I have seen that. So when it comes to the problem of evil, I would only say, who can tell the mysterious ways of God? Of course I can point out philosophically and intellectually that what you call suffering and misery is really nothing, that there is no such thing. But that doesn't help when you are suffering.

We cannot deny any experience, no matter how much anybody can say it is not true. When I am in a dream and experiencing happiness or suffering, no amount of argument at that moment will help. When I wake up, my heart may still palpitate for a while, even though I know the dream was not real. You see, there are degrees of reality.

Then again, there is an experience which is not contradicted by any other experience, but which contradicts all other experiences. In our wakeful consciousness, we experience so many things, but we wake up to the experience of the reality that is timeless, beyond space and relativity. That experience contradicts our waking experience; in it there is neither good nor evil, neither happiness nor suffering. To quote from the Chandogya Upanishad: "This Infinite is the Self. The Self is below, above, behind, before, to the right, to the left. I am all this. This infinite is the Atman, the Self. One who knows, meditates upon, and realizes the truth of the Self – such a one delights in the Self, revels in the Self, rejoices in the Self. He becomes master of himself, and master of all the worlds. Slaves are they who know not this truth."

So we are caught in the wheel of karmas, both good and evil, and there is no escape as long as we are within ignorance. The world will continue as it is, good and evil. You know, if there were no evil, there would also be no good. There is an interesting parable of Sri Ramakrishna. Sita and Rama were seated together and Sita said, "Rama, I went out into the city to see the condition of the people, and I saw that there are houses that are dilapidated, and poverty. All this must be removed." So Rama had the city rebuilt. After some time the masons and carpenters and plumbers came and complained, "We have no jobs!" So Rama told Sita, "You see how it is."

The world will go on as it is. To expect a millennium is to expect the impossible. Individuals have to come out of the world. And there is a way out. As Buddha taught: there is suffering, there is a cause of suffering, there is a way out of suffering, and there is a way of peace. My master once told me, "Meditate, meditate, meditate. Find the mine of bliss. Then you will realize how people suffer for no reason, when in every one there is that mine of bliss." (28)

REINCARNATION AND IMMORTALITY

Whence? Why? Whither? These are the eternal questions. Whence have we come, why are we here, whither do we go? The naturalist philosophers want us to be realistic and point out, "Why bother about such questions? Live your life. Make the most of it." These people think that they are very practical and that those who inquire into such truths and devote themselves to finding a solution are dreamers.

But you see a man walking the streets with a big load on his head and you ask him, "What is that load?" "I don't know." "Whence are you coming?" "Oh, I have no idea." "Whither are you going with this load?" "I don't know. I don't care to know." Would you consider such a fellow practical or realistic?

We have this life. What is the meaning of it? Why are we born, and what is the meaning of death? Every day we know that people are dying; we read the obituary notices, but the most peculiar thing is that none of us believe "I will die." We are constituted in such a way that we cannot think it.

The real solution to these problems is not to be had through theological doctrines, philosophy, or even scriptures. The only solution is to be found within yourself, when you realize the nature of your true self as birthless and deathless, when you realize the true nature of the Atman or Self as one with the

Universal Self, Brahman. Only the mystic who has realized that unity behind this manifold appearance has solved the problem. And each one of us individually has to solve that problem as well.

Today you hear everywhere in the Christian world how Christ rose from the dead. Each one of us has to rise from the dead. In other words, we have to overcome death and attain to immortality by knowing the true nature of the Atman. We are buried in this physical body, this physical consciousness, and we have to rise above that. That is resurrection, that is the attainment of immortality. (29)

There is a story that the king of the gods, Indra, once became a pig wallowing in maya. He had a she-pig and a lot of baby pigs and was very happy. Then some gods saw his plight and told him: "You are the king of the gods. You have all the gods under your command. Why are you here?" But Indra said: "Never mind. I am all right here. I don't care for heaven while I have this sow and these little pigs." The poor gods were at their wits' end. After a time they decided to slay all the pigs one after another. When all were dead, Indra began to weep and mourn. Then the gods ripped his pig body open. Indra came out of it and began to laugh when he realized what a hideous dream he had had. He, the king of the gods, becoming a pig, had thought that pig-life was the only life!

I tell this story to indicate to you the ultimate nature of every one of us. In the Upanishads we find the great seer addressing all mankind this way: "Hear, ye children of immortal bliss!" [Svetasvatara Upanishad] You are the children of immortal bliss! Your true nature is infinite! Not that you exist, but that you are existence itself! Not that you love, but that you are love itself. Not that you know, but that you are knowledge itself. Infinite knowledge, abiding love, and immortal bliss – that is your nature; that is everyone's nature. That is the true being in ourselves. But, through ignorance, we have forgotten.

Wake up to that nature. You are dreaming this hideous dream. You are afraid of death, suffering, and misery, you are afraid of meeting this world. Everywhere there is only fear, but this only is a bad dream! Wake up! Where is God? You are God! Where is Christ? You are Christ! Let that Christ be resurrected in you!

You ask, what about my personality? Do you want to hug that pig body? What is that personality? Your character? Your individuality? What you are? Do you want to stay as you are? Can you continue to stay as you are the next moment? Are you not dying to your personality every moment of your life? Consider: when you have intense sense pleasure, you forget yourself, don't you? It is by forgetting your little self, your so-called personality, that you find your true Self.

That ocean of existence, knowledge, and bliss is what you are. That is your true personality. In that ocean is the fulfillment of everything that you are seeking and desiring. When you reach that, you will laugh, just like Indra the king of the gods, laughed: "What a bad dream it was!" I want every one of you to think of that true nature of yours and meditate upon that. Do not consider yourselves mortal human beings, subject to disease and death – that is not you. Meditate upon your true divine nature.

If you cannot identify yourself with that, if you cannot meditate upon this truth, "That thou art" or "I am Brahman, the ocean of existence, knowledge, and bliss absolute," then try to think and believe. If you believe in anything, believe in the truth that the kingdom of heaven is within. Live in that consciousness. That is religion, that is resurrection, that is attainment of perfection. Through such meditation, you come face to face with the Reality, which is your divine nature. Let the dream vanish!

Sri Krishna says in the Bhagavad Gita: "There was never a time when I did not exist, nor you, nor any of these beings. Nor is there any future in which we shall cease to be." In the Svetasvatara Upanishad we read: "This vast universe is a wheel, upon it are all creatures that are subject to birth, death, and rebirth. Round and round it turns and never stops. It is the wheel of Brahman. As long as the individual thinks that it is separate from Brahman, it revolves upon the wheel in bondage to the laws of birth, death, and rebirth. But when, through the grace of Brahman, it realizes its identity with him, it revolves upon the wheel no longer. It achieves immortality."

What is that experience? Shankara expresses it: "The ocean of Brahman is full of nectar – the joy of the Atman. The treasure I have found there cannot be described in words. The mind cannot conceive of it. My mind fell like a hail-stone into that vast expanse of Brahman's ocean; touching one drop of it, I melted away, and became one with Brahman. And now, though I return to human consciousness, I abide in the joy of the Atman."

This is the experience of those who are free while living. That is the ideal – to attain that knowledge of Brahman, of our true nature, while living here. Then, it is said, those people devote themselves to God, meditate upon him, and live in the consciousness of God. Either while living, or at the moment of death, they will attain the vision, they will have *samadhi*. Again, failing to achieve that, they will be born in higher and higher realms of consciousness until they come to the highest plane, called *brahmaloka*. There they realize their oneness with Brahman and do not return. This process is called gradual liberation.

Whatever one thinks at the moment of death is most important, because that thought has been the most predominant throughout life. A person attached to money will think of money. Be attached, but be attached to God. To quote the Gita: "At the hour of death, when a man leaves his body, he must depart with his consciousness absorbed in Me. Then he will be united with Me. Be certain of that. Whatever a man remembers at the last, when he is leaving the body, will be realized by him in the hereafter, because that will be what his mind has most constantly dwelt on during his life. Therefore, you must remember me at all times and do your duty. If your mind and heart are set upon Me constantly, you will come to Me. Never doubt that. Make a habit of practicing meditation and do not let your mind be distracted. In this way, you will come finally to the Lord, who is the life-giver, the highest of the high." (30)

Those of you who know the history of Christianity will remember how the idea of reincarnation was accepted by some priests and bishops for five hundred years. Not only that, they held the belief that this creation has no beginning and no end. They also believed, like Hindus, that everyone ultimately will attain that Reality. But eventually that view was voted down and since then, the idea of reincarnation has become an anathema to the Christian Church.

It is very difficult to translate the word *karma* into English. According to the particular usage of the word in a sentence, it means different things. But when it comes to the law of karma, the word karma means actions or work. This action includes thoughts as well: thinking is a process of action. Again, it is not only what we think consciously, but also subconsciously, because subconscious thoughts become habitual thoughts and actions.

Karma, again, has two kinds of affects. One is that it forms character, good or bad, or a mixture of good and bad, because what you may call good karma has something bad in it. The other effect is either happiness or suffering and misery. For instance, one may complain that people are hostile (there is a persecution complex), but the question arises: do you love these people? If you love, you will find love; if you yourself are hostile, you get the reaction of hostility. We read in the Old Testament,[9] "Even as I have seen, they that plow iniquity, and sow wickedness, reap the same;" and from Manu the lawgiver of India, "Thou canst not gather what thou dost not sow. As thou dost plant the tree, so will it grow."

The English philosopher, John Locke, said that the mind is a *tabula rasa*, a blank piece of paper, but other Western philosophers have disagreed. In the words of Plato, "If your favorite doctrine, Socrates, that knowledge is simply recollection, is true, it necessarily implies a previous time in which we learned that which we recollect – but this would be impossible unless our soul was in some place before existing in human form."

Immanuel Kant said, "There is no religion in this world which does not believe in immortality." And Schopenhauer points out that if you take the first birth theory and claim your soul is immortal, you are saying, "an infinite stick with one end in view."

It is a great blessing that we do not remember our past. Yet there comes a time in everyone's life in the course of progress when the past comes to you like in a moving picture, but you are not affected by it. You are detached from it.

There is a misunderstanding, in India as well as in the West, that the law of karma creates bondage, so let us give

---

9. Job 4.8.

up karmas, all actions, they say. But Sri Krishna in the Gita emphasized that giving up of actions does not mean renunciation of action: we have to act, nobody can live without action, but Sri Krishna gives us the secret of action. It is as if, through action, we unwind our karmas. By karma we are winding bondages. Unwinding that thread of karma, we obtain freedom from karma through renunciation of the results of the action, by offering everything to God.

The illumined soul, whose heart is Brahman's heart, thinks always, "I am doing nothing." No matter what he or she sees, hears, touches, eats – whether moving, sleeping, eating, grasping, opening the eyes, or closing the eyes – the illumined soul always knows, "I am not seeing, I am not hearing: it is the senses that see and hear and touch the things of the senses."

There is in Judaism, as well as in Christianity, the idea of immortality. From the Psalms: "Consider and hear me, O Lord my God. Lighten my eyes, lest I sleep the sleep of death." Then there is the quote from the Gospel according to St. John: "Verily, verily, I say unto you, he that heareth my words and believeth on Him that sent me, shall have everlasting life, and shall not come into condemnation, but is passed from death into life. If a man keep my saying, he shall never see death." And there was the conversation at the well: "Whosoever drinketh of this water shall thirst again, but whosoever drinketh of the water that I shall give him, shall never thirst, but the water that I shall give him shall be in him a well of water springing up into eternal everlasting life."

St. Paul pointed out: "Flesh and blood cannot inherit the kingdom of God. Neither does corruption inherit incorruption. Behold, I saw your mystery, we shall not all sleep, but we shall all be changed, when this corruptible self hath put on incorruption and this mortal shall have put on immortality. Then shall be brought to pass the saying that is written, 'Death is swallowed up in victory.'" (31)

While we are pursuing the fulfillment of legitimate aspirations in life which are desirable, attractive, sweet, and lovable, at the same time throughout our life, we must have the discrimination that these are passing, that we shall have to renounce them some time or other.

The supreme goal of life is to reach liberation, to unfold the divinity that is within each human being in the universe. It is the same ideal that Jesus set forth: "Be ye perfect, even as the Father which is in Heaven is perfect." St. Paul said: "Ye are complete in Godhead." To realize God, to realize the Atman, the Self, which is one with God, is to attain immortality. Here and now, not after the death of the body.

Christ pointed out: "The kingdom of Heaven is within." Then he said: "Except a man be born again, he cannot enter into that kingdom of God." It is a new birth. But you don't have to die to have that new birth. And it has to be a direct experience. You cannot have any idea of the beauty of the moon by looking at a painting of the moon, as you cannot appease your hunger if somebody else eats for you. Similarly, there are these exemplars – Christ, Buddha, Krishna, Ramakrishna, and all the great mystics of the world in every age – but simply believing in them will not help you. You have to reach That yourself.

Now let us consider, what after death? Or what is death? In the Bhagavad Gita we read: "Just as the dweller in the body passes through childhood, youth and old age, so at death, he passes into another body. Wornout garments are shed by the body. Worn-out bodies are shed by the dweller within this body. New bodies are donned by the dweller, like garments."

There is another truth in the Upanishads: "The knots of ignorance of the heart are cut asunder, all doubts cease to exist, effects of karmas become exhausted, when he realizes him who is both far and near." [Mundaka Upanishad] (32)

I'd like to explain to you in the words of Swami Vivekananda the true nature of the human soul and of the universe. He says that there is nothing outside Brahman. Nothing at all. All this is He. I am looking at you; what am I seeing in reality? God, God, God – everywhere. He is in the universe, He Himself is this universe. "Thou art the man, thou art the woman, thou art the young man walking in the pride of his youth, thou art the old man tottering on his staff."

In the New Testament you have the conception: "In Him we live, move, and have our being." The idea is: God is immanent in the universe, the very essence, the heart, the soul of things. He manifests himself, as it were, in this universe. You and I are little points, little channels, little expressions, all living inside that infinite ocean of existence, knowledge and bliss. We are all living in that ocean of Brahman all the time. The difference between one person and another, between angels and human beings, between humans and animals, between animals and plants, between plants and stones, is not of kind – because everything from the highest angel to the lowest particle of matter is but an expression of that infinite Oneness. The difference is only in degree.

You and I are both outlets of the same Brahman, the same ocean that is God. You are of the same nature as God by your birthright, and so am I. You may be an angel of purity, I may be the blackest of demons. Nevertheless, my birthright is that infinite ocean of existence-knowledge-bliss absolute, and so is yours. You have manifested your power. Wait, I shall manifest mine, for I have it all within me.

Thus every creature from the atom or the worm that crawls under our feet to the highest manifestation that we find in Christ or Krishna, in Buddha or Ramakrishna, each one will unfold that same divinity. The only difference between an *avatara* or a Christ, a Son of God, and you and me, is not in kind, but in degree of manifestation.

This reminds me of an incident. Swami Turiyananda was walking on the streets of New York with a disciple. With great force and in a loud voice, he said, "Gurudas! Come out like a lion from this cage of the bondage of ignorance!"

The meaning of resurrection, as Plato pointed out, is that we rise from being buried in ignorance. Every one of us has to be resurrected, by rising from ignorance, by transcending the different sheaths of ignorance – the mind, body, sense organs, ego. When we transcend all these, then there is resurrection, then there is the identity of self with Brahman. Sri Krishna pointed out to his disciple Arjuna, "You cannot see me and my total reality, in my universal form, but I shall give you divine sight."

Arjuna asks Sri Krishna, "Suppose a man has faith, but does not struggle hard enough, his mind wanders away from the practice of yoga and he fails to reach that perfection. What will become of him then?" There are always some, you know, who practice yoga, meditation, and then fall away from that and become worldly. "When a man goes astray from the path, he has missed both lives, the worldly and the spiritual. He has no support anywhere. Is he not lost, as a broken cloud is lost in the sky? This is the doubt that troubles me, Krishna, and only you can altogether remove it from my mind."

Sri Krishna says: "No, my son, the man is not lost, either in this world or the next. No one who seeks Brahman ever comes to an evil end." Even if you have struggled a little, you are not lost. "Even if a man falls away from the practice of yoga, he will still win the heaven of the doers of good deeds and dwell there many long years. After that he will be reborn into the home of pure and prosperous parents. He may even be born into a family of liberated, illumined yogis, but such a birth in this world is more difficult to obtain. He will then regain his spiritual discernment which he acquired in his former life. And so he will strive harder than ever for perfection. Because of his practices in the previous life, he will be driven on toward union with Brahman, even in spite of himself. For the man who has once asked the way to Brahman goes further than any mere fulfiller of the Vedas. By struggling hard, cleansing himself of all impurities, the yogi will move gradually toward perfection through many births, and reach the highest goal at last." (33)

What is meant by evolution? It is like the illustration of a reservoir with a dam. In order to flood the field, you just cut the dam and the water flows in. Similarly, there is divinity, God, within each one of us, but there is the dam of ignorance. Remove that and your life is flooded with joy and freedom. Then you reach your immortality.

Reincarnation is nothing but the chance to unfold divinity. There is no such thing as a sinner forever and ever. Accumulated dirt and dust are not your nature; they will be washed away.

Why are we not born with knowledge? Why this ignorance, this maya? Nobody can answer that question. It is said to be a statement of fact. But what maya is, is beautifully illustrated by a story as told by Swami Vivekananda: "Narada once said to Krishna, 'Lord, show me maya.' A few days passed and Krishna asked Narada to make a trip with him to the desert. After walking for several miles, Krishna said, 'Narada, I am thirsty. Can you fetch some water for me?' 'I'll go at once, sir.' So Narada went and at a little distance found a village. He entered the village and knocked at a door, which was opened by a most beautiful young girl. At the sight of her, he immediately forgot that his master was waiting for water. He forgot everything and began to talk with the girl. All that day he did not return to his master. The next day he was still at the house, talking to the girl. That talk ripened into love, he asked the father for the daughter, and they were married, lived there, and had children. Thus twelve years passed. The father died, and Narada inherited his property. He lived, as it seemed to him, a very happy life with his wife and children, his field and his cattle and so forth. Then one night the river rose until it overflowed its banks and flooded the whole village. Houses fell, men and animals were swept away and drowned. Everything was floating in the rush of the stream. Narada had to escape. With one hand he held his wife, and with the other, two of his children. With another child on his shoulders, he tried to ford this tremendous flood. After a few steps he found the current was too strong, and the child on his shoulders fell and was borne away. A cry of despair came from Narada. In trying to save that child, he lost his grasp upon one of the others, and it also was lost. At last his wife, whom he clasped with all his might, was borne away by the current, and he was thrown onto the bank, weeping and wailing bitterly. Behind him came a gentle voice, 'My child, where is the water? You went to fetch a pitcher of water, and I am waiting for you. You were gone for a good half hour.' 'Half an hour!' Narada exclaimed. Twelve whole years had passed through his mind and all these scenes had happened in half an hour. This is maya."

We have been passing through many lives in ignorance. When we wake up, time will not exist. We will realize that we are always this, all the time we were free, blissful, immortal.

In the Upanishads we find "the path of return" and "the path of non-return." The path of return means reincarnation. When one is dying, a part of the mind is already in another world. The illustration is given of a leech moving; the leech does not give up what it is leaving without catching hold of something else first. It catches hold, then gives up, catches hold, gives up, like that. So a part of our consciousness is already in the next life. Then again, we are not born immediately as human beings, but there are certain karmas – good as well as bad – which have effects in the afterlife, but do not create any effect in this life. After the exhaustion of the effects of these deeds, we are thrown back into this world and given another chance. This is the path of return.

Now in the path of non-return, you do not have to come back. That is the ideal. The aim of life is to travel the path of non-return. (34)

In the Aitareya Upanishad we read: "Of what nature is this Self? Is he the self by which we see form, hear sound, smell odor, speak words, and taste the sweet or the bitter? Is he the heart and the mind by which we perceive, commend, discriminate, know, think, remember, will, feel, desire, breathe, love, and perform other like acts? Nay, these are but adjuncts of the Self, who is pure consciousness. And this Self, who is pure consciousness is Brahman. He is God, all gods; the five elements – earth, air, fire, water, ether; all beings, great or small, born of eggs, born from the womb, born from heat, born from soil; horses, cows, men, elephants, birds, everything that breathes, the beings that walk and the beings that walk not. The reality behind all these is Brahman, who is pure consciousness."

It is while living on earth – not after death – that we have to attain immortality, which is beyond time and space. You have to realize the Atman. How can that be realized? When the divine sight opens.

The question remains, how? Jesus says: "Blessed are the pure in heart, for they shall see God." In every scripture you hear of this condition, purity of heart. What does that mean? To be freed from attachment and aversion and the clinging to this surface life. To go beyond good and evil. Does that mean we retire from the world and go to a cave of the Himalayas or the Gobi desert? No, no, no, no. Wherever you go, you take your mind and your character. There is the story of a king and a holy man. The holy man asked the king to follow him, and the king said, "Look, dear sir, if I go to the forest with you, I shall build a kingdom there." It is in the mind.

So what is the way? The idea is to move amongst the objects of senses, but neither to be attached to them nor have aversion to them. When the senses thus become purified, the heart becomes purified. What, then, is the nature of that person? There is constant recollectedness of God. And when there comes that constant recollectedness of God, the truth becomes revealed, all bonds are loosened, and he attains to freedom.

When I asked my master about *samadhi*, he pointed out: "You know what? When *samadhi* happens, this is what happens." And then he quoted this verse from the Upanishads: "The knots of ignorance of the heart become loosened, all doubts cease to exist, the effects of all deeds are wiped out, by him who has known that Reality." This has to be attained here and now. I have seen such souls. Complete freedom! Oneness with Brahman! (35)

Exactly what is the spiritual ideal? It is what we call *moksha*, liberation from reincarnation. Often people who believe in reincarnation think it is wonderful. But we believe it means just so many chances given to realize that same reality; that is, none will be lost. And as long as we have this human body, it is our first duty to realize the truth in this very life; otherwise, life is in vain.

There is one very important philosophical problem: all your efforts in life, all your struggles for spiritual experience, are finite. How can your finite struggles give you that which is infinite? In Shankara's commentary on the Brahma-Sutras we find: "Our ignorance is finite, and finite struggles can remove it, just as the shining sun is covered by clouds and a burst of wind comes and takes away the clouds. The sun then is shining."

What, then, is that state of experience? I shall quote to you a Christian mystic, St. John of the Cross: "Then I bowed my head, O my beloved, forgot myself and all else ceased, myself I shed. Forgotten were the lilies holed in the field."[10] That is, the whole universe disappeared from before him.

According to Sri Ramakrishna, there are different classes of people. Some are ever free-souls, but of course these are very rare. They come for the good of mankind.

To others, sudden illumination can come. You are not expecting it or thinking of God, but you have struggled for him, and sudden illumination comes. Suddenly you become perfect. The reason is that you must have done something in the past. I'll tell you an incident in the life of my master. There was an American businessman who was very busy and never thought of God, but suddenly he had a dream: go to India. Near Calcutta there is a monastery and there is one who is known as Maharaj. Go to him. So he came. Tantine [Josephine MacLeod] went to Maharaj and told him about this businessman, but Maharaj paid no attention. Then Swami Shivananda, Mahapurush Maharaj, another disciple of Sri Ramakrishna,

---

10. Ref. Christ: "Consider the lilies of the field, how they grow."

came and begged him, because the man had come from such a long distance and only wanted to see him once. He paid no attention. The rest of the story I heard from Tantine – it is not in any book. The man went by boat to Dakshineswar, where Sri Ramakrishna had lived. As he was coming back and was about to land, Maharaj suddenly appeared on the bank. As soon as he appeared, the man fell dead. You see, Maharaj knew that this man was his disciple in another life and this was his last birth – that the moment he saw him, he would die and attain liberation. But Maharaj was clever. If he died on the monastery grounds, there would have been political implications. The man died on the river Ganges, and no issues were raised.

This is called *videhamukti*, the realization of God at the moment of death. Many we have known in this country, not only in India, have realized God at the moment of death. Though they apparently became unconscious, they were chanting their mantra. There was one man in Switzerland, my disciple, who was uttering his mantra loudly, though he was unconscious. They thought he was Irish!

I'll read out to you my favorite letter of Swamiji: "Day and night think of God, and as far as possible think of nothing else. The daily necessary thoughts will all be thought through God. Eat to Him, drink to Him, sleep to Him, see Him in all. Talk of God to others. That is most beneficial. When the whole soul pours in a continuous current to God, when there is no time to seek money, or name, or fame, no time to think of anything but God – then will come into your heart that wonderful infinite bliss of love. All desires are but beads of glass. True love of God increases every moment, and is ever new. It is to be known by feeling it, and love is the easiest of disciplines. It waits for no logic; it is natural. We need no demonstrations, no proof. Reasoning is limiting something by our own mind. We throw a net and catch something and then say we have demonstrated it. But never, never can we catch God in a net!"

In conclusion I wish to read out to you from the Bhagavad Gita what Sri Krishna says, and which is a great comfort to all of us: "Though a man be soiled with the sins of a lifetime, let him but love Me, rightly resolved, in utter devotion, I see no sinner." In this connection my master said to me: "Sin? Where is sin in God's eye? Heaps of so-called sin are like cotton. If the eyes of the Lord fall, they are all turned to ashes!" To continue with Sri Krishna: "So let him but love me, rightly resolved in utter devotion, I see no sinner. That man is holy. Holiness soon shall refashion his nature to peace eternal. O son of Kunti, of this be certain, the man that loves me, he shall not perish." (36)

PEACE AND HOLINESS

There is a desire in everyone's heart to find peace, but very few know how and where to find that peace. The ideal of holiness may even seem very dull and uninteresting to many, but if we understand what holiness really means, we shall find that in being holy alone can we find peace.

We have lost our kingdom. There is a story about a king who lost his memory and was trying to find out where the king of his kingdom was. He went to everybody asking, "Where is the king?" Nobody would answer. Then at long last he went to his prime minister, who said, "You are the king." In the same way, we have lost that kingdom of Self, and we have to regain it.

In the Bhagavad Gita, you will find that the incarnation of God is urging Arjuna, the general, to fight and not to yield. Here is the true meaning: Where is this battle going on? In *dharmakshetra*, the field of holiness, and *Kurukshetra*, the field of battle. In this field of holiness, which is also the field of battle, each one of us has to fight. There are two forces within each of us. The forces of evil, as it were, are greater in number, but the general, the charioteer, the Lord himself, is guiding from within. The forces of good, though small in number, eventually will win out.

To give a modern example, Freud says that there is a conflict in us between two wills: the will to live, and the will to die. Strangely enough, he calls the will to die the will to nirvana. And he points out that nobody can get rid of this will to die, but everyone can ultimately overcome the will to live.

The Hindu standpoint is that the surface current of a river goes in one direction, and that there is an undercurrent going in the other. The surface current goes toward enjoying life, toward pleasure, and the undercurrent moves toward realizing God, freedom, peace. Buddha calls the surface current the thirst for life; Jesus says the love for this life can be overcome. But nobody can overcome the undercurrent that moves towards God. In some life or another, Hindus believe, each individual will have to face that fight, that battlefield of life in this field of holiness, and will have to overcome the evil forces and move toward the light, towards God, and attain peace. No one will be lost.

St. Paul said: "The whole creation has been groaning in travail together until now; and not only the creation, but we ourselves who have the first fruits of the spirit, groan inwardly as we wait for adoption as sons." Even though he had the vision of Christ, he was still groaning in suffering – until, he says, we are adopted as sons of God. In this connection the great Christian mystic Angelus Silesius said: "Christ may be born a thousand times in Bethlehem, but until he is born anew in your own heart, you remain forlorn." What to speak of St. Paul or any Christian mystic, greater than all these, Jesus himself said: "Ye shall have tribulations in the world." Then he added in deeply comforting assurance to troubled hearts, "But be of good cheer. I have overcome this world."

And that is the point. You have to overcome this world. A nation wants to conquer another nation. My ideal, and it must be your ideal and everyone's ideal, is not to conquer one nation or another, but to conquer this whole world. Think of that! That is my ambition: to overcome this whole world. There have been many nations that have had big empires. The Roman Empire, where has that gone? The English Empire, where is it today? But we have to conquer the whole world. Where is the world? In our mind. So we have to conquer that mind. Then we are free in this world, everywhere.

Let me quote Jesus: "Peace I leave with you, my peace I give unto you – not as the world giveth do I give unto you. Let not your heart be troubled, neither let it be afraid." What is this peace that Christ speaks of? "The peace that passeth all understanding". Our mind, intellect, senses, cannot grasp that. Again let me quote the Bible: "Glory to God in the highest, and on earth peace among men with whom He is pleased." You see, that peace, you and I and everyone can have if we please God. And how can we please God? "Love the Lord thy God with all thy heart, with all thy mind, with all thy strength." That is the way: to love the Lord, who is the soul of our souls, who is not way out there. Before any thought even arises in you, he knows it. You can't deceive him. And he does not get mad at you: he is love itself. If you move one step towards him, he moves a hundred steps toward you. He listens to every prayer. And every prayer is granted; it may take time, according to your earnestness, your sincerity. Pray for that love. (37)

It is said that God created the senses outgoing, so we can't help ourselves from always going out. When we seek God, we think we can find him outside, also with the senses: when we seek peace, we seek for it outside of ourselves; we want to find peace and harmony in the world. And we believe that if there is no war, there will be peace. But there have been times of no war; did people find peace? There is always conflict and chaos in the world. Swami Vivekananda once said: "What is this world but a dog's curly tail! You straighten it today, the next moment it curls again." That is the nature of the world. The idea of millennium is not possible.

Suppose there is only light. Can we know what light is without comparing it with darkness? Suppose there is only good, can we recognize it without evil? Pairs of opposites have to exist in the world. When there is unification, one-ness, there is destruction of the world. But in the midst of the pairs of opposites, we must learn to find peace and harmony within each one of us, in our own individual lives. Are you at peace within yourself? Is there not a conflict going on? That is human nature. But that does not mean that it has to exist continuously. Each one of us has to be turned into the divine, because that is our true nature.

Christ and Buddha are steps to be attained by each individual. Christhood is not limited to Jesus, Buddhahood is not limited to Buddha. That Christhood or that Buddhahood is your true nature. Take the idea of evolution: in evolution there is nothing added, but what is already involved becomes evolved. In the highest evolution is a Christ, a Buddha: it is involved in every one of us.

When Swamiji was in this country, the well-known atheist, Ingersoll, told him, "If I'd been God, I'd have created health contagious, instead of disease." Swami Vivekananda replied, "Don't you know that health also is contagious?" Peace *is* contagious. That is why there is stress on associating with holy people – so that you pick up their holiness.

Let me quote to you from the Beatitudes: "Blessed are the peacemakers, for they shall be called the children of God." I shall give you an illustration from the life of my master. One time in our organization in Benares – it was a huge organization, forty or fifty young men living together – cliques were formed, and so disturbances arose. The General Secretary went there to inquire and he found the guilty ones. He wrote my master, who was then the President, that these are the guilty ones; if we expel them, perhaps there will be peace. The President said, "Don't do anything, I am coming." He did not go to find out who was guilty and who was not; he simply gave this one order, "I want all you boys to come and meditate with me every day." So they came and they would sit and meditate every day for a month. He didn't say a word about the fights or quarrels and after a month, he left. There was complete peace and harmony – no more trouble.

You see, there really are peacemakers. If there were a few dozen such souls in one age, this world would be blessed. And it is our plan that each one of you realize that peace within yourself and spread that peace – be peacemakers. (38)

When I was a little boy, I read these words, which are indelibly impressed on my mind: "Wanted: Reformers – not of others, but of themselves." We think if we can reform everybody else to our way of thinking, to our way of life, to our way of belief, then there will be peace on earth. Suppose it were so and we all believed the same way, we all lived the same way, we all thought the same way. It would be like looking at Egyptian mummies!

The reformation has to come within yourself. You have to find peace and harmony and love within yourself. In the words of one of the great thinkers of the West, Ralph Waldo Emerson: "There are two laws discrete, not reconciled, the law for man and the law for things. The last builds town and fleet and it runs wild, and doth the man un-king." How true it is. We build towns and fleets in order to have harmony and peace, and the result is that we dethrone ourselves, as it were.

There is a beautiful story in one of the Vedanta books. Ten friends swam across a river that was flooded. When they got to the other shore, they wanted to be sure that all ten of them had arrived safely, so they began to count: one, two, three, four, five, six, seven, eight, nine. Everybody counted to nine. The tenth was missing. So they began to weep and wail that they had lost a friend. A stranger passed by and inquired why they were weeping and wailing. "Oh, there were ten of us and as we swam across, one has been drowned. We are only nine now." The stranger counted, "One, two, three, four, five, six, seven, eight, nine, ten. You are the tenth." You see, each one forgot to count himself. And that is the situation with us. There is a mine of bliss within, and we have forgotten. So the search has to be turned within.

Of course we can't blame anybody, because our senses have been created outgoing. You see, this body is known as the city of Brahman, the city of God, and there are gates, senses, through which the mind goes out. But there are some wise ones who control and turn their gaze within themselves and find that King of Kings dwelling there. We weep and wail for no reason, we find disharmony and discord for no reason; it is all our own doing.

The first and most important thing in trying to find that divinity within ourselves – in whom there is peace, in whom there is infinite and abiding happiness – is to understand that there is no happiness in the finite, that in the Infinite alone is happiness, the Infinite is the source of all happiness. In order to reach that, the first and foremost thing is discrimination. Each one of us must learn to discriminate between that which is eternal and that which is not eternal. You seek pleasure and happiness and peace in the outside world. You get it, and when there is satisfaction of a particular desire, you are at peace with yourself, but only for the moment. It doesn't last. Why? Because abiding peace is in realizing that which is eternal.

Plato defined love as the love for the whole. That means love for the Infinite. If you love a part, you become frustrated. You have to direct your love towards that which is Infinite. In the book of Job we read: "Acquaint thyself with Him" – that is, God – "and be at peace. Thereby good shall come unto you."

If we believe in dogmas and doctrines and follow certain rituals, will that peace come to us? Whatever name you may give makes no difference, but that reality has to be realized, and it is an experience within one's own self. A vision of God is not enough. You can see God, yes, but you have to acquaint yourself with him, you have to talk to him, you have to attain your union with him. That is the fact of religion. In this present age Sri Ramakrishna demonstrated by his life that no matter to what religion you belong, if you follow the path, you will reach that ultimate reality. Belief does not help you, dogmas do not help you. Why is there so much confusion in churches of today? They insist upon formulas, doctrines, and dogmas. Why don't they teach how to find God?! That spirit is forgotten. As the saying goes in our country, there were fruits in the basket, and when the fruits are gone, they fight over the basket.

Where is the world? In your own mind. There is a beautiful truth taught by the great seer-philosopher Shankara. He asks this question: "By whom is the world conquered?" And the answer he himself gives is: "By him who has conquered his own mind." That is the conquest that we have to achieve. There are things within yourself which have to be overcome. Then only will you find that the world also is overcome. (39)

Where is God? Every religion points out that He is the very soul of your soul, nearer than hands and feet. To quote from the Gospel according to St. John: "The Light shineth in darkness, but the darkness comprehended it not." There is that Atman, that Brahman, who is *Sat-chit-ananda* – pure love, abiding joy, infinite happiness, immortal life. That is your inner nature, your true being. That is what you are, but that has been covered by ignorance. And this ignorance brings forth first ego, then attachment and aversion, then clinging to this surface life.

In the Bhagavad Gita Sri Krishna says: "The uncontrolled mind does not guess that Atman or God is present within the shrine of our own heart. How can it meditate? Without meditation, where is peace? Without peace, where is happiness?"

So what is the way? Simple: to discipline our own minds. There is no easy way, my friends. You have to have patience and perseverance. Old habits and tendencies will try to gain control over you, but create new habits and give a fight in this battlefield of life! That fight has to go on within your own self. And you will win! There is no failure in spiritual life as long as you keep up the struggle. Have patience and perseverance and practice, practice, practice! (40)

It is very difficult to understand even intellectually exactly what peace means and what it is we are seeking. We seek it without knowing what it is. There is some idea in our minds and hearts, but it is not clear.

Of course the word *peace* conveys the idea of a state of quiet and tranquility or of spiritual contentment, but what that really is we cannot define or express. It is something we can feel and experience, but not within the domain of the senses. That is why Christ calls it "the peace that passeth understanding." The intellect cannot grasp it or conceive of it, yet we seek it. A simpler understanding is that it is synonymous with union with God. It is the same as experiencing God face to face. In that sense, peace and God are identical.

To approach it in a negative way, Kapila defined it as "the complete cessation of suffering and misery." The wall does not suffer, and animals on the lower scale of life have less suffering. At one time I thought of contentment as the peace of a contented cow. That is not the ideal!

There is a peace that is positive, but we first have to eliminate all causes of suffering. If you study the lives of great mystics, they all call this peace ecstasy. They become intoxicated with joy; they experience waves of bliss striking them – something very definite and very positive. If you have any glimpse of what God is, you will know he is happiness, peace, joy, *ananda*. There is no word to convey the exact meaning of *ananda* but in the Upanishads we read: "From joy springs this universe, in joy dwells this universe, and unto joy goes back this universe." [Taittiriya Upanishad] Nothing but joy; from joy everything has come out.

When the mind is attached to the senses and sense-pleasures, we have troubles and worries: even our enjoyments and pleasures are not free from suffering and pain. Now center that same mind in God. It will be quite different. You will be always in the sanctuary, where nothing can affect you.

You know what to do. It is very simple to know how to do it, but to *do* it is the difficulty. Our uncontrolled mind revolts against it. And though we seek happiness and peace, we cannot have them unless we learn to control the mind. In the Gita we read: "When, through the practice of yoga, the mind ceases its restless movements, and becomes stilled, he realizes the Atman." How simple! "It satisfies him entirely. Then he knows that infinite happiness which can be realized by the purified heart, but is beyond the grasp of the senses. Utterly quiet, made clean of passion, the mind of the yogi knows that Brahman, his bliss is the highest." (41)

In the higher scale of evolution you suffer because you become more sensitive. And then there comes that great struggle to overcome all that suffering. You see, it is not merely the complete cessation of suffering, but there is a positive experience of joy and delight. Joy covers the whole universe. The fact is that everywhere – in the minutest atom, in the blade of grass or, as Shankara put it, "in that stump of a tree, from that pillar down to Brahma, the highest evolution, there is that presence of Brahman, of God." What is the nature of God? *Ananda* – bliss. (42)

SAINTS AND MIRACLES

You will find that all the great teachers and saints of the world claim to have seen God, to have talked with him, to have reached union with him. For instance, Christ "spoke with authority, not as the scribes and Pharisees." Where did he get that authority? He had reached union with God. We find Buddha saying: "Brahman I know, and I live in the Brahman-world." In this age when the young Swami Vivekananda approached Ramakrishna and asked, "Sir, have you seen God?" he replied, "Yes, I have seen him. And he is more real than I see you. And everyone can see him." That is the truth emphasized since the most ancient time of the Vedas and the Upanishads.

The point is that nobody has seen God with these eyes or has heard the voice of God with these ears, but we read in the Bible: "He who hath eyes to see, sees; and he who hath ears to hear, hears." It is a new vision. In yoga psychology and in the Upanishads it is brought out that within the three states of consciousness that we are familiar with – waking, dreaming, and dreamless sleep – the reality of God cannot be known or experienced. We have to go beyond the three states of consciousness. That state which transcends the senses and the ordinary mind is known as the Fourth.

The mind has to become purified, completely freed from all past impressions and thoughts. That is what Christ meant when he said, "Blessed are the pure in heart, for they shall see God." To see God is literally a truth, and that is religion. It appears as supernatural, as a miraculous phenomenon, and so the idea of saint and miracle have become, as it were, synonymous.

Of course if we read the lives of some of these great teachers, we find they did perform certain miracles. We find Jesus walking on water, feeding the multitude with a loaf of bread. He healed the sick and raised the dead. But in my opinion, in my understanding – and of course I am no authority on the Bible – when the dead were raised, what happened to them? Didn't they die again? So what good was it? I would explain that he gave them perfection, made them whole, gave them the attainment of God. That is the special power, the greatest miracle, of a saint or a teacher or a prophet – to transform the lives of people. And we find every saint doing that. Christ and Ramakrishna and Buddha, as well as their disciples, transformed the lives of the people who came to them.

Now again, to come to miracles, multitudes identify saintliness with miraculous power, but we find that the great ones don't encourage it. We read in the Bible: "Then certain of the scribes and of the Pharisees answered, saying, 'Master, we would see a sign from Thee.' But he answered and said unto them, 'An evil and adulterous generation seeketh after a sign, and there shall no sign be given to it.'"

Here is the point: people perhaps accept and recognize a saint – one who can walk on water, read the thoughts of others, see what is at a distance and tell their past, present, and future – and they follow. But they do not follow the teachings. In the Bible you read: "From that time, many of his disciples went back and walked no more with Him. Then said Jesus unto the twelve, 'Will ye also go away?' And Simon Peter answered him, 'Lord, to whom shall we go? Thou hast the words of eternal life.'"

Let me explain to you what miracles are and how they can be performed. In fact, you don't have to be spiritual to gain powers. I saw one fellow who demonstrated power, asking you to think of any fragrance and then if you touched his toes, your fingers would smell of that fragrance. I was a boy of about thirteen or fourteen, and I got so excited that I wanted to be his disciple. But there was an elderly man who watched my enthusiasm and he said, "Come here. You have read Swamiji. Go and read Raja Yoga and see what kind of people they are who show these powers. Read that book!"

Patanjali, who lived about two centuries before Christ, was the first yogi to edit and organize all the spiritual disciplines known at that time. He mentioned that occult powers can be achieved, and he gave methods and means by which one can attain such powers. The only condition, he pointed out, is that one must gain the power of concentration, not necessarily through spiritual practice. If one can gather the power of intense concentration, then the concentrated mind can be applied to attain particular powers. By concentrating on the subconscious mind, one obtains knowledge of the past and the future – just as, what you had been in the past, you will attain in the future. "By making *samyama* on previous thought waves, one obtains knowledge of the past lives. By making *samyama* on the distinguishing marks of another man's body, one obtains the knowledge of the nature of his mind." It is not merely thought reading; you can know the whole character of the individual. "If one makes *samyama* on the form of one's body, obstructing its perceptibility and separating its power of manifestation from the eyes of the beholder, one's body becomes invisible. By making *samyama* on the hollow of the throat, one stills hunger and thirst." Then lastly he points out, "They are powers in the worldly state, but they are obstacles to *samadhi*."

You cannot have the vision of God if you are interested in those powers. You can obtain them without being spiritual, but the door to spiritual progress becomes locked. Sri Rama-krishna used to give a parable: There were two brothers. One renounced the world in order to practice yoga. After twelve years, he came back. The lay brother said, "Now tell me, you renounced the world and practiced such hard austerities for so many years. Tell me what you have achieved." The first brother said, "Come with me. I'll show you." Both of them went to the riverside, and the yogi brother began to walk on the water and crossed the river. The lay brother called for a ferryboat and for a nickel he crossed over. When the yogi brother said, "Look what I did!" his brother replied, "Yes. It is worth a nickel!"

One of the disciples of Sri Ramakrishna, when he was a young boy, would practice meditation and suddenly feel a power of clairvoyance and clairaudience a hundred miles away. Something would open up, and he would see a friend and what he was doing. He told Sri Ramakrishna, "Take this! It is a great obstacle to my meditation. I can't think of God

when all this comes to me." Sri Ramakrishna said, "Stop meditating for some time and you will lose the power."

Another time Sri Ramakrishna told Swami Vivekananda
that he'd like to transmit some occult powers to him. Swamiji
asked, "Would they help me to find God and live in the bliss
of God?" "No. But you might need them for your preaching work." Swamiji said, "I don't need them. I will not have
them."

It is not that you have to concentrate in a particular way
to gain certain powers. Any aspirant, as his concentration
grows, may suddenly feel a power. We are told just to test it
once to see the truth of it – and then forget it. To those who
are seeking God, Sri Ramakrishna says, "These powers are
rubbish. Avoid them."

So the fundamental question arises: What is saintliness?
Is there any criterion by which we can know and recognize
a saint? Saintliness is an inner unfoldment, and in that unfoldment one experiences sweetness in the thought of God
and bliss in his vision. But how do we recognize a saint? It is
very difficult, very difficult. The only external manifestation
that you see in a saint is love, compassion, sympathy. A saint
does not look upon anybody as a sinner, and does not reject
anybody. As a general rule I would say that multitudes do not
recognize a saint. To recognize, one has to be a spiritual aspirant, one has to yearn for God. Only holiness can recognize
holiness. If you live in the company of a saint, you will find
your mind is raised up. Sri Ramakrishna gave this illustration:
You go to a lawyer, and you begin to think of litigation. You
go to a doctor, and you begin to think of medicine. When
you meet a holy person, your mind goes to God. That is the
sign. When we sat at the feet of the disciples of Ramakrishna,
we felt it was so simple to realize God, as though we had the
fruit in the palm of our hands.

Another characteristic is that a saint belongs to no sect or creed or any particular religion. If you live in the presence of a holy person, you find neither a Hindu nor a Christian nor a Buddhist nor a Muslim, but someone established in God. One who remains sectarian has not known God, has not realized anything.

And then there is the sign of continuous consciousness. In the words of Shankara, "There is a continuous consciousness of the unity of Atman and Brahman." That is also the means: to have constant recollectedness of God. You see, if you seek powers and you are looking for miracles, you will never reach God. You have to seek God and God alone. Your mind has to be attuned to him – in the beginning as often as you can. Gradually you come to a state where there is a continuous stream of thought.

This vision of God which makes one a saint is to be attained while living on earth, here and now. Sri Krishna describes an illumined soul: "He knows bliss in the Atman, and wants nothing else. Cravings torment the heart, he renounces cravings. I call him illumined." Such a person has no desires left. "Not shaken by adversity, not hankering after happiness." Not thrown off-balance. "Free from fear, free from anger, free from the things of desire, I call him a seer, illumined. The bonds of his flesh are broken. He is lucky and does not rejoice. He is unlucky and does not weep. I call him illumined. The tortoise can draw in its legs, the seer can draw in his senses. I call him illumined. The abstinent run away from what they desire, but they carry their desires with them. When a man enters Reality, he leaves his desires behind him."

A spiritual aspirant tries to gain self-control, but there is lingering desire, so it is necessary to keep away from all kinds of temptations. But the illumined soul is free from all desires. Desires may arise for the moment, but they do not disturb;

they have become completely absorbed. So the teaching is, think and think of God, learn to love him, keep recollected-ness of him, and at long last be absorbed in him, and you become a saint in this very life. (43)

It is the ideal and purpose of human life to become a living saint. But what is a saint, what is one who has attained free-dom from all bondages of life and death? How is it possible for every one of us to attain that state of saintliness?

A misunderstanding which exists all over the world, in India as well as in the West, is that in order to be a saint, one must perform miracles. Of course we know that Jesus performed certain miracles and the multitudes followed him. Then what happened? The multitudes see the signs and mira-cles, but they are not ready to follow the teachings. One time Jesus came back to a village and saw a man rolling in the mud. Jesus said, "What are you doing there?" The man said, "Master, I was a leper and you healed me. What else am I to do?" Then he saw a man chasing a girl and he said, "What are you doing?" And the man said, "Master, I was blind and you gave me eyes. What am I to do?"

Sri Ramakrishna said, "Yes, one can have these powers, and suppose I get the power of healing, what will happen? This place will be a hospital. Then how can spiritual life be given and taught?"

Is there no way to judge? Yes. In the presence of the holy, your mind goes naturally Godward. If you are a spiritual aspirant who finds it difficult to pray and to meditate upon God, you find it becomes easier to think of God in holy com-pany. That is one sign.

Another sign is that a holy person does not hate any so-called sinner. You see this in so many examples: Jesus, Bud-dha, Ramakrishna. Max Mueller, who wrote about the life and teachings of Ramakrishna, met a Brahmo devotee from India who had known Ramakrishna. Max Mueller asked what he thought of him. The Brahmo devotee replied, "Well, he was a good man, but in the end he got spoiled." "What happened?" "Well, he became friends with alcoholics and even a prostitute." Then Max Mueller jumped up and said, "Now I know he was a man of God, he was a divine incarnation! Now I know!"

A friend of mine who was very devoted to Maharaj, but who did not join the monastery, felt he had made a very grave mistake. He was attracted to Maharaj but had a guilty conscience. So he would come stealthily when he knew Maharaj would be resting. He would do certain small things and go away. One day Maharaj waited for him and caught him. "Now don't run away. Come here." Then he asked, "Have you seen a buffalo?" "Yes." "Have you seen how big its horns are?" "Yes." "Do they feel anything?" "No." "Well, I have bigger horns than a buffalo. I don't mind any flies or mosquitoes. I can throw them out any moment." You see, to him there is no sinner. This I have seen in my life. And we hear stories about the lives of these great ones – Jesus and Mary Magdalene and Buddha. Buddha, you know, died eating some pork at the house of a prostitute. He refused to go to a rich man's house but went to the poor prostitute instead.

And then, of course, Sri Ramakrishna. You know how Girish Chandra Ghosh was completely transformed. He was an alcoholic and did all kinds of mischief, so-called sin, but he was completely transformed. I met him when he was a great saint. It so happened that he had been associated with a prostitute, and one of the girls told him she would like to see Ramakrishna when he was sick. At that time no stranger was allowed to visit Ramakrishna. And so Girish Ghosh told his brother to take the girl and dress her as an English boy.

In the evening, he took her upstairs and took off the disguise. Sri Ramakrishna had a good laugh over it, and then gave her a touch, which transformed her whole life. Some prostitutes came to my master and, through his grace, those women were completely transformed. I have met them. You see, that is the greatest miracle that the great saints perform – transforming people's lives. (44)

In this country it is understood that somebody becomes a saint after he's dead and gone, but our ideal is to become saints while living on earth.

Shankara said: "There is no longer any identification of the Atman with its coverings." In other words, he has realized the Atman, the Self, as one with Brahman. "All sense of duality is obliterated. There is pure, unified consciousness. The man who is well established in this consciousness is said to be illumined. A man is said to be free even in this life when he is established in illumination. His bliss is unending. He almost forgets the world of appearances. Even though his mind is dissolved in Brahman, he is fully awake, free from the ignorance of waking life. He is fully conscious, but free from any craving. Such a man is said to be free even in this life. For him, the sorrows of this world are over. Though he possesses a finite body, he remains united with the Infinite. His heart knows no anxiety. Such a man is said to be free even in this life. Though he lives in the body, it seems merely like a shadow following him. He is no longer troubled by the thought of 'I' and 'mine.' Such are the characteristics of a man who is free even in this life."

We do not merely read about saints in books, but there are living souls who are that. The main point is that every one of us must try to achieve this state. You may ask why we don't see many people like that, and the answer is very simple: how many struggle? In fact, how many know that the purpose of life is to realize God? I have heard many ministers say that practical religion is to love thy neighbor, to do good. Of course I do not object to doing good, but what is the objective? To see the Self in your neighbor, to see the one Atman in your neighbor. How can you see that until you learn to see the Atman within yourself? See God within yourself, and see God in every being: that is the ideal. (45)

CAST OUT FEAR

The world in which we live is a world of incessant fear and constant worry. We are beset with fear at every step, and worries follow us constantly. If we overcome one difficulty, there is another. Thus it goes. We are afraid to face life itself for its uncertainties, and we are afraid to die. If we have a job, we are afraid of losing it; if we have no job, we are afraid that we might not get one. If we have economic security today, we are afraid that we might lose it tomorrow; if we don't have it, we are afraid that we may not get it.

The world by its very nature is ever changing. The Sanskrit word for world is *jagat*, which means that which changes and passes. There is nothing in this world that we can hold on to. As Buddha once pointed out, can we attempt to make the clouds stay? It is the nature of the river to flow; it is the nature of this world to flow. There are always uncertainties, and with them come fear in every life.

We find the rise and fall of nations and empires. In individual lives we find rise and fall. We seek beauty, health, happiness, position, economic security, intellect, advancement. We find them – but how long can we hold on to them? They pass away.

I am talking like a great pessimist because I don't see any-thing in life that we can hold on to as something of eternal value. But then, as I shall point out, religion makes us the greatest of optimists. In order that we attain that optimism with certitude, we have to be pessimistic with regard to what we see and experience only with our senses. In short, whether we want to call ourselves pessimists or optimists, this is the experience of everyone: we live in fear. There is no question about that. It is a fact we have to face. The ostrich in the fable may hide its head in the sand when it faces danger, but that does not free it from danger. We may hide ourselves – drink and get intoxicated to forget the worries of the world – but we have to wake up and face our situations.

Some religions play on our fears to make us fear God. We are afraid not only of this life and death, but we are afraid of the next life. We are not only afraid of the future while we are living here, but afraid of what will happen to us when we die. Religion may play on our fears, but if we go to the source of every religion, we shall find out differently.

If you read the Upanishads, there is one note running throughout: become fearless! Upon what grounds can we be fearless is the question. The Upanishads are very clear upon that point: Knowing the bliss of God, one casts out all fear. The mark of genuine religion is freedom from fear. It is not a question of bravado, but of grounding ourselves upon something where we positively become fearless, know-ing there is no danger, no worry, no troubles. That is what religion seeks to give us. The mark of genuine spiritual life is that fearlessness.

Recall the incident of the meeting between Alexander the Great and a holy man of India. Alexander was impressed by this man's wisdom and wanted him to return with him to Greece. He refused. Alexander tempted him with wealth and enjoyments. The holy man refused again, saying, "What need have I of those things? The trees of the forest supply me with fruits and food; the water in the river gives me drink; the grass is my bed; the sky my room. What need have I of anything else?" When no temptation could win this man, Alexander said, "Do you know what power I have? I can force you to come with me. If you don't, I'll kill you." The holy man laughed loudly right in his face and said, "That's the greatest lie you have uttered in your life. You say you will kill me? Nothing can kill me! Fire cannot burn me, sword cannot wound me, water cannot wet me, wind cannot dry me! I am the eternal Spirit."

We read this as a story of ancient India, but I am telling you of modern India. I have sat at the feet of such holy men who possessed nothing of this world – no power, no kingdom, no wealth – who possessed only one thing, and that is the bliss of God. Not only were they themselves fearless, but anyone sitting at their feet could feel that fearlessness in themselves. My master used to tell us, "Be fearless yourself, and spread that fearlessness to others. Let none be afraid." And that is the ideal of spiritual life. What is there to fear if you can touch eternity?

What is the real source of our anguish and bondage? The cause is nothing but ignorance, the tragedy is that we are not conscious of our ignorance. It is ignorance that causes fear and bondage, but what can take it away? Darkness can be removed by light; ignorance can only be removed by knowledge. Changing the circumstances and conditions of your life will not take away fear. If you free yourself from immediate troubles, newer troubles arise. What are you going to do about them? It is only when you know the reality behind this appearance, when you reach God, that you become fearless.

You have to rise above this phenomenal appearance and phenomenal self. At present our consciousness is, as it were, out of focus. If you consider yourself the body, and most of us do, then you try to keep it as you love it. However, you cannot: it is just like bidding the clouds to stay. But if you can reach the real Self, which is not subject to surface life or death, which is not affected by the happiness or misery of the world or by virtue or vice, which is beyond relativity, then you become grounded in a reality where fear itself fears to approach. There is a prayer in the Upanishads: "Lead us from the unreal to the real; lead us from death to immortality; lead us from darkness to light." [Brihadaranyaka Upanishad]

So, what is ignorance? To see the world only partially. We see the events and happenings in the history of mankind and of our individual lives only partially. Partial truth is not truth at all; it is even more dangerous than falsehood. Take, for instance, a beautiful painting. Instead of looking at the whole painting, you look at one point. This world that we experience with our finite consciousness is only a part of the whole. In that part we find all these worries, troubles, wars, changes. In our individual lives we see only a portion of our life – chaos, misery, life, death. As long as we live within this portion, which is on the surface, there is no escape.

There are those who believe they can straighten out the world and straighten out their individual lives. That is a good ideal, to face the facts of life. But after you have done all that, what happens? Is it not like the dog's curly tail? You straighten it out, and again it curls; that is the very nature of the dog's tail.

What makes the world appear to me as it does? When I see the world as always changing, it is my ignorance that makes me see that. How can my ignorance be removed, and who can remove it? Only I can remove it. Then all this dreaming of evil and change departs like a dream. There is a veil over our eyes, a veil over our senses; what we see and know is darkness. If that darkness is removed by illumination, we shall see what is behind the changing phenomena and behind our individual selves. The Upanishads call that *Sat-chit-ananda,* infinite existence, infinite happiness, and eternal consciousness.

God can be known, not merely intellectually, but directly and immediately. It is only when we come nearer, when we get a glimpse of God, that fearlessness comes into the heart. It is an actual experience that has to come. Before you attempt that, believe wholeheartedly, "I can know God!" In him we find the source of light, happiness, and freedom. If you believe that first, then there will come the urge to devote yourself to reaching that ideal. And this is the fact: if you make the attempt, you will find yourself moving toward that light. It is a fact, just as two plus two makes four.

When you know the true world and the true Self, then you shall find there is a perfect harmony between this world and God. They are not separate: God is everywhere. When we reach that, we become free from fear. (46)

DIVINE INCARNATION

We find the germ of the idea of divine incarnation in the Upanishads. It is fully evolved in the Bhagavad Gita. Three great major religions of the world believe in divine incarnation: Hinduism or Vedanta, one sect of Buddhism, and Christianity. There are differences in their ideas.

To the Hindus and Buddhists, it is essential to realize God, or attain super-conscious vision. They both advocate many paths. To worship a divine incarnation is one of the paths, especially for those who follow the path of devotion. In Christianity it is a fundamental belief that unless you accept Christ as your personal savior, there is no hope for you. And, according to Christianity, there is only one divine incarnation, Jesus. But according to Hindus and Buddhists, there are many; it is the same God, the same Reality, that comes in different ages in different garments.

The Christian theory of divine incarnation is to be found first and foremost, I would say, in the Gospel according to St. John. "In the beginning was the Word, and the Word was with God, and the Word was God. And the Word was made flesh and dwelt amongst us. And we behold His glory, the glory as the only begotten of the Father, full of grace or truth."

The theory of the Word or Logos was first evolved in the Western world by the Greeks, and it underwent many changes, until we come to Philo, an Alexandrian Jewish philosopher, who was a contemporary of Jesus. Philo harmonized and reconciled the immanence of God with Plato's transcendental idea of Godhead. He called it "the divine reason or wisdom which is immanent in every individual." In other words, the Logos, or Word, as divine reason, dwells in every human being. The idea was developed to breach the gulf that exists between man and God, between that which is known and that which is unknown. It was Philo who, for the first time, used the phrase "first begotten of the Father," referring to the Logos or Word. We find that St. John took the whole idea from Philo and changed it to suit the theological needs of Christianity by identifying the Word, "the first begotten of the Father," with Jesus.

We find this theory of Logos or the Word evolved in India many centuries before the Greeks. In the Vedas we find the identical sentence as we find in the Gospel according to St. John: "In the beginning was the Creator God. Second to him was the Word. This Word is identical with Brahman, with God." Again, according to the Hindus, this Word is made flesh in every being. In other words, it is immanent, it dwells in every one of us, and with the help of the Word – which they say is *Om* – one can realize the ultimate truth. This Word is also known as the cosmic Word. Whether Christian or Buddhist or Hindu, one who meditates in silence, with the mind absorbed, can hear this sound of Om. Hindus also believe, like St. John, that the Word was made flesh in an *avatara* or descent of God, a special manifestation of God as man, in order to show how to ascend towards Godhead. So by worshipping an *avatara*, a divine incarnation, in whom is to be found manifested this Word, one can attain the supreme.

Now let us try to understand why Christians believe that Jesus was the one unique divine incarnation. In support of their theory a Christian theologian will quote the words of Jesus: "I am the way, the truth, and the life. No man cometh unto the Father but by Me." But as we study the sayings of some of the other world teachers, we shall find identical claims. For instance, Sri Krishna, who lived before Christ, said: "I am the goal of the wise man, and I am the way. I am the end of the path, the witness, the Lord, the sustainer. I am the place of abode, the beginning, the friend, and the refuge. Fill your heart and mind with me, adore me, make all your acts and offerings to me, bow down to me in self-surrender. If you set your heart upon me thus, and take me for your ideal above all others, you will come into my being."

Buddha said: "You are my children, I am your Father. Through me you have been released from your sufferings. I, myself, having reached the other shore, help others to cross the stream. I, myself, having attained salvation, am a savior of others. I comfort others and lead them to the place of refuge."

In this present age Swami Vivekananda, who did not believe in divine incarnation, was seated at Sri Ramakrishna's bedside as he was dying. He was thinking to himself, "If now you say that you are a divine incarnation, I'll believe you." Suddenly he heard the voice of Ramakrishna saying: "Naren, still you have this disbelief? He who was Rama, he who was Krishna, is born in this body as Ramakrishna." At other times he said he was also born as Christ. He further said: "I am the sanctuary. Those who take refuge in me attain the Supreme. Whosoever thinks of me achieves everything." These are the direct words of Ramakrishna.

Now when Jesus or Krishna or Buddha or Ramakrishna used the word *I* or *me*, they did not use it in the sense of an individual being, but in the sense of "I" as one with the impersonal Brahman. As such, Hindus do not see any contradiction in their sayings, and there is no quarrel about them. Swami Vivekananda at one time said, "You have a room in which Christ, Buddha, Krishna, Ramakrishna are all seated together and they will embrace one another, but you have a Jewish Rabbi, a Hindu priest, a Christian minister, and their followers will come out fighting."

In the Bhagavad Gita, Sri Krishna pointed out: "It is I who am born in many ages." Especially in this age, Ramakrishna emphasized that they are all one and the same. But at the same time you must have one-pointed devotion to your chosen ideal; it does not mean that today you worship Christ, tomorrow you worship Ramakrishna. That will not do. When you accept Christ as your chosen ideal, in Christ you must learn to see Krishna, Buddha, Ramakrishna. And it is not that only in your particular chosen ideal is there the impersonal Brahman. The personal and impersonal are not separate; it is the same being, the same Reality.

Now again, where lies the difference between a human being and an incarnation of God? Sri Krishna points out that a person is forced to be born by past karmas, but a divine incarnation chooses to be born. Sri Krishna declared: "I am the birthless, the deathless, Lord of all that breathes. I seem to be born, it is only seeming, only my maya. I am still master of *prakriti*." He goes on to say: "He who knows the nature of my task and my holy birth is not reborn when he leaves this body; he comes to Me."

Let me explain why an *avatara* comes many times. The Hindus have a theory that civilization, whether material or spiritual, goes up and down, like waves rising high and then subsiding. Today we believe we have made such progress in science, but is there any proof that in another cycle of existence, the same progress was not made and then lost? In spiritual culture, whether in Hinduism or Christianity or Buddhism, there is rise and then gradual fall. People are satisfied by theories and dogmas and doctrines rather than in spiritual life: believe in Jesus or believe in Krishna, accept Christ as your personal savior and you are saved.

Sri Krishna points out that God chooses when to be born: "When goodness grows weak, when evil increases, I make myself a body. In every age I come back to deliver the holy, to destroy the sin of the sinner, and to establish righteousness." From time to time Pharisees and Sadducees abound and religion becomes just a formula, a theory, a dogma. Then God descends in human form to re-establish the eternal religion. It is nothing new; it is the same truth, but its form changes to suit the needs of the particular age.

So, in the first place a divine incarnation is not bound by karmas and is born with the knowledge of God. Then we find such a great soul undergoing spiritual disciplines in order to show us what practices to follow in order to realize God. In this connection Sri Ramakrishna said: "What I have done, if you do a part of that, you will attain."

The divine incarnation is born with perfect memory of the past. In the Bhagavad Gita Arjuna asks Sri Krishna, "How is it that you, born in this age, say you have taught this truth to such and such who lived many centuries before this time?" Sri Krishna answered: "You and I, Arjuna, have lived many lives. I remember them all: you do not remember." Or take the words of Jesus: "Before Abraham was, I am."

Now again, the greatest characteristic is that the divine incarnation is able to transmit superconscious vision – immediately – by looking at or by touching a person. Such is the power. We "small fries" have to take the help of the name of God and ask you to undergo certain spiritual disciplines for realization, but by a touch the incarnation gives it. We find in the lives of the disciples of Sri Ramakrishna that to each one he gave the highest *samadhi* by a touch or a look. Yet he made his disciples undergo disciplines.

Another characteristic is that divine incarnations are conscious of their mission throughout their life.

Lastly, there is transfiguration. In the Gita Arjuna said: "I must know, I must realize." Then Sri Krishna said: "You cannot realize with these eyes, but I shall give you divine sight." By his touch, as it were, he gave him that divine sight, and then Arjuna saw Sri Krishna transformed into the universal form.

Those of you who are acquainted with the teachings of the Bible will remember how Peter, James, and John saw Jesus transfigured. In the life of Ramakrishna we find that at one time there were arrangements made for the worship of the Divine Mother Kali in his room, but no image was brought. Sri Ramakrishna didn't ask anybody to bring an image. The disciples were seated around him, wondering what he would do next. In the meantime Girish Ghosh, the great Bengali dramatist saw Ramakrishna as Mother Kali and he offered flowers at his feet. Immediately there was transfiguration. Then all the disciples saw that and offered worship to him as the Divine Mother. It is not recorded, but my master saw Sri Ramakrishna transfigured in many forms.

One time my master was in a spiritual mood and his brother disciple, Swami Saradananda, came to him and said: "Maharaj, I'd like you to come and see the statue of Sri Ramakrishna. The model has been made." Maharaj answered, "But which form?"

Let me point out that Krishna, Christ, Buddha, Ramakrishna are still living. One can see them. Christ reveals himself to his devotees as Christ and also as the supreme Brahman. Then the devotee does not remain Christocentric. That is why churches do not encourage mysticism. In the same way, Krishna and Ramakrishna devotees, when the real vision comes, do not remain Krishnacentric or Ramakrishnacentric.

Let me quote St. Paul: "For in him dwelleth all the fullness of the Godhead bodily. And ye are complete in him, which is the head of all principality and power." And Sri Krishna says: "Who knows me birthless, never beginning, Lord of the worlds; he alone among mortals is stainless of sin, unvexed by delusion. ... Who truly knows me, in manifold being everywhere present and all-pervading, dwells in my yoga that shall not be shaken: of this be certain. I am where all things began, the issuing-forth of the creatures, known to the wise in their love when they worship with hearts overflowing: mind and senses are absorbed, I alone am the theme of their discourse: thus delighting in each other, they live in bliss and contentment. Always aware of their Lord are they, and ever devoted: therefore, the strength of their thought is illumined and guided toward me. There in the ignorant heart where I dwell, by the grace of my mercy, I am knowledge, that brilliant lamp, dispelling its darkness." Then Arjuna, his disciple, says: "You are Brahman, the highest abode, the utterly holy." (47)

10

Let us try to understand what Christ is, and then we shall come to his teachings. To understand intellectually is almost impossible. This reminds me that once a disciple asked my master, "Tell me something about Sri Ramakrishna, how you feel about him." He said, "What can I say? When he reveals himself to you, then only will you know." To know a Christ, a Ramakrishna, to know God, revelation has to come. Until then we have to have some initial understanding to proceed; there must be a parallelism.

Now, nobody can intellectually understand God in his reality. Attempts have been made and are still being made, but God has to reveal himself to you, because there is no parallel, no comparison. But when we come to his aspects, his expressions, then we see parallelism.

God is too much of an abstraction to define. All we can say is "Absolute, Impersonal," and so on, but that doesn't mean anything. There is the story of a little boy whose grandmother put him to bed at night and then put out the light. The little boy said, "Oh, Grandma, you're leaving me alone?" And Grandma said, "No, you know, Johnny, that God is with you." Johnny replied, "Yes, Grandma, I know God is with me, but I like to see a face!" You see, God is too much of an abstraction for us human beings to love, so he comes to us as something concrete, like one of us, whom we can love and who can love us.

From a philosophical standpoint I can tell you that Atman, the Self, is Brahman. True. But how can you worship the Atman? The eyes cannot see themselves; you have to have a mirror to see your eyes, to look at your face. And the mirror has to be clean and pure to give a perfect reflection. Christ is that mirror. Krishna or Buddha or Ramakrishna is such a mirror that reflects the Atman. And Jesus and Krishna and Ramakrishna taught us to love them, to worship them.

So what is it to come unto him or to take refuge in him? Christ says: "Abide in Me, and I in you." Sri Krishna says: "Be absorbed in Me. Lodge your mind in Me. Thus you will dwell in Me – do not doubt it – here and hereafter."

Learn to love and meditate. Love God in any one of these forms and he will reveal himself to you. Through him or in him, the supreme truth will be revealed. Christ is not way up there, but within the shrine of your own heart. My master taught me this: "As long as you seek God outside, you will not find him. He is neither in a church nor a temple, nor in books, nor in scriptures." Pointing to his own heart, he said: "When you find him here, you find him everywhere." And that is the ideal: to realize God, to attain union with God. (48)

INCARNATIONS AND TEACHERS

BUDDHA

To bring peace to the hearts of all mankind was Buddha's only purpose. In spite of all the luxuries, comforts, and worldly happiness that he experienced, with a beautiful wife and son and kingdom, he realized that the world is full of suffering. Nobody can escape disease and death. How could he bring immortal life, eternal freedom, and peace not to himself alone, but to all mankind?

In one of the Buddhist scriptures we read that the Tathagata, Buddha or the illumined one, had no theories. He didn't believe in speculation or doctrines or dogmas. Anybody who came to him to satisfy idle curiosity would go away frustrated and disappointed. But to anybody who came to him to find the way of peace, to overcome suffering and misery and death, he gave the way to nirvana.

Buddha's teachings are the highest aspect of nondualism: "There is an unborn, an unoriginated, an unmade, an uncompounded; were there not, O mendicants, there would be no escape from the world of the born, the originated, the compounded." Sri Ramakrishna said: "When one attains *samadhi*, there is no power of speech left by which to express Brahman." Just so, Buddha could not express definitely what is impossible to describe.

Then again, he urged his disciples to depend upon that reality within and not on any other authority. You see, when you accept authority, you think you have known it, but the truth is within; you have to unfold that truth. Buddha said in the most famous of his teachings, which is often quoted, "Therefore, O Ananda, be ye lamps unto yourselves, be ye a refuge to yourselves. Hold fast to the truth as a lamp, and whosoever, Ananda, either now or after I am dead, shall be a lamp unto themselves, shall betake themselves to no external refuge but, holding fast to the truth as their lamp and holding fast as their refuge to the truth, shall look not for refuge to anyone besides themselves. It is they, Ananda, among my *bhikkus* who shall reach the very topmost height – but they must be anxious to learn."

And he said, "You must recognize that there are four noble kinds of truth." This recognition has to come: there is suffering in the world, there is a cause for the suffering, the suffering can be overcome, and there is a way to peace. This is not acceptance on mere faith or authority; it has to be experienced for oneself. Suffering is a universal experience. Old age, disease, and death, nobody can escape – but they can be escaped. The longing for that escape, however, does not come until we find that the world cannot give us what we are seeking. Every one of us holds to this surface life as something eternal. (49)

Buddha did not claim to be an *avatara*. On the other hand, he said that Buddha is nothing but the Awakened One. We are asleep – ignorance is compared to sleep – and we have to be awakened. His most emphatic teaching is that it is possible for everyone to be awakened and be a buddha.

The most distinguishing characteristic of Buddha was his big heart. He was called "the compassionate one." He was ready to sacrifice his life for the sake of a lamb or a goat. Another distinguishing characteristic of Buddha – and of all great teachers and illumined souls – was that he pointed out that religion is very practical. He said: "If ye walk according to my teachings (he did not say "believe in me"), ye shall even in this present life apprehend the truth itself and see face to face." Not after you die, but in this life. As Irving Babbitt, inspired by Buddhism, said: "The Buddhists would like to take the cash and let the credit go." Whatever we get in life is the most important thing.

And Buddha pointed out: "The greatest sin is to be lazy." You see, when there is a way to escape suffering and you do not struggle to do it, that is laziness. Shankara pointed out that it is like suicide – and this is the universal truth taught by all great teachers. He also said, "You have to be awakened." Any great illumined soul will insist that you have to experience the truth for yourself: no matter how you do it, do it.

Nirvana is not a vacuum, not nothingness. A disciple who, once had an experience of nothingness, went to Swami Turiyananda, one of the disciples of Sri Ramakrishna, and said: "I have attained Buddhist nirvana; there was vacuum, nothingness." Swami Turiyananda said: "No, no, no, no, no. He said, 'Purna, purna, purna – fullness, fullness, fullness.' Now go back and meditate some more." Buddha himself attained that fullness. He said: "How can there be any escape from this if there were not the fullness, the reality?"

Buddha based his whole philosophy not on any theory, but on the simple psychological experience of suffering. "Not in the sky, nor in the depths of the ocean, nor in the caves of the mountains, nor in any place in the whole world may a man dwell without being overpowered by death. How is their laughter? How is their joy? As the world is always burning, why do you not seek a light, ye who are surrounded by darkness? The body is wasted, full of sickness and pain; life indeed ends in death. It is the path which opens the eyes and bestows understanding, which leads to peace, to higher wisdom, to full enlightenment, to nirvana." Just mark those words: no nothingness. He says: "Which opens the eyes." You get divine sight. (50)

On the full-moon day in the month of Vaishak (some time between the middle of April and the middle of May), the first month of the Indian year, Buddha was born. On this day he attained his enlightenment, and on this day final nirvana or liberation.

The Buddhist scriptures were written after the death of Buddha. All his disciples gathered together for the first time and wrote whatever they had heard directly from him and put what they wrote down in one of three baskets. They were then gathered together, edited and organized, and then published as Buddha's teachings. We call these his scriptures, because his teachings are revelations. They are known as *Tripitaka*, "three-baskets."

Buddha was born a prince. In India, even today, when any child is born, astrologers are asked to cast a horoscope. When the astrologers cast the horoscope of this child, they said that there were two alternatives for the boy: either he would be a great monarch ruling over the then-known world, or he would be a beggar. Of course, no father wants his son to be a beggar, especially a king. The astrologers pointed out that if the boy saw old age and disease and death, the suffering of mankind, he would renounce everything and be a beggar.

So the king built a vast estate where everything was beautiful: plants, trees, shrubs, and young, healthy people. In time the prince married and lived a luxurious life with all the comforts that anybody could want. He had one son.

One day he told his attendant, "I'd like to see how people live outside." So the two rode on horseback into town. One after another he met with old age, a man tottering on his limbs; sickness, a leper; and death, people carrying a corpse on their shoulders. He was horrified. "Does that happen to everybody?" "Yes, if you live long enough, die one must."

That was the beginning. These three universal worries had so stunned him that while his wife and son were asleep, he went away with the resolution, "I must bring to mankind the way to overcome suffering; I must show mankind the way to peace." (51)

There is suffering, and there is a way out – a way of peace. That is what religion, or spiritual life, means. Conflict and chaotic conditions arise, nation against nation, race against race, until mankind learns that we have to become spiritual aspirants and realize the truth for ourselves. If there is peace within our own hearts, we shall find that peace everywhere; and if we don't have that peace within ourselves, we shall create troubles for everybody.

Buddha was not pessimistic, nor was he optimistic in the worldly sense. The difficulty with us is that when suffering comes, we think it is going to last forever; and when we have pleasures, we think they are going to last forever. But nothing lasts. We cling to that which is ever in flux. In regard to suffering, Buddha recognizes that we must transcend our finite minds and reach the unchanging Reality, *nirvana*. Hindus call it *moksha* or *Turiya*, the (transcendental) Fourth, or *samadhi*; Christ calls it "to be born in Spirit." *Nirvana* literally means "extinction of suffering." To quote Buddha: "Wherein there is no more birth nor suffering, nor old age, nor death." He found a way to attain this.

"Be earnest in effort, and you too shall soon be free from the great evil." This state of attainment is described in negative terms. It is, in Buddha's words, a state in which we are delivered from time. There is the misconception in the West that eternal life or immortality means continuity in time. But modern science proves that the continuity of existence is there for everything in the universe. There is no such thing as complete destruction, only a change of forms and names. This existed in the past and will exist in the future; it may just become dust and go back to its elements, but it still continues to exist. Attaining to immortal life is beyond time, but it is the life of realizing the ultimate Reality, attaining perfection, while still living in the body. The *nirvana* of Buddha in positive terms means eternal peace, realizing the unborn, undying, and changeless reality.

"There are two extremes which a spiritual aspirant must not follow. The habitual practice on the one hand of those things whose attraction depends upon the passions, and especially upon sensuality; and the habitual practice on the other hand of asceticism or self-mortification, which is painful, unworthy, and unprofitable. There is a middle path, avoiding these two extremes, a path which opens the eyes and bestows understanding, which leads to peace of mind, to the higher wisdom, to full enlightenment, to *nirvana*." Buddha, Sri Krishna, Sri Ramakrishna, Jesus, all the great ones taught the middle path. That is the way of peace. (52)

Buddha lived six hundred years before Christ. Buddhism is not a separate religion from Hinduism; it is an aspect of Hinduism.

From ignorance arises the sense of ego. This ego seems to be permanent, as if it is not changing. Buddha gives the illustration of a torch. If you take a lighted torch and wave it around, you see a circle; but it is changing all the time, point by point, point by point. But again, in order to see that circle that is always changing, there has to be an unchangeable reality behind it. From the sense of ego which we cling to so definitely – "I want this, I want that; this is my possession, my life" – arise attachment and aversion, what Buddha calls the thirst for life. Patanjali calls it "clinging to life." Buddha emphasizes that this is the cause of suffering.

The middle path of moderation which Buddha teaches we also find in the Bhagavad Gita: "Yoga is not for the man who overeats, or for him who fasts excessively. It is not for him who sleeps too much, or the keeper of exaggerated vigils. Let a man be moderate in his eating and his recreation, moderately active, moderate in sleep and wakefulness; he will find that yoga takes away all his unhappiness."

I shall read to you in Buddha's words the five forms of meditation. "Said the disciple: 'Teach me, O Lord, the meditations to which I must devote myself in order to let my mind enter into the paradise of the pure land.' Buddha said: 'There are five meditations. The first meditation is the meditation of love in which you must so adjust your heart that you long for the weal and welfare of all beings, including the happiness of your enemies.'" You have to send a thought of love towards all beings in the universe. "The second meditation is the meditation of pity. It makes you think of all beings in distress, vividly representing in your imagination their sorrows and anxieties, so as to arouse a deep compassion for them in your soul. The third meditation is the meditation of joy in which you think of the prosperity of others and rejoice with their rejoicing." You have to be free of jealousy. "The fourth meditation is the meditation on impurity in which you consider the evil consequences of corruption, the effects of sin and diseases. The fifth meditation is the meditation on serenity in which you rise above love and hate, tyranny and oppression, wealth and want, and regard your own fate with impartial calmness and perfect tranquility." (53)

Buddha was only interested in showing the way of life to those who were ready to follow the way. He said: "A man is hit by a poisoned arrow. His friends hasten to the doctor. The latter is about to draw the arrow out, but the wounded man cries, 'I'll not have this arrow drawn out until I know who shot it, whether a woman or a *brahmin* or a *vaishya* or a *shudra*, to which family he belonged, whether he was tall or short, and so on." How ridiculous. There should be no speculation in spiritual life – no theorizing – but following that which will lead us to complete freedom from suffering and misery, to that ocean of blissful existence. That is what is meant by religion.

Organized religion has to have certain theories and dogmas to which millions can subscribe, but when great teachers come, such as Buddha or Christ or Ramakrishna, they are only interested in giving freedom to every individual. By their power they show us knowledge and illumination. There are scribes and Pharisees in every age, but religion is transmitted by one who has authority. Sri Ramakrishna would ask every teacher he knew, "Have you seen God? Have you gotten the command from God to teach?" Book-learning and the study of scriptures do not make one a teacher of God. A teacher has to know God. And so Buddha pointed out: "For Brahman I know, and the world of Brahman, and the path which leadeth unto it. Yeah, I know it even as one who has entered the Brahman world and has been born within it."

Buddha is called an agnostic, because he did not define the nature of God. When he was about to die, one of his disciples asked, "Holy Sir, do I understand you to say that there is a God?" He said, "Did I say that?" And another disciple said, "Do I understand you to say that there is no God?" And he said, "Did I say that?" Naturally one might conclude that he was an agnostic. But he was a true knower of God. When you say that God exists, immediately you begin to feel and think, "Oh, he exists here, he exists there, he exists in space."

But where does space come from? Take away time and space and relativity. Can you have any conception of what that truth is?

Buddha says: "From ignorance comes attachment. From attachment come the impressions of deeds of past lives. From this arises ego-sense. From ego-sense springs the false identity with mind and body. From sense contact arises feeling and sensation. From sensation springs thirst. From thirst comes attachment. From attachment spring the deeds which cause rebirth. Such is the origin of the whole mass of suffering."

Buddha then points out that suffering can be overcome by the noble kind of wisdom, by knowledge. Suffering is a direct, immediate experience through our mind and senses and body. There has to be another direct and immediate experience to come out of that suffering. Buddha calls this the noble kind of wisdom, which can be had while living here on earth. It is not just an intellectual understanding or simply having faith. It is a matter of experience.

And then he points out that this noble kind of wisdom can be attained by the noble conduct of life and the noble earnestness of meditation. Both are essential, and not until through these means the evils of ignorance and misconception become washed away can spiritual peace be attained. "Come, disciples. Lead a holy life for the extinction of sorrow."

Then again, this noble conduct of life and noble earnestness of meditation have been analyzed into an eight-fold path, which Buddha calls "the way of peace."

First is right view: to understand the first four noble truths. Unless you realize that there is suffering, that it is caused by ignorance, that ignorance can be overcome, and that there is a way of peace, you are not ready to follow the way of peace. And you must have longing, which you will have if you understand that there is suffering.

Second is right aspiration. This means that your efforts are not for yourself only. You wish to attain bliss and to free yourself from suffering, not for yourself only, but to help others to remove the suffering and to live in love and harmony with all beings. That is, wherever there is any tinge of selfishness, there is no truth of religion. Religion makes you selfless, and you feel for others. There is love.

Third is right speech, that is, truthfulness in word, thought, and deed. As you seek the truth, you have to be truthful. You may say that you can't live in this commercial, business world without telling some white lies, but that is not so. I have seen one American woman who never told a lie. But Buddha explains truthfulness by this sentence: "Abstain from lying, slander, abuse, harsh words, and idle talk."

Fourth is right conduct. Buddha emphasizes not hurting any creature in word, thought, or deed. He lays great emphasis upon that. And let me say, this non-injury is a not a negative teaching. Not hurting means to learn to love all as one's own Self, to see one's Self everywhere, to see the Atman in every being, and to love every being. At one time Buddha was invited by a very rich man, but he refused the invitation and went to a prostitute instead in order to dignify her. In her he saw no sinner.

Fifth is right livelihood. You have to make a living, but you should abstain from any forbidden occupation, such as trading in weapons, dealing in slaves, being a butcher, publican, or poison-seller; I would say dope sellers in these days.

Sixth is right effort: not to allow distracting thoughts while you sit to pray or meditate; instead, to control them. Buddha gives one method, which is also in Patanjali's Yoga: In the beginning, watch your mind run after distracting thoughts. Keep watch, be the witness, and then gather the forces of the mind and concentrate.

Seventh is right mindfulness. This means seeing the ephemeral nature of everything through discrimination and then
concentrating upon the truth that is eternal, focusing on one
of the spiritual centers of the body, just as in yoga practice.

And eighth is right contemplation. It is what we call *dhyana*,
meditation. It means concentration of the mind so that there
is a continuous flow of consciousness, without any break. An
illustration is electric light; the current comes continuously
and you see a steady light, but if there is a break in the current, the light will flicker. The very nature of the mind is to
run from one thing to another, changing all the time. But let
the current of the mind flow towards only one thought continuously, like oil poured from one vessel to another; then
there is continuity. Similarly, where there is steadiness, like
a flame sheltered from wind, then the noble kind of knowledge arises. Then you are free from suffering, and you attain
peace. (54)

There are two ideals: one is striving, and the other is depending upon divine grace. Throughout the teachings of Buddha, we find that he lays great stress on the ideal of striving,
of having to struggle.

Buddha insists on taking refuge within oneself – not in any
being outside – because Brahman is within yourself. Swami
Vivekananda pointed out emphatically that our prayers are
answered – but who answers the prayers? You yourself. He
meant God, the divine being. The Atman, which is one with
Brahman, answers the prayers from within. So take your refuge in that Self within.

Nirvana is misunderstood as extinction of life. It is the
extinction of suffering and misery and the attainment of the
Absolute – eternal life, absolute knowledge, and bliss – the
same as Vedanta or Christianity or Sufism or Judaism. Chris-

tians often say that Buddhism is pessimistic and that Christianity is life-affirming. But what did Jesus teach? "He who loves this life shall lose it." Buddha would say: "Find it here and now!" Not after death. (55)

We Hindus worship Buddha as an *avatara* or divine incarnation, though we are not Buddhists. I'll relate to you a vision, a spiritual experience, of Swami Vijnanananda. I heard this directly from him and wrote it in my diary. He said, "I went to visit Sarnath, near Benares, where Buddha preached his first sermon after illumination. Suddenly I lost all physical consciousness. My mind seemed almost to have vanished. I was enveloped in an ocean of light, the light that is vibrant with peace, joy, and knowledge. I felt, as it were, I was living in Buddha. I do not remember how long I remained in that state. The guide thought I had fallen asleep. As it was getting late, he tried to awaken me, and so brought me back to normal consciousness. Later, when I went to the temple of Vishwanath in Benaras – Vishwanath means the Lord of the Universe, it is the stone image of Lord Shiva – I thought to myself, 'Why have I come here? To look at a stone?' When this same vision opened up, it was as if Vishwanath were telling me the light is the same here as there. Truth is one." (56)

What is meant by discrimination? To realize at least intellectually the ephemeral nature of everything, how everything passes. That was what Buddha emphasized: you can hold nothing. To give the simile Buddha used: "It is like bidding the clouds to stay." You have happiness today, and you think it is going to last forever, but it is just like bidding the clouds to stay. Happiness is not to be found in that which is passing. Happiness and suffering follow each other; neither is permanent. Suffering comes and we get upset. But know that it is also a passing phase; it won't stay.

Buddha strongly accepted a fundamental theory of the Hindus – what is known as karma and reincarnation. He pointed out, like the Hindus, that the ideal is to rise above karma and rebirth. As long as we are within that wheel, we suffer. We have to come out of that wheel of karma and rebirth by attaining the noble kind of wisdom, as he calls it. (57)

What Buddha taught was really the Upanishads. We see the teachings of the Upanishads echoed through and through. We find in the Upanishads the noble kind of wisdom that Buddha taught – that which words cannot express and from which the mind comes away baffled. That is the wisdom to be sought – transcendental experience, *nirvana*. And that is the *samadhi* of the yogis, and what is called *Turiya*, the Fourth, in the Upanishads. By Jesus it is called "being born in spirit."

Buddha pointed out that there is this difference between ignorance and the noble kind of wisdom: the difference between sleep and awakening. You are asleep and dreaming. All kinds of dreams come to you. While you are asleep there is no understanding, no knowledge. And when that sleep breaks and you wake up, you see things differently. But this waking state is also a sleep. We have to be awakened. It is not vision or lights or things like that. It is beyond all that. It is the pure experience of being.

Ramakrishna said about Buddha's silence: "When one attains *samadhi*, then alone comes the knowledge of Brahman." In that realization all thoughts cease, one becomes perfectly silent; there is no power of speech left by which to express Brahman. (58)

At the outset I must tell you I'm not a Buddhist, and yet all Hindus worship Buddha as one of their divine incarnations. It is similar to the relation between Christ and Christianity. Christ was born a Jew, and Christianity at one time was a small sect of Judaism. Eventually a new religion was formed. Buddha was born a Hindu and Hindus accepted his teachings. But the followers of Buddha took him and his teachings in new directions, and so you find Buddhism developed later without the background of Vedanta. This has often been misunderstood, but I would say that Buddha and his teachings in their original form are still followed by Vedantists.

When Buddha was born, there was a degeneration of the religion of the Vedas. It had become priestcraft. There was not that urge to realize the truth of God. And so Buddha insisted upon experiencing the truth. He even went so far as to suggest throwing away your Vedas if you don't live what they teach. What need have you of scriptures if you cannot struggle to find God? What need of teachings if you forget the ideal?

Here is the point. You have to be anxious to attain the truth. You have to desire to free yourself from suffering and ignorance. You may ask, "Does not everyone seek freedom from suffering?" Not always. Let me give you the illustration of the camel. There may be green grass and a thorny plant, and the camel will run for the thorny plant. It will suffer, it will bleed, but nevertheless it will run for that thorny plant. Now consider our minds, which run after objects of pleasure. We know they give us pain and suffering, but we still run after them.

Buddha urges us to wake up. One time when he was asked, "Are you a man?" He said, "No." "Are you a God?" "No." "Are you an angel?" "No." "What are you?" He said, "I am Buddha, the awakened one." He never claimed that the attainment was exclusively his. There have been many in the past who were

11

buddhas, and there will be many in future. In fact, each one of us has to become a buddha. (59)

Sri Ramakrishna explained buddhahood as having our mind and heart absorbed in *bodha*, "pure consciousness." That is the ideal. It is very difficult to explain what pure consciousness is. We are conscious. I know I am conscious because I see this book, I am conscious of this light, of my surroundings. I know only the contents of my consciousness. But it is the pure light of consciousness that gives light to everything. I am using that light, you are using that light of God for any experience in life, good or bad – but the light remains unknown. Now, we become freed from all suffering and misery (*nirvana* means "extinction of suffering") when we are awakened to that pure consciousness. (60)

Buddha defines the state of *nirvana* as "deliverance from time." There is nothing but Brahman, but the mind is limited by time, space, and causation – by relativity. When we see Brahman percolating through time, space, and causation, we see the appearance of the universe. So when Buddha points out that *nirvana* is deliverance from time, that means the transcending of maya. To rise above time is immortality. And Buddha's words are that *nirvana* is eternal peace, the peace of realizing the unborn, undying, and changeless reality. The practical spiritual solution to life's suffering, according to all the great religions of the world, is to go beyond the physical and the finite to that reality which is infinite and unchanging.

You see, if you follow the teachings – not merely understanding them intellectually – and live life as taught by the great teachers, you will apprehend the truth here and now. (61)

CHRIST

Before I begin my subject proper, I'd like to tell you how I got interested in Christ and his teachings. Being a Hindu, I was taught to respect all religions, prophets, divine incarnations, and teachings that lead towards God. But of course that didn't mean I was actively interested in Christ or his teachings.

After graduating from high school, I went to Calcutta where the Bible Society presented a copy of the Bible to all the graduates. When I opened it and read all the "begats," I got tired, and that was enough of the Bible.

Later I took a course on philosophy at the university and had to study theosophy and Christian theology. I was a headache to the professor. The theological arguments and ontological arguments to prove the existence of God didn't appeal to me. They did not talk about experiencing God. I studied them in order to pass my examination, that's all. I have forgotten everything now. Then I took up Hindu philosophy.

When I joined Belur Math, it was during the Christmas vacation. In every monastery of the Ramakrishna Order in India, Christmas is observed. It was on Christmas Eve – I remember it vividly – in a large hall facing the Ganges at the Belur Math. Most of the disciples of Ramakrishna were present. I want you to feel that. Suppose you were in the physical presence of the direct disciples of Jesus: Mathew, John, James, Peter. Imagine that! That was literally true. I was in the presence of those direct disciples of Ramakrishna.

An altar was made and a picture of the Madonna and Child was placed there. The one who was to act as the priest was Swami Shuddhananda, a senior disciple of Swami Vivekananda. I helped to dress him up like a Catholic priest. In fun we made a little cap for him of teak leaves. He was a great

soul, this disciple of Swamiji. He entered and took the seat of
the priest to do the worship, and then Swami Brahmananda,
Swami Premananda, Swami Turiyananda, and Swami Shivananda – these great disciples of Ramakrishna – came and were
seated. The hall was filled with brahmacharis and swamis of
the Ramakrishna Order.

Christ was offered the worship with the following items:
flowers, perfume, light, incense, food, and a cigar. The food
offering was Christmas cake, which we bought in Calcutta.
While the worship was going on, Maharaj (Swami Brahmananda) asked us to meditate upon Christ within our hearts
and to feel his living presence in the place. And it all happened
so suddenly! Our minds really were lifted up and – I can tell
you my personal experience – I felt that Christ was as much
our own as Krishna or Ramakrishna.

Of course all this happened in our hearts and in silence.
Then I heard Maharaj talking to Swami Shivananda: "Wasn't
that wonderful!" And Swami Shivananda replied: "Wasn't
that something!" In other words, they had had the vision of
Christ.

Now let us try to understand what Christ is, and what his
message is. I am not interested in Christian theology, but I
am interested in Christ and his direct teachings. One truth
he pointed out was: "I come not to destroy, but to fulfill." In
other words, he was a Jew. He was born a Jew and he died a
Jew. He never became a Christian. And he fulfilled; he did
not destroy anything. In the Gospel according to St. John
is this passage: "Moses gave the law. Grace and truth came
through Jesus Christ."

There is a claim made that Christ was unique. I would corroborate that claim. Yes, Christ was unique. So was Rama,
so was Krishna, so was Ramakrishna – because each one of
them was a form of the one God in different garments.

The philosophical background of the *avatara* from the Christian viewpoint is found in The Gospel according to St. John: "In the beginning was the Word, and the Word was with God, and the Word was God." This Word is the Logos. Strange as it may seem, in the ancient scriptures of the Vedas, preceding the Bible, we have almost the identical words: "In the beginning was the creator. The Word was second to him. This Word is Brahman."

Now according to the Gospel according to St. John: "This word became flesh in Christ, in Jesus." And it is also claimed that he was the only begotten of the Father. If you are students of philosophy, you will remember how Philo, the Alexandrian Jewish philosopher, explained the Logos: "First begotten Son of God: the Logos." St. John practically took verbatim the idea of this philosopher. So let us remember that the only begotten Son of God is the Word, the Logos.

There is one eternal religion, one eternal truth, and this truth becomes forgotten. In the Western world especially, the truth has become forgotten. It is not emphasized that God can be known and experienced. It is said that Christ spoke with authority. What does that mean? He had seen God, he had experienced God. And he wanted everyone to see and experience God. In the Vedas we find the same: "I have known that truth, you also can know it." And then it is that you go beyond the dual throngs of life.

Now let me quote to you: "Philip said unto him, 'Lord, show us the Father, and it suffices us.' Jesus said unto him: 'Have I been so long with you, and yet hast thou not known me, Philip? He that hath seen me hath seen the Father. How sayest thou then, 'Show us the Father?'" And St. Paul said: "For in Him (Jesus) dwelleth all the fullness of Godhead, bodily, and ye are complete in Him, which is the head of all principality and power."

Now let us try to understand the nature of his birth. He said: "Ye are from beneath, I am from above." In other words, we have to unfold that divinity which is within us; from which he is descent. "You are of this world. I am not of this world." Sri Krishna says the same thing: "I am the birthless, the deathless Lord of all that breathes. I seem to be born. It is only seeming, only my maya."

Religion would remain an abstraction if there were not these exemplars. They come – God descends – in order to show us how to ascend towards Godhead. For instance, there is the vibration of light everywhere, even in darkness, but how do you see that light? In the electric bulb. In the same way, there is that divinity in every one of us, but we have to see it where it is manifest. Jesus said: "I am the light of the world. He that followeth Me shall not walk in darkness, but shall have the light of life." Sri Krishna says: "He who knows the nature of my task and my holy birth is not reborn when he leaves the body, he comes to me. Flying from fear, from lust and anger, he hides in me, his refuge and safety. Burned clean in this blaze of My being, in Me many find rest." Just note how similar the words are.

Again, Jesus said: "Come unto Me, all ye that labour and are heavy-laden and I will give you rest." Sri Krishna said: "Lay down all duties in Me, your refuge, fear no longer, for I will save you from sin and bondage." In this age Sri Ramakrishna said: "I am the sanctuary. Take refuge in Me." And then he used the Bengali word: "I am *kopala-mochana*: I wipe out karmas of those who take their refuge in Me." Now what does it mean to take refuge in Christ or Krishna or Ramakrishna? It is to take refuge in Brahman.

In the Christian trinity, I think of Father as Brahman; son as the *avatara*, divine incarnation; and Holy Ghost as the Atman, divine Self. And this is one and the same. So when you worship a Christ or a Krishna or a Ramakrishna, you are worshipping Brahman, the Atman, within your own self – not outside. It is the eternal Christ, the eternal Krishna, the eternal Ramakrishna, the eternal Atman – that is, your Self that you are worshiping.

Religion means realization, experience of God. There is this beautiful truth taught by Jesus: "Blessed are the pure in heart, for they shall see God." That is the condition of experiencing God – purity of heart. We find an explanation for purity of heart in the Upanishads: "When the senses are purified, the heart is purified; when the heart is purified, there is constant and unceasing remembrance of the Self; when there is constant and unceasing remembrance of the Self, all bonds are loosened and freedom is attained." [Chandogya Upanishad]

In the words of Jesus also: "Verily I say unto you, inasmuch as ye have done it unto one of the least of these my brethren, ye have done unto me." This is not humanism. Sri Ramakrishna at one time said: "Help. Help. Who am I to help another? Isn't God in every being? Can I help God?" Then he said: "Serve Him. Serve God. Serve God in everyone." In other words, see God within yourself, see God in every being, and serve God. When we go with the idea of helping another, instead of helping, we sometimes only become busybodies. Go with that ideal of serving God when you offer something to anybody. (62)

There are special reasons why Christmas Eve is observed in every monastery of the Ramakrishna Order. It is not that Hindus observe Christmas Eve, but our monasteries do. Those of you who have studied the life of Ramakrishna know how he once saw the picture of the Madonna with the baby Christ and how that picture became living. He became absorbed in the living presence of Christ.

There was another event in the lives of the disciples of Sri Ramakrishna. Sri Ramakrishna made monks of some of his young disciples by giving them the gerua cloth. After his passing away, the disciples wanted to take formal vows of *sannyasa*, so one evening they lighted a fire, sat around it, and took their vows. Afterward, Swamiji began to talk about Christ and his ideal of renunciation and what a great yogi he was. These disciples were imbued with that ideal of renunciation that Jesus taught. At the time they did not know that it was Christmas Eve; they learned that later.

Now to quote the words of Christ: "Blessed are the pure in heart, for they shall see God." What a wonderful truth! In this connection Swami Vivekananda remarked, "If all the scriptures were forgotten but this one beatitude of Christ remained, religion would remain alive in this world." That purity of heart is the one condition in every teaching of all the great ones in every scripture. My master one day told us this secret: "It is not this gross mind that can see God, but the subtle mind. When this gross mind becomes purified, that subtle mind becomes evident, and through it, one can have the vision of God." A Tamil saint, though an untouchable, said: "Be pure in heart. All righteousness is contained in this one commandment. All other things are naught – an empty display."

So what is this purity? Try to think of God, and what happens? Your mind is restless; for only a moment can you think of him, then it goes away. Restless is the human mind. Why? Because we have so many desires and ambitions. In one of the Upanishads we read: "When the food is purified, the heart is purified. When the heart is purified, there is constant recollectedness of God. And when there is the constant recollectedness of God, his truth becomes revealed."

"Food" does not mean only what we eat through our mouths, but what we gather through all our senses. It is not by stunning our senses or caning our bodies that we can achieve God. Move among the objects of senses and at the same time learn to give up attachment and aversion. That is the secret. For instance, a young man sees the face of a beautiful girl and immediately wants to possess her. He becomes attached. Instead of seeing that surface beauty, see how God dwells in that, and you will see your whole outlook change. As you think of God within yourself, you learn to think of God existing everywhere, in all beings. That is how the food becomes purified. Then there comes purity of heart.

There are two commandments you are all acquainted with: "Love the Lord thy God with all thy heart, with all thy soul, with all thy strength, and love thy neighbor as thyself." When you love God with all your mind, with all your heart, with all your soul, with all your strength, how can there be any attachment for something else? And then when you love your neighbor as yourself, you will see the same God dwelling everywhere. (63)

SHANKARA

Shankara was born in the seventh century A.D. into a very orthodox *brahmin* family. He became a saint, a philosopher, and a great poet. Anyone who learns Sanskrit and reads what he wrote will find how simply and in what a melodious way he explained the most abstruse subject of his philosophy.

His birthplace was the village of Kalady in Kerala in Southern India. He was a child prodigy. When he was only six years old, he memorized the Upanishads, the Bhagavad Gita and the Brahma Sutras. Later, of course, he wrote commentaries on all of them. As a young boy of seven, he would hold discussions with great scholars of the age, who would come from distant lands to see this child prodigy and discuss philosophy with him. But gradually he became disgusted with scholarship. He realized that all these great scholars and teachers spoke lofty philosophy, but their life examples were different; they were materialistic and pleasure-seeking.

At this period his father died, so Shankara began to think deeply about the problems of life and death. Of course he had studied all the scriptures by that time and knew intellectually how to attain immortality. In his youthful zeal, he wanted to realize the truth for himself and to set an example for others on how to spiritualize life. He wrote a beautiful poem called "The Shattering of Delusion" (*Charpata-Panjarika Stotra*). In it he says: "Behold the folly of man: in childhood, busy with toys; in youth, bewitched by love; in age, bogged down with fear and always unmindful of the Lord. The hours fly, the seasons roll, life ebbs, but the breeze of hope blows continually in his heart. Birth brings death, death brings rebirth. This evil needs no proof. Where then, O man, is thy happiness? This life trembles in the balance, like water on a lotus leaf, and yet the sage can show us in an instant how to bridge this sea of change. The son may bring thee suffering, thy wealth is no assurance of heaven. Therefore, be not vain of thy wealth or of thy family, or of thy youth. All are fleeting, all must change. Know this and be free. Enter the joy of the Lord. Seek neither peace nor strife with kith or kin, with friend or foe. O beloved, if thou wouldst attain freedom, be equal unto all."

There are many legends that gathered around Shankara's life. It is very difficult to know whether they are true or not, but I'll mention one. When he was young, his mother had to walk a long distance to bathe in the river. He felt sorry for her and wanted the river to turn its course and come nearer to her house. He went out and prayed to the river. The legend is that the river turned its course in a zig-zag way and came around just by his home before again joining the course. I have been to Kalady where he was born and saw with my own eyes how the river changed its course in an opposite direction.

When he was eight years old, as he realized the vanity of life, Shankara begged his mother to allow him to renounce the world and enter into monastic life. The widowed mother had just this son, so it was only after great entreaty that she gave her permission, with the promise that before her death, he would come visit her. Shankara kept that promise.

He went out in search of an illumined teacher. He went to the river Narmada, where even today there are huts where holy men live and practice spiritual disciplines. My master also lived there for quite a few years.

According to legend, Shankara approached Gaudapada, a great saint and philosopher, who was absorbed in *samadhi*. When he woke up – he knew this young boy would be coming to him – he said that he was not accepting disciples anymore, that the boy should go to his chief disciple, Govindapada. Shankara did so, and in a short period he attained *nirvikalpa samadhi*. He stayed in that *samadhi* for six days and six nights. It was then his turn to go out and teach.

He went to Benares, still a well-known place for scholars and holy men. There is an interesting story about this period, which is not legend, but fact. It seems that Shankara still had some caste prejudice, though he had attained the highest *samadhi*.

Caste prejudice is very strong in Kerala. I never saw it until I went there. While we were still moving on the road, it got dark. We heard a peculiar noise and when I asked my friend what it was, he said, "Oh, they're the untouchables. They make that noise to find out if there are caste people walking on the street. If so, they move away." I said, "Don't make any sound. Let's not tell them we are caste people; let's approach them." But this inferiority complex was so inborn in those people that as we approached – there were about a dozen of them and we were only three – half of them jumped to one side of the field, and the other half to the other side. One of the men, whose guest I was, was very rich. I told him he had to invite those untouchables for some good food and good clothing. He did, but the untouchables sat far away. I asked them to come nearer, inside the house, but they would not come. So I tricked them. I ran and got hold of a baby, so they followed me into the house. Later the zamindar, the landlord, opened a school and boarding houses for boys and girls, and another friend of mine became the headmaster. He was a very educated man; he became Swami Tyagishananda, who wrote a beautiful and learned commentary on the Narada Bhakti Sutras. Now, with the influence of the Ramakrishna Mission and Mahatma Gandhi, untouchability has become illegal and is not observed anymore.

But Shankara had that caste instinct in him. As it happened, as he was going to bathe in the Ganges, the road was blocked by an untouchable with four dogs playing around. Shankara ordered him out of the way. The untouchable, in a very gentle manner, addressed the dogs: "Look, you don't even know what intelligence you have and he asks us to move. He says there is one Atman. Where is one to move? Where is the place? Is not all filled by one Atman, one Brahman? Isn't that what he teaches? And he says to move away!" Suddenly it dawned on Shankara, and he saw before him that this *chandala* was none other than Lord Shiva and the four dogs were the four Vedas! After that, of course, Shankara had no prejudice. He wrote a famous poem, the refrain of each verse, being: "He who has learned to see that the one existence everywhere is my master, be he *brahmin* or *chandala*."

Then Shankara began teaching among the scholars of the day. There was one great scholar named Mandana Mishra, who was well-versed in the Vedas and who believed in Vedic rites and ceremonies. He believed that the householder's life was greater than the life of a monk. Shankara, who was then about fifteen years old, realized that unless he could convert this man, it was not possible for him to spread his teachings. But when Mishra would do any rites or ceremonies, he would close all the doors; he had a high wall, so no intruders could come in.

Shankara climbed a nearby tree and jumped over the wall. Mandana Mishra got mad and said, "From where comes this shaven head?" Shankara teased him, saying, "Don't you have eyes to see? It comes out from the neck here!" There were other scholars there who said, "Now look, this boy is not ordinary. Whatever he says has a scriptural background, so ask him what he wants." Mishra quietened down and asked, "What do you want from me?" Shankara said, "I want to debate you. And there is one condition: if you defeat me, I'll become a householder and marry a girl; and if you are defeated, you have to renounce the world and become a monk."

Mandana Mishra thought that if he could convert this fellow, it would be a wonderful thing, so he agreed to a debate, but he asked who was to be referee. Shankara said, "I'd like to have your wife as referee." Shankara knew that the wife was a great scholar. She agreed, but she was in a dilemma. On the one hand, her husband was God himself; on the other hand, a monk is God himself. So she played a trick. She put a garland around her husband's neck and another one on Shankara, saying, "The garland of whoever is defeated will dry up quicker."

The debate continued for some days, and then Mandana Mishra's garland began to wither; he realized he was defeated. He said, "You win. So I must keep the condition." But Shankara said, "No. You can't take monastic life on condition. I made that condition, true, but I don't want you to become a monk just to fulfill it. If you feel dispassion, then only will I accept you as a monk." Then Mandana Mishra said, "Yes, I see the ephemeral nature of everything. I want to follow you." So he followed and became one of Shankara's most devoted disciples. His annotations of Shankara's commentaries are very famous. They are known by the name of his wife, Bharati.

Shankara died at the early age of thirty-two at Kedarnath Temple, high in the Himalayas. It is a most wonderful place of pilgrimage, where Kedarnath – Lord Shiva – is honored.

In his short life, Shankara organized what is known today as the *Dashanami* monastic order. Monks existed from Vedic times, but they were independent. There were only guru and disciple, but no organized monastic order. All monks of the Ramakrishna Order belong to one such order. They are differently named: Puri, Bharati, Saraswati, of Shankara, and so on. We are Puri. My full title is: Swami Prabhavananda Puri, because we come from Totapuri, you see.

Then he established four monasteries in the four corners of India. Every monk is supposed to visit all these places of pilgrimage, but most monks don't visit all four. They leave out one with the expectation that at the moment of death, they will think that they have to go there and they will think of the Lord.

As I have often told you, there are four *mahavakyas* or great sayings: *Tat twam asi*: "That Thou Art," *Aham Brahmasmi*: "I am Brahman," *Ayam Atma Brahma*: "This Atman is Brahman," and *Prajnanam Brahma*: "Pure Consciousness is Brahman." Every monk is given one of these *mahavakyas*, and there is a special *mahavakya* for each order. Shankara based his whole truth upon these *mahavakyas*. These are the sayings of the Upanishads which hold the same idea, that the Self, the true being in man, is one with the Divine; in other words, behind this appearance, there is one divinity, one Atman.

Shankara's literary output was tremendous. He wrote commentaries on the Upanishads, on the Bhagavad Gita, on the Brahma Sutras, and then many original works, including Vivekachudamani and Upadesha Sahasri, the thousand verses on the teachings of advaita, nondualism. People don't know that he was also a great devotee. He wrote many prayers, including a prayer to the Divine Mother and one to Shiva. Many of his prayers, as well as many minor works, are chanted by devotees in India. Of course Shankara preached no new doctrine, no new philosophy, no new creed, but he was the greatest propounder of nondualistic philosophy, which is the main principle in the teachings of the Upanishads.

It is believed by many that Shankara said, "That which has been taught in hundreds of scriptures, I shall speak in half a line: 'Brahman is real; this universe of appearance is unreal; the *jiva*, the so-called individual, is no other than Brahman.'"

Now, Shankara does not say unreal in the sense that something does not exist at all, such as a barren woman having a son. But there are degrees of reality. Even a mirage has some reality as long as we see it, but when we come near, it vanishes. A dream has a reality greater than a mirage, but when you wake up, the dream vanishes. Now again, this waking state has a reality, an empirical reality, but as soon as we enter into *samadhi*, the higher state, the universe disappears. But your consciousness, which is Atman, is unchangeable, continuing, and always present. Without the presence of that pure consciousness, you would not be conscious of objects and things. Without that pure consciousness, there would not be the possibility even of dreaming. When you are in deep sleep and seemingly unconscious, there is still that pure consciousness – the Self, Atman. It is present in every one of us: we are carrying God with us all the time.

Just as you know a piece of gold, whatever shape or form it may have, the reality behind names and forms is Brahman, but somehow we have forgotten through what Shankara calls *avidya*, *maya*, ignorance. Ignorance is beginningless and, he points out, is simply a statement of fact. How it happened, why it happened, we do not know. Shankara says it is inexplicable but it is a fact of everybody's experience. You think you cannot mistake light for darkness, but it happens. The Atman – the subject – and the object of experience – body, mind, possessions – have been identified with each other. We don't know how it happened, but it is the experience of everybody. Even the greatest intellects who know that they are separate from the body still identify with the body in all behavior.

Shankara says that only by transcending the three states of waking, dreaming, and dreamless sleep can one awaken to the Fourth and realize the truth. But we cannot realize this truth of Brahman by simply uttering the word *Brahman*. It doesn't happen. He says, if there is a buried treasure and you say, "Treasure, come out!" it doesn't come out; you have to take a shovel and dig. Then you get the treasure. Similarly, there are methods and means, spiritual disciplines, which we have to practice for this ignorance to break.

But first, Shankara gives three conditions: human birth, the desire for the truth of God, and the grace of a guru. These three steps, which we first find in the Upanishads, Shankara brings out in the following passage: "Then the disciple must hear the truth of the Atman, and reflect upon it and meditate upon it constantly without pause for a long time. Thus the wise man reaches that highest state in which consciousness of subject and object is dissolved away and infinite unitary consciousness alone remains. He knows the bliss of *nirvana* while still living on earth."

Shankara points out that as you meditate, you go beyond the three sheathes, and the consciousness of subject and object is dissolved away. That is, in "I know this," there is subject and object and the process of knowledge. As long as there is the distinction between the subject and the object, you do not know the thing-in-itself. So to realize God is not for the "I" to see God as an object, but for subject and object to be dissolved into infinite, unitary consciousness. That is *nirvikalpa samadhi*, the transcendental consciousness. There are lower experiences and visions where there is a distinction – not a separation, but a distinction. You may have a vision of Christ or Krishna or Buddha, but that is not enough.

Shankara, as well as all the great teachers, points out that steadfastness in devotion is what is most important, whether or not you have any visions or experiences. And in order to attain that, he emphasizes meditation. He said: "Certain knowledge of the reality is gained only through meditation upon right teaching, and not by sacred ablutions or almsgiving, or by the practice of hundreds of breathing exercises."

He also points out that success depends upon the qualifications of the aspirant. He gives certain qualifications we have to acquire. As you try to understand what these qualifications are, you feel, "Oh, how impossible!" In fact, one time when I was studying Shankara with Swami Saradananda, a knower of Brahman and disciple of Sri Ramakrishna, I asked, "But if one has these qualifications, then, practically speaking, he has attained that supreme knowledge!" And he said, "That is true. But you must struggle to gain these qualifications. Try to meditate, struggle. You may fail many times, but at long last, you attain the qualifications and you have the knowledge of Brahman."

12

So I will give you the qualifications in summary. First is discrimination between the eternal and noneternal – that is, to understand that Lord, God, Atman, Brahman alone is the unchangeable reality, that everything else today is and tomorrow is not. When you have this discrimination, you renounce the enjoyments of the effects of your actions here and hereafter. You do not even want heavenly pleasure and you do not want the effects that may come from good deeds. You offer all actions to God.

Then again you have to acquire the following virtues: tranquility, that is directing the mind from objective things, seeing imperfections in them, and turning it steadfastly towards Brahman instead; then self-control, which is the power to withdraw the senses and keep them in their respective centers; and poise in the midst of the pairs of opposites of life – poise is most important. In order to be able to gain that poise, you have to hold onto the pillar of God, as it were, by which you gain equilibrium. Then faith in the words of the scriptures and in the words of your teacher, without which you cannot proceed. You also have to have faith in yourself, that you can attain it: others have attained it, and so can I. Then self-surrender, that is to keep your mind and heart fixed in God as often as possible. And of course, lastly, *mumukshutva*, the desire for liberation. If there is a little desire, the intensity of longing grows through the practice of the disciplines and through the practice of meditation.

To sum up, in the words of Shankara: "Faith, devotion, and constant union with God through prayer and meditation, these are declared by the sacred scriptures to be the direct means of liberation. To him who abides by them comes liberation from that bondage which has been forged by ignorance."

You see, ignorance, which has covered our eyes, has no reality. It vanishes, just like darkness. There may be darkness for thousands of years, but bring in the light once and the darkness immediately vanishes. In the same way, when direct experience comes, all ignorance vanishes immediately. Shankara describes the experience of an illumined soul in these beautiful words: "The ego has disappeared, I have realized my identity with Brahman, and so all my desires have melted away." How can there be any more desire? In Him everything is fulfilled. "I have risen above my ignorance and my knowledge of this seeming universe. What is this joy that I feel? Who shall measure it? I know nothing but joy – limitless, unbounded. This ocean of Brahman is full of nectar. The joy of the Atman, the treasure I have found, cannot be described in words, the mind cannot conceive of it. My mind fell like a hailstone into that vast expanse of Brahman's ocean. Touching one drop of it, I melted away and became one with Brahman. And now, though I return to human consciousness, I abide in the joy of the Atman."

So my prayer for all of you is that you may realize, while living on earth, that joy of the Atman. (64)

RAMANUJA

Ramanuja was a great saint-philosopher, associated with the system known as qualified monism, Vishishtadvaita. His influence, in Southern India especially, is very great. There are people who worship him as an illumined soul, and throughout India, he is regarded as one of the greatest philosophers the country has produced.

Ramanuja was born in South India in A.D. 1017 and lived for one hundred twenty years. His mother was the granddaughter of one of the well-known saints of the age, Yamunacharya. Yamunacharya was a great devotee and illumined soul and the head of a famous temple in South India. He lived to see his great-grandson, Ramanuja, grow up to be a young man. His one desire was to see him become head of the temple.

There is an interesting story of how Yamunacharya, on his deathbed, sent for Ramanuja. Unfortunately he passed away before Ramanuja arrived, but there was something peculiar about the dead body of the great saint: three fingers on one hand were closed. When Ramanuja inquired as to why that was so, his disciples told him that his great-grandfather had an unfulfilled desire, which was that Ramanuja write a commentary on the Vedanta Aphorisms. Ramanuja was a young boy at that time. He promised that before he died, he would do it. And then at once the fingers opened.

When he came of the age to be sent to school, he went to study under a well-known teacher of the time, a great and learned man, but just a scholar who did not have the realization of God. Ramanuja studied with him for some time, especially the Vedanta Aphorisms, but he became dissatisfied. As he pondered over the meaning of these texts, he found a better explanation than the teacher could give. When he talked about his ideas on the Vedanta philosophy to the other disciples, they found his explanation more logical and satisfactory. When the teacher learned of that, he became jealous and made it difficult for Ramanuja to continue as his student.

So Ramanuja left the school and went back home. His mother wanted him to be married and, as he was very devoted to her, he did so. But he was not happy in his marriage: his whole heart was drawn to the realization of God. Unfortunately, instead of aiding him in his ideals and ambitions, his wife created difficulties, so he ran away from home. He became a monk in order to devote himself completely to God and his service.

Ramanuja went to the temple of Srirangam where his great-grandfather had been the head at one time. Naturally, he attracted attention, and people would come to him to discuss the Vedanta philosophy. They were pleased with his logical explanations and great intellectual ability, but Ramanuja himself was not satisfied. There was a hunger in his heart to know God. He understood the philosophy intellectually, but it did not give him real satisfaction.

In order to realize God, he needed a guru. It is said that he went to the temple and prayed that he might find an illumined teacher. The story goes that the head priest of the temple was suddenly inspired, and from his lips came out a beautiful verse, which gave him the indication of a teacher and also summarized the whole truth of God in a few words. The verse, translated simply, means this: God said, "I am the Supreme. Surrender yourself completely." Mention was made of an enlightened man; his name was Gosthipurna. He was not very well known; though an illumined soul, he remained hidden. But Ramanuja learned of him and approached him. This great teacher lived a life of simplicity, with no outward expression of his greatness, but Ramanuja recognized a great teacher and wanted to be taught by him.

The teacher refused, and Ramanuja left disappointed, but he went back again and again. Some authorities say that he went back six times. In any case, the teacher was not anxious to accept him as a disciple, but Ramanuja persisted. At long last he was initiated by Gosthipurna and told that he must not reveal the mantra to anybody. That is the custom in India. The mantra is nothing but the name of God, a sort of prayer or a formula which anybody can learn from a book. But when you receive a mantra from the lips of an illumined soul, it has great effect on the life of the disciple. Through it the guru transmits spiritual power to the disciple. The mantra itself is simple, but it is charged with power and becomes living as it comes from the lips of a teacher.

Ramanuja asked his teacher, "Suppose I reveal this mantra. What will happen?" The guru said, "In that case, whoever hears it from your lips will attain salvation but for you there will be condemnation." Ramanuja did not say anything. He went back to the temple of Srirangam and asked that all the people in the town gather there at a certain time. He said that he had something to give and that whoever would come would find salvation. And so thousands of people gathered at the temple, where Ramanuja stood on a pedestal and uttered that sacred mantra in the hearing of them all.

Then Gosthipurna approached him angrily and said, "What are you doing? Don't you remember that you will suffer in hell by doing that?" Ramanuja got down from the pedestal, prostrated before his teacher, and said, "Yes, I know, but I would gladly suffer if, by my suffering, so many people would be saved." Then his teacher said, "That is what I expected of you." And he blessed him and said, "From now on this school of thought to which you belong, the philosophy of qualified monism, will be known as Ramanuja's philosophy."

And then, as he had promised his great-grandfather, Ramanuja wrote the commentary on the Vedanta Aphorisms. He presented the philosophy in a systematized form – very rational, very logical. He is the accepted authority of qualified nondualism. Ramanuja also wrote commentaries on the Gita and some other treatises that are studied by all students of philosophy in India.

Now, to come to the philosophy, qualified monism in simple words means "unity in difference." Ramanuja gave this dictum first: Brahman is *tattva*, the truth. Brahman is the *hita*, the means and methods. And Brahman is the *purushartha*, the supreme goal. So his dictum was: Brahman is the truth, Brahman is the way, and Brahman is the goal.

In explaining that Brahman is the truth, Ramanuja said that Brahman is defined in the Upanishads as *satyam*, infinite truth, infinite being, infinite consciousness, and infinite bliss. He only differed from Shankara in this particular respect: Shankaracharya explained those as identical with Brahman, not as attributes or qualities. Knowledge, for instance, is not knowledge that is relative, but knowledge itself, identical with Brahman. It is not that Brahman knows, but that Brahman is knowledge itself. Whereas Ramanuja said, "Brahman knows – that is its attribute, its quality."

In positive terms, he explained that Brahman knows, exists, and is full of bliss or love. And Brahman is the basis of all existence; that is, He is the first cause of this universe and, as cause, He is the material cause as well as the efficient cause. Here we find a different explanation from Christian theology, which says that God created the universe out of nothing. Ramanuja says that the material is also God himself, that it is he who has become transformed into the universe. This philosophy of creation is known as transformation. We also find passages in the Upanishads which give that idea: "As the spider weaves its thread out of its own womb, as hair grows out of man, so does this universe come out of Brahman."

Ramanuja does not believe that there is any beginning to the creation, but that it is all beginningless and endless; it merely passes through stages of evolution and involution. God withdraws the universe unto himself and there is dissolution; again, He brings forth this universe out of himself and that is the beginning of a cycle of creation. He says that in the universe there are two kinds of objects or things: one is sentient, the individual soul; the other is what we call insentient.

So God has become this universe, yet remains distinct from it. In other words, what in Western philosophy is known as the immanence of God and the transcendence of God: God is distinct, but not apart, from the universe. Ramanuja gives the illustration of a man who has a physical body and a soul. As the soul is related to the body, God is related to the universe. The whole cosmos is like the body of God, and He is the Soul of all souls. In that is the "unity in difference."

With regard to individual souls, he points out that they are the attributes or molds of God, related to God as parts to the whole – never the whole. Just as the wave is not the ocean, still it is not separate from the ocean. There is division, but unity. So individual souls are related to God like waves are related to the ocean.

Then he says that, unfortunately, we have forgotten in our ignorance that we are related to God, are parts of God. We have detached ourselves from that vast ocean and attached ourselves to the part. We attach ourselves to matter, and this is ignorance. If we can really free ourselves from our attachment to matter and attach ourselves to God, there is salvation. But there will always remain the distinction, though no separateness. In ignorance we have separated ourselves from God; in knowledge we unite ourselves with God, but never do we become one with him: we remain as parts to the whole. The ideal, according to Ramanuja, is not oneness, but living in the service of God.

As the method, he emphasizes what is known as bhakti yoga, the path of love and devotion: that only through love and devotion can we attach ourselves to God and be united as parts to the whole. He points out that devotion and love mean constant remembrance of God – what is known as constant contemplation, to pray ceaselessly. He gives the illustration taken from Yoga philosophy of oil poured from one vessel into another. It is continuous, and there must be the same continuity of the flow of our thoughts towards God. He explains remembrance or contemplation as seeing God. Remembering

God, then, means to see him constantly and to feel that presence. We are just like people asleep. Our friend is next to us, but we do not see him because we are asleep. Just so, God is present, is omnipresent. Know it, see it. All we have to do is feel and recognize him.

Then he gives us the truth which is given by every system of thought – that purity is the most important thing to achieve, and that is because we are really always attached to God: we live, move, and have our being in him. We are just not conscious of it, but run after things and objects, forgetting God.

Ramanuja makes a distinction between love, devotion, and self-surrender. He uses the word *prapatti*, which can be translated as surrendering ourselves completely and wholeheartedly to him so that there is no more will of our own left in us. He says that comes through love, devotion, and the practice of moral disciplines. He says that the ripened stage of love is the same as complete surrender. Then we live as complete and total instruments in the hands of God. But that is a stage we have to arrive at. The knowledge of the will of God comes to us at that stage of development – when we have completely, through our love and devotion, surrendered ourselves to him. There is no more ego left in us. Ego is wiped out.

Like all devotees, Ramanuja emphasized divine grace, that without it, you cannot surrender yourself, nor can you love and devote yourself to God. Furthermore, he points out that divine grace is not partial, but is present in every one of us. It is only because of our impurities that we do not know of it. The moment we achieve purity, we feel that grace, and we know that it is through his grace that we devote ourselves to him, and that it is through his grace that he becomes revealed to us.

In comparing the philosophies of Ramanuja and Shankara, you find an apparent wide divergence, but if we can understand, it is dissolved. In my opinion the difference is that Ramanuja had only the lower *samadhi*, *savikalpa samadhi*, whereas Shankara had *nirvikalpa samadhi*, the highest. Every philosophy propounded by our great teachers is based on experience. As such, we find that Shankara had the experience of the attributeless Brahman and, having merged himself completely in him, found himself one with him: Atman is Brahman. In that experience the universe is annihilated, there is no world, no matter, no mind, no individual souls; they are all one.

Now in the lower, *savikalpa samadhi* that Ramanuja had, there is the distinction between the individual and God. In it, you see yourself a part of the whole, so the universe is not completely annihilated. You see a relation of the universe to Brahman, to God. Ramanuja rationalized that experience in terms of the philosophy that the individual soul, though not separate from God, is a part of God and distinct from him. The universe as we see it is, of course, not true, because what appears in that lower *samadhi* appears as a part of God. Naturally, then, in his philosophy the universe is like the body of God – the cosmos is the body, and he is the soul. And we are related to him as parts to the whole. To Ramanuja, *bhakti* is the ideal, not knowledge, because he considers knowledge relative. You see, he did not have that transcendental, absolute knowledge. He did not experience that truth. So he teaches that devotion which makes us completely forget our little ego and have self-surrender.

In the beginning we may look on God as separate from ourselves; then we are a dualists. Then we see ourselves as part of God [qualified nondualism]: "I am the vine, ye are the branches." Later, when that love becomes very deep, the lover, beloved, and love become united in one and we realize, "I and my Father are One." (65)

CHAITANYA

In Sri Chaitanya we find the highest expression of divine love. He was the founder of the sect in Bengal known as Vaishnavism, which is the religion of love. His influence is very great in Bengal. I can say that this love that Sri Chaitanya preached got into the very blood of the people of Bengal.

I will tell you how Sri Chaitanya influenced me when I was a little boy. I was only fourteen years old, and it was the first time I had read any religious book or life of a saint. I read *The Life of Sri Chaitanya*. I did not understand much, but this I remember: that as I read it, there was such sweetness that I would weep over every line. His life, more than his philosophy, had the greatest influence on me.

To Sri Chaitanya, all are creatures of God. He made no distinction between a sinner and a saint. To him everyone was a child of God. Those who were outcastes, who were destitute, whom people would not even speak to, were the ones who gathered around this great soul and found the greatest consolation and the highest illumination. Even today, those who have nowhere to go are accepted by the followers of Sri Chaitanya.

He was born in the year 1485 in a town called Navadwip, in Bengal very near Calcutta and at that time a seat of great learning. There was a Hindu university, which was especially famous for the study of logic and grammar. Sri Chaitanya went to study in this university under the well-known teacher Vasudeva. Another brilliant student, Raghunath, was a classmate of Chaitanya. Raghunath stands in the history of India as the founder of the Neo-logic school of Bengal. This logic is still studied throughout India.

There is a story told that one day the two boys were riding in a boat. Sri Chaitanya had with him a manuscript in which he had written about logic. He was reading out the manuscript to his friend, but Ragunath became depressed. Sri Chaitanya asked him why. Did he not like the manuscript? Ragunath said, "No, it is not that. I have also written on the same subject, but your writing is so good that I will have to throw mine away." Sri Chaitanya said, "Well, you don't have to worry about that." Right then and there he threw his manuscript into the river, and Ragunath became the founder of that famous school of logic associated with his teacher, Vasudeva.

Though he had not finished his studies, at the age of sixteen Sri Chaitanya opened a school of his own to teach grammar and logic. He became so famous that many went to him to study. From sixteen to twenty-two he was known as the greatest grammarian and logician of the age. During this period in his life, he was married. He was also notorious for his atheistic views. Devotees of God dreaded him. He would ridicule them and sometimes persecute them. Before his logic, they could not stand.

And then at the age of twenty-two he went to the famous place of pilgrimage, Gaya, where Buddha had gained his illumination. He went there because his mother wanted him to do some ritualistic ceremony; it was not because he believed in God. But when he went into the temple, something happened. He found himself suddenly illumined. There was a great saint standing near him, a monk belonging to the order of Shankara. He knew Sri Chaitanya as a great logician and also as a notorious atheist. As he watched, he felt that Sri Chaitanya attained realization, so he held him; he took him out of the temple, and initiated him into the worship of Krishna.

When Sri Chaitanya came back to his hometown, his students gathered around him, but the great debater, grammarian, and logician was dead. Instead, there was a serene devotee, ecstatic. The boys wanted lessons on grammar. He looked at them, his eyes filled with tears of ecstasy, and he began to chant the name of Krishna. He composed a chant which is widely sung in India, just giving the different names of Krishna and his attributes. His students were amazed. He told them, "Brothers, go to some other teacher. I can't teach anymore." So the school was dispersed and all those devotees who were at one time persecuted by him gathered around him.

Thus it went on for two or three years, and then the ideal of burning renunciation seized him. He could not live at home any longer. He renounced the world when he was twenty-five. Today in Bengal you find dramas depicting this period of his life, that of his renunciation.

Sri Chaitanya was very beautiful, with a fair complexion. He had a beautiful wife; he had name and fame – and he renounced all that in order to devote himself completely to God.

There is a story told that the reason renunciation took hold of him was that in a vision, he received a *mahavakya*, a great mantra of the Upanishads: "Thou art That." So he went out in search of a guru who could initiate him into the monastic life. He met Keshab Sharata, who belonged to the school of Shankara, who gave him the same mantra that he had received in his vision.

Now if one reads Chaitanya's life and teachings and then the teachings as explained by his followers, one gets a little confused in regard to his philosophy. Occasionally, in *samadhi*, he would say, "I am God." When he came back to the normal state, he could not even bear the idea, but would think, "I am a servant, I am a lover, of God." We find in him these two extreme sides – nondualist and dualist, a lover. Sri Ramakrishna used to explain that just as an elephant has two sets of teeth – one to chew, and the other, the tusks, to protect itself – so Sri Chaitanya had this double personality. He had the realization of the highest truth of nondualism, but then he realized that for most people, the philosophy of dualism is the path.

There is a well-known place of pilgrimage called Vrinda-ban, where Krishna had his divine play. In an ecstatic mood Sri Chaitanya went in search of Vrindaban and he began to see Krishna and his divine play. He marked each place in that little village of Vrindaban where a particular incident occurred. Today Vrindaban is considered a great place of pilgrimage, and Sri Chaitanya's marking of the different places is still accepted.

But he did not stay in Vrindaban for long; he went to Puri. We find Chaitanya's great influence there in the famous temple. Anyone entering the temple finds such an ecstatic atmosphere that he or she cannot but feel the presence of God. Sri Chaitanya lived in Puri for many years, most of the time in a state midway between the highest *samadhi* and normal consciousness. His passing away is shrouded in mystery, but the story is told that in an ecstatic mood he ran into a temple near Puri and disappeared. Nobody ever saw him after that, so there is the belief that he still lives in that temple in the form of the deity.

Sri Chaitanya did not give much consideration to the problems of God or soul or universe. He had no theory of God, Sat-chit-ananda Brahman. But he was a God-intoxicated man. He did not try to expound a philosophy of God. To him, God was Krishna, the youthful, enchanting Krishna, and not the Krishna of the Gita, the great harmonizer of philosophy and religion who propounded such great truths as *karma* and *jnana* and devotion. To Sri Chaitanya, Krishna was the God of Love. If you wish to understand this aspect that Sri Chaitanya realized, you will have to study the Bhagavatam, which he made popular. He was asked to write a commentary on the Vedanta Aphorisms and he said, "Why should I write a commentary? There already is a commentary: the Bhagavatam, that is Vedanta."

He gives the simple truth that the Krishna of Vrindaban is the playmate of the shepherds and shepherdesses, and the playmate of everyone. That Krishna is the Soul of souls. Where is this Vrindaban where Krishna played with the shepherds and shepherdesses? It is the heart of mankind. The eternal Vrindaban and Krishna, the eternal God, dancing, singing, playing his flute and drawing mankind unto Himself – eternally within the heart of mankind. That was his simple philosophy.

He pointed out that the intense love which brings out that sweetness, that joy, that ecstasy, is the way to mystic union with God. And the love that brings that union is in the heart of everybody; it is only that it is covered, because the mind runs after the senses. Here you find no difference between the philosophy of knowledge and the philosophy of love. Shankara, for instance, preached knowledge as the supreme goal, the knowledge that brings union with the divine. And he said that the divine consciousness in every one of us is the Atman, which is one with Brahman, but remains covered in ignorance. To uncover that, he advocated the path of knowledge.

Sri Chaitanya used the word love instead of knowledge – love that brings union with the Divine, with Krishna. And he taught how to uncover that. He called the method bhakti, disciplinary love: "Be humbler than a blade of grass; be forbearing like a tree, give honor to all, take no honor for thyself, and chant the name of God all the time." That was his dictum.

He explained that there are five stages of divine love. The idea is that we have to enter into a relationship with God. Love means that there is a relationship. The first stage is *shanta*, a peaceful sort of love, in which the relationship has not yet grown; you have not yet felt that God is your own, but you are trying to love him.

Then you enter into a relationship of father and child or mother and child.

When that love deepens, there comes the idea of friendship with God. This is the third stage. You see, in the beginning there is a glamour about God. He is omnipotent, omnipresent; he is the ruler of the universe. And then we try to enter into a relationship with him: I am his preacher, I am his child. But then as love deepens, who cares for his greatness? He is my friend; he is my own. You see, awe and reverence separate us from God. To think of his greatness may be good in the beginning, but as we begin to love God as our own, that greatness falls away. A son does not care for the greatness or glamour of his father, he knows the father as his own. So when we become familiar with God, we forget his greatness. He is a friend to us, we are his playmates. Sri Chaitanya said that real love begins here.

Then there is another stage in which God, instead of being either great or equal, is inferior to us: he is my child and I have to take care of him. That is a higher stage of love. There are devotees in India who worship Krishna as their child; they serve God as their own child.

Then there comes a stage of sweet relationship, which is the greatest expression of love – the love between husband and wife, lover and beloved. When we can attribute that kind of love to God, it is the culmination of divine love. In this, one is completely free from the consciousness of the body. In worldly relationships there is the sweetness of relationship, but there is always a sex-connection behind this love. When that love grows, according to Sri Chaitanya, mystic union comes: the lover, the beloved, and love become united.

In this connection I would like to read out to you a famous discourse with one of his disciples, Ramananda. Sri Chaitanya asked him, "What is the goal of life?" The disciple answered,

"A man must follow the rules and injunctions as prescribed in the scriptures. This is the means of attaining devotion." Sri Chaitanya said, "That is the external part of religion. It is only the means, not the goal." In almost every religion you find a sort of degeneration when the scriptures are taken as everything. To worship the book is no religion.

So Sri Chaitanya asks, "What next?" and the disciple says, "Surrendering the fruits of action to Krishna." The Gita teaches to work, to live in the world, to attend to your duties, but to surrender the fruits of your action to God. Sri Chaitanya says, "This too is external. What next?" The disciple says, "The devotion that arises from self-surrender, when we forget our ego, allows us to give ourselves completely to God." Sri Chaitanya says, "This too is external. What next?" The disciple says, "Devotion with knowledge, but there must be self-surrender with understanding." Sri Chaitanya says, "This too is external. What next?" The disciple says, "Your devotion which knows no reason."

You see, first there is the devotion with knowledge, and the next step is no knowledge in the sense that you are thinking of how great God is, or that this is the one purpose of life. If you ask a devotee, "Why do you love God?" the answer might be, "I love God because that will bring me salvation, will free me from suffering in life, and I'll attain to immortal life." But all that is forgotten when you love God for the sake of love. If you ask such a devotee, "Why do you love God?" the answer could be, "I don't know."

Sri Chaitanya asks the disciple to go further, and then the disciple says, "Loving devotion is the best." Here we find greater absorption. Sri Chaitanya says, "That is good. Go further." The disciple says, "The spirit of service to Krishna." In that loving devotion, everything has become Krishna, and you serve Krishna everywhere, in every being. Chaitanya says,

13

"That is good. What next?" "To love Krishna as a friend." That is a higher relationship. Chaitanya says, "That is very good. What next?" "To love Krishna as a child." "That is good also. Go further." "To love Krishna as the beloved bridegroom." Chaitanya says, "This is no doubt the furthest goal, but tell me if there is any attainment further than this." The disciple answers, "My understanding does not reach beyond this, but there is another stage." "Beyond that," Sri Chaitanya says, "there is something. There are different interpretations with regard to that."

One interpretation is that it is not merely to love God as your husband, but as a man loves his mistress. There is greater attraction there. Others say that as you begin to love God as your beloved, there arises a sweetness, and from that sweetness there comes a mystic union that leads to the supreme realization of oneness with God. (66)

TOTAPURI

Whenever Sri Ramakrishna wanted to learn about any particular religion or path, a teacher who had attained illumination through that path would somehow come to him. First came a woman teacher who was well-versed in the Tantra. That path leads through both devotion and knowledge, and through it, Sri Ramakrishna attained the highest realization. Then Vaishnava teachers who attained God through simple love and devotion came. Sri Ramakrishna followed the paths of the different divine aspects of God as Father and Mother, as child, as beloved, as friend, and attained union. Then it came to his mind that he must follow the exclusive path of knowledge that we find in the teachings of Shankara, which emphasize the teachings of the Upanishads. At that period a great teacher, Totapuri, came.

Very little is known about Totapuri. He was born about a hundred and thirty years ago, and I calculate that he was a little older than Sri Ramakrishna. Nothing is known about his parents, only that he was born in the province of the Punjab in northern India and lived in a monastery from childhood. There is a custom in northwest India, according to which a couple vows that the first-born will be dedicated to a monastery for the service of God. That is what must have happened with Totapuri. This monastery is near the battlefield of Kuru-kshetra of the Gita.

Totapuri used to speak to Sri Ramakrishna about his life in the monastery. This is how we know about his early life and practices. When he lived there, there were seven hundred monks under one spiritual teacher. His guru was very well known at that time, and even today the people from surrounding villages come once a year to the monastery to show their reverence for the teacher.

Totapuri belonged to the school of thought known as nondualism, the principle that Brahman is real and everything else is unreal, and that the individual is none other than Brahman.

This is not mere philosophy. These people try to practice that philosophy in their lives. In order to practice, what must they do? The first thing is to question: This universe is unreal. What is it then? How do we experience it? Through the senses. And how do the senses act? As we attach our mind to the senses, the senses go out through their doors. Then the universe is presented before us, and we experience it. But when you are told the universe is unreal, that Brahman alone is the Reality and you are one with Brahman, in order to live that philosophy, you will have to close the doors of your senses and withdraw your mind from this apparent world. But even that is not enough. You must occupy your mind with the thought of that Reality.

So these monks were taught these two principal things: one, the withdrawal of the mind from the objective universe, and two, meditation upon oneness with Brahman. The process of practicing that meditation is what is called *neti neti* in the Upanishads – "not this, not this." Whatever comes to your mind is not Brahman. Whatever you conceive of is not Brahman. Whatever you know is not Brahman. There comes a detachment from all knowledge, from all objects, when the mind is completely freed from all thoughts and impressions. Then the mind knows that which is unknown, but it needs many, many years of striving and practice to attain that.

Totapuri said some very interesting things about some of the practices in their monastery. He said that in order to practice meditation, one must sit comfortably, so he was given a very soft cushion to sit on. He was given foods that he liked, proper dress to protect himself from the weather, and all the comforts of the body. At the same time, he was required to sit and meditate. The reason, Totapuri said, is that in the beginning the mind is not drawn to God easily. If you practice physical austerity – for instance sitting on hard ground – you begin to feel pain in your body, and as your mind goes to the body, you can't think of Brahman. If you don't eat enough, or have to eat food that you don't like, you don't feel well. And then the mind is on the body. So all the comforts were supplied, but the young monks were to meditate and make their minds absorbed in Brahman.

After some months or years of practice, when the mind became absorbed, the monks were taught gradually to forget the body and outside comforts. Gradually they were made to sit on hard ground, to eat any food, and not to be affected by the weather. As their bodies came to bear any weather, gradually they learned to live without any dress at all. There are, in India, monks walking the streets completely naked. They don't usually come to the big cities or towns, but in some places on the bank of the Ganges there are hundreds and thousands of monks living without clothing.

When the guru of that order passed away, the person who would become the next head of the order had to have attained the state of *paramahamsa*, which means "great swan." According to fable, if you give a swan water and milk mixed together, the swan has the power to drink only the milk; the water will be left. A person who has attained the knowledge of Brahman can live in the world; the unreal appears as unreal to one who can live in the midst of the unrealities of life without being disturbed. A monk who attains that stage becomes head of the order. We are told that Totapuri lived in that monastery for forty long years. After strenuous practice and struggle for all those years, he attained to the state of *paramahamsa*, the *nirvikalpa* state, and became head of the order.

Sri Ramakrishna used this example to explain the *nirvikalpa* state. Take seven vessels filled with water on which the sun is reflected. Break one vessel after another until there is only one vessel. This is the lower *samadhi*, when you see the reflection of the sun, but you still have the ego, the reflection. You see God and talk to God, but this is still the lower stage. Now break that vessel also and there remains nothing but the one sun. There is no more reflection – just one reality.

In the same way the Atman or Brahman is reflected on us. We have many vessels, as it were: the body, the senses, the mind, the ego. Upon all these vessels Brahman is reflected. My body moves and feels, is conscious, but what is this? Reflected consciousness of Brahman. Your senses can feel and sense because of the reflection from Brahman. Your mind is conscious because of the reflection of Brahman. Your ego feels that you are so-and-so. What is that? Only a reflection of Brahman, not the Reality. Now break these vessels, one after the other, through meditation, and through deep absorption you rise above this consciousness of body, and above the mental plane. Then just one vessel is left. Consciousness of ego is there, and you have the vision of God. Break that ego. What remains? Brahman, the infinite existence, infinite bliss. There is none there to see anybody, to hear anybody, to teach anybody. This is a state of direct, immediate experience, and it is one attained after great struggle.

We find in the case of Totapuri that he struggled from his childhood with a one-pointed mind. He did not know anything of this world; from his very childhood he learned to be absorbed in God and knew nothing but God. Having attained that state, one usually lives only for a short while. Sri Ramakrishna used to say that such a person can continue to live for only twenty-one days; after that, the body falls away like a dry leaf. But there are free souls who, having attained to that realization, come back to teach mankind. Totapuri was such a free soul.

He came naked to Dakshineswar and lived near the temple. Wherever these monks go, they build a fire by which they eat and sleep, and they meditate there. Totapuri built a fire under a tree in the Panchavati. That is where Sri Ramakrishna used to practice his spiritual disciplines. It is a cluster of huge trees whose branches spread for about a block. There you find shade, and if there is a heavy rain, only a few drops fall through.

It was Totapuri's habit to lie down, apparently asleep, in the daytime by the fire, covering his body with a sheet. At midnight, when the whole world had gone to sleep, he would get up and sit by that fire, absorbed in meditation the whole night. One night as he sat for meditation, a tall, lustrous, and effulgent figure came, which he recognized as no human being. Totapuri, being fearless, asked him, "Who are you?" "I am an attendant of the Divine Mother. I live here." Totapuri answered, "Come and sit down. Let us meditate on Brahman. I don't care who you are or what you may be, but you are Brahman. I am Brahman. Come on. Sit down. Let us meditate together." Instead the figure disappeared. When Totapuri told Sri Ramakrishna about his vision, Sri Ramakrishna said, "Yes, I know about him. I have seen him often. He lives here."

At this period Sri Ramakrishna asked Totapuri, "You are a free soul. You have attained knowledge. Why do you have to practice meditation like this?" He replied by pointing to a brass vessel near him. "Look at that vessel. I have to clean that every day. If I don't clean it, it can't shine like that." Sri Ramakrishna said, "Yes, that is true. But suppose the vessel is made of gold. Then you don't need to clean it every day, it shines always." Totapuri said, "That is also true."

Now I will tell you about Totapuri's first meeting with Sri Ramakrishna. Sri Ramakrishna was sitting on the bank of the river on the temple steps when he saw this naked monk. When the monk, Totapuri, saw Ramakrishna, he recognized in him a great soul. He came directly to him and said, "Look. Would you want to be my disciple? I would teach you how to know Brahman." Sri Ramakrishna said, "Wait a minute. Let me go and ask my Mother about it." Totapuri thought, of course, that he was going to ask his earthly mother, so he said, "All right. Go ahead and ask her." Sri Ramakrishna went straight into the temple while Totapuri watched. When he came back, he said, "Yes, Mother said that she brought you here to teach me about Brahman." Totapuri was confused. He thought to himself that the young man must be a little superstitious. But he thought the superstition would go as he followed the teachings.

So Totapuri initiated Sri Ramakrishna and the very first day taught him the meditation upon Brahman, the Absolute.

Sri Ramakrishna had a little difficulty and said, "I try to meditate upon Brahman, but the blissful Mother comes to my vision, and I can't do it." Then this teacher said, "What! You can't do it?" There was a piece of broken glass where they were sitting, and Totapuri took it and pressed it between Sri Ramakrishna's eyebrows, saying, "Now, concentrate your attention there." Again the vision of the blissful Mother came. Then, as he described it, Ramakrishna took the sword of discrimination and cut the blissful Mother, whom he had worshiped all these years, into pieces. And then his mind went into the formless, the Absolute, and he attained *nirvikalpa samadhi*. Totapuri was surprised. "How could it be possible? I struggled for forty years to come to this, and this young man gets it in a few minutes! What divine *maya* is this?"

They were in a small hut which Sri Ramakrishna had built with his own hands. His teacher closed the door and locked it so that no one could disturb him. Every hour or two he would go to find out if Sri Ramakrishna had come out of *samadhi*. Generally people do not live in that consciousness for many hours. Three days and three nights passed in that way. Totapuri knew, of course, how to bring him back to normal consciousness, and he began the process. He began to chant the name of Brahman, and Sri Ramakrishna came back to normal consciousness. The story is told how, after that, Sri Ramakrishna in a way lived continuously for six months in the consciousness of Brahman. During that period he was fed forcibly. He would be brought back to normal consciousness and given a little milk or be forced to take a little food. In six months it became such a natural state that he could go into it any time he willed. It is one of the greatest feats in the life of an *avatara*, which no human can do.

Totapuri wanted to take leave of his disciple, because he had done what he came for and did not need to stay there any longer. But he could not; something obstructed him. He would talk with Sri Ramakrishna about the knowledge of Brahman, but he could not say goodbye to him. This went on for about eleven months. It has been pointed out that Totapuri did not believe in a personal God and did not believe in loving God. Who is there to love whom, since the Atman is everywhere? So to him, loving God as Divine Mother or Divine Father was all superstition. Once, Totapuri noticed Sri Ramakrishna's habit of clapping his hands and chanting the name of Hari every evening. He said, "Now what are you doing? Preparing chapattis?" Sri Ramakrishna rolled in laughter and said, "You fool! I am taking the name of God!" And of course Totapuri also laughed.

Totapuri also felt that, though it was nonsense that Ramakrishna still went to the temple, worshiped, and put flowers at the feet of the image, there must be something to it. But he did not ask Sri Ramakrishna about it. Then one day he became very ill with colic pain. He was given medicine and every care was taken for some time, but he still could not free himself from that pain. He thought he would go into *samadhi* and forget the body. He could, with the effort of will, go into *samadhi*, but this time he failed. He tried again and again with all his will, but could not. So he thought, "After all, this body is the greatest obstacle to living in the consciousness of *samadhi*, so let me go and throw it in the Ganges."

With that object in view, at night when it was dark, he jumped into the Ganges and was surprised that the water was only knee-deep. The Ganges is a big river, but that night he walked from one bank to the other – in knee-deep water. He thought, "What is this divine *maya*? I can't do anything that I wish to do! I have no will of my own." And suddenly a vision opened up, and he saw the Divine Mother. He saw her in suffering and in happiness, in health and in disease. He saw Mother in all appearance and as one with Brahman, beyond this apparent universe. Then he came back and passed the night in meditation on the Divine Mother. When it was early morning, he went to see Sri Ramakrishna, who noticed in his face a bliss that he had never seen before. Totapuri said, "I have known your Mother. I have recognized our Mother. She came to me!" Both of them went to the temple and prostrated themselves before the image of Kali. Then Totapuri departed from the temple of Dakshineswar. Nobody ever knew where he went. (67)

RAMAKRISHNA

The Vedas, the Bible, the Koran, the Tripitaka are there; that does not prove anything. You have to prove the truth of these scriptures in your life. This is what is most emphasized by Sri Ramakrishna in this age. In that sense he gave new life to all the religions and scriptures of the world. All his search and struggles were not for himself, he was born with the knowledge of God, but he did struggle. He went through great austerities and spiritual disciplines in order to show us the way to reach the ideal.

When he was only seven years old, he had the vision of God: "I was walking alone in a paddy field, carrying a small basket of puffed rice. While eating the rice and looking overhead, I saw that the sky was covered with rain clouds. Suddenly I noticed snow white wild cranes flying in a row against that dark background. I was overwhelmed by the beautiful sight. An ecstatic feeling arose in my heart and I lost all outward consciousness. I do not know how long I remained in that state. When I regained consciousness, I was in my own home, brought there by some friendly people."

When Christ was twelve we know how he had a discussion with the priests in the temple. He said he was attending to his Father's business. And Sri Ramakrishna, when he was nine or ten years old, heard some scholars discussing certain points on the truth of God. When they were not coming to any conclusion, this young boy whispered into one scholar's ear where the solution lay. The scholar immediately saw it, took the boy on his shoulders, stood up, and said: "Here is the solution, given by this boy."

Again we find him searching, searching, searching, and restless for God. He did not go to any theological seminary or study scriptures or books to find religion. He engaged himself as a priest in a temple, and there he would weep before the Divine Mother. All day he would struggle, practice meditation, and then when the evening bells rang, he would say: "Ah, another day is gone and I have not found you."

He performed the daily duties of a priest, but his inquiring mind longed for something more, and he questioned within himself: What is all this for? Is the Divine Mother real? Does She listen to my prayers? Or is this mere imagination conjured up by human brains? He yearned increasingly for the direct realization of God, the Mother, and soon life became unbearable without her. He would rub his face on the ground, as if gripped by pain, and cry. Finally, one day she revealed herself.

Sri Ramakrishna was born with the knowledge, but then he struggled to attain the experience, the realization. Teachers came to teach him the different ways of approaching God. First, a woman teacher. This is very interesting because especially in this country, I have been asked many times, "Is it possible for women to realize God?" If you go to the Vedas, uttered by the ancient sages, many of them were women. In this particular age we find Sri Ramakrishna accepting a woman as his teacher. And she recognized in him the *avatara* or descent of God. She was not the first to recognize this. In his village there lived an old man who was highly developed spiritually, and he also recognized in this young lad the divine incarnation. One day, without the knowledge of anybody, he knelt down before the young boy and worshiped him as God. He said: "I will not live to see your divine play, but I have lived just long enough to see you and worship you."

The woman teacher taught him the Tantric disciplines of spiritual life. She made him go through all the different practices of Tantra in order that the methods and means as given in the scriptures, when followed and as taught by a teacher, would lead to the ultimate goal.

Then he practiced Vishishtadvaita, the worship of Rama and worship of Krishna. After that there came an extreme Vedantist – extreme in the sense that he believed in the oneness of God, in nondualism and "I am That." Totapuri belonged to a monastic order of Shankara, and he initiated Sri Ramakrishna into this order. In a very short time, Sri Ramakrishna reached the ultimate *samadhi*. His teacher couldn't believe his eyes. He said: "What took me forty years to attain, he has reached in such a short time."

But this was not enough. He then wanted to practice religions outside the fold of Hinduism. A Sufi mystic living at Dakshineswar initiated him into Islam. In Sri Ramakrishna's own words: "I began to repeat the holy name of Allah and would recite the Namaz regularly. After three days I realized the goal of that form of devotion." First Sri Ramakrishna had a vision of a radiant person with a long beard and a stolid countenance – Mohammed. Then he experienced Brahman with attributes, which finally merged into the impersonal, attributeless Brahman.

Some years later he wanted to explore Christianity. A particular devotee used to explain the Bible to him whenever he came to Dakshineswar. Thus, Sri Ramakrishna became drawn to Christ and Christianity. One day while he was seated in the drawing room of Jadu Mallick's garden house, he saw a picture of the Madonna and child. He fell into a deeply meditative mood and the picture suddenly became living and effulgent. A deep love for Christ filled Sri Ramakrishna's heart, and there opened before him a vision of a Christian church with devotees burning incense and lighting candles before Jesus. For three days Sri Ramakrishna was under the spell of this experience. On the fourth day, while he was pacing near the Panchavati grove at Dakshineswar, he saw an extraordinary-looking person of serene countenance approaching him with his gaze intently fixed on him. From the inmost recesses of Sri Ramakrishna's heart came the realization: "This is Jesus who poured out his heart's blood for the redemption of mankind. He is none other than the *rishi* Christ, the embodiment of love, the Son of Man." At this, the Master went into *samadhi*. Thus was Sri Ramakrishna convinced that Jesus was an incarnation of God.

He practiced all these different faiths, not with the idea of proving the truth of every religion or of establishing the harmony of religions – he had no such idea. He just wanted to explore. But when he was asked, was not one path enough by which to reach the supreme goal, he answered: "The Mother is infinite. Infinite are her moods and aspects. I sought to realize her in all of them, and she revealed to me the truth of many religions." His life demonstrated that harmony.

In this connection I shall read out to you what he said about the ideal of harmony: "So many religions, so many paths to reach the same goal. I have practiced Hinduism, Islam, Christianity, and in Hinduism again, the ways of different sects. I have found that it is the same God towards whom all are directing their steps, though along different paths. The tank has several *ghats*. At one, Hindus draw water and call it *jal*. At another, Muslims draw water and call it *pani*. At a third, Christians draw the same liquid and call it water. The substance is one, the names differ, and everyone is seeking the same thing: every religion of the world is one such *ghat*. Go with a sincere and earnest heart by any of these *ghats* – that is, paths – and you will reach the water of eternal bliss. But do not say that your religion is better than that of another." In other words, the harmony in which we can find unity is in God, in the ideal – not in the path. We are babies in religion until we realize God. It is better to be an agnostic than a believer who does nothing about it. To realize Brahman is to come face to face with the ultimate truth. Therein lies the experience of perfection. (68)

Sri Ramakrishna was born a Hindu, practiced Islam and Christianity, and went beyond all boundaries and limitations of any religion or sect. In other words, he was a God-man. And the ideal he placed before us, we have seen realized in the lives of his disciples. I had the blessed fortune to meet and to sit at the feet of most of them. You could not label them Hindu or Christian or Muslim; they were men of God. That is the ideal that we have to strive for and attain.

Sri Ramakrishna practiced severe austerities and went through great hardships, weeping and crying for God, but he himself lived in the bliss of God: it was all for mankind. He declared that in this age—no matter to what religion a person may belong, no matter what that person may believe or not believe – anybody who sincerely desires God, with that as the only aim in life, will easily find him.

Sri Ramakrishna later described his first vision of the Divine Mother: "House, walls, doors, the temple, all disappeared into nothingness. Then I saw an ocean of light, limitless, living, conscious, blissful. From all sides waves of light with a roaring sound rushed toward me and engulfed me, and I lost all awareness of outward things." You and I and everyone can have this experience. It is not unique, not so special that only Ramakrishna or Christ could have it, and not you and me. It is possible, and it is desirable, and that is what we must aim for.

If you go to the very source of every religion, you will find the one goal is to know God. In the words of the Upanishads: "Realization, the experience of Brahman." In the words of Christ: "To be born in spirit, to enter the kingdom of God." The harmony is in that goal, in that ideal. Paths are different dogmas, doctrines, theories. They are all right, they are necessary for some people, but through any of these, Sri Ramakrishna pointed out, you reach the same goal. The sky is the same sky, whether in Hollywood or anywhere else. (69)

I heard from my master, Swami Brahmananda, who lived with Sri Ramakrishna for quite a few years, that if one attains to the highest *samadhi*, he has attained the very highest. He said he saw Swami Vivekananda going into *samadhi* only twice in his life, and he saw Sri Ramakrishna going into *samadhi* every day.

After Keshab Chandra Sen came to Sri Ramakrishna, he began to preach for the first time the greatness of Sri Ramakrishna. And then of course many people came, but Sri Ramakrishna was not satisfied. He would go to the roof and cry, "Where are my own people? Come! I am waiting for you!" He was waiting for the young disciples who became monks. And they came, one by one. The interesting thing is that whenever any of them came to him, he recognized them. The youngest was known as Khoka Maharaj – Baby Maharaj. To him Sri

Ramakrishna said, "Say, Khoka, do you not come from the family of so-and-so?" He answered, "How do you know?" "Well, I knew that you would be born in that family thirty years before you were born."

Let me tell you one incident in the life of Sri Ramakrishna. When Swami Vivekananda was present, he was muttering to himself a saying of another great saint: "To chant the name of the Lord, and to have compassion for all beings." Suddenly Sri Ramakrishna said, "Compassion, compassion, compassion. How can you have compassion for God? Is not everybody God? Serve God in all beings!" Vivekananda overheard it and said if he lived, he would give this truth to the world. In this way secular humanism has been spiritualized by the teachings of Sri Ramakrishna. When you offer anything to anybody, any kind of help, consider that you are serving the Lord, that the Lord is giving you the opportunity to come before you in that aspect. (70)

In one of the prayers that Swami Vivekananda wrote, he used the epithet for Sri Ramakrishna "He who is the embodiment of all religions." What exactly does it mean?

Hindus of many sects came to Sri Ramakrishna, and they all recognized in him their respective ideal. A Vaishnava would come and realize that here was the embodiment of the truth of Vaishnavism. A Shakta would come and think he was a Shakta. A Shaiva would come and would consider him the embodiment of Shiva. A Christian would come and see in him the embodiment of Christ. A Muslim would come and find in him the Muslim ideal. He helped each of them proceed in their own respective ideas and ideals. How was it possible for him to do that? Generally, any great teacher, be he an incarnation or a prophet or a saint, can direct us in one way, the way in which he achieved his perfection. But Sri

Ramakrishna used divergent ways and methods, according to the ideas and ideals each individual cherished.

He had a band of a few monastic disciples and a few house-holder disciples. That is what happens in every case. Multitudes followed Christ because he showed miracles, but what happened? They left him. Then only a few of his disciples gathered around him, only a few. Christ seemed to have been depressed and said, "Are you also going to leave me?" St. Peter said, "No, master. You have the words of eternal life!" And that is the truth of religion, not miracles. What is the greatest miracle these great ones performed? Not healing the sick, because you heal the sick and again they get sick and die. Or you raise the dead – do they not die again? The greatest miracle is to transform the lives of individuals so that they attain eternal life. That health is immortal: that happiness is abiding.

Sri Ramakrishna said, "He is born to no purpose who, having the rare privilege of being born a man, is unable to realize God." In other words, it is possible for every human being to realize God. Have the desire: "I must know him, I must see him face to face, I must talk to him, I must realize the bliss of union with him!" That is what religion means.

We have to experiment to experience the truth. As Sri Ramakrishna said, "There is butter in the milk, but if you simply cry, 'butter, butter,' that does not give you butter. First you have to have the milk, turn it into curd, and then churn. Only then can you get butter." We have to struggle, to strive, to practice spiritual disciplines to realize that eternal treasure.

If you study any religion of the world, you will find it falls within the category of one or the other yogas, but Sri Ramakrishna emphasized that there must be a harmonious combination of all of them. In other words, we must be active as well as meditative; we must be devotional as well as discrimina-

14

tive. Then again, emphasis can be laid upon one or the other – upon action and selflessness; or upon knowledge and discrimination; or upon meditating on the impersonal; or upon love and devotion. But there must be a combination.

Then again, he pointed out that very few can follow the path of knowledge exclusively. You have to consider this whole universe as illusion, as unreal. That is not so easy. As long as we have the sense of ego, as long as we have physical consciousness, it is not so easy. So he says that the path of devotion is the natural path that can be easily followed by most people – not that he excluded the path of knowledge.

He emphasized meditation, no matter what path you follow. You must keep your mind and heart fixed on God. Not only with closed eyes, but with open eyes, you must learn to see that indwelling God everywhere in the universe. Meditation also does not mean that you sit for only a few minutes or hours; you must try to have constant recollectedness of God. My master used to emphasize that: while sitting idly, while lying, while walking, try to keep your mind in God.

The basis of harmony is in the experience of God. When we reach that transcendental attainment, there are no divergent views to reconcile. You see, as Sri Ramakrishna said, "All jackals, in their highest pitch, have the same cry; you can't distinguish them." Just so, every great mystic of the world, whether Christian or Hindu or Muslim or Parsi, as he reaches transcendental consciousness, finds no divergence to be reconciled. Only in the lower levels of con-sciousness are there divergent views, such as determining the nature of God and the universe and their relationship and so on.

You find that God is said to be personal or impersonal, with form or without form. Some think the universe is unreal; others that it is the creation of God. There are so many divergent views; how can they be reconciled? Sri Ramakrishna reconciled them from the standpoint of a mystic, not from a theological standpoint. He did not try to give doctrines or one theological idea to the exclusion of the rest: Infinite is God, infinite are his expressions. He who lives continuously in the consciousness of God knows that he is personal as well as impersonal, he is with form as well as without form, and also he is beyond, where speech cannot utter. His name is Silence.

So let there be divergent doctrines and dogmas. You cannot modify them and bring them to one doctrine, or it would again be another dogmatic religion. I have said many times that the world will not be saved by Christianizing it, or by Hinduizing it, or by making everybody a Buddhist or Muslim. The world can be saved, individuals can be saved, only by realizing God. And when you realize God, you are neither a Christian, a Hindu, a Buddhist, nor a Muslim. You are a man or a woman of God. That is what I have seen in my life – men and women of God.

There are two watchwords Sri Ramakrishna set before mankind: renunciation and service. *Renunciation* is a forbidding word, but he taught the ideal of renunciation and service to both monks and householders. You can understand how monks can renounce, but what about householders? Does renunciation mean you take your husband and drown him in the ocean? We have a saying that in order to kill a mosquito that is biting your nose, do you take a gun? No. So what is the way? What is the truth of renunciation? To deify, to see God in the husband, the wife, the children – to try to serve God in the husband, wife, children, family, and friends. (71)

Sri Ramakrishna emphasized this truth: that divinity, that Atman, is the reality within. "The fellow who considers himself a sinner becomes a sinner," he said. What you think, you become. There is this urge in every one of us to become God – because we are already that – but we must unfold it.

Simply believing in that does not help. Sri Ramakrishna used to say, You hear about milk. That's something. Then you see milk. That's again something more. Then you drink milk – and you have to drink milk." The same with God. You hear about God – God exists, yes, God is within, that's one thing – but to see him, to feel him, to experience him, that's something more. Then to attain union with him, to realize the ultimate truth that "I and my Father are One" or "I am He" is again something more – and that's the ultimate truth. Sri Ramakrishna used to say, "To those who pray to God outside, 'God come down,' religion has not yet begun. But when you begin to feel, 'Here is God,' that is the beginning."

Sri Ramakrishna said, "So many religions, so many paths to union with God." We call this path of union yoga, which is a Sanskrit word meaning union, yoking ourselves – just as religion in its root meaning is *religio*, "a binding back, a re-uniting." There are four yogas, four ways of union – the path of love or devotion, the path of knowledge or discrimination, the path of meditation, and the path of selfless service. But these are not to be differentiated and separated into air-tight compartments. Sri Ramakrishna emphasized in this age that we must harmonize in one life all the yogas. But again, he reduced them to two: the path of devotion or love, and the path of discrimination or knowledge. Then he pointed out that they unite. The path of meditation and the path of self-less service you have to follow no matter what path you follow, whether of devotion or knowledge. In other words, the essence of these paths can be reduced to two words: contemplation and service.

But you will find three attitudes in religion. There is what is known as dualism, I am separate from God. Next, I am a part of God. Last, I am one with God. In the teachings of Christ you will find each of these attitudes. When he said, "Our Father which art in Heaven," he was a dualist. When he said, "I am the vine, ye are the branches," he was a qualified monist. When he said, "I and my Father are One," he was a nondualist. Sri Ramakrishna said, "When I think of my physical self, then of course I am separate from God. But when I consider myself as an individual soul, God is the whole, I am the part. And when I consider myself as the Atman, I am one with him." When this revelation comes, then one sees the Atman as one with Brahman. This is realized in the highest revelation, *samadhi*.

Exceptionally great teachers such as *avataras* or *ishvarakotis* can give you realization by a touch. Sri Ramakrishna gave that touch to all his disciples and they attained *samadhi* by it. In some of the disciples that power was manifest to a certain degree.

Sri Ramakrishna pointed out – and this is unique – that to attain liberation or salvation for yourself, or to live absorbed in *samadhi*, is a lower ideal. The higher ideal is different. After having attained *samadhi*, if you come down, your whole life has changed, your whole viewpoint, the values of life have changed: you see Brahman everywhere, so you live in the service of all. He didn't say to do good to the world. In fact, whenever anybody said anything about doing good to the world, he said, "Who are you to do good to the world? Is the world such a small place? Serve God in the world! Service!" (72)

One time when Sri Ramakrishna was seated with his disciples, he said, "Do you know what I see? I see Rama everywhere." When he was worshiping in the temple, what did he experience? Everything was full of consciousness: the image, the shrine, the altar, the flowers, the bricks that made up the temple; everywhere there was that presence of consciousness – Brahman, Brahman. It is not a unique experience of Ramakrishna, but is the experience of every great saint, teacher, prophet, or incarnation. You read in the Upanishads that the sages, having attained that, say, "Brahman is above, Brahman is below, Brahman extends to the right, Brahman extends to the left, Brahman is everywhere. All is Brahman." [Chandogya Upanishad] That is the fact, the truth. Not one moment in your life have any one of you, for even a fraction of a moment, been apart from God. Try to feel that! Realize that!

Religion has to be living. That is what Sri Ramakrishna emphasized: "I have seen him. I have known him," he said, "and you can know him!"

He pointed out that the revelation in the scriptures is possible for you and for me, for everyone – not by chance, but by training ourselves to reach that transcendental consciousness.

I have quoted Sri Ramakrishna, that if you follow certain spiritual disciplines, revelation will come to you, but all the great teachers tell us that without grace, it is not possible. There must be grace. So what are spiritual disciplines for? Here is the illustration given by Sri Ramakrishna: A magnet constantly attracts, but if the point of the needle is covered with dirt, it doesn't feel that attraction. So what is to be done? The point of the needle is to be cleaned. If you clean it, immediately it feels the pull of the magnet and it goes to it. The needle will say that the magnet drew it there. Sri Ramakrishna used to say, "Cry, cry, weep, weep for God, and let your tears wash away all the dirt and dross from the mind! In other words, yearn for him!"

That yearning has to come from inside, to grow from within. For that longing to come, you practice spiritual disciplines. Then a greater longing will arise in your heart for the truth of God. When that yearning comes, you have the vision, the realization. It is not just a vision. Along with it comes a complete transformation. Your whole character changes, your viewpoint, your values. In other words, a human being becomes God. There is a saying of Sri Ramakrishna, "The Atman, or God, in bondage is the man; and that man is Shiva when freed from bondage." (73)

It is generally thought that Ramakrishna followed all the paths to prove to mankind the universality of religion, but the other day I was reading some teachings of Holy Mother, and she said: "No. It happened this way. He did not strive to follow or experiment with the religions with the idea of showing the universality or harmony, but he just followed the many religions because he wanted to know how others, by following other paths, taste the bliss of God."

Of course there is nothing unique about him. You go to the Upanishads, the Bhagavad Gita, the teachings of Jesus and of Buddha, and they all have that idea of universality and harmony. Jesus said: "In my Father's house are many mansions." Sri Krishna said: "Whatever path you may follow, you reach only Me." In the Rig Veda it is taught: "Truth is One; sages call it by various names." But it was left to Ramakrishna to demonstrate this truth.

Of course if you are a Vedantist and at the same time do not struggle to realize God for yourself, you are not a Vedantist. If you call yourself a Christian and do not struggle to realize the kingdom of God here and now, you are not a Christian. Upon that truth of realization is built the universality or harmony of religions.

Why do religions quarrel? Why do they say you have to follow my way? Because they have not followed their own way; they only talk about it. You see, if you worship Krishna or Christ, when you have the vision and realization, you will find there are so many ways to reach that roof of the house. You will not say that Christ is the only way or Krishna is the only way. You go on quarrelling as long as you do not follow your own religion.

After Sri Ramakrishna had the supreme knowledge, the Divine Mother instructed him: "Remain in *bhava samadhi, bhava mukha*." You see, there is the supreme experience where there is no ego left – complete union with God. This is *nirvikalpa samadhi*. And then there is a lower *samadhi*, the *savikalpa*, where there remains a sense of ego: I see God, I have the vision of God. *Bhava mukha* is the state between the supreme, *nirvikalpa*, and the lower, *savikalpa*, *samadhi*. So his mind plied between these two states. In other words, he lived in *samadhi* all the time, only occasionally coming down to teach. And while teaching, he would again go into that, and then come back, then again go into that. This was unique. (74)

All the disciples of Sri Ramakrishna were given *samadhi* by his touch. Swami Shivananda, the second president of our Order for instance, said that one day Sri Ramakrishna asked him how his meditation was. "Oh, I can't meditate. I try, but so much distraction! So difficult to meditate!" Sri Ramakrishna told him, "Go and sit under a tree in the *Panchavati* and try to meditate." He went there, and while he was meditating, Sri Ramakrishna came and stood by him and watched. And things began to happen; he attained *samadhi*.

Sri Ramakrishna gave the vision and experience of the highest truth of God in so many ways. Another disciple, Swami Vijnanananda, was a wrestler and athlete. When he came to Sri Ramakrishna, Sri Ramakrishna said, "I want to wrestle with you. Come on." And he began to act like a wrestler. Swami

Vijnanananda thought, "What is the matter with this man? I can just crush him." But Sri Ramakrishna would not let him alone. So he agreed, and Swami Vijnanananda held him and of course pushed him to the wall. And then Swami Vijnanananda said, "Then I became just paralyzed, helpless!"

Sri Ramakrishna taught his disciples not how to become Vedantists, but how to find God. But though they had realized God, we still find them practicing hard austerities. In the life of my master, he went day and night with very little food, without any comfort, absorbed in meditation. What is the answer to that? Sri Ramakrishna said that they were like some fruits that come out first, then flower: they have the fruit – that is, the knowledge – and then come the disciplines.

So why did the disciples practice austerities if Sri Ramakrishna had done it all for them? It was a problem I could not solve for a long while, but then the answer came. You see, all these disciples are not separate from Sri Ramakrishna: they are one body. They're the limbs of Sri Ramakrishna, and they came to this earth to give a new impetus to the Eternal Religion. By their austerities, they let a current into this world. For centuries anybody who is struggling to realize God will receive their help. It will be easier to realize God in this present age. I am telling you, it is possible!

One time I complained to my master, "Sir, you give teachings, then you don't do anything about it." He said, "How do you know that we don't do anything about it? Are you struggling a little? Are you practicing a little what I told you to do? If you do, then you will know how we are helping you." This does not mean just a few disciples – they did not come for just a few disciples, but for everyone. They may not know from where this help is coming. The main thing is this: are you desiring God? If you strive to realize God, then you will receive help without name, without denomination. (75)

SARADA DEVI

You may read the Bible, the Upanishads, the Koran, or the Tripitaka, and you will find principles and theories of religion and philosophy, but you will still not understand the highest truth. You may read the Sermon on the Mount, or chant the Bhagavad Gita every day of your life; it will not make you spiritual. What spirituality is, and what religion is, is a life in God – knowing and living in that consciousness of God continuously. How can you do that unless you see exemplars before you?

And so, great ones come from time to time to prove the truth of religion and to show us the way. I will quote just two sayings of our Holy Mother. "If one loves the Lord, he becomes steady in meditation, and he clearly sees the Lord in his heart. He hears his voice, then he sees God everywhere; this makes one truly humble." You see, these few sentences give us the substance of the whole of religion. Then she says "God is our very own. It is the eternal relationship. One realizes him in proportion to the intensity of one's love for him."

My master, Swami Brahmananda, the spiritual son of Ramakrishna, said that it is very difficult to recognize the greatness of Holy Mother unless she reveals herself to you. I tell you, all these great ones are still helping, if only we will open our hearts. Mother lived a life in silence. She spoke few words; she gave religion in silence.

Once Holy Mother went to South India to visit a monastery, a huge place with beautiful gardens. She went out for a ride and while she was out, about a thousand men and women gathered to visit her. When she came back, she stood before them and said in her own language, "I am so sorry that I can't speak your language." And then she mentioned another holy woman who, if she had been there, could have spoken to them in English." When this was interpreted to the audience, they said, "Look, we don't want to hear you speak anything. Just stand there for a moment. Let us see you." They felt something – all of them.

In silence she transmitted spirituality: by her presence one's heart would be filled with love and reverence. She made no distinction between sinner and saint. One time a young lady snatched away the plate of food that Holy Mother was going to take to Ramakrishna. When she brought it to him, he couldn't eat that food because this young lady didn't lead a very pure life. Holy Mother said to Sri Ramakrishna, "Eat that." "I can't eat. Why did you let her bring it?" "You have to eat it; you can't make a distinction like that." So he had to eat it, he had to bless that girl. And then Sri Ramakrishna said, "You should not associate yourself with such and such people." She said, "Look here, I'll obey you in everything, but not in this. They're also my children." The whole of humanity were her children; she never made any distinction.

I will tell you another interesting story. At one time when there was a great political movement in India, we young boys joined the movement and we would not buy any English goods; we boycotted all their merchandise. But Holy Mother gave some money to a young man and said, "Go buy some Manchester cloth." The young man said, "But Mother, we have boycotted that, so we cannot buy it." "Well, that's all right for you," she said, "but you should recognize that English people are also my children. I cannot boycott. Go and buy Manchester cloth for me."[11]

Another thing: there was a notorious robber – Holy Mother said he committed murder too – who became devoted to her. Of course his life was transformed, but Holy Mother's women relatives who lived with her looked down on him as wicked. One day he came and Holy Mother asked one of the girls

11. This cloth was asked for by the relatives of the Holy Mother.

to serve him food. The woman practically threw the food at him. Holy Mother exclaimed, "What are you doing?" She took the food tray and began to serve him herself. She said to the woman, "Look here, this man is my child as much as Saradananda (a monastic disciple of Sri Ramakrishna who was taking care of Holy Mother)." She made no difference between them.

One of the disciples of Ramakrishna said to us, "You know, the poison that we cannot swallow, we send to Holy Mother." One time my master, Swami Brahmananda, sent a man with a letter requesting Holy Mother to bless him. When Holy Mother saw him, she said, "Oh, Rakhal also sends a man like that!" He was so impure! But of course Holy Mother accepted him, blessed him, and transformed his life.

One man in our little town was ostracized because of his life and character. Do you know, Holy Mother became his guest and the life of this man was completely transformed. I saw this with my own eyes. This man would not even touch Mother, he felt so impure, but from a distance he would bow down to her; after Holy Mother stood somewhere, he would go and touch that ground.

Great incarnations, while living on earth, are recognized by only a few. Christ had only twelve disciples who followed him to the end, and then one of them betrayed him. And Rama-krishna also did not have too many disciples, but Holy Mother made at least a thousand. And here is something unique: no *avatara*, no divine incarnation, was worshiped while living the way Holy Mother was worshiped. She was worshiped as the Divine Mother, but she was still a simple country woman.

A devotee once asked her, "Are you our real Mother?" "Yes." And we have a closer relationship with her – our Eternal Mother – than with our own Mother. She made us feel that way.

When she was about to give up her body she said, "I tell you one thing. If you want peace of mind, do not find fault with others. No one is a stranger, my child. The whole world is your own." She was the embodiment of this truth.

Another teaching: "If one loves the Lord, he becomes steady in meditation and clearly sees the Lord in his own heart." You see, to love the Lord means to meditate on him. And what is that? To think of him. You have to fall in love with God. You fall in love with a man or a woman, but the intensity doesn't last. With God, the intensity grows and grows and grows until one goes into ecstasy.

Holy Mother was Mother Eternal. Whether you recognize her or not means nothing, but if you worship Christ, you are worshiping our Mother; if you worship Krishna, you are worshiping our Mother. (76)

When I was fourteen or fifteen years old, I was going out for a walk with a friend. We saw Radhu, Holy Mother's niece, who was about twelve or thirteen, standing and holding onto a pillar on the porch of an inn. Then we saw a holy man seated there surrounded by women, and we criticized him for it. When we came back, they were still seated there. My friend went on his way and I was supposed to go to my house on another road, but something drew me back. I went and bowed before the holy man, who said, "Do you wish to see Holy Mother?" I asked, "Holy Mother?" I got excited because I had read *The Gospel of Sri Ramakrishna* and knew about her from it. I said, "You mean the wife of Paramahamsa Ramakrishna?" He said, "Yes. There she is, seated right there."

So I bowed down to her and touched her feet. She, like our own mother, kissed me as Indian mothers do – they put their three fingers on the cheek and then kiss the fingers. She said, "Son, haven't I seen you before?" Mother knows

her own children, but unfortunately children do not recognize her. I said, "No, Mother, this is the first time I've
seen you."

When I was a college student in Calcutta, Holy Mother
used to stay at the Udbodhan office for six months; and for
six months she'd stay in her own village, Jayrambati. During
her time in Calcutta, one day every week was for men to see
her and another for women. They stood in rows, one by one,
to wash their hands and then go to her. Holy Mother had a
veil on her head, and you could only see her feet. I used to
go because as I would touch her big toes with my fingers, I
felt something like an electric shock. It was very pleasant and
soothed my whole body. They say that power is transmitted
in that way – I didn't know all that – but I used to go every
week for those six months, not because I was attracted to her,
but because I got the sensation.

When Holy Mother was at her home in Jayrambati, about
twenty miles from our town of Vishnupur, I went to see her
with a friend, Paresh, a disciple of Maharaj as I was. He became Swami Amriteswarananda. We were late arriving, because we had stopped at another little village, Koalpara, where
we saw a picture of Holy Mother, which she had installed and
worshiped herself. We bowed down to it.

There were no telephones, and we didn't write any letters
to her, but she told her attendant Rashbehari Maharaj that
"two of Rakhal's children are coming. They'll be arriving late.
Keep some food for them." So when we arrived, she welcomed
us – she wore no veil then – and she sat with us like our own
mother. Here is a very interesting situation. Everybody who saw
her face saw the reflection of his own mother's face. And she fed
us like a Hindu mother: if you liked something, she would give
you more. When we had finished eating, we tried to take our
leaf plates, but Mother said, "What are you doing?" "Oh, we

couldn't leave these plates here." "What would you have done if your mother were present?" Naturally we left them.

We stayed there for three days and three nights, and she made every arrangement for our comfort, just like a mother. When we left, she stood at the door and gazed upon us as long as she could see us, just like our own mother.

One time in Calcutta some volunteers were needed, so I got some college students and we stood in rows as Holy Mother passed by. Four swamis carried her in a chair: Maharaj, Swami Saradananda, Mahapurush Maharaj, and Swami Premananda. They carried her upstairs to the shrine room, and of course they worshiped her, but nobody was allowed to go there.

While she was living, she was worshiped by hundreds and thousands of people as a goddess. Once a funny incident happened. A brahmin priest came to worship her as if she were an image. It was summer, and Mother was perspiring. When Golap-Ma noticed it, she dragged him out of there and said, "Do you think she is an image that you can revive and give life to?" She threw him out.

Another interesting incident happened at the Udbodhan office, where Mother was staying upstairs. A holy man from another order went up and prostrated before Holy Mother; then he came down and Mother sent him three fruits. He kept quiet, but he would not move. The people in the office tried to move him away, but he would not go. He sat silently. Then Holy Mother sent another fruit after an hour, and when he got that fourth fruit, he began to dance in joy, saying, "So Mother gave me liberation at long last!" (Three fruits are *dharma*, merit; *artha*, fortune; *kama*, what you desire; the fourth is *moksha*, liberation.) And then he went away.

I saw her once more, without a veil. When Maharaj sent us to Mayavati, he said, "Go and take the blessings of Mother." Her bed was in the shrine room itself. It was there that we saw her face. She kissed us and gave flowers from the shrine to each of us. After the flowers dried up, I threw them away.

We would go and touch her toes, but when Swamiji went to see her, he didn't think himself pure enough. Think of that! He would dip himself in the Ganges at least seven times and then, in wet cloth, he would go and touch her. We have seen Maharaj, when going to see Holy Mother, just like a naughty little boy, nervous to approach her. He would compose himself, and she would say, "Hello Radhi, how are you?" Then he would bow down and want to come away, but Mother would make him sit. Then she would ask how he was and all that. Swami Yogananda, who was also an ever-free soul, would not touch her feet. He would only take the dust from where she stood. With what reverence these disciples of Sri Ramakrishna looked upon her!

An untouchable boy came and wanted to be initiated by her in Jayrambati, but Mother said, "Wait. Go to Calcutta. Here the villagers do not understand." And the untouchable boy said, "When you were in danger, you could show your grace to the dacoits, but now you behave differently!" Then of course Holy Mother initiated him.

There was a drunkard who was with Girish Ghosh's theater. He would get drunk and come to her. Swami Saradananda would not allow him to enter, but as long as Holy Mother was there, at twelve o'clock at night he used to sing a song: "Cherish my precious Mother Shyama tenderly within, O mind; may you and I alone behold her, letting no one else intrude." And then he would say, "Let not that rascal Sarat (Saradananda) intrude." And Mother would hear the song and open the door and come out and look at him. Then she would say, "Now Padmalochan, go back home." And he would be all right – he was not drunk anymore – and he would go.

One time Swami Turiyananda told me that Holy Mother's mind never came down from the *vishuddha chakra*. That means she was always in *samadhi*. But externally nobody knew it. At the same time she could do housework and was conscious externally. See her greatness!

One time when Holy Mother was going to Kamarpukur from Jayrambati, Shibuda, Ramakrishna's nephew, was carrying her bag with a stick. Suddenly he stood in front of her and said, "Mother, who are you?" "Shibuda, what are you talking about? I am your aunt." "If you are only my aunt, here is your bag, carry it yourself!" Then she said, "I am Mother Kali." And he bowed down and chanted some verses for Mother Kali.

Another time he did the worship for three days and then came to Holy Mother. She said, "Shibhu, why did you come here now?" "Oh, I have finished worship for three days and three nights. I am going to stay here for three days and three nights." "Oh, no, you can't do that. You have to go back. You can't do worship that way. It is a family deity. You have to do the worship regularly, on time." And so he was forced to go, but he said, "What you said that time: are you really that?" And Mother said, "Yes."

One time Holy Mother came to Belur Math during Sri Ramakrishna's birthday. Maharaj went into *samadhi* and all the swamis tried to bring him out of it, but none of them succeeded. Then they reported to Holy Mother and she said, "Let him stay that way." After a while she touched him with her hand and said, "My child, Rakhal, I have this *prasad* for you." And Maharaj woke up immediately.

In Benares Maharaj went to prostrate before Holy Mother upstairs and, as he came down, Golap-Ma asked him, "Rakhal, Holy Mother is asking you to tell her why Mother is to be worshiped." He danced a little and said, "Mother holds the key to the knowledge of Brahman." Another time in Benares she asked

15

Rashbehari Maharaj to get gerua cloth for all the disciples of Sri Ramakrishna, but she said, "For Rakhal, get a silk cloth." Rashbehari Maharaj asked her, "But, Mother, are not they all your sons?" "Yes, they are all my sons, but Rakhal is my *son*."

I can remember her saying one time, "I must be very old. I saw my mother die, I saw my father die, I saw my grandparents die. I must be very old." She never mentioned her husband, Sri Ramakrishna, dying.

Maharaj, Holy Mother, and her attendants went to Sarnath, where Buddha gave his first sermon. Maharaj was in a motor car and Holy Mother went in a carriage, but he saw something while going there and asked Holy Mother to take the motor car on the way back; he would come back in the horse carriage. While coming back, when Mother passed by in the motor car, the horses of the carriage Maharaj was seated in shied and the carriage fell over. It didn't hurt anybody much, but Holy Mother said, "You see, Rakhal took the suffering from me on himself."

It is interesting how Holy Mother received Swamiji's Western disciples. I think it was Tantine and Mrs. Leggett and Sarah Bull that he brought to her, and they were all sitting at her feet. There was a cloth spread and silver plates and many sweets. While these Western women were eating their sweets, Swamiji stood at the door. Suddenly Holy Mother bent down and, while they were eating, took one sweet and ate it herself. Even Swamiji was shocked. Of course Swamiji knew that she accepted his Western disciples.

During her *mahasamadhi*, when she was passing away, only the disciples of Sri Ramakrishna were allowed to see her. Maharaj did not come, because he was at Bhubaneswar. Somebody asked Swami Saradananda, "How is it that you are all here, but Maharaj is not?" He replied, "Maharaj is not like one of us." You see, Maharaj had the power to leave his body and come and visit in a subtle body. Holy Mother saw him.

Just at the moment she passed away, Maharaj said to Surji Maharaj, Swami Nirvanananda, "Surji, Mother just passed away." And then he received a telegram that confirmed that exact hour. (77)

Sri Ramakrishna discriminated and selected his disciples, but Mother initiated everybody who came to her. She said one time, "Just like ants, they are all coming to me." She saw no sinner or saint.

I will translate for you a Bengali song which comes to me whenever I think of her:

"In all my life I never longed for Thee, but, seeing me destitute, Thou sought me out. Before I called for Thee, Thou, through Thy grace, revealed Thyself to me." (78)

To review her life in short, Holy Mother was married to Sri Ramakrishna when she was just a little child. You see, they were trying to find a bride for Sri Ramakrishna because they thought he was going insane, becoming crazy for God. To bring his mind down, his mother and older brother thought that if he could be married he would settle down. But everywhere they looked, the dowry was so much that the poor mother couldn't afford it.

Sri Ramakrishna – as if nothing about him was happening – said in fun, "You want a bride? Just go to the home of such-and-such person in Jayrambati (that's the village where Mother was born), and you will find a girl marked out for me." So they went and saw a little child, practically five years old. Her parents didn't want much money, so they were married.

When she was fourteen years old, she came to Kamarpukur when Sri Ramakrishna was also there. During that period Sri Ramakrishna initiated her and transmitted spiritual power. Holy Mother said about her life at that time that she felt like a pitcher brimful with ineffable bliss. And this continued. When Sri Ramakrishna returned to Dakshineswar, she was left with her parents.

When she was eighteen, people began to whisper about what bad luck Sarada had, that she'd gotten a husband who was crazy, all the time weeping for God. In the little village they all stared at her and talked about her. So she told her father that she had to go and see her husband. Her father took the girl, and because they were poor people, they had to walk all the way. On the way, she got a high fever. Lying in bed with the fever, she saw a young girl like herself approach and place her hands on her, curing her. "Who are you?" she asked. "I am your sister." "Where do you come from?" The girl replied, "I come from Dakshineswar." "Oh! You know my husband?" "Yes. I live in the temple and take care of him for you." Then suddenly she disappeared, and Mother realized that Mother Kali had come to her and talked to her.

So she came to Dakshineswar and Sri Ramakrishna welcomed her. As she went to her room at night, Sri Ramakrishna said, "Have you come to draw me down to the flesh?" She said, "Oh no! I have come to help you in your spiritual growth and not to drag you down." In later years Sri Ramakrishna used to say about her, "If she had not been so good and pure, I do not know if I could have remained as pure." That was Holy Mother.

During this period, one evening – it was the night of Kali Puja when the Divine Mother is worshiped – Sri Ramakrishna asked his nephew, Hriday, who was taking care of him, to arrange for all the paraphernalia of worship in his room. Flowers, sandal paste, fruits, garlands, everything was brought to the room. A little table was placed there for the Goddess. But Sri Ramakrishna didn't ask his nephew to get any image, so nobody knew what he was going to do. He asked Holy Mother to come at a certain time and then told her, "Sit down there." Holy Mother became half-conscious and was seated on that seat. If you go to India, you will find this seat at the Belur Math. When Ramakrishna began to utter the mantras, Holy Mother went into *samadhi*. Sri Ramakrishna also went into *samadhi*. And so they had a spiritual union in the domain of the spirit, beyond all physical consciousness.

Holy Mother lived for some time in the same room with Sri Ramakrishna, but he would go into *samadhi* often at night and it was difficult for her to sleep. Realizing that, he said, "You had better go and stay in the nahabat." That little building is still there. She lived there for some time and then went back to her village.

Another time she went to Dakshineswar with a party of travelers, but she couldn't walk as fast as they could and was left behind. It got dark at a place infested with what in India are called *dacoits*; they rob and kill. Holy Mother was alone. When she saw a big man with a big stick approaching, she said, "Hello. I am your daughter. I am going to your son-in-law and have lost my way." She touched his wife and said, "I am your daughter, Sarada." And you know? Both were changed. They took care of her, took her to a place where she could rest, brought food, and then took her to meet her companions. Of course their lives were transformed. We are told that later they came to Dakshineswar and got the blessing of Sri Ramakrishna.

It is the custom in India that a widow dresses differently; she does not wear any jewelry or cloth with a border, or a certain red mark of a married woman. After Sri Ramakrishna's *mahasamadhi*, she was discarding her bracelets, which were given to her by Sri Ramakrishna, when he came to her and held her hand, "Don't do that. I am not dead. I am just in the other room." And so she never wore the dress of a widow, but for the sake of the customs of the country, she was careful and had just a small border on her cloth, and she kept the red mark, but hidden on the side of her head.

Vivekananda used to say that Mother lived in transcendental consciousness all the time. She behaved like any other woman – just like a mother – but she was in communion with God all the time. Swami Turiyananda said, "Holy Mother had difficulty bringing her mind down to the plane of the throat." On that plane you become established in God-consciousness; it is called *vishuddha*. Swami Turiyananda said, "We have difficulty bringing our mind up to that center, and Holy Mother had difficulty bringing hers *down* to that center." Just think of that!

She said, "The more intensely a person practices spiritual disciplines, the more quickly he attains God. Open your heart to him, shed tears, and pray sincerely: 'O Lord, draw me toward you; give me peace of mind!' He who has really prayed to God even once has nothing to fear. By praying to him constantly, one gets ecstatic love through his grace. This love is the important thing in spiritual life." (79)

VIVEKANANDA

Soon after Naren met Sri Ramakrishna – I think on the second or third visit – Sri Ramakrishna took him into a private room and chided him, saying, "Why didn't you come earlier? I have been waiting for you." As Naren later described it, "He took me into the room and began to talk with me as if I were one of his longtime acquaintances." Suddenly Sri Ramakrishna's mood changed and, with folded palms, he began to pray to Naren: "Lord, you have assumed this human form to do good to mankind." "I am the son of Vishwanath

Dutta, and my name is Narendra!" he said to himself. "What is he talking about?"

Though he still felt greatness in Sri Ramakrishna, he thought he was not exactly in his right mind. He decided he would not visit him anymore. But the attraction was so great that he could not resist and had to go again and again. But that love was tested. As you read in the Gospel, Sri Ramakrishna paid great attention to Naren when he visited. Sometimes he would even go into *samadhi* looking at him. But then for months he paid no attention to Naren at all. One day Sri Ramakrishna asked him, "Why do you come? I don't pay any attention to you, I don't even look at you!" He said, "Because I love you."

To corroborate his intuition, Sri Ramakrishna touched him, and Naren went into a condition where he was not conscious of himself. He began to talk, and as he talked, he told about his past and present, and he corroborated the intuitive knowledge Sri Ramakrishna had. Then Sri Ramakrishna said to him, "Now I keep the key with myself and you will not know who you are. The moment you know who you are, you will give up the body – but only after you have fulfilled the mission for which you have come."

As it happened, on his last day Naren sent Maharaj on an errand to Calcutta because he felt if Maharaj were present, he might create an obstacle to fulfilling his wish. He talked to Swami Premananda and walked with him, telling him many of his plans for the future. Swami Premananda suddenly asked, "Brother, do you know now who you are?" "Yes." And then of course he sat in meditation in his room and asked his attendant not to come into his room until he called for him. While in meditation, he passed away. When the disciple was not called for hours, he told the senior swamis, and they all came into his room. At first they thought he was in *samadhi*. They tried to wake him up, but it was not possible. The doctor was called in and pronounced him dead. In the meantime Swami Ramakrishnananda, who was in Madras, had a vision of Swamiji saying to him: "Brother Sashi, I have spat out my body."

This was the man or God-man Vivekananda was. He is still living; he is still helping humanity. It was his master who recognized the greatness of Swamiji, that he was an ever-free soul born to give a universal message.

As a monk Swamiji traveled from one place of pilgrimage to another. In Madras quite a few young men gathered to see an educated monk; and they witnessed a great spiritual power in him. One was a young professor who was an intellectual and an atheist. He came to Vivekananda and argued with him, and Vivekananda could not defeat him. But then Vivekananda held his hand and said, "Kidi, don't you see that God is?" He shook him, and the man was completely transformed. Of course that was the end of him. He renounced everything. He had a wife, a career, and children. The Ramakrishna Monastery had to support the wife and children.

These young men learned about the Parliament of Religions, which was going to be held in Chicago, and they insisted that Swamiji must represent Hinduism. They collected funds and gave the money to him, but he distributed the funds! Again they collected funds. But you see, Swamiji was waiting to get the command from God. Then he had a vision. He saw Sri Ramakrishna on the ocean beckoning to him to come. He wanted to corroborate his vision, so he wrote to Holy Mother. He didn't tell her about the vision, but that the young men were insisting that he go to America to represent Hinduism and to spread Sri Ramakrishna's message.

Holy Mother, having a Mother's heart, thought he was so young – he was twenty-nine – to be sent to a distant, unknown land with no friends. She was going to ask him not to go when

Sri Ramakrishna appeared to her and said, "Permit Naren to go." It was when Swamiji received a letter from Holy Mother that he went. You know, Buddha preached his first sermon near Benares where there was a gathering of great scholars from all over India. Through these scholars, his message was spread all over the country, then to the world. Vivekananda gave his first sermon in Chicago, of all places! In this most materialistic country and in that city, he gave his first message.

He had a message for India and the East, and he had a message for the West. He is often misunderstood in India as well in the West. In India they regard him as a patriot saint, as if he came for India. As he traveled from one part of India to the other, he felt spirituality was alive, but he saw poverty, dirt, laziness, *tamas*, in the name of spirituality. So he gave his message in one way to that country. But in this country, he gave a message which is the eternal truth, the core of Hinduism, Buddhism, Christianity, Judaism, Islam, and all the religions of the world.

Inside, Swamiji was all *bhakta*, outside a *jnani*. My master told me that of all the disciples of Sri Ramakrishna, Swamiji was the greatest devotee. He mentioned that Swamiji would sometimes sing a song which says: "I am thy slave, thou art my master, Lord." Again he would sing: "Whatever I see, it is thou who hast become everything, and everybody." If you study Swamiji carefully, you will find that he was not one-sided, but was a harmonious combination of *karma, bhakti, jnana*, and meditation, as were all of Sri Ramakrishna's disciples.

His message to the West was that of a practical religion. He had no use for theory, dogmas, and doctrines. He said that, yes, they may help, but religion means practice in order that you can realize in your own life what the books and scriptures talk about. He could not accept the Bible as the word of God, or the Vedas as revelation, but he insisted that what is said in the Vedas, the Bible, and the Koran must be practiced, and the same truth realized. If it was possible for the seers of India of ancient times, possible for Moses or Christ or Krishna or Buddha, to realize God, then it is possible for you and me and everyone to realize that truth of God within ourselves. That is what he meant by practical religion. (80)

Some think Vivekananda didn't believe so much in religion and God. For instance, he said, "You will be nearer to God by playing football than studying the Bhagavad Gita." Or he would say just to worship God in man – give shelter, food, and so on. Then again, he said, "Forget God or religion for fifty years. Make India your Motherland, your God." You see, you can quote Swamiji for anything.

But he is none of these. As he said, "I belong not to India, I belong to all the countries of the world." That also is not the final truth. He again said, "Why has a man to deal with the world? I belong not to this world." He would teach according to the individuals coming to him. But his one aim was to teach people how to be God themselves, and how to help others become God. That was the final message he gave.

As Vivekananda said, only another Vivekananda could understand Vivekananda. But whenever I think of Vivekananda, I see him absorbed in meditation, completely lost to the world in his love for God. Then again, opening his eyes, I see him seeing God everywhere and helping others to unfold that Godhead within themselves.

He came to preach Vedanta. If we take away the names and call that religion *Sanatana Dharma*, the Eternal Religion, that is what he came to preach. He did not give theology or doctrines, but he showed us how to find God. If you read his lectures, you are inspired. "Sinner? It is a sin to call a man sinner! Children of immortal bliss!" A brother disciple of his told me that even a bad man would wake up when he heard Swamiji.

So what do I mean by *Sanatana Dharma*? Vedanta is the religion that takes the Vedas as the authority. That is Hinduism: you have to accept the Vedas as the authority, just like Christians have the Bible as their authority. But he said: "The Vedas are beginningless and endless. Can these books be beginningless and endless?" It is the Eternal Religion that is beginningless and endless. Simply stated: God is, and he dwells within each human heart; in fact, God is your true Self. And to realize that, to unfold that divinity, is the purpose of human life and living.

Within that fold there is room for Moses, for Mohammed, for Christ, for Krishna, for Buddha, for Ramakrishna, for every saint, and even for every sinner. It does not discard anybody. Whether you are a saint or a sinner, God dwells within you, and the duty of a man or a woman of God is to discard the sinner. Do you hear of any teacher, any great soul, any prophet, that hated a sinner? They came not for saints, but for sinners, to show them how to unfold that divinity which is their very birthright. That was Vivekananda.

A man came to Swamiji to become a monk. He was as old, or older, than Swamiji and didn't have a very good reputation. Most of the disciples of Sri Ramakrishna knew him. Swamiji told him, "All right, I will make you a monk. Go shave your head. I'll give you initiation into monastic life." One of the disciples of Sri Ramakrishna was horrified and said, "Swamiji, if you give *sannyasa* to that man, I'm leaving this monastery." Swamiji said, "Good. You see, wherever you go, you can build monasteries, but what about this man? Who will give him shelter if I don't?"

Swamiji's meeting with Sri Ramakrishna was very wonderful. You see how the East and West met together in a sense. Sri

Ramakrishna did not know a word of English except "thank you." He had gone to school for a little while to learn to read and write, but he said, "What will I do with this learning? It will help me to earn my living – bundles of rice and bananas." He didn't want that kind of knowledge. And Vivekananda was a student of a Western university, well versed in Western philosophy and psychology. He was steeped in Herbert Spencer. But he wanted to know if God is, and if God is, if anybody had seen Him. In other words, could the truth of what is said in the scriptures be verified?

So when he came to Ramakrishna and asked him, to his surprise, Ramakrishna said, "Yes. I have seen Him, with a clearer vision than I see you before me. And I can show you." Vivekananda was sold forever at the feet of this man. And Ramakrishna recognized him as his apostle. He saw him as a free soul, an ever-free soul.

You see, there are three classes of people: souls bound to their life in this world as the be-all and end-all of existence; those who long for liberation – spiritual aspirants; and then those who attain that in this life. They are called *jivanmukta*, free while living. Then again there are some who fail to achieve that while living but at the moment of death, they have attainment. They are called *videhamukta*, liberated at the moment of death. Then there is a class of very rare souls who only come with an incarnation of God, and they are called ever-free souls, which means they never were in bondage to this world. Sri Ramakrishna gives the example of a bird called *homa* which lives way up in the sky. When its egg begins to fall and the chick comes out, while falling, it sees the ground and soars up high.

So these ever-free souls are born on earth, but they see the world as it is; they soar high in the sky. That is, they have the attainment already, but it becomes unfolded. And ever-free souls come with one purpose in life – to free others. That is the objective of their lives.

In a sense Vivekananda was an agnostic, and then he became devoted to God. He was brought up in the Brahmo Samaj, which is something like the Unitarian Church. He was a theist in that sense: to think that I am divine or that everything is God would be blasphemy. That's how Vivekananda thought at the time.

One day he and Hazra were making fun of the idea of Vedanta: "This hookah is Brahman, this fire is Brahman, I am Brahman, that smoke we are breathing out is Brahman." And Sri Ramakrishna came and touched Vivekananda, who later said: "That touch immediately brought a complete revolution of my mind. Wherever I looked, I saw Brahman, and I lived in that consciousness the whole day. I returned home, and the same experience continued when I sat down to eat: I saw the food, the plate, the server, and myself – all were Brahman. I took one or two morsels of food and again was absorbed in that consciousness. All this while – whether eating or lying down or going to college – I had the same experience. While walking in the street, I noticed cabs plying but did not feel inclined to move out of the way. I felt that the cab and myself were made of the same substance. When this state changed a little, the world began to appear to me as a dream. While walking in Cornwallis Square, I struck my head against the iron railing to see if it was real or only a dream. After several days, when I returned to the normal plane, I realized that I had had a glimpse of nondual consciousness. Since then I have never doubted the truth of nondualism." That is religion. You have to experiment and experience the truth for yourself. Then only, believe.

When he had attained the bliss of *samadhi*, one day he was asked, "What do you wish to be?" "Oh, I wish to live absorbed in *samadhi*, and occasionally get up and eat something for the sustenance of life, and then again be absorbed in *samadhi*." Sri Ramakrishna said, "I am ashamed of you! I thought you were greater than that!" And he pointed out the ideal that, after attaining *samadhi*, you come back and live in the service of God in all beings.

In this connection I must point out how Vivekananda learned the ideal of service. There is the ideal of philanthropy, but what he taught was not philanthropy; it was something completely different. This we misunderstand. He was with Ramakrishna one day when Ramakrishna was repeating the teachings of another great saint: "Compassion for mankind. Compassion for mankind." Sri Ramakrishna said to himself: "Compassion? Compassion? Compassion? No, why should I be compassionate? Is not everyone God? Serve, serve, serve. Serve God." Vivekananda came out of the room and said to some of his brother disciples: "I have learned something today, something unique. If I live, I'll give this truth to mankind." (81)

I remember one time when I was a member of the revolutionary movement, I was asked to write a leaflet to incite the youth of India to wake up and throw off the British rule. I quoted a sentence from Vivekananda: "It is better to wear out than to rust out."

To every disciple Sri Ramakrishna gave the whole truth – dualistic as well as nondualistic. From nondualism, he taught Vivekananda the dualistic aspect. When Vivekananda's family was suffering terribly, he asked Sri Ramakrishna to help him and was told to go to the temple of the Divine Mother. He was told that whatever you ask of Mother, She will give you. So he went to pray and as soon as he went into the temple, there was a revolution in his whole mind. The whole universe began to

disappear, and Mother became a living reality. And he forgot
to ask anything but for devotion, for knowledge. When he went
back to Sri Ramakrishna, he saw his face completely changed,
and he asked, "Did you ask of Mother?" "No, I forgot." "Go
back again." So he went back again and the same thing happened. He was sent back three times, but he forgot every time,
his whole being overwhelmed with the love of Mother. Then he
said to Ramakrishna, "I can't do anything, you have to do it."
And Sri Ramakrishna said, "All right. They'll have no wants;
the necessities of life your family will get always. (82)

I heard a disciple of Sri Ramakrishna, Swami Turiyananda,
say about Vivekananda that whenever he used the word "I," it
was the universal "I" – that he kept his union with Brahman
all the time. And at the same time he was full of fun. For instance, he said this about himself, "When I am feeling well,
I say I am one with Brahman; when I have a stomach ache, I
cry, 'Oh Mother!'"

Whatever Vivekananda said was not theory, not opinion.
His message was, and is, the definition of religion: "Religion
is the manifestation of the divinity already in man." Your true
being is free, pure, and divine, but it is hidden, and you have
to discover that.

You don't have to tell people they are weak; they know they
are weak. But Vivekananda emphasized this truth: "There is
that lion within every one of you." All these weaknesses don't
mean a thing. A diamond can remain covered for centuries but
does not lose its luster: it is just that dirt has accumulated. That
is not its nature. Wash it and it shines. So it is not enough to
learn this truth that you are pure, free, and divine: you have
to unfold that, realize that, have that experience.

Swamiji not merely emphasized unfoldment or realizing
God for yourself, but also dedicating your life, to the service

of God in all. He preached all through his life: "He who seeks for his own liberation is full of narrowness. Seek for your liberation; at the same time, you must live for the good of mankind, for the happiness of others."

These are two ideals: realizing God, and serving God in humanity. Serving God in that way is a most wonderful truth that Vivekananda gave to the world. It is not philanthropy, not doing good to others, not saving the world, but serving the world. Not helping people, but serving God in them. The big difference is the attitude. You see, you are not compassionate to God, you serve God, you worship God, you adore God – and where is he? In so many forms: in the form of the sick, in the form of the depraved, in the form of the ignorant. Serve God in all of them.

This reminds me of the scolding of my master when I wanted to live a life of contemplation. He said, "Swamiji did not want you boys to be like those wandering monks, thousands of whom are walking the streets of India. Where would you find God, unless you find it within yourself? Then learn to see God in others, and serve mankind."

Speaking of God-realization, Swamiji gave his message of the ideal of a universal religion: "It has been proved to the world that holiness, purity and charity are not the exclusive possession of any church in the world, and that every system has produced men and women of the most exalted character. In the face of this evidence, if anybody dreams of the exclusive survival of his own religion and the destruction of the others, I pity him from the bottom of my heart, and point out to him that upon the banner of every religion will soon be written, in spite of their resistance, "Help and not fight." "Assimilation and not destruction." "Harmony and peace, and not dissension." "A sage is no sage if he does not hold a different opinion." "You have to think independently." "Freedom is the watchword of growth." (83)

Swami Vivekananda spoke of himself and of his master, Sri Ramakrishna, in the following terms. He said Sri Ramakrishna was all knowledge inside, that he had the full awareness of his identity with Brahman all the time; and outside he was a devotee of God or Divine Mother. And about himself, he said, "Inside I am a lover of God, but outside I am a knower of Brahman." In other words, in each of these lives there was a perfect harmony between knowledge and devotion. Generally the followers of the path of knowledge denounce those who follow the path of devotion, saying that they are weaklings. And those who follow the path of devotion say that those who follow the path of knowledge are just dry intellectuals. Neither is true. Knowledge means becoming a knower of Brahman; one becomes one with Brahman. At the same time, as Sri Ramakrishna explained, "I see a universal ocean of bliss, and there's a stick here that divides me as a devotee, and on the other side is the Divine Mother – but it is all one ocean of bliss."

In the life of Vivekananda we find harmony, but those who are narrow-minded and one-sided generally do not understand him. They find contradictions in him. But here is the point: he was a follower of the path of knowledge, the path of devotion, the path of action, and he also was perfect in contemplation. So when he talked about *jnana* yoga, he was all *jnana*. And when he talked about *bhakti*, devotion, he would be all devotion. You have to see the man as a whole, and if you do, you see a perfect harmony in all his teachings.

He never spoke about anything which he did not realize or experience in his own life. Just as the great Buddha said, "Tathagata has no theories," in the same way Vivekananda had no theories. Whatever he uttered was his experience, not mere intellectual understanding. The truth about the divinity in each human soul is something that he first experienced and then taught. (84)

Sri Ramakrishna said Swamiji was born *dhyanasiddha*, perfect in meditation. One day Girish Ghosh saw Swamiji meditating under the tree at Dakshineswar; his whole body was covered with mosquitoes like a blanket. He was not conscious of it, he was so absorbed in meditation. So Girish began to fan him.

Sri Ramakrishna said to Swami Turiyananda, who told me this story: "You say that everything is *maya* and only Brahman is real, but put your hand on the thorn and it will prick. But if Naren says it is *maya*, there will be no thorn, it won't prick him."

There is a book called the Ashtavakra Samhita which is extremely nondualistic. Sri Ramakrishna asked Naren to read it to him. As he was reading, Naren said, "Why, this is blasphemous! How can it be? How can everything be God?" You see, he was then a young man going to the Brahmo Samaj, which was theistic. Sri Ramakrishna replied, "Never mind. I am not asking you to read it for you, I want to hear." You see his way of training.

One time Swamiji was lecturing in Southern India and talking about harmonizing the three schools of thought: dualism, qualified monism, and nondualism. In that connection he pointed out how the great teachers – Shankara, Ramanuja, and Madhva – were, in a sense, one-sided and tortured texts to fit in with their own way of thinking. His audience took objection and said, "But none of these teachers said what you are saying!" He replied: "No, they did not. They left it for me to harmonize." (85)

BRAHMANANDA

I shall make an attempt to speak about my master, Swami Brahmananda, who used to be known as Maharaj. I shall confine myself to my personal experiences with him, the times

I lived with him, what I received from him, what love and grace I received from him. Of course it will be a sort of auto-biography, so you will forgive me if I use the pronoun *I* many times, but I want you to understand that this pronoun *I* that I shall be using is not a separate individuality or ego, but this ego belongs to him whose servant I am.

Those of you who are acquainted with the Ramakrishna and Vivekananda literature are well aware of what place Maharaj had in the Ramakrishna Order. He was considered by Sri Ramakrishna as one of the free souls; that is, he was born to help mankind to attain liberation. He was liberated himself from the very beginning of his life, and he comes again and again with what we call divine incarnations to give liberation to others.

When I was fourteen years old, I was introduced to *The Gospel of Sri Ramakrishna* in its original form and original language. I was attracted to two names, the names of Naren and Rakhal. Of course Naren was already gone; only Rakhal was living at the time. There were many other disciples living then and I had the opportunity to meet most of them. At this age also I had the opportunity to meet Holy Mother. But it was Rakhal that attracted me, the very name.

When I was sixteen years old and had graduated from high school, I came to Calcutta to study at college. I used to go to Belur Math regularly, but Swami Brahmananda was not there. About a year later I learned that he had arrived in Calcutta and would be at Belur Math. I went to visit him at Balaram Mandir, the devotee Balaram's home, but from the stairway I saw a big crowd and left. I waited for an oppor-tunity when he would be at Belur Math without a crowd. I took what you may call "French leave" from college and went there on a weekday.

I saw Maharaj seated in an easy chair on the veranda up-stairs, facing the room preserved in honor of Swami Viveka-nanda. Of course I didn't dare approach him immediately. I felt shy, and then I thought to myself, I can stand in this corner and watch Swamiji's room. This is public property; nobody can tell me anything. And so I was watching, but I was also glancing at Maharaj. He watched me for a while, and then he said, "Come here, boy."

The moment I prostrated, he said, "Can you take off these stockings and place them in the sun?" He gave me the op-portunity to serve him immediately. I remember the maroon-colored stockings. I placed them in the sun, then he asked me, "Haven't I seen you before?" "No, Maharaj." And that moment I felt such love, such fulfillment, in one moment. I felt, "That was it!"

Once a disciple asked Maharaj, "Won't you please tell us something about Sri Ramakrishna?" His answer was, "What can I say? And how would you understand? Unless he reveals himself to you, it is not possible to understand." I'd say the same thing about my master, that unless he reveals himself. ... This was something unique with my Master: whomever he accepted as a disciple, he accepted the very first moment he saw him. This I have learned from most of the disciples of Maharaj. There is that saying of Jesus: "Ye have not chosen Me, I have chosen you."

Then I used to visit Maharaj every Saturday and Sunday. I was studying in a college which was very puritanical; it was run by the Brahmo Samaj. They would not allow a student to go out in the evenings or stay out on Saturdays and Sundays, because these are the evenings for theaters in Calcutta, and they were against anybody going to the theater. So when Ma-haraj said, "You had better come on Saturday and stay here in the evening," I said, "But it might be difficult for me to get a leave of absence from the principal of the college." He said, "Oh, just ask him; he'll let you come."

So I wrote an application, which had to pass through the superintendent of the hostel where I was living; then I submitted it to the principal. He was very strict, very puritanical, so I was nervous. He read the letter and said, "Correct your English." He handed it back to me. I read and re-read it, but I couldn't find any mistake, so I went to the Professor of English and asked him to correct it. He looked at it and said, "Put a comma here." So I put the comma and then took it back to the principal. He granted me permission immediately, without any question. That was how it was possible for me to go to Belur Math almost every weekend.

When Maharaj would rest after lunch, I'd go and give him a massage. Then I'd give Swami Turiyananda a massage. I was good at it. One day Maharaj said, "Go give a massage to Swami Premananda." He was lying on his bed. He would never accept personal service from anybody; that was his principle. But Maharaj sent me. I sat on his bed and began to massage his feet. He got up and said, "Get away from me! Go to Maharaj. Get away, get away!" I said, "Oh no, Maharaj has ordered me to give you the massage." There was some tug of war between us for some time. You see, I was quite a young boy, seventeen years old. Then he said, "Oh, you win!"

After two months Maharaj went away to Kankhal, the Ramakrishna Home of Service at the foot of the Himalayas. It was during the month-long Durga Puja vacation, and I had no intention of continuing my studies. I just ran away from college. My father had sent money for the college fee and boarding expenses, but I wrote him, "Send my brother and pay off all these debts and take away my books." I was going to Maharaj at Kankhal.

I broke my journey in Benares. I thought Swami Turi-yananda was there, but he was not, and I didn't know anybody. In that period there were boys with the revolutionary party, so our monasteries had to be very careful about accepting guests. The abbot was firm and said, "No, I can't have you here. We don't know you; you might get us in trouble." Then the abbot asked me, "Have you a letter from Maharaj? Did you write to him that you were coming?" I said, "No, I didn't let him know." "You must get his permission. Go back home." There was another young swami who took compassion on me and talked to the abbot. He let me stay there for two nights, and I took rest.

I arrived at Hardwar Station at about three in the morning. When I arrived at the *ashrama*, it was about four o'clock, still very dark. There are so many buildings in that *ashrama*, but somehow I went straight to one building. I didn't wish to disturb anybody, and as I was placing my blanket from my bundle at the door and was about to sit, Maharaj came out. Then his secretary came out from another door and Maharaj told him, "Here is a *brahmachari*, a novitiate. Make room for him." No questions asked.

I stayed on and had a great opportunity. The young *brahmachari* who was Maharaj's personal attendant at that time was to be engaged to learn the worship of Mother Durga, so Maharaj asked if I could take care of him for a month. Of course I was very glad to do that. But here is my first day's experience. Maharaj asked me to ask a boy servant to draw water from the well and heat it for his bath. I was sort of jealous of this boy and said to myself, "Why should I ask him to do that?" So I did it myself – drew water from the well and built a fire and had it all ready – but the water was very hot. When I told Maharaj it was ready, he asked me "Which vessel did you use to heat the water?" I said, "One of those." "Oh no,

I have a special vessel for that." So, you see, I didn't obey his first order, so the whole thing was rejected. The boy servant had to do everything anyway.

This was the time I received Maharaj's grace: he initiated me. One day I was feeling hungry for Bengali sweets, which you can only get in Bengal. Maharaj said, "You know, if you just chant the name of the Lord and wish for anything, it comes." I was wishing for the sweets, you know. So he chanted – he counted – and within an hour three Bengali women came with sweets of different kinds. From my boyhood I was sort of a doubting Thomas, so I approached these women and said, "Did you tell Maharaj that you were coming?" They said, "No, we wanted to surprise him." Then I asked them, "Do you ever bring the sweets you brought this time?" "No, this is the first time. We wanted to surprise him." Of course I knew he was not surprised.

After the worship of the Divine Mother, there is an immersion ceremony. It was to be in the Ganges. All the swamis went, and many boats were hired. Maharaj stood on the bank of the river and didn't go, and I stayed with him. He said, "Aren't you going?" I said, "No." In the evening Maharaj had the habit of having Ganges water sprinkled on him. He would stand at the time with closed palms and think of the Lord for a length of time. That evening he wanted me to take some Ganges water from the river and sprinkle it on him. I took that opportunity to prostrate before him. We all consider it a very sacred occasion to prostrate before the guru by the Ganges.

I wanted to join the monastery, but he said, "No. You had better go back home and finish your university education. Then come." So I had to go away. And then I got mixed up with politics and joined the revolutionary movement. But I still kept in touch with the monastery and with Maharaj.

I continued my studies. Swami Brahmananda was at Belur Math. It was the year 1914 during Christmas vacation. I came again to study Vedanta with a disciple of Swami Vivekananda, Swami Shuddhananda, who was a great scholar. During that period I had no idea of joining the monastery. I had made up my mind to fight the British and get them out of the country. This Swami used to argue with me; he wanted me to join the monastery. I'd argue against him, saying, "Oh, you swamis are lazy people. You're not following what Swamiji wanted the people of this nation to do." He couldn't convince me. Then one day an old man who used to be present during our discussions followed me when I went to prostrate before Maharaj – every morning we used to bow down to him. As I went this day, this old man asked Maharaj, "When is this boy going to join the monastery?" Maharaj was silent for a minute. He looked at me, up and down, and said, "Whenever the Lord wills." And all my ideas were revolutionized. Immediately I made up my mind to join the monastery. I didn't tell Maharaj anything, but I went down and told Swami Shuddhananda, "I've joined the monastery." He said, "What?" "Yes, I have joined." "Have you told Maharaj?" "No." And so I stayed on.

At that time I dragged one of my friends from the college and he also joined the monastery. And then, within a month, the *brahmacharya* ceremony was to be held and all the boys who would be given vows were asked to get permission from Swami Premananda. He looked at us and said, "You don't have to ask any permission." So he gave us *brahmacharya* after a month.

During this period I remember two incidents. One was that there was to be a trustees' meeting; the disciples of Ramakrishna were the trustees at the time. Of course Swami Brahmananda was the president and Swami Premananda was the vice-president; Swami Saradananda was the general secretary. The morning of the trustees' meeting, Swami Saradananda, who stayed in Calcutta, came to Belur Math. When he came, I happened to be present. He asked me, "Where is Swami Premananda?" I said, "He's upstairs. He's gone to the shrine to meditate." You see, Swami Premananda did not want all these meetings, so in order to avoid this one, he went to meditate in the shrine. Swami Saradananda went upstairs – I followed him – and he got hold of Swami Premananda, who was meditating in seated posture, and quietly lifted him up and carried him downstairs; he just threw him into the courtyard. You know, they're full of fun, these people. And then he stood and began to dance as if in *kirtan*, singing a sentence from a song. And then Maharaj, Swami Turiyananda, Swami Shivananda, all the disciples of Sri Ramakrishna gathered immediately from nowhere. And Maharaj became the center. They began to dance in ecstasy; they were all in ecstasy. Maharaj was improvising words and they were repeating and singing for thirty minutes or more. Then of course they had the trustees' meeting later.

Another incident I remember during that period is the following. Two young boys who joined the monastery had fought with one another. First words, harsh words, and then they came to blows. I was seated by Maharaj, and Swami Premananda came to him and said, "Maharaj, you know how much love we have for one another. Did we ever pass any harsh word between us? But you see these boys have come to blows. We must get rid of them." Maharaj looked at him and said, "They didn't come here perfect, they have come here to attain perfection. You are here to transform their lives." Then Swami Premananda said, "Yes, brother, you are right." So he went out and called all the swamis and *brahmacharis* and brought them to Maharaj with folded hands: "Maharaj, you have to bless them all." And then he ordered them one by one to bow down before Maharaj. Maharaj was in a great spiritual mood. He just put his hand out over the head and did something very difficult to explain.

My parents objected to my joining the monastery, but I would not go back home. They said, "Why not come just for a little visit?" So I went. Maharaj was living in Calcutta at Balaram Mandir, and I went to see him. I had my head shaven, you know, and the son of Balaram Babu was seated by Maharaj. Maharaj introduced me to him, and then he wanted to prostrate before me. I wanted to prostrate before him – you see, he was an older man. And then Maharaj got hold of me and put his hand on my bald head and made a little fun. But, as he did so, an electric current passed through my whole being. That's all I can say. Anyhow, I went home, and then it was very difficult for me to come away. I had no money, so I asked a friend to give me some. While everybody was asleep, I left the house stealthily, went to the railway station, and bought a ticket. As I got into the train, somebody dragged me down. It was my brother. He said, "Mother is weeping. Come back and then in a few days, go." So I had to go back. Then, of course, Mother also agreed.

Paresh Maharaj was the friend I had dragged with me to Belur Math. Maharaj asked Paresh, "Say, what is happening to your friend?" "He has not written me, he has not let anybody know, so I believe he's not coming back." Maharaj said, "No, he will be here this morning." And, sure enough, I came that morning.

Then Maharaj sent me to Mayavati in the Himalayas and I was there for two years. I felt very lonely and the abbot of the monastery didn't want me to go, but I wrote to Maharaj and he gave me permission to come back. But the abbot was mad at me and wouldn't give me enough money to go to Puri, where Maharaj was living. He gave me enough money to go to Calcutta, and then of course a little extra for my food. You know, I used this little extra for my train fare and arrived at Puri, where Maharaj was.

One morning, Swami Shankarananda, Maharaj's secretary, handed me a bill and said, "Take it to the railway station and give it to the station master." On the way I met the young *brahmachari* who used to do that job. I asked him, "This was handed to me. What am I to do?" He said, "Oh, there's nothing to do. Just give it to the station master, and when the basket comes, he will send it." So I handed it to the stationmaster, and, as I was coming back, I approached the gate. I saw all the swamis watching, waiting. Somebody asked me, "Where is the fish?" I said, "Fish?" Then Maharaj's secretary took a cab and went to get the fish. It was to be cooked for Maharaj's lunch. The whole day – that was the first time – Maharaj just went after me, scolding and scolding and scolding. "He has no intelligence." Like that, he went on. I just listened; in my heart I knew I was innocent, but I didn't say a thing. In the evening, when Maharaj and Swami Turiyananda were having their supper outside, I was fanning to keep away the insects, and Maharaj was still going on. I kept quiet. And then Swami Turiyananda said to me, "Do you understand why Maharaj is scolding you?" I said, "Frankly speaking, I don't." Swami Turiyananda said, "You see, the disciple is asked to do something, and he does it. That's a third-class disciple. Then the disciple can read the thoughts of the guru and does it. That's a second-class disciple. Before the thought has arisen in the mind of the guru, the disciple accomplishes it: that's a first-class disciple. Maharaj wants you to be a first-class disciple." Then Maharaj – his comment was very interesting – said, "Yes, brother Hari, I have become very old, so they don't obey me. You pour a little intelligence into their heads."

One day in Puri, I was seated in a big hall; I saw Maharaj walking up and down. Always when Maharaj walked up and down, he would be in a very high spiritual mood. The whole monastery would vibrate with spiritual fervor. He looked very compassionately at me, and the next morning I received a letter from my mother that father had passed away. I read the letter to Maharaj. Later I felt that when he was walking up and down and looked at me the day before, he knew my father had died, and he was giving him liberation. That's my personal belief.

You know, after a father or mother dies, the sons and daughters are supposed to observe the occasion by cooking their own meal in one pot. In one pot rice, dal or lentil, and any vegetables are cooked together. You are not allowed to sleep on a bed, but on straw. The idea is to pray and live a very pure life, think of God, and pray for the departed soul. Maharaj had said, "You don't have to do anything, you are a *brahmachari*." And then again he said, "Take *prasad* from the Jagannath Temple." And then he said, "Take my *prasad*." So I was there for three or four days, and suddenly Maharaj looked at me and said, "Why are you here? Go to your mother." He bought the ticket and sent his secretary to put me in the car with food from the Jagannath Temple. When I arrived home, my mother and brothers and sisters said to me, "Something happened. As soon as you came, our grief was turned into joy." All grief was gone. It became a festive occasion. So, Maharaj must have sent something through me. That is my belief.

When I came back to Belur Math, Swami Premananda wanted me to remain as an assistant to Swami Saradananda and to learn the job of secretary. He told me, "We are getting old. You boys have to conduct the whole work. So stay with Swami Saradananda." I agreed. And then I got a letter from Maharaj saying to come to him immediately. I told Swami Premananda and he asked me, "Write to Maharaj that you won't go." I said, "I can't do that." Then he said, "What! You won't obey me?" I said, "When it comes to obeying Maharaj and obeying you, I have to obey Maharaj." Then – you see, his love was so great – he got excited and said, "Get away from me! I can't look at you!" And so I went and bought some shoes and when I came back, somebody said, "Go upstairs. He is waiting for you." Swami Premananda gave me some sweets and water and then asked, "Are you mad at me?" I said, "Why should I be mad at you?" "Well, I scolded you." "But, Maharaj," I said, "your scolding is a blessing." And really I always felt that way. Then he said, "Don't tell Maharaj that I scolded you. You see, this is the last you will see of me." And then he said, "Of course, I had some plans for you, but Maharaj has some others, so go."

As soon as I arrived at the feet of Maharaj, he asked me, "How is brother Baburam?" I answered that he was sick and suffering. And then he said, "Did he ask anything of you?" I answered, "Yes, he asked for some of the Lord's bathwater from the temple." Maharaj exclaimed, "And you have kept quiet! Such a great soul asking for such a little thing and you kept quiet all this time?" Then he turned to his secretary to get the *prasad* water and to send it to him immediately. He said to me, "Do you know how great he is? If he looks in one direction, that direction becomes purified."

After I was at Puri for some time, he sent me to Madras. You know he always considered me not very intelligent, not very practical, so he used to take care of me in a very motherly way. He was sending me to Madras, but he said to his secretary that since it was a long way to go, I must break my journey at such-and-such place. He wrote a letter to a disciple and asked him to arrange for my stay with him. One of the swamis said, "But he came all the way from Mayavati alone!" Maharaj would not listen to such a thing, so it was arranged that I would break my journey at Kokanadah (Present Kakinada) and stay at a disciple's home for three days. The Madras

Mail does not stop in that railway station, so Maharaj wrote to this disciple, whose brother was a member of the Legislative Assembly. The brother sent a telegram to the governor, and the governor sent a telegram to the superintendent of railways, and the Madras Mail had to stop for me. Then, later, it had to stop again to take me to Madras. I was the guest of some very rich people who had a special guest house. They engaged a cook especially for me, because they knew I didn't eat hot food. They advised the cook not to use chilies, but even the morsel of food I took, cooked especially for me without chillies, burned from here to there! (86)

I'll tell you why Swami Brahmananda was called Maharaj, Raja-Maharaj. While Sri Ramakrishna was lying on his deathbed, he organized the Ramakrishna Order. That was the time when all the young boys got together in order to serve their master. Of course Sri Ramakrishna was training Vivekananda to become the leader, apostle, and during that period, he said, "Rakhal has the intelligence of a king to rule over a kingdom harmoniously." So Vivekananda came down and announced to all the disciples gathered together, "From today, Rakhal is our *raja*, ('king')."

The great scientist Einstein read the life and teachings of Maharaj. One of our brother disciples went to visit him, and Einstein said, "Maharaj emphasized meditation." And this brother disciple said, "Well, he talked about work also." Then Einstein said, "Well, look here, as Maharaj said very well, 'You don't have to ask people to work, they will work anyway,' but he emphasized meditation: meditate, meditate, meditate."

Vivekananda used to say, "Look, Rakhal is Thakur's son, we are his disciples." A special regard was given him by all the disciples of Ramakrishna.

One time Sri Ramakrishna prayed to the Divine Mother, "Mother, bring me somebody who will be like myself, with whom I can talk, who can understand me, who can talk to me." The day before he came, Sri Ramakrishna had a vision of Sri Krishna dancing with a young boy. How sweet the vision was, how wonderful and beautiful! Of course he went into *samadhi*. And then Rakhal came by boat. As soon as Sri Ramakrishna saw him, he recognized him as the companion of Krishna with whom he danced, in his vision, and also as the one who would be like himself – his spiritual son.

Maharaj was considered a *nityasiddha*, ever-free. There were six disciples of Ramakrishna who were considered ever-free souls – that is, not just ordinary human beings who attained through struggle to the knowledge of Brahman, but were born with the knowledge of Brahman.[12] They come in every age with the divine incarnation for the good of mankind. Some came with Christ, some with Buddha, some with Krishna, again some with Ramakrishna – because there is one and the same God that incarnates in different ages, in different forms, and with different names. As such, the disciples are born with the knowledge of God also. This is what Maharaj told me one day: "I see everything as Brahman or God playing in so many masks: thief, murderer, saint, holy man." Everyone God, one God in so many masks – the mask of a wicked man, the mask of a saint. That is why these great souls never look down on anybody.

We read in the Upanishads: "Brahman is above, Brahman is below, Brahman is to the right, Brahman is to the left. Brahman before you, Brahman behind you. All is Brahman." [Chandogya Upanishad] Maharaj said to me, "When I am in that state,

---

12. The six are: Swamis Vivekananda, Brahmananda, Premananda, Yogananda, Niranjanananda, and the householder disciple, Purna Chandra Ghosh.

who am I to teach whom? Can God teach God?" Then he said, "I come down to this normal plane, and then I see your mistakes and I correct you." But when he came down to the normal plane, it was not exactly normal; he was always living in God. In other words, he lived in two states. In one state he would see Brahman everywhere, he himself would be Brahman, that is, the nondualistic experience. And then again, in the lower state, he would be a devotee of God, that is, the dualistic attitude. I am going to tell you of this dualistic attitude.

When Maharaj was in Madras, he wanted to go to headquarters, so he asked me to get an almanac and find an auspicious day for leaving. Of course we young boys used to think that was superstitious. Anyway, I brought the almanac, and then he said, "Find out between such-and-such dates which is the auspicious day to leave." I began to laugh. He said, "Hey, what's the matter with you, laughing like that?" I said, "Well, Maharaj, you will look at the date and settle on one, but I know you are not going then." And he said, "What can I do? These people are pressing me all the time when I shall go, so I have to satisfy them; but I don't do anything unless I get the direct order from God, unless I know the will of God." And then I cross-examined him. I said, "Do you mean to say that for everything you do, every moment, you ask the Lord, you see him? You know, we also may think intuitively that something is right and it is the will of God; is that what you do?" "No." "Do you see him and talk to him and he tells you everything?" He said, "Yes." Then I asked, "Well, that you accepted us as your disciples, did the Lord tell you to do that?" He said, "Yes." Just think how I felt at the time – that the Lord knows about us through him! I often remember that.

After his *mahasamadhi,* the first monks' conference was held. There were many disciples of Ramakrishna living, and the younger swamis and *brahmacharis* gathered together.

Swami Saradananda, a direct disciple, who was then the general secretary of the order, said, "From now on, whatever we ask you to do, do not accept immediately, but reason it out. And if you think it is not right, come to us again and talk it over. While Maharaj was living, whatever he said, without any question we obeyed, all of us, because we knew that that was the will of God."

One day, which was the special celebration of the Divine Mother, our monastery invited swamis and monks from many different orders to come and partake of the *prasad*. Maharaj had a special chair, and I did not want anybody to sit on it, so I took it from the house and way out onto the lawn. I had it upside down. Suddenly I saw an old monk sitting on the chair, so I ran to him and said, "Oh, please, you cannot sit there. That's Maharaj's seat." "Oh, Maharaj won't mind." Then I said, "But I do. *I* mind!" Then he said, "If I don't get up, what will you do?" I was getting excited; I took his hand and lifted him up. He got up, smiling. Then I went to prepare seats for everyone and I got Maharaj's special chair. That is when he said, "Oh, no, no, no, no, the same seat for everybody. There are two holy men here who are knowers of Brahman." This old man, you see, was talking to Maharaj, and I was standing there. I couldn't follow what they said (they were speaking in Hindi), but I knew they were having a good laugh at my expense.

In Madras my master's disciplining of me went on for three months. I usually felt joy inside, but one time I got a little tired and thought I'd just run away. So I came to bow down in the morning, and as I was backing out, he said, "Come, sit down. Do you think you can run away from me? The Mother holds the child on her lap and spanks it. The child cries, 'Mother! Mother!'" Then he said, "Our love is so deep we do not let you know how much we love you." (88)

Maharaj wanted to send me to live in Allahabad with another disciple of Ramakrishna, Swami Vijnanananda. Maharaj told me that he was a knower of Brahman who kept himself in hiding and didn't let anybody know that he was great. To prove how great he was, and what a great devotee of Ramakrishna he was, Maharaj told me a story: "You know how greatly devoted to Ramakrishna he is? I was visiting his ashrama, and a young boy came and wanted instructions. I said, 'I'm nobody here. There is the abbot, go to him.' And so the boy went to Swami Vijnanananda who said, 'I am the abbot here, but look, he is the head of the whole organization. Go to him.' So the boy came back, and again I sent him back to Swami Vijnanananda. Do you know what he did? He said, 'Wait, I'll give you instruction.' He went to his room, opened a trunk, and brought a photo of me (Maharaj). He gave it to the boy and said, 'Every day before this photo pray to be guided, to be instructed. I don't know any higher teaching than that.'" And then Maharaj said to me, "Do you see what a great devotee of Ramakrishna he is?" You see, there was no distinction in him as separate.

One time Maharaj had to sign a document. After three or four days, his private secretary said, 'Maharaj, this is the last day. I have to give that document back. Please sign it." Maharaj said, "I get confused about my name, what to sign." You see, he was so identified with Ramakrishna. (88)

There is a prayer written by Shankara to the guru. In that prayer he describes the guru and how the guru teaches his disciples. In one of the verses he says that the guru is seated under a tree in silence. The disciples are seated around him in silence. The guru is young; the disciples are old. Doubts are being dispersed; knowledge, wisdom, is dawning in them, and their hearts are becoming filled with the bliss of the presence of God. The guru is young, because the truth that is eternal is ever young. The disciples are old, because doubts and superstitions, the karmas of many, many past lives, are old. But all doubts are dispersed, knowledge dawns, hearts become filled with bliss of the presence of God.

This fact I have witnessed in the life of my master. He would remain seated silently, his disciples seated around him. Sometimes he would speak, but not of God. He would make fun, cut jokes, and make us laugh. And then again there would be silence, complete silence. As you went out of the room, all doubts had gone, all problems had suddenly been solved. This I witnessed from day to day: that in his presence he made us feel that the realization of God is not only the goal of life, but so easy, like God were the fruit in the palm of our hands. We could feel that.

And then another great characteristic I have witnessed is that wherever he would go – from one monastery to another, and he would stay for some months in each monastery – there would be festivity. All the time it would be full of joy. Whoever entered within a certain orbit would feel that joy, as if on a festive occasion. Even when Maharaj would chastise us with harsh words, thundering at us, even then there would be a current of joy inside us.

Once a professor from Colombo came to visit our monastery. After one week he said, "I can't stand the atmosphere anymore. I want a little worldly atmosphere. I don't know what kind of people you are, you boys, but if you can stand him from day to day like this, you must be great!" The fact is, I came to him as an adolescent. I tried to think lustful thoughts and I couldn't. Lust and greed, such ideas, would not arise in your mind, such was his power. Of course these are rare souls.

When Maharaj came to Madras the first time, Swami Ramakrishnananda was the abbot. In Southern India they are crazy about lectures, just as in this country. So some people came to inquire when Maharaj was going to give a speech. Swami Ramakrishnananda said, "Look here, he speaks to us just one sentence, and we expound that sentence for years before you! What would you understand if he speaks?" You see, religion is something that is transmitted in silence.

He just put his hand over the head of each one of us and something happened to everybody. I can speak of my own experience, and that was as if my body was burning in great heat and a cool spray of water went over it, soothing it. Thus it was that these great souls could transform the lives and characters of people.

While Maharaj was living, if somebody went astray, the one punishment was, "Come and stay with me." I must say, that is not as easy as it sounds. The soil must be ready. For instance, in the life of Sri Ramakrishna we read how many visitors would come, and only a few of them would be interested to sit by him. The others would get restless and say, "When are you going home? We will wait in the boat." In the same way we have seen people want, and yet couldn't see anything, couldn't feel anything. They were not ready.

In the scriptures we read, "Not by study, not by learning, not by austerities, can you find God, but whom he chooses, by him is he known." Now again, whom does he choose? Is he partial? No. He who longs for him. In other words, you have to be a *mumukshu*, one who is desiring. But I must confess that I was not a *mumukshu*. All I knew was that I had read *The Gospel of Sri Ramakrishna* when I was a boy of fourteen or fifteen, and the names Naren and Rakhal attracted me. I don't know why. Naren was gone, but Rakhal was living: that is what attracted me. And then he gave me, he gave his disciples, that desire, that longing. He said to me, "What is to be done for you, I have done already; but if you want to enjoy bliss while living, you have to struggle, you have to work hard." But in my experience I have seen that through his grace, without much struggle, he gives, he fulfills, me.

While I was at Puri, Maharaj gave me the charge to take care of two young women who were his disciples: to take them to bathe in the ocean, to take them to the temple, in other words to show them the place of pilgrimage. One day they wanted to go visit the famous monastery established by Shankara, but they did not dare approach Maharaj. They asked me to ask permission of him. His reply was, "Shankara. Shankara will give you liberation. Go and meditate!" Of course these women ran away! And he told me, "Meditate, meditate, meditate. Then you will find that people suffer for no reason when there is the mine of bliss in everyone's heart. Then your heart will go out in sympathy and compassion for everybody."

He emphasized what is known as the easy path to realize God. That is to keep recollectedness of God as often as possible. You see, we pass our time idly. We have time for everything else – we can sit and gossip for hours – but we have no time to meditate! That is the situation. But if you are a spiritual aspirant, the best method is to keep remembrance of God as often as you can, and remembrance means to feel the presence of God. Of course Maharaj emphasized work also – work and worship, work and meditation. As he said, "With one hand hold on to God, and with the other hand work."

While I was in Madras with him, and knowing how all the disciples of Ramakrishna practiced hard austerities, I was inclined to practice austerities also. So one day I asked his permission. He told me to go to such and such place, and he fixed a date for me to go. I didn't realize at the time that he did not mean it, and so I made every arrangement to go. I had my blanket all folded and tied and ready, and when I came to say goodbye to him, he asked, "Where are you going?" He got nervous like your own mother. He said, "The boy is going astray, running somewhere!" And as if he could not manage alone, he said, "Get Tarak-da (Swami Shivananda)."

Maharaj told him, "You see, brother, what a foolish boy this is! He says he wants to practice austerities. What does he know about austerities? And why does he have to practice austerity? We have done all that for him!" He went on talking for three hours, and all the swamis and *brahmacharis* of the Order came. For three hours he talked about many things of spiritual life. And then I followed Mahapurush Maharaj (Swami Shivananda) out and he said to me, "You poked the honey comb; I learned many things I did not know."

When Swami Shivananda became the next president, after Maharaj's passing away, he never considered himself president. He had the shoes of Maharaj, he said. "He is the president." That is, his brother disciples had such regard for him.

After my master's passing away, I wanted to practice austerity in Almora, in the Himalayas, and Mahapurush Maharaj, who was then president of the order, gave me permission. I was getting ready when they called me back. The result was that I came to this country. So here they sent me to practice austerities!

You know, when Maharaj was practicing hard austerities, there was another great soul who used to visit Sri Ramakrishna. He said to Maharaj, "Why do you have to practice such austerities? Didn't the Master do everything for you?" He said, "Yes, that's true, he did everything for us. But I want to make it my own."

He lived in *samadhi* in the normal state. One time I was arguing with my brother disciples about some experiences or visions that Gopaler-Ma had. I said, "Of course those visions were in *samadhi*, when he was in ecstasy." Maharaj heard us arguing, and when he heard that, he came out of his room and said, "Ah, I see you have become omniscient!" Then I said, "Maharaj, do you meant to say that with these eyes one can have such visions?" He said, "Show me a line of demarcation where matter ends and spirit begins." You see, it is that we don't see the spirit, we don't see God, we see matter. But there is no such thing as matter. When the eye of the spirit opens up, then everything is spirit. We have seen how Maharaj lived in that blissful consciousness and at the same time carried on his duties as president of a vast organization.

When we first joined the monastery – we were the largest number of young boys to join, twenty-four of us at one time – one of the older disciples of Swamiji came to Maharaj. I was seated nearby and heard him say, "Maharaj, we must make some new rules for the conduct of these boys." Maharaj said, "But didn't Swamiji make some rules already?" "Yes, that's true, but not enough." Then Maharaj said, "Look, you don't need rules. Enough rules. What you need is to intensify your love for others." And so our order was founded on the basis of love. But of course now they have made rules and regulations. I am not aware of what they are.

Maharaj's place amongst the disciples was unique. Swamiji was the chief disciple, and Maharaj was the spiritual son. When Swamiji came back from this country to India, the first thing he did was to give Maharaj all the money he had gotten to build a monastery. He said, "Now, this is your property. You keep it." And then he prostrated before him, saying, "The son of a guru is to be regarded as guru." And Maharaj also bowed down to Swamiji, saying, "An elder brother is to be regarded as the same as the father." That was the relationship they had. And you know, often when Ramakrishna would look at Naren or Rakhal, he would go into *samadhi*, just seeing either of them. Just think of that!

Remember that Sri Ramakrishna had a vision about Maharaj before he came, that he was dancing with Sri Krishna. One day when he prayed to Mother, "Mother, bring me somebody who is like me," he saw Divine Mother Kali placing a little baby on his lap, saying, "This is your son." He was shocked and said, "My son? Everybody is my mother, how can I have a son?" And the Divine Mother smiled and said, "Not in that sense." So he was regarded as *manasaputra*, spiritual son.

Religion or God remains an unknown quantity. We have scriptures, but there must be living examples. The truth has to be demonstrated. These examples are the children of light, light themselves. Sri Ramakrishna used to say they are like doors and windows through which you peep into the Infinite. Before Maharaj passed away, he declared, "I am the bridge that spans the chasm between man and God." And of course liberation is very little. Maharaj taught us, "Pray for devotion, pure devotion and supreme knowledge." When you come to that, it is all the same.

One day I complained to him, "You teach us in five minutes and then you don't do anything about it." He said, "How do you know? If you practice what I have taught you, you will find that you are receiving help." This is the truth that I am telling you: the divine incarnations and their associates, these *ishvarakotis* or their associates, are still living. One can see them. They are still helping mankind. There is no barrier to him who seeks that help, whoever opens his heart. You see, there is good air on one side of a window, and bad air on the other side. Open the window. That is, if you begin to think of God and holy thoughts, you will find that you get greater help. If thoughts come to you, they become intensified. (89)

A guru of the highest order can recognize the past, present, and future of the disciple. In the life of Sri Ramakrishna you find that he knew the past, present, and future of each of his disciples intuitively, and then he corroborated that intuition through other means. I know that Maharaj also did that. For instance, he touched a disciple, who began to talk and went on talking without knowing what he was talking about or for how long. Then he became conscious and realized that he had been talking to Maharaj for a long time, but he couldn't remember what he had said.

In the scriptures we read that a combination of three things are needed. One is human birth, another is longing for God or liberation, and another is the association or grace of a holy man. Of course it is said that if you have the longing for liberation, then you meet your guru. But I must confess that I did not have any longing for God. It was the love of Maharaj that attracted me, and he infused that longing. That was the power that Maharaj embodied.

He said, "Swamiji did not want wandering monks, like the thousands of monks all over India; he wanted you to realize God and at the same time do selfless service for mankind." In that connection he pointed out, "Why make yourself restless to go here or there? He who finds him here (pointing to his own heart), finds him everywhere; and if he does not find him here, he does not find him anywhere."

The relationship between Vivekananda and Maharaj was most touching. One night he came to Maharaj and said, "Raja, these young boys don't know how to serve. I can't sleep. You take the fan, and fan me so I can sleep." And Maharaj fanned him all night. Swamiji slept deeply.

You know, just before his passing away, Maharaj did not know his true nature as the shepherd boy of Brindavan who danced with Krishna – Sri Ramakrishna kept that secret from him because he knew that if Maharaj knew, he would go. At the last moment, he had that vision.

I had the opportunity of seeing him dancing in a big hall in Madras. There was nobody there and he was dancing as if he were holding somebody. As I looked, I felt such a thrill. But then as he approached me, I felt a little nervous. I thought I was not pure enough, that he might lose that mood. So I closed the door and ran away. Later I thought I should have gone and prostrated before him and I could have received more blessings. Of course I received plenty of blessings. (90)

By learning to love one of the divine incarnations, one can attain divinity, perfection. Not only by loving one of them, but by loving any one of the *ishvarakotis*, the ever-free souls, one attains that. My master was an *ishvarakoti*. I remember once when I was arranging flowers in his room, he came and whispered into my ear, "Lovest thou me?" I was completely paralyzed. Through that, he gave me some power, and then twice he said, "Love me."

My Master did not care for study; he did not even pass the entrance examination. But his knowledge was unparalleled – on any subject whatsoever! An engineer would come and take some ideas from him. A businessman would come and take ideas from him. His intelligence was unparalleled. One time I was in the home of a well-known professor with Maharaj and Swami Turiyananda. The professor said to me, "You, being a graduate of the university, sit at his feet?" I said, "Look here, Mister, what knowledge have you got? You have studied some books and you have written a book, that's all. But they are knowers of Brahman. B.A.s and M.A.s and PhDs should roll at their feet!" (91)

When I was sent to this country, I was only twenty-nine years old. I asked Swami Shivananda, who was then the president, "What do I know?" He said, "You have seen the son of God, you have seen God!" I have seen religion transmitted through silence. Teachers of that type do more good to mankind than many preachers like myself, who become hoarse speaking. Yes, in silence, something is transmitted and you become renewed in spirit. I must say, it is not so easy as it sounds.

Any time we would feel that majestic greatness in Maharaj, he would do something, say something, and make us laugh and forget. Had that feeling continued in us, we could not have given him the personal service we had the privilege to give. He would be like one of us, he would come down to our plane and then give us a lift from there.

All of you are acquainted with the life of Christ, how multitudes followed him but only a few intimate disciples stuck by him. My master once said to us, "We have the eternal treasure to offer, but what do people come for? They come to us for potatoes and onions." How many really seek that eternal treasure? As Sri Ramakrishna used to say, we are enamored by this creation of God; very few want to know the Creator. One time Maharaj said to us, "They talk of joy of life, but what can people of the world understand by the joy of life? Where is the joy of life? Only in that which is infinite. 'In the Infinite alone is happiness; there is no happiness in the finite.'" He often said to us, "Give up the pleasures of a few days to attain that eternal joy, that abiding joy, which knows no sorrow." He emphasized meditation. As in all scriptures and the teachings of all great teachers, he emphasized, "Seek for the eternal amongst the noneternals of life. Seek for that highest abiding joy in the midst of the fleeting pleasures of life."

Though he emphasized meditation, he did not minimize service to others. What Swamiji pointed out, Maharaj also emphasized: See Narayana – see God – and serve God in every human being.

Whenever Maharaj would show the signs that he was about to go into *samadhi*, he would control it and would walk; at that time nobody could approach him. The whole monastery would be shaking. Only one time did I see him completely absorbed in *samadhi*. There was a convent run by an old holy man, who invited Maharaj to visit. Maharaj, Swami Shivananda, and Sri Ramakrishna's nephew, Ramlaldada, with Maharaj's retinue, went there. There was a big hall and many young nuns. They brought a vessel of scented water to the feet of Maharaj and placed it near him. Then they began to dance, singing a song to baby Krishna. As they were singing and dancing, they came and washed the feet of Maharaj and wiped them with their hair. Maharaj was absorbed completely in *samadhi*. They were singing the song to baby Krishna and pressing a vessel of milk to his lips. But of course he was in *samadhi*. The whole place was charged with something indescribable. He brought *samadhi*, as it were, into the normal plane. As Shankara has said beautifully: "Our perception of the universe is a continuous perception of Brahman, though the ignorant man is not aware of this." (*Vivekachudamani*, verse 521) Try to feel this, that what you are seeking, what I am seeking, all this is really nothing but Brahman.

The relationship between Swamiji and Maharaj was unique. Whenever Swamiji wrote to Maharaj, he wrote in Bengali, "My one unbroken heart." I happened to find a letter that Swamiji wrote to Nivedita which is very interesting. He wrote: "I recommend none, not one, except Brahmananda. That old man's judgment never failed. Mine always does. If you have to ask any advice or get anybody to do your business, Brahmananda is the only one I recommend. None else, none else. With this, my conscience is clear." (92)

I want to tell you why almost invariably I use this chant: "Our salutations to that Supreme Being who is one without a second." One time I was standing by Maharaj and he was chanting that prayer with his most musical voice. When he would chant the name of God, or any prayer, it would melt any heart. So that chant stuck in my mind.

Maharaj was seated in an easy chair and Sri Ramakrishna's nephew, whom we used to call Ramlaldada, was sitting in another chair. A young man who was also a disciple but not a monk had come to visit Maharaj and was seated on the floor by Maharaj. The young man asked, "Maharaj, tell us who you are." And Maharaj said, "Well, how do I know? You ask Ramlaldada." Ramlaldada said, "I don't know. Ask Maharaj!" I was thinking at the time, why do we have to know who Maharaj is? Then Maharaj looked at me, and I felt shy that he was going to ask me – so I just walked away.

You read something about a man, and you may form an opinion about him, but the inside feeling is something else again. When you meet the man, when you see the man and are in his presence, what you experience is what matters. To try to express to you when I first saw Maharaj – I was a lad about sixteen or seventeen years old – I felt a magnetic attraction, just as a moth would feel for the fire. You couldn't resist. And such love poured forth when he looked at me!

You may ask what the general characteristic was that I felt in his presence. To put it into words would be like a dumb man having a perfect dinner and trying to describe how it tastes. What can he say? When it comes to the spiritual domain, what you feel and experience you cannot utter, it is impossible to define. The characteristic we all felt was that he hardly talked, and yet he talked about many things, not only about religion or God. It is like a girl who is in love with a boy; she may be talking about many things, but her mind is on the boy. In the same way Maharaj's mind was in God, and one could feel that. I saw this from day to day. Every morning he would be seated in his room, where devotees, *brahmacharis,* and swamis would gather around him. We would have problems, but if you'd go and sit in his presence – you didn't have to tell him about your problems – when you came out, your problem would be solved. Everybody's experience was like that.

You see, religion is something that is transmitted. This is very hard to understand. We have the idea that we can learn of religion from a teacher teaching, lecturing, speaking – but that and books only arouse our interest. Real religion is something that is transmitted by an illumined teacher to the disciple, and that transmission is in silence, not in words. I have to convince you with reason and book knowledge, but go to a Christ and you feel the presence of God. Not only that, you feel that God is something that can be known and experienced. This man talks to God! You feel that way. And I can also talk to God. This is exactly what Maharaj made every disciple feel in his presence. There would be no question about the existence of God, but in the presence of the exemplar of God, you'd feel that it is so easy to realize God. That is the greatest feeling I can express to you. You felt the presence of God, and you felt you could realize God for yourself if you made a little attempt. Maharaj taught the same truths that you read in the Gita, the Bible, the Upanishads, the Koran – but when he spoke, it had a power. That is the difference.

He would make us very free with him. He would make fun and tease us, and then again at times you couldn't approach him. And the whole monastery would just be shaking. And you felt he was not of this world.

Maharaj taught: "Spiritual life begins after *samadhi.*" After you have the vision of God in *samadhi*, then you become a real benefactor to everyone. Then you can serve God in every being. You see, Maharaj pointed out how this *samadhi*, the supreme supernatural experience, is to be brought down, as it were, into the normal plane.

With our physical eyes what do we see but physical things, sensual things? But when you go into *samadhi* and attain the eye of the spirit, with that eye of the spirit you see God. And we saw that example in Maharaj. He would remain immersed in that bliss of God, and at the same time he would be very normal – he was the president of a big organization and he would conduct the work.

One time Maharaj was berating me; of course, he was giving me many teachings, but I said, "But Maharaj, I am hopeless. I can't do it. You don't help us. You only talk. You don't help us!" You know what he said? "How do you know that we are not helping you? First try to do what I have asked you to do. Make a little attempt. Then you will realize how we are helping you." In other words, you have to take one step, and then you will find the Lord is taking a hundred steps toward you. Self-effort is important! But ultimately it is grace. (93)

Let me point out my own experience and how I look upon it. You see, if we think of God with his glories and almighty power, it is very difficult to approach him. But I believe God comes to us as a friend, as one amongst us. And this is how I looked upon Maharaj. Whenever I'd be near him and any sense of awe would arise, he would say something or act in such a way that he would take away that feeling. He would be just like our own father, but more approachable than even our own friend. He used to make us laugh with his jokes. One time he said something and pointed out to another disciple, "Look how he is laughing: he giggles like a girl." Then he nudged me and, you know, I rolled on the ground in laughter!

Another time a devotee brought a tin of cigarettes – English cigarettes, fifty in a tin – and asked me to keep it. I knew Maharaj didn't smoke cigarettes, so we boys finished the whole tin. The next morning when I approached him, Maharaj said, "Hey, would you bring a cigarette for Ramlaldada?" I didn't know what to do. You see, the monastery was so far away from the shopping district that I couldn't run and buy some more, so I just stood still there, and he got the whole idea. He said, "You see, Ramlaldada, we have a saying that the mother who is pregnant is given some special food and privileges, and she receives them in the name of the baby. But in this case, it is just the opposite: in the name of the Mother, our babies get things."

The writer of *The Gospel of Sri Ramakrishna*, M., told one of my brother disciples, "Look at Maharaj when he is in a very light mood, when he makes fun. Watch him. Sri Ramakrishna used to do that with the young boys after he came down from the highest *samadhi*. Maharaj is like that, too, so watch him during those periods."

What is it that attracted all the disciples of Maharaj? They will all say with one accord that it was his love. He was a magnet, a great attraction. One day I asked Swami Subodhananda why we felt that attraction – that Maharaj loves us more than our own parents and friends. His answer was, "God is love, and that God is manifest in his heart. As such, you see that love, you feel that love."

It is very difficult to recognize the greatness in the great, to recognize a holy man – unless he reveals himself. I must be frank about it, we disciples did not see as much greatness in Maharaj as his brother disciples saw. One time Maharaj said something that I thought was just not right, but Swami Shivananda, who was also present, said, "Yes, Maharaj." As he came out, I said, "You are like a yes-man to Maharaj!" You know what he answered? "Look here. In Maharaj you see Maharaj. But what do we see? Sheathes of Maharaj – filled inside with nothing but Ramakrishna. That's what we see."

Why is that so difficult to recognize? Unless you have the longing for God and the desire for the truth, you don't see the inner life, inner unfoldment. You can't go by externals. I'll tell you an incident. Maharaj was a guest in Balaram Bose's house – he was a rich man who had oriental rugs, thick carpeting, and beautiful bedding. Maharaj used to smoke a brass hookah, which the disciples kept so polished it shone. A professor who had read *The Gospel of Sri Ramakrishna* learned that Maharaj was staying at Balaram Bose's house, so he came to visit. Just then Maharaj's attendant, Surji Maharaj (Swami Nirvanananda) was away. The professor walked in and saw Maharaj smoking that hookah amidst all sorts of luxury. He received a shock. He went out and sat on the porch and thought: "This is the spiritual son of Sri Ramakrishna. What did I expect to see? That he would live an austere, simple life. But what do I see?" Thus he was cogitating when Surji Maharaj came back and asked him if he would like to visit Maharaj. Of course he didn't say, "I already went into the room." He said, "Yes, I came to visit him." So he went in, and Maharaj talked to him. When he left the room, he told Surji Maharaj, "What a mistake I would have made if I had gone away, having received that first shock. I tried to judge a holy man with my ideas of holiness!" And then that professor became a devoted disciple of Maharaj.

This is what we have found out from our own experience. God and ever-free souls—Maharaj was such -- are still living and helping all of us who want help. I know Maharaj is not dead, but living, and he helps whoever seeks that help. These great holy ones are bridges that unite the known with the unknown. They help us to realize that which is unknown. (94)

SCRIPTURES

UPANISHADS

WHEN WE FIND that there is no happiness in the finite, that there is no freedom as long as we live within the limitations of our senses, when we come to such understanding, then we want to "seek for that eternal amongst the noneternals of life." We try to "realize that highest abiding joy in the midst of the fleeting pleasures of life."

Not many subjects have been dealt with in the Upanishads – only the nature of Brahman or God, the nature of the universe, and the nature of the Atman or Self. Always the emphasis is upon realizing the truth for yourself. To quote the seer of the Upanishads: "Hear, all ye children of immortal bliss: I have known that truth. Having attained it, I have reached immortal bliss! In the same way, you also, having known that truth, go beyond all darkness." [Svetasvatara Upanishad] That is the spirit of the Upanishads – to attain that knowledge of Brahman, to go beyond the bonds of ignorance and be free.

In different Upanishads (or even in the same Upanishad) are different ideas about the relationship between Brahman and the universe. A scholar will try to force one meaning and ideal because he wants no contradictions. But, you see, the Upanishads are revelations, not ideas thought out. Their authors, called "seers," record what they see, and there are different stages of mystic experience, of unfoldment. Accordingly, you see their different pictures. Suppose you take a picture of the sun from here, then move up into a jet plane: they are different. But they are both pictures of the same truth. (95)

In the West the word *philosophy* means speculative thinking, a process. The proposition is to reach the unknown from the known. First the philosopher studies the universe and the mind, and from such study tries to come to an understanding as to the nature of reality.

For instance, Hegel, through reasoning, established that there is a reality, which he calls the Absolute. From our standpoint we would say that it is Hegel's idea or opinion, and as far as he goes, his process of reasoning is correct. Another philosopher comes along and says no, he is not correct, because in all processes of his own reasoning, he has come to another conclusion. They are both ideas. Is there any guarantee that either idea is a matter of fact? You may conceive with your eyes closed what this desk looks like, and you may come and touch it, but you don't know it. You come to a conclusion that it is this color, this size, and so on, but it is still an idea until you see it perfectly with all your senses. Theological doctrines and dogmas have developed and evolved throughout the centuries, but they are only opinions and ideas.

Eastern or Indian philosophy is defined as experience and not as a process of reasoning. So when I say the philosophy of the Upanishads, it may be misunderstood if we take it in the Western sense. The teachings of the Upanishads bring some effect in life: you realize that you are the Atman, which is immortal bliss, and you experience that immortal bliss. You experience infinite wisdom and have infinite love and compassion in your heart. These are the effects. (96)

Every religion is based upon revelation, every major religion has its revealed scriptures. The Hindus have the Vedas, the Christians have the Bible, the Muslims have the Koran. If we go to the source of every religion, we shall find that the revealed scripture does not claim that the revelation is limited to the books alone, but it is the Vedas which emphasize that the truth is to be revealed in each human soul. It is said that the Vedas are beginningless, meaning that God's revelation is beginningless and endless. It will continue – God's revelation is not finished – but will continue to be revealed in the hearts of mankind for eternity.

But revelation must not be accepted without question. True revelations can be verified: what cannot be verified is not to be accepted as revelation. If scriptures contain things which cannot be proved or which are impossible, they should not be accepted as revelation, but as symbolic. Revelation is beyond reason, but it is not unreasonable: it transcends reason, but it does not contradict it.

When I was a young boy of about seventeen, my master quoted to me a verse from the Upanishads which explains exactly what happens when we realize God: "The knot of the heart, which is ignorance, is loosened, all doubts are dissolved, all evil effects of deeds are destroyed, when he who is both personal and impersonal is realized." [Mundaka Upanishad] The knot of the heart that binds and limits us – ignorance – is loosened. Doubts continue in every one of us no matter how much faith we may have, but with this experience all doubts cease. You become a free soul. No karma resulting from what you have done in the past can bind you. That is what we have to achieve in life.

The Vedas are divided into two parts: the work portion and the knowledge portion. The work portion speaks of lower ideals: performing sacrifices, good deeds, and so on, so that you can enjoy life in heaven. But the Vedas point out that life in heaven is not the ideal: you may go to heaven for your good deeds and enjoy their effects, but after the exhaustion of their energy, you are thrown back into this world again.

So the ideal is to have knowledge of God, of the Self. Where is God? Within, without, everywhere. But only when you find him within can you see him everywhere. This is taught in the Upanishads, the latter or knowledge portion of the Vedas. The Upanishads are known as Vedanta, *anta* meaning the latter portion or end of the Veda.

All the different sects which have arisen in India since beginningless time are based on the Upanishads. Translated literally the word means "sitting near devotedly." Sitting near whom? Sitting near an illumined teacher. In other words, religion is not book learning. The Upanishads cannot give you religion, but one who has attained the wisdom of God can transmit that truth to you by showing the way, though you don't realize it immediately.

Another meaning of the word *upanishad* is "secret teaching." "Wonderful must be the teacher, wonderful must be the disciple." What is the main characteristic of such a disciple? Longing for God. When you have that longing for the truth of God, you find your guru, God comes in human form to teach you. That longing does not come all of a sudden; it comes only when you become completely desireless of anything else. Such growth has to come, and it is a great growth. When great yearning comes, immediately there is the vision of God.

Shankara gave the illustration, also given in the Upanishads, that we are walking all the time where a treasure is buried. If you say, "Come forth!" it does not. You have to take a shovel and dig, and go on digging until you hear the noise of your shovel touching metal. Then, having found the treasure, you are happy. In the same way, there is buried treasure within each heart. If we simply say, "God, come forth!" he doesn't come. You have to desire him earnestly. That earnest desire comes when we pray, chant his name, meditate, devote ourselves to selfless action, and make every action a worship of God. The two main disciplines from the Upanishads are mastery of one's own mind and meditation. Through meditation, of course, self-control comes.

Shankara gives us another meaning of the word *upanishad*: The knowledge of Brahman, the knowledge that destroys the bonds of ignorance and leads to the supreme goal of freedom. In other words, *upanishad* means "knowledge of Brahman" – not knowledge contained in books, but that which unfolds in your thought.

Just as I have a body and a soul, this whole universe is the body of God, and Brahman is the soul of the universe: "Heaven is his head, the sun and moon his eyes, the four quarters his ears, the revealed scriptures his voice, the air his breath, the universe his heart; from his feet came this earth. He is the innermost Self of all." [Rigveda]

Again we find: "Thou art woman, Thou art man, Thou art the youth, Thou art the maiden, Thou art the old man tottering with his staff; Thou art fire, Thou art the sun, Thou art the air, Thou art the moon, Thou art the fiery firmament, Thou art Brahman Supreme: Thou art the waters, Thou, the Creator of all!" [Svetasvatara Upanishad] He is the Creator, and again he is in his creation.

In another verse is brought out: "Filled with Brahman are the things we see. Filled with Brahman are the things we see not. From out of Brahman floweth all that is, From Brahman all, yet is he still the same." [Taittiriya Upanishad] He has not exhausted himself in the universe. He transcends the universe.

There is a story in the Upanishads of a disciple who came to his teacher and asked to know of Brahman. The teacher remained silent. The discipline asked him a second time, and a third time. Then the teacher said: "My boy, I have been teaching you all this time. You don't understand me. His name is Silence."

This reminds me of a personal experience. Sometimes when we sat at the feet of Maharaj with a doubt or problem, no opportunity arose to tell him. Maharaj would be speaking of mundane matters, or sometimes he would keep completely silent. But when we came out of the room, our problems would be solved. We have also seen how, in the silence of his presence, the mind was lifted up. At one time I consciously tried to think lustful thoughts, and I couldn't. Such was his power. So in silence the truth is given.

These are facts of experience. It is not that you take these words and try to understand them intellectually, for they would have no meaning. You have to meditate to come to the experience. And there are varied experiences at different stages of growth. But the three states of consciousness – waking, dreaming, and dreamless sleep – have to be transcended. The ultimate experience is reaching that whose name is Silence. When you come out of that, you see everything as Brahman. Sri Ramakrishna said: "In that ecstatic realization all thoughts cease; one becomes perfectly silent; there is no power of speech left by which to explain Brahman." And again he said: "The jnani or follower of the path of knowledge analyzes the universe of senses, saying 'Brahman is not this, not that.' Thus does he attain the knowledge of Brahman. He is like the man who, climbing a stairway, leaves each step behind, one after another, and so reaches the roof. But the vijnani who gains an intimate knowledge of Brahman has his consciousness further extended. He knows that the roof and the steps are of the same substance. First he realizes that all is not, God is; next he realizes that God is all." Of course he realizes that within his own soul.

The Upanishads point out the difference between the individual self and the Atman, the universal Self that is identical with Brahman: "Like two birds of golden plumage, inseparable companions, the individual self and the immortal Self are perched on the branches of the self-same tree. The former tastes of the sweet and bitter fruits of the tree; the latter, tasting of neither, calmly observes." You see, we are tasting the sweet and bitter fruits of this tree of life, but the Atman, the upper bird, is observing calmly. "The individual self, deluded by forgetfulness of his identity with the divine Self, bewildered by his ego, grieves and is sad; but when he recognizes the worshipful Lord as his own true Self, and beholds his glory, he grieves no more. When the seer beholds the effulgent Self, the effulgent One, the Lord, the Supreme Being, then, transcending both good and evil, and freed from impurities, he unites himself with Him." [Svetasvatara Upanishad, Mundaka Upanishad]

The main question is how to achieve this. How is it to be found? "By the pure heart is he known. The Self exists in man within the lotus of his heart, and is the master of his life and of his body. With mind illumined by the power of meditation, the wise know him, the blissful, the immortal."

"None beholds him with the eyes, for he is without visible form, yet in the heart is he revealed, through self-control and meditation. Those who know him become immortal. When all the senses are stilled, when the mind is at rest, when the intellect wavers not, that, say the wise, is the highest state. This calm of the senses and the mind has been defined as yoga. He who attains it is freed from delusion." [Svetasvatara Upanishad]

The form of meditation is also given in the Upanishads: "Om is the bow. The arrow is the individual being. Brahman is the target. With a tranquil heart, take aim; lose thyself in him even as the arrow is lost in the target." [Katha Upanishad]

In one of the minor Upanishads, the disciple asks: "Master, teach me the knowledge of Brahman. I hear that this is the supreme knowledge hidden and sacred, sought by the wise, and that he who seeks it is freed from impurities and attains the supreme being." Just see, even he who seeks it becomes freed from impurities. The teacher says: "Seek to know Brahman by acquiring faith in the words of the scriptures, and in your guru. Be devoted to Brahman, meditate on him unceasingly. Not by work, nor by progeny, nor by wealth, but by devotion to him and by indifference to the world, does a man reach immortality. The supreme heaven shines in the lotus of the heart, they enter there who struggle and aspire. Understanding the spirit of the scriptural teachings, they renounce the world.

"Retire into solitude. Seat yourself on a clean spot and in erect posture with the head and neck in a straight line. Be indifferent to the world." Just you and God exist, nothing else. "Control all the sense-organs. Bow down in devotion to your guru, then enter the lotus of the heart and there meditate on the presence of Brahman, the pure, the infinite, the blissful.

"The mind may be compared to a fire stick, the syllable Om to another; rub the two sticks together by meditating on Brahman, and the fire of knowledge will burst into flame." [Svetasvatara Upanishad] (98)

BHAGAVAD GITA

The Bhagavad Gita is regarded as the Bible of India and is one of the most important scriptures of the Indo-Aryans. It has been translated into many languages. Most of you have probably had at least a glimpse of the book.

At the outset, as he opens the very first chapter of the Gita, a Western student is confronted with the problem of war.

There are people who are not in favor of any war, so they close the book. Then again, there are people who like to fight and feel they have got something here. I have known those who are in favor of war to quote the Gita in support of any and every war. But to us who have been brought up traditionally on the teachings of the Gita, war is incidental.

The Gita is primarily and fundamentally a *shastra*, that is, a sacred scripture that teaches how to attain liberation. It insists upon the performance of duty, and also how to rise above the very sense of duty. Every Hindu understands that duty is not the same for every individual. The one fundamental truth brought out in the Gita is that temperaments of individuals differ. All people are not equal; they are born with different characters, different tendencies and in different levels of growth and evolution.

There is, however, a fundamental unity in this diversity, a unity in the spirit, in God, that dwells within every individual. In the unfoldment of that divinity is the diversity. One duty, one teaching, cannot apply to everybody. Take, for instance, the ideal of non-resistance, which Jesus taught. Who can deny the ideal of non-resistance? Yet, if we insist that everybody follow this teaching, the lack of resistance of a coward who cannot resist because of lack of power will be seen as a virtue. You must first gather the strength to resist before you can practice that ideal. Every beggar wants to give away a million dollars: first have something to renounce before you talk about renunciation.

In the very beginning of the Gita we find Arjuna, the disciple, not wanting to fight. His words against fighting are most convincing. But what was his feeling? He talks like a wise man, but he was nervous and fearful. He was a coward. As he himself says: "O Krishna, as I look upon these men here ready to fight, my limbs weaken, my mouth dries up, my body trembles, and my hair stands on end; the bow Gandiva slips from my hand, my skin is burning, I cannot stand upright, my mind seems whirling round and round." By being a coward, you do not become spiritual.

The teachings of the Gita, then, have nothing to do with fights and battles. The central teaching is to become a yogi, which means to be completely united with God. In the words of Sri Krishna, the key to the whole teaching of the Gita is in giving up all formalities of religion and taking refuge in him alone: "Occupy your thoughts with me, be devoted to me." That is what we have to do – always, every moment, to live in union with God, to act with the consciousness of God.

The question is, therefore, what is God? What is the ultimate Reality? The Gita summarizes the teachings of the Upanishads. It is not exactly an independent scripture, but a summary of the sacred scriptures called the Vedas. The Upanishads are the records of revelation in transcendental consciousness. There are said to be one hundred eight Upanishads, so instead of studying the whole mass of them, you can study the Gita.

The conception of God that we find in the Gita is the same as we find in the Upanishads: Atman, the Self within, is one with Brahman. And the ideal is to realize this – not merely to say "God is within me" or "I am divine." It is by realization that we attain religion and understand the scriptures. The vision of the Reality is not to be experienced through the eyes of a saint, a Christ, or a Krishna, but by the Atman, by your own Self, just as you have to appease your hunger by eating for yourself.

Scriptures not only give you the truth, but also the way to reach that truth, to attain that ideal. There is one peculiarity in the teachings of the Gita. Other scriptures tell you how to attain God, but in the Gita we find not just one method, but a combination of all ways. Fundamentally, there are four methods, which we call yogas: karma yoga, the path of work; raja yoga, the path of meditation; bhakti yoga, the path of devotion; and jnana yoga, the path of knowledge. Any religion on earth can be classified within these four yogas, but in the teachings of the Gita alone, you find all the yogas, and you find the insistence that you make your life a harmonious combination of them all. There are four streams, and they all reach that one goal, the ocean of God.

First we find the insistence upon karma yoga, the performance of duty and work, activity. Each individual has heart and intellect which want to be active as well as tranquil. You can't sit idly, and at the same time you must gain tranquility; you must rest. You must have faith, but that faith must be based on sound reason and facts. So you must be active – laziness is not religion – but at the same time, you must learn tranquility and absorption in the consciousness of God.

Along with karma yoga, you have to learn to occupy your thoughts with God. As you do this, *dhyana*, the yoga of meditation, becomes simple; the mind naturally becomes inclined to think of God. In the Gita meditation is compared to a lamp sheltered from the wind; the flame is steady. That comes through purification of the heart through work: your mind stands steady in the presence of God.

Still, even that is not enough. When you learn to meditate, tranquility comes, and sweetness, devotion, and love come. There is one eternal reality – God. When you turn your love towards God, it finds its purpose and grows in intensity. It finds its fulfillment. This is called bhakti yoga, the path of devotion.

With bhakti yoga you attain to a stage which the Gita calls *sama darshana*; you begin to see oneness everywhere. You see the Atman, which is the Reality within you, as the Beloved within your own heart. You begin to feel that in the heart of everybody. You no longer see the distinction between a saint and a sinner. And that is the beginning of jnana yoga, the path of knowledge. It leads you to the ultimate vision, what we call *advaita darshana*, the vision of oneness. That is the ideal: you are divine, you are the Atman. Know yourself to be the Atman. All bondage, all limitation, is caused by illusion, ignorance. Remove that ignorance and you are God. [For full discussion on the yogas, see "Path of Meditation," "Path of Action," "Path of Devotion," and "Path of Knowledge." Ed.] (98)

TANTRAS

The word Tantra literally means "that which saves by that which spreads." It refers to the knowledge, by the spread of which all ignorance is dispelled and one attains freedom or liberation. The Tantras are regarded as the auxiliary scriptures of the Hindus.

First we have the Vedas, then we have the Smritis (the Puranas, the Tantras, and auxiliary scriptures). The Puranas illustrate the truth of the Upanishads by means of myths and by examples from the lives of saints, sages, and divine incarnations. The word *smriti* literally means "that which is remembered" – not direct revelation, but something heard and then written from memory. Tantras deal with the practical application of the truth as recorded from direct experience in the Upanishads. The Upanishads, being part of the Vedas, are the most authentic of the scriptures. The authority of the auxiliary scriptures depends upon their conformity with the revelations of the Upanishads.

There are three classes of Tantras, depending upon the deity chosen to worship – there are various conceptions of God or deities. This does not mean that there are so many

Gods, but that in one aspect or another one worships the One, Absolute, indefinable Truth.

There are the Vaishnava Tantras, for whom the deity is Vishnu, God as the preserver. But as one worships Vishnu in that aspect, the worshiper worships him also as the creator and the one who dissolves the universe. Then there are Shaiva Tantras, for whom Shiva is the deity. In Shiva the worshipers find all the aspects as one with Brahman. And then there are the Shakta Tantras, where the aspirants worship God as the Divine Mother. The Shakta Tantras are the most popular; it is these that we will discuss.

As I pointed out, the Tantras deal with the practical application of spiritual truths. They can be said to be religion in practice. It does not matter to what particular sect one may belong. In India all the practical spiritual disciplines adopted and practiced by the different aspirants are taken from one of the Tantras. One may be a Vaishnava or a Vedantist, or one may not belong to any religion, but in practice, the whole of India practices the religion of Tantra, because the Tantras give us the practical disciplines of worship and meditation.

There are three sections to the Tantras: the philosophy, the sadhana or spiritual disciplines, and siddhi – what is to be attained. We will first deal with the philosophy, which is based upon revelations in the Upanishads. In other words, it is nondualistic. Nondualism explains that the Atman, the Self within, is identical with Brahman.

There is a slight difference between the nondualism propounded by Shankara and the nondualism of the Tantras. According to Shankara the creative power is *maya*, which has no absolute reality. The creation that we find is an appearance, but that does not mean it is an illusion. Shankara points out that there are degrees of reality. Even the reality of a dream is real as long as we are dreaming, but it is unreal as soon as we wake up. For all practical purposes, this empirical experience of the universe is to be accepted as real, but it is only relatively real. It becomes unreal as we reach the absolute truth of oneness – of Brahman and Brahman alone. This, in short, is Shankara's philosophy.

The Tantras give absolute reality to the creative power. They call that power Shakti, or Mother – God the Mother. They point out that Brahman and Shakti are inseparable, as fire and its power to burn are inseparable. That is, the power to create, preserve, and dissolve is inseparably united with Brahman.

According to Tantra, Brahman has two aspects. In its transcendental aspect, there is no creation; Brahman and Mother are united. Now, Shankara's nondualism and Tantra are not contradictory philosophies, but Shankara refers to one aspect only. Tantra refers also to the immanent aspect of Shakti, the power that has become transformed as this multiple universe.

This Mother is described as having three gunas, and also as being beyond the gunas. The three gunas – sattva, rajas, and tamas – unfold as the universe. Every object in the universe of mind and matter is composed of the three gunas and can be reduced to these three energies. God the Mother is not bound by the gunas, and the whole universe, according to the Tantra, is her play. What you call good or bad, destruction or creation, are all the Divine Mother's play. Of course we dread destruction, but without destruction, there is no creation. In order for the plant to grow into a tree and bear flowers and fruit, the seed has to be destroyed.

And so we find that all these aspects – creation, preservation, dissolution – are attributed to the one Godhead, God the Mother. She is dancing the dance of creation, preservation, and destruction. As Sri Ramakrishna said, "When I meditate upon God, Brahman is at rest; then there is no creation, no preservation, just God alone. And when I meditate on God as the creator, then it is God the Mother" – the immanent God. But there are not two Gods, immanent and transcendent; it is one and the same, the only difference being the way you approach it.

Another very important idea brought out in Tantra is that in this whole universe of form, Mother's play is for two reasons. One is to give us the taste of an experience of enjoyment, and another is to give us liberation from everything. First there is *bhoga*, enjoyment; then there is complete detachment and the attainment of infinite, eternal, formless bliss. From atom to man we are all rushing towards that one goal – freedom and infinite bliss. As such, the different forms of life, from the mineral kingdom to the vegetable and animal kingdoms, are like so many stairs to climb into that height where there is no more form, but infinite, eternal bliss. The whole universe is running toward that.

Now we come to what are known as *sadhana* and *siddhi*. Sadhana literally means striving for a particular purpose or goal; attainment is called *siddhi*. Attainment is said to be freedom from the bondage of ignorance. Perfection, knowledge, divinity are not something you don't have; union with God does not mean that God is somewhere else and you have to go to him. God is within you, and your very nature is godly. All our striving and struggle, all the spiritual disciplines we have to practice, have that one purpose: to remove ignorance. The sun is shining, self-luminous, but clouds cover its luminosity. What is needed is a gust of wind to drive the clouds away. Without that gust of wind, the clouds will stay. So *siddhi*, or attainment, is the attainment of our own kingdom of God. Ignorance is a direct experience, and so is the attainment of the Atman or Brahman a direct experience.

The Tantras lay great stress upon what is known as *kundalini yoga*, the awakening of the sleeping energy within each individual. You find the philosophy of this serpent power elaborately explained in the Tantras. The principle is that there is a psychophysical relationship and that the divine energy, the Mother power, is coiled up, asleep, at the base of the spine. Along the spine are six centers of spiritual consciousness, the highest being in the brain, where Shiva or Brahman dwells. That Reality is directly experienced when the divine energy, the Mother power, becomes united with Father in the *sahasrara*, the thousand-petaled lotus in the brain. When union is achieved, there is the revelation of the truth of Brahman.

Sri Ramakrishna summed this up from his own experience in a few words. He said that the *kundalini*, the Mother energy, lies asleep at the base of the spine and that an individual ordinarily lives within the three lower centers: at the base of the spine, the root of the genitals, and the navel. As such, no higher thoughts, no pure thoughts, come, but attachment to worldliness – lust, greed, and power – remains. When spiritual awakening comes, consciousness is in the region of the heart. There one has the vision of God as formless, blissful light, and wonders at the beauty, the grandeur, and the great joy of that experience. Then when the *kundalini* reaches the next higher center in the region of the throat, that person becomes completely detached from worldliness and cannot bear worldly talk; the mind dwells in God. When the *kundalini* rises to the next higher center between the eyebrows, ecstasy is attained, and *samadhi*, a complete vision of God. But there is still a sense of duality, the sense of "I." The supreme truth of Brahman is experienced, but there is a thin glass partition, as it were. When that partition is gone and the *kundalini* becomes united with Shiva in the center of the brain, the individual experiences unified consciousness. Of course this experience is indescribable and indefinable.

The Tantras point out that in order to follow spiritual practices, we must be initiated by a competent teacher. We find two kinds of initiation. One is called *shambhavi*, the other *mantri*. I have no way to give English equivalents to these words, but in *shambhavi* initiation the guru just looks at the person, and the person becomes illumined immediately. Another kind of *shambhavi* initiation happens by a wish or a touch. Only *avataras*, divine incarnations, can give that kind of initiation.

Mantri initiation is with the help of a mantra – the word, God's name. The competent teacher transmits it in a seed form, which we call seed mantra. Spiritual power is transmitted with the help of that seed word. But of course the disciple has to chant and repeat that mantra in order for it to develop into a flowering and fruitful tree.

Individuals vary in capacity, temperament, and levels of growth, so Tantra has given different spiritual disciplines for the different grades of people. It has classified humanity into three general divisions: *divya*, or divine; *vira*, or heroic; and *pashu*, or animal. Accordingly, practices differ. The animal class has not yet learned any kind of control, so the advice for people of this class is to keep away from temptations and to devote themselves to worship and meditation.

The higher class, called the heroic, have attained some self-control. The mind of people of this class naturally flows more towards God than toward enjoyments, so the teaching that has been given them is to test their life of control – to live amidst temptations and at the same time to keep control and have thoughts flow towards God. Let me point out frankly that at a certain period in the history of India, in many people who thought they were this type, we find great degradation in the name of religion. Sri Ramakrishna reformed that aspect of Tantra by his practices of living in the midst of temptations and at the same time showing how to be above them by see-ing the motherhood of God.

Then there is the highest class of people called *divya* or divine. They have attained self-control, and their mind flows towards God and becomes absorbed in God.

There are four forms of worship and meditation in the Tantra. The highest is the meditation on the identity of the Atman with Brahman: "He lives absorbed in the conscious-ness of identity, unity, with Brahman." We find that aspect in Vivekananda. He could sit to meditate and become absorbed in that identity. That is the supreme way of worship.

Lower than this is meditation on the chosen ideal, in which the mind flows naturally towards God and there is no longer any distraction in the mind.

Next is what we call *japam*, chanting the mantra and trying to meditate along with the chanting.

The lowest class of practice is said to be ritualistic wor-ship. But let me point out that there are ways and means by which you can raise yourself to the higher levels. Some be-lieve that ritualism is religion and is an absolute necessity. For example, without attending mass, you cannot attain salvation. Another school of thought wants to do away with all kinds of ritualism. But as Swamiji pointed out, their ritu-alism is the book; it has become so heavy that they cannot think for themselves.

Tantra, which advocates ritualism, does not say that ritu-alism is necessary for everybody, but that for some to try to meditate on their divine identity would be like breaking their necks. As my master said, you have to go to the roof of the house, but if somebody throws you there, your limbs will be broken. So you have to begin from a lower rung of the ladder. From there, you are trained to move higher and higher into that supreme realization. (99)

BIBLE: THE NEW TESTAMENT

The Beatitudes

The central theme in the Beatitudes, as well as in the entire Sermon on the Mount, is brought out in one Beatitude: "Blessed are the pure in heart, for they shall see God." That is the central theme of all religions of the world: *for they shall see God.*

A disciple of Sri Ramakrishna once said to me that when he was a young boy studying the scriptures, he was trying to find out the purpose of living. One day he came across a passage in the teachings of Shankara: "A man is born, not to desire life in the world of the senses, but to realize and enjoy the bliss of an illumined soul." He said, "That fixed me. From that very moment, I was determined."

What is the way? Christ gives the main principle: "Blessed are the pure in heart, for they shall see God." The mind is restless, distracted, full of dirt and dust. God is within every one of us, but we are not aware of it. If a mirror is dirty, its reflection is not clear. Sri Ramakrishna used to say, "Weep and weep, so that the dirt of the mind can be washed away." What a simple truth.

You find many good and virtuous people in this world. They are moral and ethical, but that's not enough. Christ himself brought out this truth in one passage: "The Light of the body is the eye: if therefore thine eye be single, thy whole body shall be full of light." You see, that light has to be single. You will understand what that means immediately if I tell you something to experiment with: With a single eye, concentrate upon the presence of God. What happens? You can't do it. In a flash you can think of the presence of God, then your mind is distracted, thinking all kinds of thoughts, because your eye is not single. You have poured so many thoughts and deeds into your mind that it is full of impressions, and those impressions come out the moment you try to concentrate. You may say, "But when I try to concentrate on how much I have in the bank, other thoughts don't come to me!" True, because you are interested in that. In the same way you have to create an interest in God. Then your eye will become single.

Now let me read out to you: "And seeing the multitudes, he went up into a mountain: and when he was set, his disciples came unto him. And he opened his mouth, and taught them, saying, 'Blessed are the poor in spirit: for theirs is the Kingdom of Heaven.'" Just mark: *and seeing the multitudes.* You see, he went away to the mountains, and then only to his disciples did he give these supreme truths of religion. Almost every teacher has two sets of teachings. I learned this from a disciple of Sri Ramakrishna when I first joined the monastery. He said, "You know, the elephant has two sets of teeth – tusks and teeth. With his tusks, the elephant protects itself from enemies, and with his teeth, he chews his food and digests it." Similarly, these teachers have two sets of teachings: one to clear the path and create an interest, and the real teaching, which is given to the intimate ones.

"Blessed are they that mourn: for they shall become comforted." Sri Ramakrishna used to say, "Men weep rivers of tears because a son is not born, or because they cannot get riches, but who sheds even a single drop because he has not been fortunate to see the Lord?" For anything else you have to labor hard, and you may not achieve it, but here there is no failure, because the treasure is right within you. So weep, weep, and let the dirt and dust of your mind be washed away. That treasure is yours if you desire it. And you know, as you mourn for him, there arises intense desire, intense longing.

So Christ teaches: "Blessed are they which do hunger and thirst after righteousness: for they shall be filled." Sri Ramakrishna used to say "a hunger and a burning thirst." When that comes, when you feel you cannot live one moment without God, then you are filled. Of course that great yearning comes through the practice of spiritual disciplines for months and years. When anybody asked Sri Ramakrishna, "What is the way?" he would say, "Yearn for him with a longing heart." But this yearning is not so easy to have. It is a state of growth that has to come.

Righteousness does not mean moral virtues, but righteousness itself. When somebody said to Christ that he was good, he said, "Why call me good?" You see, God alone is goodness itself and righteousness itself. That is what is meant by righteousness: it is God.

Then: "Blessed are the meek: for they shall inherit the earth." This is the most difficult to understand. How do the meek inherit the earth? Who rules over empires? The meek? No. This meekness is the humility that comes when your heart is filled with the love for God. You become freed from the sense of vanity, from an ego. In this connection, there is a beautiful truth taught by Laotze: "Of all the soft and weak things in the world, none is weaker than water. But in overcoming that which is firm and strong, nothing can equal it. That which is soft conquers the heart; rigidity and hardness are companions of death. Softness and tenderness are companions of life."

Now, what does "for they shall inherit the earth" mean? As I said, empires were not built by the meek. Patanjali also says: "The man who is confirmed in non-stealing becomes the master of all riches." Stealing does not mean what we ordinarily mean by thieving, but that you steal if you even consider anything that you own or possess as yours, because nothing belongs to you, everything belongs to Nature or to God.

Next we find: "Blessed are the merciful: for they shall obtain mercy." Here again I quote a parallel passage from the Yoga Aphorisms of Patanjali: "Undisturbed calmness of the mind is attained by cultivating friendliness toward the happy, mercy and compassion for the unhappy, delight in the virtuous, and indifference toward the wicked." Just follow this. How does "undisturbed calmness of the mind" come? "By cultivating friendliness toward the happy." What happens, you know, is that somebody is very happy or gets something, and I become envious. But be happy with that person's happiness! Or if we are miserable, we sometimes become indifferent, so have mercy and compassion for the unhappy. Sometimes if somebody is virtuous and good, we don't like it. But delight in the virtuous. And if we see a wicked person, be indifferent.

"Blessed are the peacemakers: for they shall be called the children of God." It is the illumined souls, you know, that are the peacemakers. There is a beautiful truth in the Bhagavatam: "He in whose heart God has become manifested brings peace and cheer and delight everywhere he goes." I'll tell you an experience of mine as to how these great souls are peacemakers. When we first joined the monastery, Swami Premananda came to Maharaj and said, "Maharaj, you'll have to throw these two boys out. They're not only quarrelling, but they have come to blows. You know how much love we always had for our brother disciples, but they come to blows. Throw them out." Maharaj said, "Brother, they have come to you to transform their lives." And Swami Premananda said, "You are right, Maharaj." He then went downstairs and gathered all the swamis and *brahmacharis* together and they came in a procession to Maharaj. "Maharaj," he said, "bless them!" One by one everybody came and Maharaj held his hand out. What I felt was just like on a hot day when your body is burning and you take a cool shower. And peace was restored.

"Blessed are they which are persecuted for righteousness' sake: for theirs is the Kingdom of Heaven. Blessed are ye, when men shall revile you, and persecute you, and shall say all manner of evil against you falsely, for my sake. Rejoice, and be exceeding glad: for great is your reward in Heaven: for so persecuted they the prophets which were before you." What should the attitude of the spiritual aspirant be? Not to react. It is but natural that people of the world do not understand the life of a spiritual person. Of course they will say they do understand, and they think a spiritual person should behave in such-and-such way. If they don't, they persecute them. The natural tendency of people is to believe the worst of others. People do not understand that there is a possibility of motiveless love. We have lived with such holy men. Their love was enormous, something that you can't find in anybody else.

So what should our attitude be? Christ taught by his own life: "Father, forgive them, for they know not what they do." He taught to forgive, not ten times, but hundreds of times. I will tell you one instance from the life of Sri Ramakrishna which is higher than the idea of forgiveness. It was not human really, but something divine. There was a priest who became very jealous of Sri Ramakrishna for what Mathur Babu, the owner of the Dakshineswar temple, was doing for him. The priest thought Ramakrishna knew some kind of magic to charm Mathur Babu, so he approached Ramakrishna and asked, "Would you teach me that magic which you have used on Mathur Babu?" And Sri Ramakrishna said, "I don't know any magic. I have no secret." Of course the man didn't believe it and when he found Sri Ramakrishna alone in his room one day in ecstasy, he kicked him and kicked him until he fell down completely unconscious with blood coming out of his mouth. Of course, Sri Ramakrishna revived, but he didn't mention it to anybody for a long time. One day, in course of conversation, when that priest had been discharged from the temple for some reason or other, Sri Ramakrishna told Mathur Babu about the incident, and Mathur Babu said, "But Father, why didn't you tell me? I would have just killed that man!" "That's why I didn't tell you." And then he added, "Look, you can't blame him. I failed to convince him I was telling the truth." You see, he took the blame upon himself.

In the Bhagavatam there is a passage called the Song of the Mendicant. A monk is going through a village, and the boys in the village persecute him, throwing stones at him. He says: "Even if thou dost think another person is causing thee happiness or misery, thou art really neither happy nor wretched, for thou art the Atman, the changeless spirit. Thy sense of happiness and misery is due to a false identification of thyself with the body, which is subject to change. The Self is the real Self in all. With whom should thou be angry for causing pain, if accidentally thou dost bite the tongue with thy teeth?" What an attitude! (100)

I Am the Way, the Truth, and the Life

The goal is freedom! Freedom from the bondages of the pairs of opposites of life – birth and death. We have to realize that we are unborn and undying. We have to realize that we are filled with the bliss of God. This freedom is the goal, and in order to realize it we have to know the truth. This is known in the Upanishads as "the truth of all truths." There is nothing beyond that.

I am reminded of the rich man who came to Jesus and said he had followed all the laws and codes, but he found no peace. Christ said to him: "Sell all thou hast and give to the poor and follow me." But the poor fellow could not follow him because he had many riches.

The power to attain transcendental knowledge is in every one of us. In the Psalms we read: "As the hart panteth after the water brooks, so panteth my soul after thee, O God. My Soul thirsteth for God, for the living God: when shall I come and appear before God?" Jesus said: "Ask, and it shall be given you; seek, and ye shall find; knock, and the door shall be opened unto you: For every one that seeketh, receiveth; and he that seeketh findeth; and to him that knocketh it shall be opened."

But the point is, how many seek God? For those who are satisfied with what this world of senses can offer, the time has not come. It is not that they will be lost, but it is said that one will be born again and again until, through many experiences, through much frustration, at long last one realizes that to seek the eternal amongst the noneternals of life, to find the highest abiding joy in the midst of the fleeting pleasures of life, is the only goal of life.

As I said, how many seek him? Jesus says: "And he said unto another, 'Follow me.'" But he said, "Lord, suffer me first to go and bury my father." Jesus replied: "Follow me, and let the dead bury the dead." Another said, "Lord, I will follow thee, but let me first go bid farewell to those which are at home at my house." Jesus said unto him: "No man, having put his hand on the plow, and looking back, is fit for the kingdom of God."

But one has to be ready. The intensity of longing does not arise all of a sudden. In the teachings of Jesus there is a beautiful parable: "Behold, a sower went forth to sow; and when he sowed, some seeds fell by the wayside, and the fowls came and devoured them. Some fell upon stony places where they had not much earth: and forthwith they sprang up because they had no deepness of earth. And when the sun was up, they were scorched; and because they had no root, they withered away. And some fell among thorns; and the thorns sprung up and choked them. But others fell into good ground, and brought forth fruit, some an hundredfold, some sixty-fold, and some thirty-fold."

The question arises as to how to make ready the field. In the words of Jesus: "If any man will come after me, let him deny himself, and take up his cross and follow me. For whosoever will save his life shall lose it: and whosoever will lose his life for my sake shall find it. For what shall it profit a man if he shall gain the whole world and lose his own soul? or what shall a man give in exchange for his soul?" So the first condition is that we must learn to deny ourselves. What does this mean? This little ego.

Christ says: "Come unto me, all ye that labour and are heavy-laden, and I will give you rest." In *The Imitation of Christ* by Thomas-à-Kempis we read: "O Lord God, when shall I be made one with Thee, and be molten into Thy love so that I wholly forget myself? Be Thou in me, and I in Thee, and grant that we may so abide always together in one." (101)

Thomas, the disciple, once asked Jesus, "What is the way?" And the answer given by Jesus was, "I am the Way, the truth, and the life. No man cometh unto the Father but by me."

Naturally the question arises, "Way to what?" Of course both Jesus and the disciple knew that he was asking for the way to the knowledge of the truth and to the attainment of eternal life.

The Atman is the way, the Atman is the truth. Meditate on the Atman. How do you find the Father, Brahman? "By me." Within yourself. Nowhere else. You have to find that Reality, that God, within yourself. Then you find him everywhere. Religion is within yourself; that kingdom of God is within you. And it is "by me," by that Self alone, that you realize

Brahman. This is the attitude of the knower of the path of knowledge.

Christ is a perfect mirror in which to see yourself. Furthermore, this Christ is to be worshiped as one with the Atman, because, where is Christ but within yourself? "The Light shineth in darkness, and the darkness comprehended it not." That light is shining, Christ is there, hidden within every one of us, but we do not comprehend because of the darkness of ignorance. See Christ within your own heart. This we call the chosen ideal. Infinite is God and infinite are his aspects. You choose an aspect, and in that one aspect see all aspects. Then, for the follower of the path of love, "I am the way, I am the truth, I am the life," refers to his *ishtam* or chosen ideal.

When we come to an ultimate understanding of what "I am the way, the truth, and the life" means, or when we read the words of Krishna, "I am the end of the path, the witness, the Lord, the sustainer, and the place of abode, the beginning, the friend and the refuge," the devotee realizes that it is a growth in consciousness, that God is all in all. You know the prayer I repeat: "Thou art our loving mother, thou art our compassionate father, thou art our true friend and constant companion. Thou art our only wealth, and thou art our only wisdom. Thou art all in all." This is the understanding that has to come: "Thou art all in all."

Let me first explain what is meant by "I am the truth." Everything that I sense and perceive is true, but only for the moment; the next moment it is gone. But truth is the changeless Reality, the eternal Reality – call that Brahman or Atman or Christ. Whatever name you may give, there is one changeless Reality that is the truth. So there must be discrimination between the eternal and noneternal. That means we must try to feel before we can experience. Before we can grow spiritually, we must try to feel that God alone is real. You know, there is nothing new in any religion, every religion teaches this, but let me quote Christ: "Lay not up for yourselves treasures upon earth, where moth and rust doth corrupt, and where thieves break through and steal: But lay up for yourselves treasures in heaven, where neither moth nor rust doth corrupt, and where the thieves do not break through, nor steal; For where your treasure is, there will your heart be also." We have to come to this understanding through discrimination: that the only treasure is God, and that he is the soul of our soul.

"I am the life" does not refer to the surface life, but to life that is eternal. Continuity of existence is not life eternal. Everything is changing, but continuing to exist in some form or other. That is not eternal life. What is eternal life? It is beyond time, when there is no more birth, death, or rebirth. That is something you have to attain by realizing Christ within. In Him is the eternal life.

You find Jesus saying, "Verily, verily, I say unto you, he that heareth my word and believeth on him that sent me hath everlasting life, and shall not come into condemnation; but is passed from death unto life. ... If a man keep my saying, he shall never see death. In Corinthians we read: "Now this I say, brethren, that flesh and blood cannot inherit the kingdom of God; neither doth corruption inherit incorruption. Behold, I show you a mystery; we shall not all sleep, but we shall all be changed ... So when this corruptible shall have put on incorruption, and this mortal shall have put on immortality, then shall be brought to pass the saying that is written, 'Death is swallowed up in victory.'"

I come to the last, which is brought out first: "I am the way." What does it mean? It is beautifully brought out in the teachings of the Bhagavad Gita, "Quickly I come to those who offer me every action, worship me only, their dearest delight, with devotion undaunted. Because they love me, they are my bondsmen, and I shall save them from mortal sorrow and all the waves of life's deathly ocean. Be absorbed in me, lodge your mind in me. Thus you shall dwell in me. Do not doubt it here and hereafter." (102)

The Lord's Prayer

Before I come to the Lord's Prayer, you must hear what Jesus says about how to proceed. He says: "And when thou prayest, thou shalt not be as the hypocrites are: for they love to pray standing in the synagogues and in the corners of the streets, that they may be seen of men. Verily I say unto you, they have their reward. But thou, when thou prayest, enter into thy closet, and when thou hast shut thy door, pray to thy Father which is in secret; and thy Father which seeth in secret shall reward thee openly. But when ye pray, use not vain repetitions, as the heathen do, for they think that they shall be heard for their much speaking. Be not ye, therefore, like unto them: for your Father knoweth what things ye have need of, before ye ask Him."

I want you to note this last sentence: "Be ye not, therefore, like unto them, for your Father knoweth what things ye have need of before ye ask Him." In other words, this Lord's Prayer is not a petitional prayer, it is not a prayer to the Lord to give me this or that.

The Lord's Prayer was given by Jesus to a few disciples who belonged to that class who realize that God alone is the eternal Reality and that everything else is transitory. They had already been taught spiritual disciplines, the methods of meditation and prayer, in detail. I believe this Lord's Prayer is just like an aphorism to remind them of how to proceed step by step in their meditation and worship.

Now let us try to understand. "Our Father." There are mainly two paths to the realization of God. One is called the path of knowledge, the other the path of devotion or love. To those who follow the path of knowledge, God is an impersonal being – the absolute Reality, formless, attribute-less. But to those who follow the path of devotion, God is a personal being. Jesus taught the path of devotion. Nowhere in the teachings of Jesus do we find any reference to impersonal Brahman, except when he said, "I and my Father are one." In that he gave the ultimate truth of unity, oneness with Brahman, oneness with the Father.

As we follow the path of devotion, God is a personal being with whom we must establish a relationship. You see, he is our very own: our mother, our father, our friend, our constant companion, everything. But we have to enter into a relation-ship. Here "Our Father" means the relationship.

You have to feel God as your very own. Perhaps for a be-ginner it is good to think of God as majestic and powerful, but as you come nearer, God withholds his majesty and power and appears as your very own. Sri Ramakrishna used to say that he is not our father in the normal sense, but he is nearer, more intimate, closer than your own blood father.

"Our Father, which art." God is. After pursuing spiritual disciplines for months and years, you begin to feel that he is. He becomes a living presence.

"Which art in heaven." Where is this heaven? Every religion points out that God is dwelling within each one of us. In the words of Jesus, "Neither shall they say 'Lo here,' or 'Lo there,' but behold, the kingdom of God is within." Unfortunately, Christian theologians explain away this very fundamental truth of religion, but the fact is that he is right within us: it is his power that we all use when speaking, walking, thinking.

Of course the question comes, where is earth if heaven is within? The earth is also within. For those who have attained the vision of God, the ultimate realization, this whole universe appears as Brahman: all is God. With our physical consciousness we don't see spirit; we see matter, earth, but not the kingdom of heaven. Philosophically, we are looking at the reality, the Absolute, through *maya*, which is composed of time, space, and causation. You see, whatever you think or experience with your senses or mind is always within the limitations of time, space, and causation. If you can eliminate these three and if you can go beyond *maya* – time, space and relativity – you see the absolute Brahman. My Master at one time said to me, "Show me the line of demarcation where matter ends and spirit begins." Of course when we experience with our senses, we see nothing but matter; it is only when our divine sight opens that we see everything as Brahman: matter has disappeared.

Now again, heaven is within, and God is everywhere, in everything, but manifest particularly in what we call the centers of spiritual consciousness. "Man is the measure of all things"[13] and has the capacity to extend from physical consciousness to spiritual consciousness. It depends on where one's consciousness is. There are seven centers of spiritual consciousness. In the three lower centers, the mind experiences lust, greed, and earthly awareness. When the consciousness rises to the heart center, the love for God arises. It is said, therefore, that you should try to meditate upon God within the shrine of the heart. "Our Father, which art in Heaven." Feel that presence within the shrine of your heart.

"Hallowed be Thy name." The name is what we call the *mantra*. According to the particular aspect of God, there are

---

13. Protagoras, a Greek philosopher of the fifth century B.C.E.

different names. As Sri Chaitanya says in one of his prayers, "Various are Thy names, O Lord; in each and every name Thy power resides." The name itself is God; you learn to feel a power in it; you feel it has become alive. Every time you chant the name of God, you get a thrill; you feel the living presence. But you have to continue to repeat it for it to become living, and when you feel its power, you also feel a sweetness.

"Thy kingdom come." This is a most wonderful truth, to feel that living presence when you meditate, and to feel you are in that kingdom of God. A Hindu is taught a prayer for ritualistic worship: "As with eyes wide open you can see the sky overhead, so the seers, with their divine sight open, see the kingdom of God."

We have to convince ourselves of that. We have to have that confidence in ourselves that others have known him and we, too, can know him. You see, our limitations are not real; they are imaginary. We have hypnotized ourselves into believing them real. What are prayer and meditation? To de-hypnotize ourselves, to live, move, and have our being in God. Be aware of that.

In the ritualistic worship of the Hindus there is a beautiful process called *bhutashuddhi* which is translated as "purification of the elements." As you go to worship or pray or meditate, you have in your consciousness this physical universe: the physical body, senses, mind, intellect, and ego. In other words, you are conscious of *maya*. Now try to dissolve this consciousness of the physical universe. Mentally imagine that the elements which make it up become absorbed in the primal cause, *prakriti*. Your mind, senses, and ego all dissolve in the primal cause. Then that *prakriti* dissolves in Brahman. So your mind, senses, and ego all become dissolved in Brahman. The universe has disappeared and there is Brahman and Brahman alone. Feel your unity with him: I am He! I and my Father are one! You see: "Thy kingdom come."

Now try to feel that everything comes out of him; this whole universe is his projection. Your body, mind, senses, and ego, everything have come out of him – and so all is Spirit. You see, first "Not this, not that; Brahman alone is." Then "Brahman is all."

"Give us this day our daily bread." What is bread? Divine grace. You can't live without that divine grace. It is not that he has to give it, but that we feel it! This day – not tomorrow. Though we may not believe we are sinners, we feel our weaknesses and failings; we do not feel worthy. Therefore it is difficult to believe that at this moment we can have the vision of God. But it is a delusion that you are limited and finite. Your real nature is divine and infinite. And his grace can make you worthy. Try to feel that. There is a saying that howsoever you wash charcoal, it doesn't lose its blackness. But put a spark of flame on that charcoal and the black is gone. Similarly, howsoever you attempt to be worthy of God – to be pure – nothing can make you that. But get that flame, of God, and all blackness will be gone.

"And forgive our debts, as we forgive our debtors." Of course this is the debt of karma. As we live together, we affect others, and we are affected by them in turn. No matter how innocent we may be, there will be some who are critical of us. A spiritual aspirant will learn not to react, but to forgive, and to pray for others. Then we are at peace with ourselves and with the universe. The law of karma is a very strong chain. The only way to free ourselves from it is to surrender to God. It does not matter what we did in the past: everything is wiped out through devotion to God. In the end, the fire of the knowledge of God burns all karmas to ashes.

"And lead us not into temptation, but deliver us from evil."
How can the Lord lead us into temptation? He is doing it all
the time. I see a young, beautiful face, and I am attracted; I
run after that face. Well, God created that person! This whole
universe is a temptation, though it is thorny also. But temptation is such that, in spite of all kinds of thorns, we run after
them. And yet passing beyond *maya*, we are delivered from
evil. Then is it that we realize: "For Thine is the kingdom, and
the power, and the glory forever. Amen." Then we feel that we
are only an instrument. It is his power, his glory, his kingdom,
and we cannot move without that power. Every moment we
feel his glory, his power, his Kingdom. (103)

Peace I Give Unto You

"My peace I give unto you: not as the world giveth, give
I unto you. Let not your heart be troubled, neither let it be
afraid." These great words of hope are the words of Jesus – and
a challenge to all. Is it because we have no faith in what Jesus says that it is a challenge? It is because we do not exactly
understand what this peace means. We know of happiness in
the world, we know of excitement which brings happiness,
but what do we know of religious peace? Is it the peace of the
graveyard, where there is no delight? We do not understand.

Then again, religion has been preached as the way of the
cross – that we have to be long-faced to be spiritual, we have
to go through suffering and tribulation, and we have to take
them for granted in our lives. Even so-called religious people
accept suffering, which is the lot of everyone on this earth,
without trying to overcome it. They think themselves spiritual
because they find consolation. Little do they know that spiritual life is to overcome suffering and tribulation: little do they
know about that peace that passeth understanding.

Any enlightened soul who has attained any illumination decries the idea that religious life is a life of suffering. It is just the opposite. Religious life is a life of joy from the very beginning. If you ever live in the company of those who have any enlightenment, you will find that the whole atmosphere is surcharged with joy. There is no worry, no trouble, no suffering. They are examples of joy and peace. Theirs is a positive experience.

What is God? If we have to have suffering in God, and bear the cross literally when we worship, why should we worship God? Who seeks suffering and misery? Jesus does not want us to suffer. He came so that we can overcome suffering. In the Upanishads we read: "This whole universe springs from joy, in joy it lives, and unto that joy it goes back." [Taittiriya Upanishad] What does Christ want us to do? He says, "Let not your heart be troubled, neither let it be afraid."

If we want infinite happiness, yes, we have to bear the cross of Christ – but what does bearing that cross really mean? It means that we have to make up our minds not to live in darkness, but to overcome all trouble and suffering. "Bearing the cross" means spiritual discrimination. (104)

Not Peace, But a Sword

In the Gospel according to St. Matthew: "Think not that I am come to send peace on earth: I come not to send peace, but a sword. For I am come to set a man at variance against his father, and the daughter against her mother, and the daughter-in-law against her mother-in-law. And a man's foes shall be they of his own household. He that loveth father or mother more than me is not worthy of me: and he that loveth son or daughter more than me is not worthy of me. And he that taketh not his cross, and followeth after me, is not worthy of me. He that findeth his life shall lose it: and he that loseth his life for my sake shall find it."

These are strong words which frighten us, but we must understand that behind them is a naked, uncompromising truth that can give us the true peace that we seek. There is peace in slumber, there is a peace in ignorance, but if we live within slumber and ignorance, there is nothing but tribulation. And then life passes into nothingness. A son of God or divine incarnation – a Jesus, a Krishna, a Buddha, or a Ramakrishna – and illumined souls who come from time to time do not come to put us to slumber; they come to wake us up from ignorance.

So the ideal that these great illumined souls place before us is not to wallow in the mire of delusion that we are happy and that our happiness lies on earth, but to take the sword of discrimination and cut asunder the attachment to the false, ephemeral things of the world. That is the sword of which Jesus speaks: the sword of discrimination between the eternal and the noneternal. This discrimination is the first step in spiritual life, and it is taught by all the seers of the world.

Jesus tells us to take the sword of discrimination and cut our worldly attachments: "He who loves his father more than me is not worthy of me." What is father? What is mother? Do we see the Reality? No. We see the name and form, the appearance; it is the shadow of a father. So renounce the shadow and see the reality. Not negation, but affirmation of the Reality is what is meant by renunciation. To hold onto God is what is meant by renunciation and what is meant by spiritual life. (106)

Be Still and Know That I Am God

"Be still and know that I am God." In this one sentence the supreme truth of spiritual life has been brought forth. But it is not so easy to understand what is meant by the stillness which gives the knowledge that I am God. Two aphorisms of Patanjali explain with greater clarity the truth of this statement. The first is: "Yoga is the control of the thought-waves of the mind." The other is: "Then he abides in his real nature."

This control, or stillness, of the mind is not superficial. To quote the words of St. Paul: "Be ye transformed by the renewing of your own mind." A complete overhauling of the mind. You see, Sri Ramakrishna used to say: "With this mind you cannot see God; but with a transformed mind, with a purified mind, you can see him." In the Upanishads we read: "Words cannot express him, the mind comes away baffled, unable to reach him." [Katha Upanishad] But again the same Upanishad points out: "By the purified mind alone, he can be known."

If we have control of the senses, we gain mastery over our mind. We are slaves to the mind, but when we gain mastery over the mind, then the ego, which is the cause of all trouble, is dissolved. And then the joy of Brahman comes to the heart. There is a beautiful truth in the Bible: "Where your treasure is, there your heart will be also." You have to consider what that treasure is: it is God, who is dwelling within. There you find fulfillment in life. (107)

A Well of Water Springing Up Into Everlasting Life

There is a famous saying of Jesus in The Gospel According to St. John: "Whosoever drinketh of this water shall thirst again: but whosoever shall drinketh of the water that I shall give him shall never thirst; but the water that I shall give him shall be in him a well of water springing up into everlasting life."

In this famous passage are contained two most wonderful truths. One is that if we drink of the water that Jesus gives us, we will never suffer thirst anymore; the other is that we shall have everlasting life. These two ideas appear to be different, but in the Upanishads they have been made one, and that is immortal bliss. You see, Brahman or God is *sat* (eternal, everlasting life), *chit* (pure consciousness, knowledge) and *ananda* (bliss, fulfillment). They cannot be distinguished: they are one and the same reality. In other words, this drinking of the water that satisfies one forever is the attainment of Christ within. The moment you realize God, you realize your true Self, you attain to immortal life. (107)

Know Ye Not That Ye Are the Temples of God?

I have taken for my subject a verse from Corinthians: "Know ye not that ye are the temple of God, and that the spirit of God dwelleth in you?" This verse expresses a significant truth. That the spirit of God dwells in every one of us and must be experienced. Religion consists in realizing that truth. We may be told of the truth repeatedly, yet it does not become an experience for us. We may believe it, but God still remains unknown.

If you see a knower of God who has experienced the identity of God within, you will immediately feel no doubt about the existence of God. As you approach such an individual, if you are a sincere seeker, you will not doubt the existence of God; you will feel, here is God. These great souls are living temples of God. They do not seek God somewhere outside of themselves, but see God within. And then every form becomes a visible God to them. To them, God is a fact, and to realize that fact is the whole truth of religion.

Let me read from Corinthians: "Let no man deceive himself. If any man among you seemeth to be wise in this world, let him become a fool, that he may be wise. For the wisdom of this world is foolishness with God. For it is written, he taketh the wise in their own craftiness."

We think ourselves clever, wise, intelligent, learned – we may be walking encyclopedias – but that is ignorance; that is not knowledge. Knowledge is the knowledge of God dwelling within us. In order to be awakened to that, we have to expand further and transcend our ego. We must learn to turn the light of consciousness towards God. All mystics in all ages insist upon the cultivation of awareness of that presence of God within.

There comes a stage of growth in spiritual life when you feel that you cannot move your finger without that light, without that power of God. But the highest expression is beyond all expression. And so silence is his name. (108)

Except A Man Be Born Again

"Except a man be born again, he cannot see the kingdom of God." In this verse Jesus brings out very explicitly the ideal of spiritual life and the way to its attainment. That ideal has been stated here as to see God. When Sri Ramakrishna was asked about the purpose of life, he said, "to see God, to talk to him, to reach your union with him."

We find exemplars who have claimed such attainment. Jesus said: "I speak that which I have seen with my Father. Yet ye have not known him, but I know him. And if I should say I know him not, I shall be a liar like unto you, but I know him and keep his faith." In the Upanishads we find a great seer saying: "I have known that truth which is beyond darkness." [Svetasvatara Upanishad] Then he says: "You also, having known that truth, attain to immortality." Christ repeats this same truth: "Ye shall know the truth, and the truth shall make you free."

Without the experience of God, religion does not mean a thing. It must be something that gives you peace that goes beyond normal understanding, beyond our senses, beyond our reach. That peace is eternal. And realizing God and divine love in solitude, one may live in the world as well. That is why Jesus said: "Seek ye first the kingdom of God, and everything else shall be added unto you." Everything will be added unto you in the sense that you will have a different view of life; everything will be an expression of that blissful consciousness. At one time my master said to me, "Do the people who are forgetful of God and are attached to the world and worldly pleasures know how to enjoy life? They do not. It is only when you devote yourself to God and his search and you find him that this life becomes fun and there is joy in living."

We may say, "But we do not see people who have known God." The reason is that very few people seek God. Those who seek God never meet with failure. If you seek him, you are bound to find him. There is a saying that if you move one step towards God, God comes a hundred steps towards you. It is literally true.

In the history of the world, in the modern age as well as in ancient ages, we find many who have known God and whose lives have become blessed. But they don't advertise their experiences and visions. In fact, they live hidden. Take Christ, whom you worship as God. When he lived on earth, how many recognized him? Multitudes followed him, yes, but did they follow him to attain God? No, they followed for a few miracles. And when he wanted to give the real truth, just a few disciples stayed. The point is that you can recognize an illumined soul only if you are seeking for the truth of God.

What is taught in religion today is to be good and ethical, but that does not give you the peace, satisfaction, and perfection of which Jesus spoke: "Be ye perfect, even as the Father which is in heaven is perfect." He didn't say that you have to go to heaven to attain perfection, or that there is relative perfection. It is either absolute perfection or no perfection at all. Where is that perfection? Jesus said, "Ye are complete in Godhead."

There was a rich young man who came to Jesus and asked him what he would have to do to inherit eternal life. Jesus answered: "Thou knowest the commandments. Do not commit adultery. Do not kill. Do not steal, and the rest." The young man replied, "All these have I kept from my youth up." When Jesus heard this, he said: "Yet lackest thou one thing. Sell all that thou hast and distribute to the poor and you shall have treasure in heaven. Come and follow me."

You see, the riches you consider as treasure are not the eternal treasure, which is God. You have to follow Christ, and that means to be completely absorbed in Christ-consciousness. Then alone will you find peace. You can live a very good, moral, and ethical life but feel lack and frustration. "Ye shall have tribulations in the world." Nobody can escape. But you can overcome those tribulations.

In the Upanishads we read that considering religion to be the observance of rituals and acts of charity, one who is deluded remains ignorant of the highest good. It is not that you must not observe rituals and perform acts of charity but you must not consider these the ultimate aim in religious life. What is the highest good? Union with God!

But we read in the Bible: "No man hath seen God at any time." Very true – with these eyes. But "He that hath ears to hear, let him hear." You can hear the words of God and you can see him – not with these eyes, but with divine sight. In the Bhagavad Gita we find the same teaching. Sri Krishna tells Arjuna: "But you cannot see me with those human eyes. Therefore, I give you divine sight."

A divine sight has to be opened up, and that is possible for every one of us. All the great teachers have taught that God is the spirit within us and our true self, so consider yourself as one with the spirit: in spirit you can worship God as spirit. Where is bondage and where is freedom? In the mind. If you consider yourself flesh, you are flesh; if you think of yourself as spirit, you are spirit. But in order that the birth in spirit can be achieved, Jesus points out: "Verily, verily, I say unto you, except a man be born of water and of the spirit, he cannot enter into the kingdom of God. That which is born of the flesh is flesh; and that which is born of the spirit is spirit."

So to be born again is an actual birth – not by dying and entering into the womb of another, but while living here on earth. In India human beings and birds are both called *dvija*, "twice born." Birds, you know, have to break through their shells. If they remain in their shells, they rot. There is nothing more rotten than a rotten egg! Now human beings are born in flesh, but there is the shell of an ego, which makes us think we are human individuals. If we remain human individuals, we rot in this shell. We have to break through the shell of an ego to be born again. Of course Jesus points out to be born of water and spirit, water being a symbol of purification. A sprinkling of water is also used in India for what we call initiation. It is what Christians call baptism.

There is a Chinese saying, "Peace is not on the mountain-top, noise is not in the marketplace; both are within the mind." Mind is the measure of everything. And Jesus said: "The kingdom of God cometh not with observation, neither shall they say, 'Lo here,' or 'Lo, there,' for behold, the kingdom of God is within you." (109)

SPIRITUAL PRACTICES

VEDANTA IN PRACTICE

EASTERN RELIGION IS charged with emphasizing renunciation and contemplation. I'd like to include Christianity in this charge in that Christ emphasized these two ideals as well. Concerning renunciation, you remember the rich man who had fulfilled all his duties but had no peace. When he came to Jesus, he was told: "Sell all thou hast and give to the poor, and follow me." And then in regard to contemplation, remember the first commandment: "Love the Lord thy God with all thy heart, with all thy mind, and with all thy soul, and with all thy strength." If you give your whole heart, mind, and soul to God, with all your strength, is there anything else left but to contemplate God?

These are the supreme ideals taught in every religion, but we have to admit that it is not possible for everyone to renounce everything all at once and to love God with one's entire heart, mind, soul, and strength. It is not possible! That does not mean that we have to give up those ideals or drag them down to our plane; we must uphold them, but religion has to be made practical. The ideal is to come to the stage of unfoldment when we have no other craving but for God.

In this age Sri Ramakrishna points out that there are two ways, the path of the householder" and the path of the monastic. But he said that you cannot be free from desires and cravings until you have gone through some enjoyments in life. He said: "As long as you have the desire, go and fulfill it."

Swamiji said, "The goal is to manifest this divinity within, by controlling nature, external and internal." What is the effect of that? In the Upanishads we read, "The knots of the heart are cut asunder." [Mundaka Upanishad] What are those knots? Subtle cravings. You see, when you are practicing meditation, trying to love God, leading a holy life, still there are subtle cravings lurking within your heart. They are not manifest, but as a spiritual aspirant, you begin to feel them. These cravings all go away when you have attained the knowledge of Brahman. Then, all doubts cease to exist. But until we have the vision of God – by that I mean supreme unity – doubts will come. These doubts are even healthy if you do not give up the struggle. A chemist can teach you that if you mix this with that, it will have such-and-such effect. You may doubt how mixing this and that could have that effect, but experiment and see.

When realization comes, all your karmas of the past are wiped out. You become free from the law of rebirth and reincarnation; you become perfect, immortal, and satisfied forever. You realize your immortality by overcoming birth, death and rebirth, realizing that the Atman is changeless, birthless, and deathless. When you have known that Atman, when you have the knowledge of Brahman, then you attain immortality, and you are satisfied forever. Anything of this world – any object, any satisfactions that come from our contact with objects – does not last, but the contact with Brahman, or realizing your true Self, satisfies you forever. Attaining that, you have no more desire for anything. Then you become flooded with joy, flooded with true life. You grieve no more, do not become jealous of anything, and do not take pleasure in vanities.

To quote Shankara in this connection: "When a man has awakened to the knowledge of Brahman, his impure mind is dead, his thirst is gone, his ego has disappeared, and the cave of delusion has been shattered to bits. When a man has attained the place beyond passion by realizing the supreme, pure, absolute Reality, nothing either of this world or of heaven can turn him away from enjoying it." This is what is known as *moksha*, liberation. It is not going to heaven; you achieve it here and now. But your interest must be that Reality. If you have other interests, no. Swami Shivananda used to tell us: "When you go to meditate, forget everything. Just you and God." Then is it that gradually the mind becomes absorbed. (110)

HOUSEHOLDER AND MONASTIC LIFE

Without knowing the purpose of life and living, it is not possible to live an efficient life. We find three views of life, if I may generalize. One is naturalism, which believes in this life only and only accepts the validity of sense experiences. As such, this life becomes the be-all and end-all of all existence. Basically, it accepts man as a physical being.

Next there is the humanistic view of life, which holds that duty chiefly consists of the advancement of the welfare of humanity. Humanists believe in higher moral and ethical laws and in love and harmony with all beings. They stress the idea that a person is not only a physical being, but a mental being also. I would say that as a general rule, very few can actually live this philosophy of selfless service without love for God.

Then we come to mysticism. Any religion of the world, in its truest sense, is mystical; great mystics or men and women of God who have experienced God have come from all the major religions of the world. As Sri Ramakrishna used to say, to hear about milk, to see milk, and to drink milk are not the same. Similar is the difference in hearing about God, believing in him, and then seeing him, drinking the nectar, and becoming one with him.

Mysticism believes that the human being is spirit and has a body and a mind. It includes naturalism and humanism and at the same time points out the supreme ideal as the unfoldment of the divinity which is already within. It is the natural urge in every human being, whether we know it or not, to unfold this divinity. The ignorant person tries to find God without knowing it, the spiritual aspirant struggles to find God, knowing that to be the purpose of life. Who does not seek for life that is eternal? Who does not seek for happiness that is not beset by misery? Everyone is seeking abiding love and knowledge. And that is God: *sat-chit-ananda* – immortal existence, pure consciousness, abiding love and infinite bliss. The point is that the naturalist and humanist seek to express infinite reality in the finite. Consequently, they become baffled, frustrated; only at long last do they turn inward and seek God within.

In the teachings of Vedanta we find four pursuits of life: *dharma*, or duty and acquiring certain virtues; *artha*, economic stability; *kama*, certain emotional longings of the heart to be satisfied, and lastly, *moksha*, the supreme ideal of realizing God. But throughout all the pursuits of life, the ideal of *moksha* must never be forgotten. What is actually meant by *moksha* is liberation from the bondages of life and death, of misery and pleasure, and attaining complete freedom by realizing our oneness with God.

The word *kama* is translated as sex, but it has a broader meaning. It includes all desires and all longings. Psychologically, everyone is a complex of thoughts and longings of the heart. The more highly evolved one becomes, the more complex become the cravings and desires. In lower life, there are just a few desires: to eat, drink and procreate. But all desires are not approved, because we must not forget the ideal of *moksha*. Satisfying the longings of the heart is not wrong, but it is to be hedged in by *dharma*, the duties of life and acquiring certain virtues.

Life has different stages: student life, householder life, retired life, and monastic life. The same duties do not apply in every stage. There are certain virtues we have to acquire as students, which will equip us to become householders or monks. We have to cultivate virtues such as self-control, charity, compassion, and devotion to God through prayer and meditation. Acquiring secular knowledge means language, science, literature, grammar, and so on, as well as the study of the scriptures. The study of scriptures is secular knowledge as well; it is not spiritual knowledge. Spiritual knowledge can only be acquired through prayer, meditation, and devotion to God.

A householder marries. Marriage is a sacrament and a legitimate desire of the heart to be satisfied, but married life is not to be recklessly indulged in. It is an institution where, in the words of Sri Ramakrishna, one lives in a fort and, being protected by its walls, can give a good fight.

You know, when Rama was a young boy, he wanted to renounce the world. His father, Dasaratha, sent for the family guru, Vasishtha, a great sage. Vasishtha asked him, "Is the world apart?" Sri Ramakrishna used to give the illustration that if you add zeroes to zeroes, it doesn't mean anything; you must put a unit in front of the zeroes to add value. This world appearance has no value, but if we learn to see divinity behind the appearance – God underneath, as the ground of all existence – then this world becomes real. You see, to renounce does not mean that you take your husband and drown him in the ocean – Swami Vivekananda said that would be like taking a gun to shoot a mosquito on your cheek – but that you learn to see the divinity behind everything. Love God in the husband, God in the wife, God in the children. That love is to be directed towards God in every way.

If one is not trained from childhood in these virtues and has lived a wild life, is there any hope? In the Gita we find: "Though a man be soiled with the sins of a lifetime, let him but love Me, rightly resolved in utter devotion, I see no sinner, that man is holy. Holiness shall soon refashion his nature to peace eternal. O Son of Kunti, of this be certain: the man that loves me, he shall not perish."

In short, when we give up our little self, our ego, and open ourselves to the Divine, the Divine takes up the burden of life and lifts us to its bosom. In this connection, I will tell you, when I was in the Madras monastery, an old man came and told the Abbot, "I have this money. I give it to your monastery. You give me a bed to sleep in and food to eat; that's all I want." He told me that he had lived a reckless life. He was with us four or five years when Maharaj came to Madras. This old man prostrated before Maharaj, who looked at me and asked, "Where did you find this *rishi*?" From that day on, he became known as Rishi Mudebhihya. (111)

CONTEMPLATION AND HAPPINESS

Many centuries back a great seer-philosopher, Kapila, pointed out that the common goal of all mankind is to have complete cessation of suffering and misery. Mark these words: "complete cessation."

There are many causes of suffering and misery: physical causes such as disease; mental fear and worries, imaginary or real; and suffering caused by things outside ourselves, such as someone speaking harshly to us or trying to do us harm. And there are what are called acts of God – flood, fire – and also what you might call your fate, what is going to happen to you. This, of course, is linked with the law of karma: what you may have done in the past, you don't remember, but it now causes suffering that appears to have no reason. And then there is death.

How do we overcome all these? How can we reach a state of unfoldment where none of these sufferings can affect our lives? That is the common goal of everyone. Of course there is also happiness – joys and pleasures that we experience in life. As it is said in the Upanishads, whether you are ignorant or illumined, who could live for a moment if there were no joy at all in this world!

But again, to the discriminative one, whose one goal is to have complete cessation of suffering and misery, these so-called joys and pleasures are also suffering. For we read in the Bhagavad Gita: "Senses also have joy in their marriage with things of the senses, sweet at first, but at last how bitter. Steeped in *rajas*, that pleasure is poison."

Why is the spiritual aspirant who seeks for ultimate reality, for the truth and complete cessation of suffering and misery, not satisfied with a little joy or pleasure? Because every fulfillment reveals its inadequacy. As one mystic said: "The terrible thing is that we can never make ourselves drunk enough." Our hunger cannot be appeased by anything that is finite. The infinite God is present within each human soul, and nothing finite can ever make us happy: in the infinite alone is happiness.

Now there are two classes of people. The worldly-wise are practical and want to remain satisfied within their limitations. They would say, yes there are suffering and misery, but there are also joy and happiness; I must make the most of them. Yet in their heart of hearts they believe that one day they will be free of suffering and misery in heaven.

Spinoza says: "For the things which men, to judge by their actions, deem the highest good, are riches, fame and sensual pleasure." He sums up beautifully: "Of these the last, sense pleasure, is followed by satiety and repentance. The other two are never satiated. The more we have, the more we want. While the love of one compels us to order our lives by the opinions of others, if a thing is not loved, no quarrels arise concerning it, no sadness is felt if it perishes, no envy if another has it. In short, no disturbances of the mind. All these spring from the love of that which passes away, but the love of a thing eternal and infinite fills the mind wholly with joy and is unmingled with sadness. Therefore it is greatly to be desired and to be sought with all our strength."

The most wonderful truth that has ever been given to the world, by all the great teachers and prophets and in all the scriptures of the world, is in the words of Jesus: "The kingdom of God is within." Everyone who has realized the truth of God will tell you that he is right. To quote the words of Vivekananda: "After long searches here and there, in temples and in churches, in earths and in heavens, at last you come back, completing the circle from where you started, to your own soul, and find that He for whom you have been seeking all over the world, for whom you have been weeping and praying in churches and temples, on whom you were looking as the mystery of mysteries shrouded in the clouds, is nearest of the near, is your own Self, the reality of your life, body, and soul."

One time my master, seeing me restless, said: "Go anywhere you like, but you will not find God, you will not find peace, until you find him here, within your own heart. He who finds him here will find him everywhere. If he does not find him here, he will find him nowhere."

Dogmas or doctrines, theology, beliefs, and non-beliefs, have nothing to do with religion. In the teachings of Christ or Buddha, of Ramakrishna or Krishna, do you find theological doctrines? No. God is the central reality, the central truth, and that God is within each one of us. To know him and to reach union with him is the one goal of spiritual life, and the one spirit of all the religions of the world.

What is the nature of God? The term the Upanishads use is *sat-chit-ananda*. *Sat* means absolute existence, "is-ness." Where is he? In space? He is beyond space. In fact, because of his existence, this whole universe exists – you and I and every being in this universe. Then he is *chit*, consciousness. Your and my consciousness is possible because of that infinite presence. And he is *ananda*, love and happiness. And because of that presence within each one of us, there is that urge to express life and to attain knowledge. We want to know everything, to have infinite wisdom, and we are all hungry for love and happiness. But we try to realize him in the external. Ultimately we come to the understanding that fulfillment can only be had completely if we go within.

You see, he can be experienced. And this experience is wonderful; it is unified consciousness. The great seer philosopher, Shankara, pointed out that the subject and object become united. He calls it the untying of the three knots of knowledge: the knower, the object of knowledge, and the process of knowledge. That is what is technically known as *samadhi*, in which you realize your oneness with God.

We read in the Gita: "Who knows the Atman, knows that happiness born of pure knowledge, the joy of sattva, deep his delight, after strict schooling. Sour toil at first, but at last what sweetness, the end of sorrow."

We are carrying that fountain of life, joy, and knowledge, within ourselves. "Know ye not that ye are the temples of God?" Jesus said. But in order to know that, we must first toil. It is not so easy! There is one condition, as Ramakrishna said: to yearn for him with a longing heart.

St. John of the Cross said: "The more the soul cleaves to created things, relying on its own strength, by habits and inclination, the less is it disposed for this union, because it does not completely resign itself into the hands of God that He may transform it supernaturally."

You know the Lord's prayer: "Lead us not into temptation." What is that temptation? His creation, his whole creation. It seems impossible for us to be free from desire, to have no other desire but for God. When you come to that stage of unfoldment, God becomes revealed to you. He is right there, listening to every heartbeat.

But we have to practice spiritual disciplines to arouse great longing for God. Of the many millions of people, how many really have the least desire for God? Very few. If you have the least desire, blessed you are. That desire must be strengthened by the continued practice of spiritual disciplines.

You know, as we think of God often, love grows in our heart. And when love grows in our heart, it becomes easy. All of you have had the experience that if you love somebody intensely, you begin to think of that person all the time. When you have intense love for God, naturally you also think of him all the time.

When you practice a few days or a few months or a few years and you seem to be getting nowhere, do not lose heart. Stick to it. One day all the darkness will vanish – in one moment. You see, darkness may be accumulated for centuries in a room, but with one strike of a light, that darkness is gone. In the same way, if you stick to this practice of contemplation, prayer and meditation, you may seem to get nowhere, your mind may still be restless; but in the midst of the storm and stress that you may be going through in your meditation, suddenly something happens and the light is there.

Whenever we used to complain to our master, he would simply say: "Practice, practice, practice. What I have told you, continue to practice." Through such practice, you will find that

love for God grows, and when that love for God grows, everything else becomes insipid. Then it is that all desires cease.

Patiently, little by little, you must free yourself from all
mental distractions with the aid of the intelligent will. You
must fix your mind upon the Atman and never think of anything else. No matter where the restless and unquiet mind
wanders, it must be drawn back and made to submit to the
Atman only. That is the secret. (112)

In the Upanishads we read this truth: "The Self-existent
made the senses turn outward. Accordingly man looks towards what is without, and not what is within. Rare is he who,
longing for immortality, shuts his eyes to what is without, and
beholds the Self. Fools follow the desire for the flesh, and fall
into the snare of all-encompassing death. But the wise, knowing the Self as eternal, seek not the things that pass away."

Each one of us has to have our own experiences before
spiritual discrimination arises. But we all come to the main
problem: the control of the mind. It is a difficult task. My
master once said to me, "Mind is made up of the three gunas,
and every object of the universe is also made up of the three
gunas, so naturally the mind runs after the things and objects
of the senses." Swami Vivekananda compared the mind to a
monkey, jumping. But he was not satisfied with just a jumping monkey; the monkey got drunk with the wine of ego.
And even that is not enough; he also is stung by a bee – the
desires, passions.

So what is the way? Both the Bhagavad Gita and Patanjali
point out *abhyasa* and *vairagya*, practice and dispassion. In
other words, earnestness in meditation and self-control. In
order to control the mind, we need the regular habit of certain practices. What is a character, but habits and tendencies
we have created by our own deeds and actions – a bundle of

habits? Now, one bundle of habits can be replaced by another bundle of habits.

I want to share with you a part of a letter that Swami Vivekananda wrote to the two Hale sisters. It affected me very much. He wrote: "Catch a glimpse at least every day of that world of infinite beauty and peace and purity, the spiritual. And try to live that, live it day and night. Let your souls ascend day and night like an unbroken string unto the feet of the Beloved, whose throne is in your own heart, and let the rest take care of themselves – that is, the body and everything else. Say day and night: Thou art my Father, my Mother, my love, my Lord, my God. I want nothing but Thee, nothing but Thee, nothing but Thee. Thou art Thou in me, I in Thee. I am Thee, Thou art Me. Wealth goes, beauty vanishes, life flies, powers fly, but the Lord abides forever. Stick to God through the terror of evil. Say: My God, my Love. Through the pangs of death, say: My God, My love. Through all the evils under the sun say My God, my love. Thou art here. Thou art here, I see Thee. Thou art with me, I feel Thee. I am dying, take me. I am not of this world, but Thine. Leave then not me! Do not go for glass beads, leaving the mine of diamonds. This life is a great change. Why seekest thou the pleasures of the world? He is the fountain of all bliss. Seek for the highest, aim at the highest, and you shall reach the highest." (113)

HOW TO GAIN POISE

The Bhagavad Gita lays great emphasis on the necessity of gaining poise to attain passionless peace. Such peace is defined as a spirit of serenity in the midst of life's pairs of opposites – pleasure and pain, heat and cold, life and death, sickness and health. To quote the Gita: "A serene spirit accepts pleasure and pain with an even mind, and is unmoved by either."

Poise is the very first step needed to enter into the gate of the spirit. Again, it is the last step before illumination. If we take the experience of the universe as permanent and eternal, there is no possibility of gaining poise. If we accept misery as something permanent in life, how would it be possible to retain balance of mind? It is the same with pleasure, in the fear of losing it.

We live in a universe of two faces. We see only one face but, whether we are spiritual or not, we have something within that tells us that everything is not what it seems. Authors try to show the hidden, emotional experience of people; scientists invent new instruments to give them the power to observe behind the appearance. There is the urge in every one of us to probe deeper into the things and appearances of the universe.

A person of spiritual understanding says that there are two universes – the Reality and the apparent universe, which is a misreading of that Reality. We misread because we do not have the understanding to enable us to read the real correctly. If you do not observe a beautiful painting from the proper perspective, you cannot appreciate its beauty: a partial view may appear as ugly or as having no meaning. You must have a total vision to estimate truly the nature of the universe in which we live.

Illumined souls gain such a total vision and say: "This universe springs from joy; in joy exists this universe; and unto that joy goes back this universe." [Taittiriya Upanishad] They do not see the pairs of opposites, which, to them, are only appearance. They see the Reality behind – *ananda*, bliss, joy, consciousness, eternity. The seers of the Upanishads define this total vision by analogy: multiply any sense pleasure so many times and you get that joy in God, in the Atman. It is not a passive joy, but it is positive and intense.

But until you reach the Atman and are united with God, there will be the experience of the pairs of opposites. They cannot be avoided. How, then, shall we live? By bearing them patiently, keeping a balance in the midst of them, and by knowing that they are impermanent by their very nature.

It is easy to say that, and almost impossible to practice. If it is unbearably hot, I suffer. How can I bear it patiently? The teaching is to learn not to react. You are susceptible to cold and heat; make yourself so strong that you will not be susceptible. It is the same with every experience. One of my spiritual brothers once said, "Brother, act – but do not react!" That is the secret of gaining poise.

Sri Ramakrishna said, "Let the boat stay on water, but don't let the water get into the boat." You cannot avoid storms and stress; they will be there. There will be good people and bad people. You will get praise and you will get blame. That is the world. But behind these pairs of opposites, you have to gain poise. It is not something you just assume. It is far deeper, because the mind becomes the nature of the object upon which it is concentrated. A young boy looks at a young girl, concentrates his mind upon her, and he becomes attached. Lust arises. It is bound to happen; it is natural. You see, when he looks at the girl, he is not looking at the soul within, at God within. He must let his mind be given to the spirit within. Then he will get bliss, consciousness, and what is eternal.

To gain poise effectively and permanently, we have to learn to devote ourselves steadfastly to God. If you are steadfastly devoted, poise comes to the mind, and also to the body and nerves, to every cell. You have heard the expression "spiritualizing the body." It is not that the body can be made spirit and not decay, but it can be made pure. When you actually experience spiritual bliss, there is forgetfulness of the body;

but when you come back, every cell, your whole being, has enjoyed that bliss.

So in all circumstances and under all conditions, in everything you sense and whatever you experience, hold on to God. See that one reality everywhere. A moment will come when poise, control, and purity all become natural to you, and you don't have to try to control anymore. You don't have to try to be pure, because your very nature has become pure, just as the flower gives its fragrance without being conscious of it. Your character and your life become such that you become a blessing to yourself, and to others, without being conscious of it. (114)

HOW TO PRAY

Prayer is an essential means to spiritual experience. Most people believe in God or the existence of a power, but most do not pray in the sense that the great teachers and illumined prophets of the world have taught, because they accept this life on earth to be the be-all and end-all of existence. If they pray at all, they pray to enrich their lives on earth. Most people try to make their religion geocentric or egocentric. As a rule they begin spiritual life because they become distressed or because they cannot supply a lack by any earthly means and wish the intervention of a supernatural power. Their prayer is called petitionary prayer.

There is nothing wrong with petitionary prayer. It is but natural if we consider this life on earth as real and we cannot fulfill our desires. In this kind of prayer God is a means for some other end. Spiritual life itself has not yet begun. But if we sincerely believe that God is our only means, a gradual change will come in our hearts. You see, religion really is theocentric: God must be the center of everything. We must not seek life which has ebb and flow, but the life that is eternal. Spiritual life begins when that search begins.

Most people love the creator because of his creation, and they love the creation more than the creator. As long as we love the creation, the creator has not arisen in our hearts. True prayer is the reverse: when we forget the creation and long for the creator, when we see, through discrimination, that everything in this life is evanescent and that there is only one thing that is dear – God, the spirit – only then do we learn how to pray. Reaching union with the Godhead is the only purpose of prayer and the only purpose of life. Prayer is the attempt to live constantly in the thought of God constantly.

You will find that the more you think of God, the more you love him, and the more you will find how intensely God loves you. You do not have to seek his love: it is there. You do not have to pray for happiness to be given to you: you will find sweetness as you approach God, because it is his very nature. And his very nature is knowledge as well.

There are many secrets that become revealed as you begin a life of prayer. The guru, the external teacher, can only place you on the path, but you have to travel it by yourself. The guru helps you always, but as you advance, you find your own mind becomes your guru. The secrets that you have never heard through the lips of anybody become revealed to you. Sri Krishna says in the Gita: "Whoever is seeking me, I give him the intelligence by which he comes to me."

God himself teaches us and reveals the methods and means by which to reach him. The only thing needed is sincerity of purpose, single-mindedness. It does not come all of a sudden. But if you hear again and again, and then you reason upon it and practice regularly, your mind may still be distracted, but gradually a current opens up within. When this current opens up, the inner consciousness is awakened and you are born in spirit. Something happens from inside. Mystics call that the grace of God. Through the grace of God, you are lifted into that kingdom of heaven within yourself while living on earth. You reach that eternal felicity while living on earth. (115)

When Sri Ramakrishna was asked how to find God, he said: "Love and pray." The disciple asked which comes first. He said: "Love, and then pray." Now when I heard that, it struck me that it should have been first pray, and then love. But then it dawned on me that unless you have that interest in God, you would not pray. Pray does not mean "God I want this; give it to me." Pray means "How can I find him?" Pray that you can have his vision. (116)

FAITH

Many years ago, in 1923, as I was leaving India for this country, I went to pay my respects to 'M.,' the writer of the *Gospel of Sri Ramakrishna*. He was a direct disciple of Ramakrishna and a knower of Brahman. I asked him, "What have you gained, going to Ramakrishna? What did you achieve?" His answer was, strangely, "Faith." M. was a man of God, he had the vision of God, he had experienced his oneness with God, and his final word was "faith." This is the faith that comes after experiencing God. One time my master, Swami Brahmananda, another disciple of Ramakrishna, described his own vision, saying: "On the ocean of Brahman, I am floating on the leaf of faith." This faith is something that comes after a direct and immediate experience of the truth of God.

But I am going to speak to you first about what may be called working faith, the beginning faith that leads to the realization of God. First, the definition of faith as given in the English dictionary is the ascent of the mind or understanding to the truth of what God has revealed. Shankara defined faith as "the firm conviction, based upon intellectual understanding, that the teachings of the scriptures and of one's master, are true." Sages call this the faith which leads to realization of the Reality.

Before showing the differences, let me point out the common ground upon which all the religions of the world are based. You ask Christians what their faith is and they say the Bible. For them the Bible is the revelation of the word of God. You ask orthodox Hindus and they will say they believe in the Vedas as revelation, the word of God. Thus we have the Vedas, the Bible, the Koran, the Tripitaka. Each religion is based upon scriptures, which are said to be revealed wisdom. Of course, that revelation is supernatural.

We must understand that there are three kinds of proofs to arrive at the truth of anything. First there is direct perception: I see this, I sense and perceive. Then, I have not seen something, but through reasoning I can infer its existence. And a third kind of proof is what is known as revealed wisdom, or revelation.

Knowledge of the universe and our everyday behavior is based upon sense perception. The knowledge of science derives from direct perception as well as from inference. But there is a knowledge which cannot be attained either by the senses or by inference, but by a new sight – what we call divine sight. Take, for instance, the truth of God: nobody has seen God with these eyes or heard his voice with these ears, but the revelation in the scriptures tells us that to somebody this knowledge was revealed.

A student of physics or chemistry has to have a certain faith, a working faith, or there will be no urge to study. That student doesn't know physics yet but has faith in the words of scientists who have experience. What is the study? To experiment and to experience the truth for himself or herself. It is the same with religion. A religious person studies the scriptures, goes to church, and believes in God – but that is not enough. In his *Vivekachudamani* Shankara says: "What is the use of the study of scriptures if one has not known God?" And in the Upanishads we read: "The Self... is to be known. Hear about it, reflect upon it, meditate upon it. By knowing the Self, my beloved, through hearing, reflection, and meditation, one comes to know all things." [Brihadaranyaka Upanishad] Until and unless you do that, your faith is lip-faith. Mohammed, that great prophet, compared people who believe but do not struggle to experience, to asses carrying big loads of books. And Shankara mentions an ass carrying a big load of sandalwood: sandalwood has fragrance, but the poor ass doesn't get that fragrance.

So you can study scriptures and attend church, but that is not religion. You have to struggle to experience the truth of God; otherwise your faith is no faith. And the working faith that leads to the realization of the ultimate is very rare. The point is, we must have the faith that there is God, that he is the treasure, and that we must find him.

The pure truth of the Atman, which is buried under *maya*, ignorance, and the effects of ignorance, can be reached by contemplation and other spiritual disciplines such as a knower of Brahman may prescribe, but not by subtle arguments. In a very simple way the great saint Ramprasad expressed this truth: "Fix your heart in God. Then will love be awakened within. Faith is the root of all." The Yoga Aphorisms also say that faith is the root and that you have to practice spiritual disciplines with energy, will, and enthusiasm.

In the Gita we read: "When, through the practice of yoga, the mind ceases its restless movements and becomes still, he realizes the Atman. He stands firm in this realization. Because of it, he can never again wander from the innermost truth of his being. Now that he holds it, he knows this treasure above all others. Faith so certain shall never be shaken by heaviest sorrow." That is the faith that comes after achieving union with God. (117)

Swami Vivekananda used to say, "If anybody says, 'I have seen and you cannot see,' don't trust him!" And Shankara points out: "A clear vision of the reality may be obtained only through one's own eyes, when they have been opened up by spiritual insight, never through the eyes of some other man, some other seer." Through our own eyes we learn what the moon looks like. How could we learn through the eyes of others? In all the scriptures of the world you will find this truth, that you have to know the truth for yourself.

If you think you have understood but still have doubts, you must question. Doubts you will have. Faith does not mean immediate acceptance. Intellectual understanding is needed. But if we do not try to realize the truth for ourselves, it is only lip faith without sense or meaning.

Sri Ramakrishna once told Vivekananda that very few people have faith in God. Naren said, "What are you saying, sir? Most of the people I know believe they have faith in God." He replied: "Suppose there is a treasure and a thin wall, and there is a thief who wants to get hold of that treasure. If he has faith that the treasure is there, what will be his condition? Will he remain still? Will he remain quiet? To believe in God and do nothing about it is worse than not to believe in God!" As Emerson said, there is faith in chemistry, in meat and wine, in wealth, in machinery, in the steam-engine, in the galvanic battery, in turbine wheels, in sewing machines, and in public opinion – but not in divine causes. What he means is that if we have faith, we must struggle to realize, and not merely believe.

One Christian mystic said: "God's light dwells in the Self; it shines alike in every living being, and one can see it with one's mind readied." That is the one condition – to steady the mind. How? Take an interest in it! You have to have not only faith, but interest. But faith is the root of all.

Patanjali gives the different steps: "The concentration of the true spiritual aspirant is attained through faith, energy, recollectedness, absorption, and illumination." First you have to have working faith, and then you have to have enthusiasm and earnestness. You must have faith in yourself as well – the faith that you *can* do it, you *can* attain it. Bring energy and enthusiasm! (118)

According to Patanjali, spiritual unfoldment comes in seven stages. The first stage is the realization that the source of all wisdom is within. Generally when we seek anything, even the knowledge of God, we go here or there outside of ourselves. Yes, you need to go to a teacher, you need to learn how to go within, but then you must dive deep. When you do, conviction – true faith – comes to you. You have not seen God yet, but the firm conviction will come that what you have been seeking outside, what you have been praying for in churches and temples, what you have been studying to find in scriptures and books, is within your own soul. He is nearer than the nearmost. He is dearer than the dearest. He is your very Self – the conviction comes that he is the reality of your life. (119)

To realize the truth, the inner vision has to be opened, a divine sight has to come This power of divine sight is latent in every one of us. It is not the privilege of a few individuals. Please understand and remember that. Have confidence in yourself. Faith does not mean faith only in the words of the scriptures or of the guru, but faith in yourself. Others have realized this truth; it is possible for me to realize it here and now, even this moment. A room may have been dark for centuries. How long does it take to remove that darkness? One moment. (120)

STAGES OF SPIRITUAL UNFOLDMENT

The first stage of spiritual unfoldment, though it seems very simple, is the most difficult to arrive at. It is to realize that all knowledge is within, that God is within. This is not merely what you read in books or what you believe, but it is an actual experience. As you close your eyes, even with eyes open, you begin to feel a stir in your heart; you know God is there.

When you come to this first experience, something stirs up and you love to think of God, you find sweetness in it. Every religion talks of dispassion and renunciation, but in my opinion it is not something that is forcibly done; you do it because you find something greater, sweeter, than the senses can give.

In the second stage cravings become less and less. They become saltless; they have lost their flavor.

In the third stage your ego becomes humble. My master often used to quote this verse of the chant of Sri Chaitanya: "Be humbler than a blade of grass. Be patient and forbearing like a tree. Take no honor to thyself. Give honor to all. Chant unceasingly the name of the Lord." In the Upanishads it is said: "What is the nature of a man of God? He becomes humble and does not assert himself."

The fourth stage is poise and tranquility – absence of pain. Nothing can disturb your equilibrium. In the midst of the opposites of life – happiness and misery – there will be a balance. If you hold to a pillar, you can spin round and round and you will not fall. That pillar is the pillar of God. Live in the world, move among the objects of senses, but have no attachment or aversion to them. In the Gita yoga is defined as "the breaking of contact with pain."

In the fifth stage God becomes the only reality, and the world appears as a shadow. The whole view of life changes. Instead of seeing the physical aspect of something, you see Brahman inside. You learn to really love, because you are loving God – in the husband, in the wife, in children, in parents, in every being.

Then in natural sequence, the sixth stage, *samadhi*, follows. The mind and nature have ended their services. We turn back. Nature's two objectives are to give us enjoyment and to give us liberation. When Nature has finished her job – immediate with *samadhi* – karmas and the effects of karmas are burned.

In the seventh and last stage you taste the bliss of living as a free soul. Then you dedicate yourself to the service of God in mankind. (121)

As you begin to feel the presence, something stirs within you. Hindu psychologists and yogis explain it as the rising of the *kundalini*, the divine energy. There comes great joy, and at the same time, an ache in your heart. You feel that ache because you have not yet seen him, and you want to see him. Then comes greater earnestness. You feel him very near; yet you feel frustrated. There is such inner joy and at the same time an ache. It is a peculiar experience, but wonderful. Then you find that craving for sense objects becomes less and less. Things that used to give you pleasure no longer do. But you get a higher pleasure, and craving lessens as your ego becomes less and less assertive. (122)

SELF-EFFORT AND DIVINE GRACE

Divine grace is intimately related to God-realization. Any spiritual aspirant who has ever had any experience – either the ecstatic vision of God, drunkenness in the love for God, or the lower or higher *Samadhi* – feels tangible divine grace. I have heard it declared by great men of God who had attained the highest samadhi that without question it is due to unconditional grace.

As long as we remain bound by doctrines and dogmas and beliefs, so long the idea of divine grace has no sense or meaning. The Gita says: "The right time has to come." And that right time is when you are thirsty for God. My master often used to say: "If I give a cool drink to somebody who is not thirsty, he will not care for it." You have to feel thirst. And everyone will feel it. Nature has given us two purposes, one for pleasure and enjoyment, the other for freedom and realization of God.

The body is considered the city of God with nine gates through which the soul goes out in search. Of what? God. Every one of us, when we seek pleasures, when we seek life, when we seek enjoyment, is seeking God, though we don't know it. Because it is normal for the senses to go outward, we think we can find what we are seeking outside ourselves, but when we understand that it is really the God-urge, we realize that what we were seeking all the time is within our very selves.

I still hear the words of my master: "I take my refuge in thee. I take my refuge in thee. I take my refuge in thee." If you take refuge with that sincerity and earnestness, you feel divine grace. Yes, it is tangibly felt; these are not mere words. Religion is not mere listening to lectures, my dear friends, not studying books, but it is something to be practiced. And the practice is to pray, pray, pray without ceasing. Be just a *little* restless, have a *little* longing, have a *little* desire, then practice – and it will grow in intensity!

Then we understand what the scriptures tell us, for instance Christ's saying: "Ye have not chosen me, I have chosen you." It is not that he is partial, but you have to long for him, you have to thirst. "Seek and ye shall find." In the Upanishads we read: "The Self is not known through study of the scriptures, nor through subtlety of the intellect, nor through much learning. But by him who longs for him is he known. Verily unto him does the Self reveal his true being." [Katha Upanishad]

My master used to teach us to pray *in order to feel* his grace. He didn't say to ask him for his grace, he said: "His grace is there; try to feel that grace." It is a psychological and mystical experience, tangibly felt by everyone who practices any spiritual discipline in life. Of course it is felt in different ways; there is not one way for it to be felt.

My master also once said to me: "One may have the grace of God, the grace of his guru, and the grace of the devotees of God, but for the grace of one's own mind, one can be ruined." What is the grace of the mind? Self-effort. Struggle. Practicing of spiritual disciplines. But with the grace of a guru, the grace of the mind does come to you gradually. Ultimately the mind and heart will be fixed in God. There is no doubt about that.

One thing my master repeated often is: "There is no failure in spiritual life. If you move towards God one step, he moves toward you a hundred. No attempt is in vain." (123)

We find a philosophical contradiction: on the one hand, grace is the last word, on the other, self-effort is. Sri Ramakrishna reconciled the two sayings: "The breeze of grace is blowing for all. Set your sail to catch that breeze." There is no question of God being partial or impartial, personal or impersonal. He is within us, like a magnet drawing us. You know, one name for God is Hari, which means one who steals our hearts. Another Sanskrit word is *madhava*, the sweet one. That magnet is drawing us all the time, but the point of the needle is covered with dirt and dust, so it does not feel the attraction of the magnet. Therefore, as Sri Ramakrishna said: "Weep, weep, weep for God! Let your tears wash the dirt and dust of the needle of your mind. Then you will feel the drawing of the magnet."

While we are in ignorance and only hear about grace, the thought comes to our mind that it comes from a personal being. So God is personal? But to those who do not believe in God but who do believe in the impersonal, absolute Reality, Atman-Brahman, how can the impersonal have any grace? From our standpoint of ignorance we consider it something mechanical. I had one student who said she believed in the impersonal God. When I asked her to give me some idea of the impersonal Reality, she said: "It is power." I said, "Very good, but how does that power express itself?" "Oh, like electricity." You see, we can't conceive of it. But here again, let me point out that whatever conception or idea of God you have, if you sincerely believe in it, it is real. The image of God comes to you according to your growth and understanding. Even if you have no idea or conception of God, seek and pray, saying, "I do not know if you exist. I do not know what you are. Whatever and whoever you are, please reveal yourself to me. I cannot live without the ultimate Reality!"

You know, his presence is felt in every human heart. You are a conscious being: whose consciousness is it? Of course you are not conscious of that consciousness, you are only conscious of the contents of consciousness. If you remove the contents of consciousness, there is God!

Sri Ramakrishna used to say that a policeman with a bull's eye lantern in the dark sees everybody, but nobody sees him. Similarly, God within – pure consciousness – is like that bull's eye lantern with which we see, know, and cognize every object. But we don't know that pure consciousness. So Sri Ramakrishna said: "You have to tell the policeman, 'I want to look at your face. Please turn your bull's eye lantern upon your own face.'"

So if there is divine grace, what need is there of self-effort? The religions of Hinduism, Christianity, Islam, and Judaism believe in divine grace, but we find Buddha not saying anything about it. He exhorts us to struggle, to strive. You see, Buddha was very practical. His point was this: If you follow these principles, if you struggle, you will know for yourselves whether God is or is not. Follow these methods and principles, and see for yourself. (124)

We think God is way above, somewhere beyond, and that grace comes from there. But the fact is, God is within, dwelling there as pure consciousness. We are conscious of objects and things, but by what power? The power of God that dwells within as pure consciousness. We are not aware of that; we are aware only of the light that is thrown upon objects and things, the light of consciousness. I see you before me. Whose power is that? The power of God. I am conscious. Whose power is it? The power of God. When I am asleep, there is that consciousness also. When I wake up, I am the same person; I know I had a wonderful rest. That pure consciousness of God is always present.

As St. Augustine said: "God is the circle whose center is everywhere, but whose circumference is nowhere." In other words, his center is in you, in me, in everyone. We are all living in that one center. We are many forms, yes, but as the Upanishads explain: "As air, though one, takes the shape of every object it enters, so the Self, though one, takes the shape of every object in which it dwells." [Katha Upanishad] It is that Atman, that pure consciousness, present everywhere, which is one with immortal life and abiding bliss, *Sat-chit-ananda*. Such is the experience of the great mystics. They open their eyes and see that pure consciousness everywhere. (125)

Through spiritual practices one attains the illumined knowledge of God, but remember – I am quoting the words of my master – "God is not a commodity like potatoes and onions that you can buy at a price." God is not a commodity that you can buy with so much japam and so much meditation. But practice meditation, go on practicing, and then you find the grace. And, as you have any kind of experience, any kind of vision, immediately there arises the thought, "Grace, grace, grace!"

When longing comes, you feel that grace. And then you realize that you could not even think of God, meditate upon God, or chant the name of God without his grace! There is a wrong understanding that if you read the scriptures regularly, you will realize God or will at least find after death that you go somewhere. But we have a saying that when the husking machine goes to heaven, what will it do but husk? When gossipy people go to heaven, what will they do? Gossip.

Grace is a psychological experience. It comes in many different ways. For instance, while you are trying to meditate and you can't, you can't even make japam, because you are restless for some reason – suddenly your whole body becomes soothed, and you become calm. And then you feel the grace. Those of you who have meditated long enough know that at times your mind goes down deep and you feel choked, as it were, because of the clinging to life; you feel as if you are going to die. So you come up. But then there comes another time when you are struck by thunder, as it were, and you are afraid – but there is no time to be afraid; you are in another world. And then you can see a form, or you may not see any form, but an ocean of light and waves of bliss striking you – and the whole universe disappears. (126)

All realized souls admit that realization comes through divine grace, and they will point out that the struggles we have to make are also through divine grace. You see, at that level of consciousness, everything is seen as divine grace. One time a disciple of Sri Ramakrishna told me, "You know, I passed through a stage when every step I took I felt was through the power, the grace, of God." What we call ego was completely missing.

The fact is, God is personal, and God is impersonal, but not the way you and I may think of God being personal, like a human being, nor impersonal like an automaton or an abstraction. All the definition that can be given is that he is endowed with all the blessed divine qualities or, if impersonal, is beyond all attributes. No matter how you think of God, it is anthropomorphic. But it doesn't matter. No matter how you call on him, he will reveal himself to you. And until he reveals himself to you, you really cannot conceive of him. But try to think of God in your own way. You know, the Upanishads say there are thirty-three million Gods, because each of us conceives of the Divine differently.

The ultimate experience is that whatever is perceived or experienced is none other than God. Wherever your eyes fall, there is God; you see nothing but God. (127)

KARMA AND GRACE

Karma is a Sanskrit word which means work, or action. Mind is active as well as body, so thoughts are also considered work – not only conscious thoughts, but subconscious and unconscious thoughts or reflex actions. And that is not all. Any act done or any thought thought is not lost: each creates an impression in the mind.

You see, a thought arises and, though you forget it, it is not lost. It has created an impression in your mind. You do a good or a bad action and then you forget it, but that action has created an impression in your mind. The sum-total of those impressions form the character of an individual. All impressions remain in the subconscious mind. It is not that there is a conscious mind, a subconscious mind, and an unconscious mind, but that the one mind has these three levels. The conscious mind on another level is the subconscious, and on another level, the unconscious.

That is not all. Each action, each thought, not only helps to form an individual character, but certain experiences which they bring into our lives – whether happiness or misery – are the results of our past actions, good or bad. So the word *karma* refers to what we call "the law of karma": it is the law of causation. Just as in the physical world the law of causation works inevitably – put your finger in the fire and it will burn – similarly, this law of causation works on the mental and moral planes. You raise a wave of love, and it comes back to you, bringing happiness. You raise a wave of hatred, and it brings back suffering. There are both good actions and thoughts and bad actions and thoughts; we are a mixture of both.

In the Bible we read: "As a man soweth, so shall he reap." In Hindu scripture, Manu the lawgiver says: "Thou canst not gather what thou dost not sow; as thou dost plant the tree, so will it grow." You see, our suffering and happiness are of our own making. Nobody else is responsible. We have created certain tendencies in our lives and we are bound by them.

When you have formed a habit – such as drinking or smoking – you have created a tendency. You can't help yourself: you have to drink, you have to smoke.

But the law of karma teaches something further. True, you have created a tendency in yourself, no doubt, and you feel you are forced to repeat it, but there is something in the back of your consciousness that says, "No, I have the freedom to resist it." You can't exactly call that free will, because the will is a compound of our various characteristics and as such is sometimes helpless. But there is a freedom – the freedom of the Atman. This is what we must learn, and this is the most wonderful truth taught in Vedanta, that there is the Atman within, which is free by its inherent nature. Your true nature is free, and you are divine. Yes, you have formed a habit, but you can resist it; you can create another habit to overcome it. This, of course, is the freedom of divinity, the freedom of the Atman, asserting itself.

There is no individual in this world who can be so bad as to be lost forever. Howsoever wicked you may be – and you suffer for your wickedness in one life or another – freedom asserts itself and ultimately you attain freedom, salvation, liberation, union with God – whatever name you may give it.

You have the ego – ignorance – and you have to struggle with it. But there are two kinds of ego, one unripe, the other ripe. The unripe ego feels, "I am so intelligent, I am so great, I am so rich, I am so big, I am so famous." That is to be shunned. The ripe ego says, "I am a child of God, I am a servant of God." We have to take the help of that ripe ego. As in the Gita we read: "What is a man's will and how shall he use it? Let him put forth his effort to uncover the Atman, not to hide the Atman. Man's will is the only friend of the Atman, his will also is the Atman's enemy." You are your own savior, your own friend, and you are your own enemy. Savior and enemy are not outside of you.

There is a struggle to take refuge in God. Who will do that? You have to do that. Your mind has to do that. Your will has to do that. There is the misunderstanding that becoming absorbed in God, you lose your personality, your individuality. But that is not so. The ego, your individuality, has no reality, but passes away like a shadow when the reality is experienced. Edwin Arnold said that a dewdrop is mixed in the ocean, that you are a dewdrop and you get absorbed in the ocean, but that's not it. You are not a dewdrop. You *are* the ocean! There is one ocean of existence, one ocean of knowledge, one ocean of bliss – and you are that. I am that, everybody is that. Suppose you are one of the waves of that ocean. Is that a dewdrop? You are the whole ocean! Realize what you are! (128)

It is taught that you have to devote yourself to God, to fix your heart and mind in God, to meditate and meditate. Shall we, then, give up action? Shall we give up work? Shall we give up the duties of life? Shall we cease to think? Is that possible?

Now, where does karma attach itself? Let us try to find that out first. The Atman within, the indwelling God, is *sat, chit,* and *ananda* – eternal life, pure consciousness, and abiding love and infinite bliss. Its intrinsic nature is free. It is never bound. You are never bound, but you are dreaming this dream. Why? Because you identify yourself with body, mind, senses, and sense-organs. The first begotten son of ignorance is the sense of ego. "I am this body, I weigh so many pounds. I have to diet." Something arises in the mind: "Oh, I am happy," or "My mind is restless," or "I feel so lazy." We assign the attributes of the coverings of the Atman to the Atman.

How do we get out of this? Sri Krishna points out in the Gita: "Freedom from activity is never achieved by abstaining from action. In fact, nobody can even rest from this activity for a moment." Thoughts arise: that is activity. All are helplessly forced to act by the three gunas – sattva, rajas, and tamas. We are bound by them. It is three gunas that make the mind calm, restless, or lazy. We are subject to them. According to them we act, think, and behave.

So should we renounce physical actions? If the mind continues to dwell in those thoughts concerning them, that would be hypocrisy! Or, as modern psychologists point out, repression. So should we give expression to every thought that arises in the mind? Then we shall be nowhere. Does that, then, mean that we should not look at objects of senses, keep away from them, go into a cave in the Himalayas or the Gobi desert? No. We have to be able to move among the objects of senses without being attached to them or having aversion to them. Attachment and aversion are the causes of bondage to the law of karma.

There must, therefore, be a secret of action. You have to meditate, but is it possible to meditate and not perform action? Through action we must learn to keep our mind in God and be freed from attachment and aversion. We have the right to work, but we have no right to the fruits of the work. Every day after you have done your deeds and thought your thoughts, offer the effects of all these to God within you. Never forget that the ideal is to attain Brahman. The question that arises is, "But then it would be a motiveless action. How is that possible? I want to do something because I want to get certain effects out of it. Motiveless and disinterested action may be all right to read about in books, but how can I do it?" Well, it is not completely motiveless action – but there is a bigger motive in it. You see, if you ask for the fruits of action, yes, you get them. If you do not seek for the fruits but offer them to God, you will get an infinite effect. That effect is never exhausted: that effect is that you find God.

I often tell people, "Look, if I had to rob anything, I would rob a bank." If you desire anything, desire the Supreme, the highest. Then everything is fulfilled. In the Gita we read: "Perform every action with your heart fixed on God. To unite the heart with Brahman and then to act, that is the secret of motiveless action."

And the secret of that is to surrender yourself to God. That means to keep your mind fixed in God. In the Gita again we find: "In the calm of self-surrender, the seers renounce the fruits of action and so reach enlightenment. Then they are free from the bondage of rebirth and pass to that state which is beyond all evil."

And there is another method: try to consider your work itself as worship. Let me quote the Gita again: "The world is imprisoned by its own activity except when actions are performed as worship of God. Therefore you must perform every action sacramentally and be free from all attachment to results." The secret of worshiping God through action is this: "Whatever the gift you give to another, whatever you vow to the work of the spirit, lay these also as offerings before me." You ritualistically offer a flower to the Lord: now make work a flower that you offer to the Lord. When you cook, cook for the Lord. When you keep house, keep house for the Lord, because he dwells there. When you nurse the baby, consider you are feeding baby Krishna or baby Christ. And learn to see God in every action. "He who sees Brahman in every action finds Brahman."

The ultimate thing is to get rid of the ego entirely. Sri Ramakrishna used to say this prayer: "I am the machine, Thou art the operator. I am the house, Thou art the householder. I do as Thou makest me do. I speak as Thou makest me speak." But we must be sincere about this. I once asked Swami Turiyananda what religion is. He answered: "To make the lips and the heart the same." In other words, to be sincere. When you feel that you are only an instrument, that God is the operator within, you have to feel it sincerely.

My master taught me this truth: the Lord, or God, does his own preaching; you be the witness. In other words, that you are attracted to think of God is not your doing: God attracted you.

Now I must tell you how an illumined soul feels about action. The gopis, shepherdesses, were eager to go see their beloved Krishna, but the river Jamuna was flooded. They couldn't find a boat to carry them across, and they couldn't swim. A holy man came by – probably Vyasa – and they asked him, "Holy sir, please help us cross this river." He said, "Look, have you got something to eat?" They had all kinds of food, which they gave him with the hope that he would help them to cross. You know, he finished everything! And then he prayed to the river Jamuna: "River Jamuna, if I have not eaten anything today, please part." And the river parted. Because he felt he himself had not eaten.

That is what an illumined soul feels. The Gita explains this: "The illumined soul, whose heart is Brahman's heart, thinks always, 'I am doing nothing,' no matter what he sees, hears, touches, smells, whether he is moving, sleeping, breathing, speaking or opening his eyes or closing his eyes. Thus he knows always, 'I am not seeing, I am not hearing. It is the senses that see and hear and touch the things of the senses.' And he knows that he is not the senses, but is beyond the senses; he is the Atman." (129)

St. Augustine used to pray: "Free me from lust," and then he would whisper, "Not yet, Lord!"

When we are weak and cannot resist our temptations, what do we do? Pray. But you know the secret? Who answers the prayer? If done sincerely and earnestly, the answers to all our prayers come from, not God above, but God within. In other words, the Atman answers our prayers: it is you who answer your own prayer. And every prayer is answered.

` The earth moves, but what do we think moves? Through our illusion, the sun appears to move. Or clouds are in the sky and we think, through illusion, that the sun is coming out of the clouds. It is the clouds that are moving. What is born, and what dies? What is reborn again? Nature, mind, matter. The Atman is where it has always been. Witnessing. Through illusion we are deluded by identifying ourselves with the mind, senses, body, and sense organs. We think we are being born and we die. But no, we are in God all the time. We are free, immortal, pure, all the time.

The truly admirable man controls his senses by the power of his will. He moves amongst sense objects and acts, but without any attachment or aversion. So renounce the fruits of action. Keep your heart fixed in God and act. You may think, how can we concentrate our mind upon the action if we keep our heart fixed in God? To this, my master taught us: "If you meditate, then you can use eighty percent of your mind for God; if you give twenty percent to action, it is enough." (131)

RITUALISM

The highest truth is to realize our identity with Brahman, realize the true being, the true Self, within. And ritualism is one of the methods. It is not the only method, and it is not that everyone has to practice ritualism, but it is a help, especially for a beginner. Of course it depends upon one's temperament.

There are two extreme schools of thought. One identifies religion with ritualism, and that's all you have to do. When we emphasize ritualism and identify that with spiritual life, we forget why ritualism is being practiced: we forget that the ideal is to experience God. But some form of spiritual discipline has to be practiced, whether ritualistic worship or worshiping God with prayer and chanting of his name; or meditating, when there is a current of thought flowing towards God constantly, or the highest meditation on the supreme identity with Brahman.

My master said, "A man should begin his spiritual life from where he stands." If an ordinary man is told to meditate on the union with the absolute Brahman, he cannot grasp the truth of it, nor can he follow the instructions. He may make an attempt, but he will soon tire and give it up. However, if the same man is asked to worship God with flowers, perfume, and other accessories, you will find that his mind gradually becomes concentrated and he will soon experience joy in his worship. Through ritualistic worship, devotion to the performance of *japam* grows, and you begin to love to chant the name of the Lord.

The finer the mind becomes, the greater is its capacity for higher forms of worship. An aspirant moves towards the ideal by a process of natural growth. (131)

If any religion insists that ritualism is the only way, then that religion will grow into a fanatical sect. (132)

Ritualism is not absolutely necessary. It is not that everybody has to practice it to have religion or to live a spiritual life. It is according to the temperament of the individual that a method is given. I'll give you my personal experience. One day I was arranging a basket of flowers that were sent by a devotee to my master. He asked, "Have you given half of those flowers to the

Lord in the shrine?" I answered, "No." In my mind I thought, "That's only a picture. Here is the living God." He seemed to read my thoughts and said, "You think that's only a picture?" I said, in a low voice, "Yes." Then he asked me, "Have you ever done ritualistic worship?" I said, "No." "Why?" "I don't believe in it." He didn't argue with me, he simply said, "I am asking you to do it. Will you?" "Yes, of course."

Let me point out that my master didn't ask everybody to do the ritualistic worship. I'll tell you my experience, because ritualism is not something you can understand intellectually. You have to do it yourself to understand its validity. It is a matter of experience.

It happened this way. I was living a contemplative life in a monastery. The worshiper in the monastery became sick, so I learned the worship and began to do it, although mechanically. In spite of that, on the third day, the grace of my guru proved to me the efficacy of this ritual worship. It was shown to me as is taught in the Bhagavad Gita: "Whatever a man gives me in true devotion, fruit or water, a leaf, a flower, I will accept that gift as his love, his heart's dedication." Now I confess that I had no devotion when I did the worship. I did it mechanically; yet the Lord and the grace of my guru proved to me that the Lord does accept what we offer. Often I have said to people, "You offer a flower before the picture. You think he doesn't know, but you'd be surprised. The Lord does know, and he does accept."

Most people have the misunderstanding that ritualistic worship is dualistic. The fact is, when you learn to do it, you find it nondualistic. The ego disappears, the universe disappears, there is Brahman alone. Then the ego comes back, but it is the ego of knowledge; then you see everything as Brahman. This is the principle we find throughout the ritualistic worship.

In order to do ritualistic worship, you have to have some accessories: flowers, water, light, incense, and so forth. These items have two meanings. One meaning is that this whole universe is made up of five elements – earth, water, air, ether, fire. Of course not this earth, but the subtle element of earth, the subtle elements of fire, and so on. You see, the earth that we see is a combination of all the elements in a particular proportion. I need not go into that, but the idea is that these items represent those five elements, and you are giving them back to God. You are offering back the universe that has come out of him; you are saying, "Lord, take, and let me see only you."

There is another explanation: that all the items before you represent the objects of the whole universe. You touch each item, you worship it, as Brahman, as God. We have a saying, "Worship Mother Ganga with the water of Mother Ganga." It is the same: worshiping Brahman with Brahman. Now I shall explain a little of the ritual worship in detail.

You begin by sipping water. As you sip, you say a mantra: "Om Vishnu, Om Vishnu, Om Vishnu," which means you are trying to think of the all-pervading spirit, God, as consciousness everywhere in the universe. Your body, the worshiper, is also full of consciousness.

Then you touch the different parts of your body to signify that you are closing the doors of the senses so that you can see within the temple of your own heart the dweller in this city. There is an allegorical saying that the body is a city of nine gates: mouth, two ears, two eyes, and so forth. We go out through these doors of the senses in order to enjoy the world, forgetting God. Whereas, within the city of nine gates dwells the Lord of the universe. Now you close the doors of the senses with a prayer: "Om, as with eyes wide open, a man sees the sky spread before him, so the seers, with their divine sight opened, see Brahman everywhere. May I see him. May the truth of God be revealed to me." In other words, your object in worship is that God may reveal himself to you. As my master once said to me, you have to have confidence in yourself: others have seen God, I also can see him.

Then the worshiper makes some gestures with the hands and fingers. They all have meaning, because the body and mind are interrelated. For instance, if there is love in your heart, it is expressed in your body and hands and fingers. If you are angry, it is expressed also. The idea is that if you can bring those expressions in your body repeatedly, then that same feeling will arise in you. For instance, if you express love outwardly, you can bring changes in the body and in your heart also.

In almost every case, a spiritual aspirant who is struggling to realize the truth of God has some obstacles on the path. You are progressing, your mind becomes absorbed in God, then suddenly you find yourself full of lust, anger, greed, things like that. As you find in the life of Jesus: "Get thee behind me, Satan!" He was tempting him. In the life of Buddha also we find Mara tempting him. These temptations come on the way. They are the obstacles. And there are three other kinds of obstacles: evil spirits hovering around, psychic obstacles and obstacles created by gods in heaven afraid they will be replaced. Since you are struggling, they become jealous of you – that you may want their position. There are certain methods by which to remove these obstacles.

Next is worship of the guru. You meditate upon your guru because the guru is the instrument. Of course, there is one guru – God, *Sat-chit-ananda* – but this instrument is a human being. Naturally you show your respect to the guru, because guru is God himself, the same power descending.

Then comes the worship of Ganesha, who is the god who gives success.

Next, you protect yourself in your mind with a wall of fire.

Following that comes the meditation upon the identity of the Atman with Brahman. You meditate upon that divine energy called the *kundalini*, which remains in a coiled form at the bottom of your spine. You meditate upon that energy rising through the center of the spine. This actually happens when one reaches the highest, but now you try to imagine that. It rises to the center of your heart, where your individual self is just like a candle flame. You raise that candle flame with the help of this divine energy and come to the center of the brain. There is Brahman, and you merge the individual self in that light. As you practice this, you also meditate upon the idea that the physical body is merged in the subtle body, then the subtle body is merged in the causal body, and then the causal body is merged in *prakriti*, the Mother power. *Prakriti* is then merged in Brahman. And so there remains only Brahman: I am he, I am he, I am he.

You see, that is a complete nondualistic method of meditation.

Now the question arises: who is there to worship whom? The point is that you become a god to worship God. You use some seed words that make this body, which is built up of sacred words, into the deity himself that you are worshiping, your chosen ideal. You think that the limbs, the senses, and sense-organs are all those of your chosen ideal. You are no longer there; you have become one with the Lord.

And then you meditate. As you meditate, you have a *mudra* or gesture of the hand. If you look at the standing photograph of Ramakrishna, you find his fingers in a certain position. That is the meditation *mudra*. Holding a flower in this *mudra*, you meditate.

After this meditation, you put that flower on your head and worship God within. As you worship God within, you offer the different elements, your mind, your senses, your everything, to him.

Then again, you do the *nyasa* (purification), touching the body, and continue to think that it is made up of *mantra*, not physical matter.

Then you meditate with a flower. You place that flower before the image. You have breathed into it your Atman, the divinity that is within you. Through that flower, you bring the Lord from within your heart and you place it before the image. Now you see the Lord before you.

Next you offer the different items: incense, perfume, light, and so on. Then you practice *japa* of the *mantra* that has been given to you by your guru.

Lastly, you offer the fruits of everything that you have done in the worship to the Lord. And then all you seek, all you pray for, is pure devotion, pure love, and pure knowledge. (133)

OVERCOMING OBSTACLES
IN SPIRITUAL LIFE

There are five obstacles in the empirical self: ignorance, the sense of ego, attachment, aversion, and the desire to cling to this surface life. These obstacles are universal. By ignorance I mean that which covers the Reality. One may have encyclopedic knowledge, but without knowledge of Brahman ignorance remains. And to be a knower of Brahman is a direct perception, not an intellectual understanding or faith. Our ignorance is direct and immediate: we identify ourselves with the empirical self, and this has to be removed. The shadow has to fall away before the light of the Atman can shine within us. That has to be a direct and immediate experience.

The tendencies of the mind, the senses, the nerves go in one direction, and you try to change them to the opposite direction. The surface current goes toward the enjoyments of life, and the undercurrent that wants God is going in the opposite direction. Forget that surface current and go to the deeper current. Distractions or obstacles can be overcome only by practice, by concentrating on a single truth, the truth of God. Make that practice your habit. (134)

In the process of evolution, nothing is added: what is already there in potential form becomes unfolded gradually. The intelligence that you find evolved in the human being exists in the worm that crawls underfoot, but through the process of evolution, that intelligence has become unfolded.

Christ-hood or Buddha-hood is nothing special or unique. It is only that we all have to unfold that Christ-hood – God in his infinite degree. His all-perfection is dwelling within each individual soul: you and I are never separate from God. As Swami Vivekananda pointed out, in all your life you have seen nothing but God, but you have to be aware of that.

There are two words in Sanskrit: *nishkama* and *purnakama*. *Nishkama* means to be desireless, and *purnakama* means the fulfillment of all desire. They both mean the same thing. In other words, as long as you have cravings for the objective world, you cannot have fulfillment. When you renounce all cravings and desires – and by such renunciation, you raise a positive desire for God in yourself – you find fulfillment.

Where your consciousness is, there is what you experience. As long as we are in ignorance and have only the physical senses experience, that is the truth. But when we raise our consciousness, we see nothing but God or spirit. Swamiji's example is that a baby is lying in a room and a thief comes and steals something. The baby does not see a thief, because thieving is not in the baby. We see someone as bad because we see the reflection of what is in us. But if the vision has opened, then we see no sinner or saint, we see only God.

Now, what is the main obstacle? We read in the Bible: "The light shineth in darkness, but the darkness comprehended it not." The Hindu or Buddhist saint calls this *avidya*, ignorance – ignorance covering the light. And not only does it cover the light, but it creates something which has no reality – the sense of ego. As Sri Ramakrishna said: "Try to find what your ego is. Just like an onion, peel layer after layer to find out what is inside. You find nothing." Similarly, ask yourself, "Am I this body? Am I the mind? Am I the senses? Am I a combination of these?" You will find that they are all shifting and vanishing, all in flux. Yet because of a sense of ego, there is attachment to things and objects and persons that give us pleasure, and aversion to those that give us suffering.

There is a clinging to this surface life, and it is universal, a universal ignorance. We do not want to give up what we enjoy through our senses and consider so real. Though our goal is to be God-men or God-women – and while living in this body we can attain that – there is a great obstacle in the way. The Katha Upanishad says: "The Self-existent made the senses turn outward. Accordingly, man looks toward what is without and sees not what is within. Rare is he who, longing for immortality, shuts his eyes to what is without and beholds the Self." [Katha Upanishad]

As aspirants we pass through different stages to reach the goal. First, we search here and there and everywhere, then at last we realize that what we are seeking is to be found within. We learn to practice spiritual disciplines – and then obstacles come.

First there is mental laziness. And naturally doubt arises: am I not fooling myself? What is this, closing my eyes and trying to focus my thoughts on God? Do I know anything of God? Swami Saradananda, a disciple of Sri Ramakrishna, was asked by one of his disciples, "How can I meditate on God if

I don't know what God is?" Swami Saradananda answered: "Look here, if you know what God is, you don't have to meditate." It is like a person who insists on learning to swim before getting into the water.

Though we know that "vanity of vanity, all is vanity," still old habits come back, and our mind runs after sense pleasures again and again. We can't help it. So we have to keep the sword of discrimination at the door.

And then there is another great obstacle, despair, caused by the failure to concentrate.

What is the remedy for all these obstacles? There is one remedy; bundle them together. My master used to say "Practice, practice, practice." That is the only way to overcome all these obstacles. He would repeat again and again his one answer: "Meditate, meditate, meditate, practice, practice, practice, and you are bound to succeed." (135)

In actuality there is one reality. Call that matter or call it spirit, there are not two realities. There is no division between matter and spirit, that here is one and there is the other. One time my master said to me: "Show me the line of demarcation where matter ends and spirit begins." In other words, we experience only matter, but when we transform ourselves, we shall experience only spirit.

In the words of Shankara: "How can the physical eyes see anything but physical objects; how can the mind of the enlightened man think of anything other than the Reality, Brahman? See Brahman everywhere, under all circumstances, with the eye of spirit and a tranquil heart." To repeat, perfection is already in you; you are one with God. No other perfection is possible: God is the one perfect being, and that perfect being is within each one of us. In his infinite degree, not in part. You *are* God, I *am* God, there is no other God but I. This is the universal experience. As you proceed in your spiritual path, ultimately you will experience this.

St. John of the Cross said: "The more the soul cleaves to created things, relying on its own strength by habit and inclination, the less is it disposed to this union, because it does not completely resign itself into the hands of God that He may transform it super-normally."

Now, what is the way? Just as you have to have physical exercises and intellectual training, even so the training of the spirit is possible only through the exercise of the spirit. There is no other way. What is meant by exercise of the spirit? To discipline the mind in the first place. Undisciplined thinking and habits and behavior lead us nowhere. You have to discipline the mind completely. (136)

In the Kena Upanishad, we read: "Having given up the false identification of the Self with the senses and the mind, and knowing the Self to be Brahman, the wise, on departing the world, become immortal."

That is the goal to be achieved, but I find a misunderstanding in almost every student of Vedanta. They try to get rid of their egos – a wonderful idea – but how can you totally get rid of your ego, this empirical self, until you have got hold of the Atman? Only in *samadhi*, when you have attained the knowledge of Atman and have become your Self does the empirical self drop off. And without your ego, how can you struggle? How can you meditate? Who is there to meditate on whom? Who is there to worship? As long as we are in the relative plane, there has to be an ego. Self-consciousness, or ego, has to evolve before one can reach the complete unfoldment of divinity.

This ego again has two aspects, which Sri Ramakrishna described as the ego of knowledge and the ego of ignorance.

First we have to kill the ego of ignorance: "I am such and such an intelligent person; I know more than any of you; I am proud to be an American; I take pride in having this and that." This is the ego that leads to great bondage, that separates us from everybody else and distinguishes us as somebodies. That ego has to be killed. But have instead the ego of knowledge, "I am a child of God; I am a servant of God; everybody is a child of God; I am not better than anybody." At the same time have the confidence that you are pure. Then you can approach God. This ego of knowledge is very important in order to ultimately transcend it, but first we must eliminate the ego of ignorance.

So the good ego leads you to freedom, the bad ego to bondage. And according to the psychologist Patanjali, there are the obstacles of attachment, aversion, and the desire to cling to life. Considering clinging to life an obstacle will be misunderstood immediately. It does not mean that we should commit suicide, but let me quote Christ: "He who loves this life shall lose it." The clinging to this surface life is instinctive in every one of us. When you practice meditation, you find that your mind is becoming absorbed in the consciousness of God, but you have not yet got hold of it, and that makes you restless. Even if a great soul like Christ or Ramakrishna gives you the ultimate experience with a touch, you say, "No, no, no, I don't want it." Such is our instinctive desire for the surface life. Even when you are a spiritual aspirant struggling hard to find God, when the grace of God comes, it strikes you like thunder. You feel as if you are going to be killed and you say, "No, no, no!" But through the grace of God, you pass through that stage and have no more time to be afraid. You are in that other deeper life that transcends this ego, this life.

How to overcome these obstacles? The way can be likened to a dirty cloth. To clean it you need to apply soap, and then wash it in clear water. The dirt of attachment and aversion is in our minds. We have created karmas and all their impressions in our minds. Now a new character has to be formed. Patanjali points out what the soap in spiritual life is: "austerity, study, and dedication to God. These are the preliminary steps to yoga."

The practice of meditation is the water with which to wash.

But as my master said, "Who can meditate?" Meditation is next to *samadhi*; it is a constant, unbroken flow of thought towards God. In other words, we must be absorbed. That absorption is the last stage before *samadhi* – illumination, enlightened knowledge.

So here is the secret: think of your chosen ideal and chant his name. It is that simple. Your mind may be slothful, but even if you're lazy you can still lie down and chant the name of God. If you don't even have the desire for God, pray that you may *have* that desire – and chant the name! Patanjali said, "That one practice can lead you to the highest illumined knowledge of God." (137)

PATH OF MEDITATION

Meditation is not so easy – the constant recollectedness of God, when the mind thinks of God without any break. It is the most difficult task to bring the mind under complete control. Of course the main principle is to want to realize God; one has to have that desire. Sri Ramakrishna used to say: "For those who have not yet come to understand the futility of sense enjoyments and pleasures and worldly experiences, it is not possible to desire God."

So you have to have the interest for God. That interest arises only when you feel that this finitude of existence is a bondage; only then will you be interested in the struggle to find him. Practical lessons are given in the yoga of meditation, but you have to be interested to follow them.

Ultimately to realize God, meditation is the path. Whether one is following the path of action or knowledge or devotion, one has to meditate. But it is not such an easy thing to do. You may sit, close your eyes, and try to concentrate, but there are distractions. And so there must be preparations. All the spiritual disciplines have one end in view: to achieve purity of heart.

But what is that purity of heart? What does that mean? It means desiring nothing else but God. When your mind is no longer distracted and your heart loves only God, then it is pure. To quote the words of Patanjali: "As soon as all impurities have been removed by the practice of spiritual disciplines – the limbs of yoga – a man's spirit opens to the light-giving knowledge of God." It is not a matter of acceptance or belief or intellectual understanding, but of following of a path. One ounce of practice is greater than many tons of theories. As you practice concentration and meditation and as love grows, ethical principles become natural. Men or women of God do not harm any creature: the one characteristic of the holy is that they emanate such love that as you approach, you feel no enmity. It is said that the lamb and the lion will sit at their feet in harmony.

I will give you one illustration that I have seen. Two of us young boys were following my master out of the monastery, and from both sides of the road people were shouting, "Get away! Get away! A mad bull is coming. Get away!" We saw the bull approaching, and we wanted to protect our old master, so we went forward. But Maharaj just put his arms out and threw us back; he stood there and looked at the bull. The bull stood there shaking its head a few times; then it became calm and moved away.

As you begin practicing spiritual disciplines, you will feel cheerfulness and faith in your heart. A long face is not religion; from inside will come cheerfulness. There will also come the power of concentration and the power to control the passions, the fitness for the vision of God.

"Knowledge is power," says the proverb, and that is true. Until you know what the mind is doing, you cannot control it. Those who never meditate think their mind is wonderful; they do not know what a rascal the mind is. But when you try to practice concentration and meditation, you begin to realize how distracted and restless it is. Until you know what the mind is doing, you cannot control it.

Give it rein. Many hideous thoughts may come. You'll be astonished that it was possible for you to think such thoughts. But you will find that each day the mind's vagaries are becoming fewer and less violent, that each day the mind is becoming calmer. In the first few months you will find that it will have a great many thoughts. Later you will find that they have decreased somewhat. And in a few more months you will find they are fewer and fewer still, until the mind comes under perfect control. But we must practice patiently each day.

Learn to concentrate. What is concentration? Holding the mind within a center of spiritual consciousness in the body. You have to learn these centers of spiritual consciousness from a teacher and then fix the mind on some divine ideal either within the body or without.

In one Upanishad we read: "Within the lotus of the heart he dwells, where the nerves meet like the spokes of a wheel. Meditate upon him as Om, and you may easily cross the ocean of darkness. In the effulgent lotus of the heart dwells Brahman, passionless and indivisible. He is pure, he is the light of all lights. The knowers of Brahman attain him." [Mundaka Upanishad]

Of course, for this you have to sit and try to concentrate and meditate regularly. Apart from that, my master taught us what is called the simple yoga, the simple way, to attain God: "Keep recollectedness of God as often as you can. While you are sitting, standing, walking, and under all conditions, try to feel the presence of God. Keep that recollectedness of God until it becomes a habit."

Through such practice, when you come to a stage of unfoldment when your mind really can meditate, when there is no distraction, then the vision of God will come. Once you go into that state where the world has disappeared, just God is; when you come back, you are an illumined soul, and that is something that you have attained for eternity. (138)

Meditation means that your consciousness is in God continuously, without any distracting thought, just as when oil is poured from one vessel to another, there is an unbroken stream. When you reach that state of meditation, then knowledge of God comes.

Now, you do not achieve that stage all at once. You have to practice some spiritual disciplines to prepare yourself for such attainment. You have to discipline yourself before you can have real interest in God and real love for God.

What is the nature of love? To think constantly of the beloved. If you learn to think constantly of God, then you begin to love what you are thinking about. The principle behind this is discipline.

But to come to the conviction that God is within your heart takes time. When you come to the conviction that he is right here, then everything else follows. But sometimes it takes many years to come to that conviction. You see, it is not intellectual understanding or an ordinary kind of conviction. It is when you begin to feel that presence that everything begins to happen. Through such practice of concentration you come to a stage of unfoldment when your mind becomes meditative. Without any distractions, your mind runs towards God. You see, the nature of the mind is to move on and on and on. You have steady electrical light when the current comes steadily. If the current is interrupted, the light will flicker. So when we first try to concentrate, the mind flickers. We think of God, but there is a distraction, a gap. Again we try to think of God – again distractions. You cannot hold that thought long enough. But through practice, a time comes when distractions vanish and there is a continuity of consciousness. In Hindu psychology it is said that if you can have that for even twenty-seven minutes or half an hour, without any break, you attain *samadhi*; that is, you become absorbed and have the vision and experience of God. (139)

Of course you have to struggle. True it is that the grace has to descend, but the grace is always there. In order to catch that breeze of grace, you have to make an effort. And the principle is meditation.

The fundamental question is how to meditate on "that whom words cannot express, from whom the mind comes away baffled, unable to reach." [Taittiriya Upanishad] It is not possible to meditate on that which is absolute. Who sees whom? Who knows whom? When one sees another, when one talks to another, that is finite. When one sees no one, when one talks to no one – that is the Infinite! That is the blissful state to be attained.

So what are we to do? There are four different paths for different temperaments: the intellectual, the emotional, the active, the contemplative. You can't give the whole teaching to everybody, you can't teach meditation only one way.

You see, there is not one way to meditate, but many different ways according to different temperaments. In the Yoga Aphorisms, Patanjali gave many methods. He said: "You can meditate on the inner light that is sorrowless, the light that is smokeless. You can meditate on the heart of the illumined soul who is free from all passions. And you can meditate upon a dream experience, if that dream experience be of a holy personality. Some people see a holy personality or even receive *mantras* in a dream. You can meditate upon that, or even on the peaceful happiness that comes in deep sleep. Or upon any divine form or symbol that appeals to you as good and divine."

As a general rule, whatever your chosen aspect – an inner light or a divine incarnation or anything within – it has to be first within the shrine of the heart. In one of the Upanishads we read: "The supreme heaven shines in the lotus of the heart. Those who struggle and aspire may enter there. Retire into solitude, seat yourself in a clean spot, in an erect posture, with the head and neck in a straight line. Control all sense organs. Bow down in devotion to your teacher. Then enter the lotus of the heart and meditate there on the presence of Brahman, the pure, the infinite, the blissful." [Kaivalya Upanishad]

In another Upanishad, the Mundaka, it says: "Within the lotus of the heart he dwells, where, like the spokes of a wheel, the nerves meet. Meditate on him as OM and you may easily cross the ocean of darkness.... In the effulgent lotus of the heart dwells Brahman, who is passionless and indivisible. He is pure, he is the light of lights. Him the knowers of the Self attain." [Mundaka Upanishad] (140)

A few days back as I woke from my sleep, my finger began to move. Suddenly I thought to myself, "What causes this finger to move this way?" Then it suddenly occurred to me that there is the power of divinity within me, and it is because of that presence that my mind can think, my body can move, my senses are active. Without that presence, I am nothing. And then I remembered the passage from the Kena Upanishad: "At whose behest," the disciple asks, "does the mind think? Who bids the body live? Who makes the tongue speak? Who is that effulgent being that directs the eye to forms and color and the ear to sound? The Self is the ear of the ear, mind of the mind, speech of the speech. He is also breath of the breath and eye of the eye... He who realizes the existence of Brahman behind every activity of his being, whether sensation, perception, or thought, he alone gains immortality."

Just consider. It is possible for me to think and for you to listen, because of that effulgent being within each one of us. Without that presence, we are nobody. This we have to realize. And when we experience this truth, then we shall feel like Sri Ramakrishna, who said, "I am the instrument, Thou art the operator. I am the house, Thou art the householder." When we realize that, we are free from all *karmas*; we attain to our eternal life. In other words, our minds, senses, and body must learn to pay homage, as it were, to that effulgent being who is within us. That is our main duty. All religions teach this fundamental truth: "Ye are the temples of God and the Spirit of God dwelleth in you."

Now, how are we to meditate on God? What is God? What is his nature? Are we to meditate on him as absolute and impersonal, as personal, or what? Sri Ramakrishna, who followed all kinds of *sadhana*, pointed out this truth: "Infinite is God. Infinite are His aspects. If one lives continuously in consciousness of him, he knows him in his true nature. He knows him as impersonal, without attributes, and he also knows him as personal, with attributes." Then he gave a beautiful illustration: "There is a vast ocean, endless, but through

24

intense cold, some places form icebergs." So, though water has no form, it has assumed forms. And there are innumerable forms – *avataras* or divine incarnations whom we call "sons of God": Christ, Krishna, Buddha, Ramakrishna. There is a Hindu prayer: "They call you by many names, they divide you as it were by different names, yet in each one of these there is to be found your omnipotence. You are revealed through any of these."

Let me point out exactly what the state of meditation is. In the Gita it is beautifully expressed: "The light of a lamp does not flicker in a windless place. This is the simile which describes a Yogi of one-pointed mind who meditates upon the Atman. When, through the practice of Yoga, the mind ceases its restless movements and becomes still, he realizes the Atman. It satisfies him entirely. Then he knows that infinite happiness which can be realized by the purified heart, but is beyond the grasp of the senses. He stands firm in this realization. Because of it, he can never again wander from the inmost truth of his being."

And again, "Utterly quiet, made clean of passion, the mind of the yogi knows that Brahman; his bliss is the highest. Released from evil, his mind is constant in contemplation: the way is easy, Brahman has touched him, that bliss is boundless. His heart is with Brahman, his eye in all things sees only Brahman equally present, knows his own Atman in every creature, and all creation within that Atman. That Yogi sees me in all things, and all things within me. He never loses sight of me, nor I of him. He is established in union with me, and worships me devoutly in all beings. That Yogi abides in me, no matter what his mode of life."

Now before you can come to that state of meditation, which is *samadhi*, you first have to practice, and then you begin to feel the presence. He is: you become convinced of that. No more hearsay. Then you begin to feel that he is moving, living. You talk to him. These are facts. Ultimately you realize your oneness with him. In all these experiences there is a feeling that it is not through your attempt, but through his grace. Whenever any experience comes, immediately there will come this understanding: not by my struggle, not by my effort, but by that divine grace. It is a tangible experience. It is then that you become a blessing to yourself and a blessing to all mankind. Your very presence becomes a blessing to all.

In conclusion I'd like to quote Swami Vivekananda: "In meditation we divest ourselves of all material conditions and feel our divine nature. The touch of the soul can paint the brightest color, even in the dingiest places. It can cast a fragrance over the vilest things. It can make the wicked divine, and all enmity, all selfishness, is effaced. The less the thought of the body, the better, for it is the body that drags us down; it is attachment, identification, which makes us miserable. That is the secret: To think that I am the Spirit and not the body, and that the whole of the universe, with all its relations, with all its good and all its evil, is but a series of paintings, scenes on a canvas of which I am the witness." (141)

PATH OF ACTION

I never tire of defining the true spirit of religion, that it is an experience of God, that it is realizing God within one's own heart and soul, that one can see God more intimately, more clearly, than this objective universe. Of course nobody can see God with these eyes or hear the voice of God with these ears, but when divine sight opens, you see God everywhere.

You may say, "I already see God everywhere – in the flowers, in the beautiful face of a girl, everywhere in nature," but I say to you, no, you are romanticizing. The flower is not God, the flower blossoms and then dries up. Nature – shifting, moving, changing – is not God. What is beautiful today becomes ugly tomorrow. And there comes a time when the whole world becomes dissolved. Where is your God then? Swami Vivekananda made it very clear by saying: "All is not. God is." You have to realize this first, you have to experience it – and then you realize that God is all.

Make no mistake: if you want to find the truth of God, do not romanticize. We have three states of consciousness – waking, dreaming, and dreamless sleep. In none of these states you ever find God. While you are awake, you are still asleep. You have to be awakened, as Buddha pointed out, from this prolonged dream of the waking state.

But of course we cannot jump out of our bodies. While in the waking state we have to struggle, even though the attainment of God is not something that we do not have now and have to achieve. It is already there.

According to the teachings of Vedanta, there are four methods of union: the path of action, the path of devotion, the path of meditation, and the path of knowledge. But they are not to be regarded as independent of one another. You find that all religions of the world emphasize one aspect or another, but in the teachings of Vedanta, especially in the Bhagavad Gita and Sri Ramakrishna, it is recommended that the paths be followed simultaneously. Without performing actions, without attending to the duties of your life, you cannot achieve purity of heart, which is the one condition necessary to realize God. Purity of heart is very difficult to define, but its effect is that the whole heart and mind are pin-pointed on God. There are no distractions in your mind, and your heart longs for God and God alone.

Action, or work, is absolutely important to gain purity of heart. Shankara, who advocated and emphasized the path of knowledge, said: "Purity is impossible without actions or movement." Religion is not for the lazy. First you have to be active. As it is said in the Gita: "Activity is better than inertia." If you are lazy, you cannot even sustain your own body. Again, we read in the Gita: "Let him who would climb in meditation to heights of the highest union with Brahman take for his path the yoga of action; then when he nears that height of oneness, his acts will fall from him, his path will be tranquil."

The four yogas may be regarded as disciplines suited to different stages of a spiritual aspirant's development. The path of action is especially important for the beginner. Of course, it has to be selfless action – helping others, doing good, without any thought of name or fame or of reward either in heaven or on earth.

With selfless action, simultaneously you must have a regular routine of prayer, worship, and contemplation. It is not possible to do selfless and motiveless action without them. There would always be the idea of reward behind the action. So for some time you must perform the daily duties of worship, study of scriptures, and chanting of his name, just like routine work. Then you will begin to love to do them, and you will find that you cannot act without worshiping God, without meditating. Love comes into your heart, and as it does, your heart naturally goes towards God. Meditation and contemplation become natural. When they become deeper, the worshiper and the object of worship, become united; the lover and the beloved become one. That means that knowledge – *jnana* – comes to you. Action, devotion, meditation and knowledge become one united whole. That is the ideal for each one of us.

Everyone in this world works. Being busy, one often says, "When have I the time to meditate?" So we have to learn the secret of action by which the karma that binds us is given blows by the karma we are performing. Karma, of course, means both physical and mental activity. Each action we do, each thought we think, is not lost, but lies within, either in the conscious, the subconscious, or the unconscious. Each action creates an impression in the mind, and the sum-total of these impressions makes up what we know as the character of the individual. We ourselves have formed our character, not only in this life, but in past lives. Accordingly, there are tendencies to repeat the same actions, to think the same thoughts. We are caught on a wheel of birth, death, and rebirth, and there is no way out of it. You cannot pay back all your karmas because you create new karmas as you go on.

Shall we, then, give up all action? No, that is not possible. You cannot live and breathe for a moment without doing something. So we must learn the secret that will give a blow to the law of karma. To quote the Gita: "The world is imprisoned in its own activity, except when actions are performed as worship of God. Therefore you must perform every action sacramentally, and be free from all attachment to results."

This is the first point we have to understand. We have to give up attachment to the results of our actions, and offer the results of our actions to God. In other words, instead of self-centered action, let us have God-centered action. It is said in the Gita: "Whatever your action, food or worship, whatever the gift that you give to another, whatever you vow to the work of the spirit: O son of Kunti, lay these also as offerings before me. Thus you will free yourself from both the good and the evil effects of your actions. Offer up everything to me. If your heart is united with me, you will be set free from karma even in this life, and come to me at the last."

What a wonderful secret: offer everything as worship to God. You are sweeping the floor. Do it for God. When you do something for your husband or child, see God behind the form. Wherever you are, whatever you do, offer to God. To quote the Gita again: "You have the right to work, but for the work's sake only. You have no right to the fruits of work. Desire for the fruits of work must never be your motive in working. Never give way to laziness either. Perform every action with your heart fixed on the Supreme Lord. Renounce attachment to the fruits. Be even-tempered in success and failure, for it is this evenness of temper which is meant by yoga. Work done with anxiety about results is far inferior to work done without such anxiety, in the calm of self-surrender. Seek refuge in the knowledge of Brahman. They who work selfishly for results are miserable. In the calm of self-surrender, you can free yourself from the bondage of virtue and vice during this very life. Devote yourself therefore to reaching union with Brahman. To unite the heart with Brahman and then to act; that is the secret of nonattached work." These very words were told to me by my guru, Swami Brahmananda: "Hold God in one hand, and with the other hand, work."

Motiveless action does not mean that you are not seeking anything at all. You are seeking God, the Infinite! Here is the beauty of it: through each work, you get results, but if you do not seek results and you seek God, then you will get the result that is infinite. Performing the same work in one way you get a finite result, in the other way, an infinite result.

As you continue to perform action, offering the fruits to God, you gradually come to a stage of unfoldment when you begin to feel, "I am not the doer; it is all God's will." When the ego dies – the sense of 'I' – that very moment you feel everything is God's will. But this is an unfoldment. (142)

THE PATH OF DEVOTION

The path of devotion, which emphasizes love for the Lord, is said to be the most natural process and the easiest to follow.

To love God with all the heart, soul, and mind is the whole truth of what I call the Eternal Religion and a truth common to all religions. If you don't have that love for God, everything else becomes vain.

Now let us try to understand what this love is. Nobody can actually define it, because it is felt and experienced in every heart. It is something that is within every one of us, so we don't feel the need for definition. Because of this, the path of devotion is said to be the natural process of realizing God. You see, nobody lacks in love; when love appears to be lacking, it is just covered up. There are many layers of covering; nevertheless there is infinite love within each one of us, because God is dwelling in his infinite degree in each of us.

All attraction that we feel is divine attraction. But that initial attraction doesn't last long, and there is frustration until we direct the love knowingly towards God. Then we realize its true divine nature. And then it grows in intensity. One of the great teachers of devotion, Narada, said that its intrinsic nature is immortal bliss, because God is love and immortal bliss. One who gives love to God and has no more desire for anything else is free from grief and hatred. There is complete fulfillment. Can there be any room for desire when one becomes intoxicated in joy and immersed in the bliss of union with God? When you have attained this love, you have reached the highest, supreme truth. And it comes gradually; it does not come all of a sudden.

The problem is, how to love God if you don't know what God is. You'll find theologians and philosophers defining God in many ways, but they are trying to do the impossible. The moment you try to define God, you limit him and make him finite. To define God is impossible: he is indefinable and inexpressible. But he is realizable. And as you realize him, you become silent. Silence is his name: *shanto'yam atma.*

The supreme ideal is for the lover, the beloved, and love to become one. When I was a young boy, seated at the feet of my master, a man came and quoted a song: "I want to taste sugar, not to become sugar. I want to taste the bliss of God, not become one with God." To that my master replied: "You can sing that song – until you have tasted sugar. When you taste the bliss of God, then you want to be united with him." And that is the supreme ideal – not a mere vision of God. You can have a vision – God has many aspects and innumerable forms, you cannot limit Him – but a vision is not enough. You have to go beyond all forms and be united with him completely. (143)

My master once said: "Why did God create this world? In order that man can love the Lord and make his life blessed." M., the recorder of *The Gospel of Sri Ramakrishna*, said most beautifully: "Man is endowed with three bodies: physical, subtle, and causal. And all these bodies need food." In order that we can sustain the physical body, we need food: potatoes, rice, fish, and so on. And then the subtle body must be given food. One cannot remain a human being without culture: education, art, science, philosophy. These are intellectual food. Then again, one remains human by living an ethical life – not only being good, but doing good to others. This is a universal law, and it nourishes the subtle body. But let not the causal body starve! What is the food for that? To love God, to struggle and find God. I emphasize struggle – but also to find God.

Yajnavalkya taught his wife, Maitreyi, "None loves the husband for the sake of the husband, but for the sake of the Self, for the sake of the Atman or divine Reality that is within the husband. None loves the wife for the sake of the wife, but for the sake of the Self that is in the wife. None loves the father for the sake of the father, but for the sake of the Self that is in the father. And so on." But we are not conscious of that.

When we fall in love, it is the love for God. Nothing else. That's why when we fall in love for the first time, we feel, "Oh, it is a divine experience!" Wait for ten days. This love degenerates, and there is frustration. Divine love is infinite. When our love is directed towards the Infinite, towards God, and if we are aware of that, it finds its fulfillment.

Plato defined love as the desire and pursuit of the whole, that is, the Infinite. Narada, a great lover of God, expressed the very nature of love as immortal bliss. That is why, as I already mentioned, one feels a divine quality when first falling in love. There is such bliss in it. But when it is directed toward something finite and mortal, it doesn't last, it doesn't find fulfillment, and there is frustration.

When we begin to think of God, everything else gradually becomes tasteless. The path of devotion is really wonderful in this way: you don't have to struggle to gain self-control or anything of the kind. You only have to think of God, try to love him, pray that you may love him, and all the baser things of life fall away from you automatically.

You may ask at this point: "But what is God?" Both Hindus and Buddhists point out that we should not try to define God, because God cannot be defined. Again, all definitions are true. Once Sri Ramakrishna, who was intimate with God, was asked: "Holy sir, there are so many definitions of God. Some say he is personal, some say he is impersonal. Some say he is with form, some say without form. So on and so forth. Now what is God? These views are all contradictory." Sri Ramakrishna said: "Go to the neighborhood of God and then you will see that all contradictions meet in him." He pointed out that the bee makes a big noise before it sits on a flower, but as it sits and begins to suck the honey, it becomes silent. Then again, becoming intoxicated by drinking that honey, it comes out and makes a sweet humming noise. Before we have known God, we make a big noise about him, but when we sit on the flower and begin to suck the honey, the sweetness of God, we become silent. Then again, becoming God-intoxicated, some speak of him this way, others speak of him that way. In many ways the truth is expressed: truth is one, sages call that by various names.

Of course the fact is that God is within; he is your very Self. But how can you know the Self? How can you meditate on the Self? The eyes cannot see themselves. You have to stand before a mirror to see your own eyes. So God in his great mercy sends or gives full knowledge of Brahman in individuals. In every age, in every religion, there is someone to worship.

A perfect mirror is Jesus, Krishna, Buddha, or Rama-krishna. You may try to conceive of God and imagine God, but if you study the lives of these great ones, you will find that their lives are paths: any conception you may have, you see in them.

What is the method to love? You have your chosen ideal, and you practice some ethical virtues and also repeat or chant the name of the Lord. As Chaitanya's prayer says, "Chant the name of the Lord and His glory unceasingly, that the mirror of the heart may be wiped clean, and quench that mighty forest fire, worldly lust." As Meister Eckhart said: "The soul in her hot pursuit of God becomes absorbed in him, and she herself is reduced to nought, just as the sun will swallow up and put out dawn. Whoever would see God must be dead to himself, and buried in God." (144)

Now here is the point: only spiritual aspirants can feel and experience and express love. In human love there is nothing but the attraction of God. Swami Vivekananda said: "Do you think that the molecules arranged in a particular way would attract somebody?" No. It is the divinity that attracts us. We cannot say that we love God. However we may try, we feel we cannot love him. But do you know what happens? If you have any experience that makes you absorbed in the thought of God, you feel that attraction. It is something tangibly felt, and you go into ecstasy. That ecstasy that comes, you enter into, not because you love God, but because God's love is so overwhelming that you feel it. And then you cannot but love him.

The intensity in human love sometimes lasts for ten days, but with God that intensity grows ever more intense. And intoxicating madness in love comes when you learn to love him for love's sake. This comes only after you have had at least a glimpse of him.

What are the spiritual disciplines on the path of devotion? Chanting the name of the Lord, meditating on him, serving him, serving him in others, learning to see God in others, and serving the God within them. These are the preparatory methods and means. Of course you have to have ethical principles also: truthfulness, chastity, freedom from greed, things like that, but here is the point: if you can just chant the name of the Lord and think of God and meditate on him, your life naturally becomes ethical. You don't have to struggle to have self-control. The more we advance towards God, the less craving we have for objects of the senses.

The supreme ideal is the complete union and absorption in God, wherein love, lover, and beloved become one. Ultimately, the paths of knowledge and devotion meet in one place: knowledge becomes love, and love becomes knowledge. (145)

On the path of devotion you enter into a relationship with God. There are many kinds of love in the world. For instance, a child's love for its mother, a friend's love for a friend, a

mother's love for her child, or the love between lover and beloved. These are different expressions of the same love. For
instance, the mother has a baby, and she has her husband. She
loves both, but her love is expressed differently, though it is
the same love. Just so, we must enter into a relationship with
God. He is our father or mother. I mention mother purposely,
because there is a teaching given in the *Gospel of Sri Ramakrishna* about the image of Kali. There was a sacred thread
on her body. Now a sacred thread is not used by women, only
by men. One fellow came and said, "What is this nonsense.
You have put a sacred thread on Mother's body!" And Sri
Ramakrishna said, "Well, brother, perhaps you are the one
who knows what Mother is – whether Mother is mother or
father – I do not know." God is both mother and father, and
then he is friend and playmate, and also the most beloved,
the bridegroom.

With the understanding that Christ, Krishna, Ramakrishna, or Buddha is myself, you worship him, meditate on
him, and chant his name. And as you practice, you will begin
to feel a love as if you were receiving it from him, and your
heart will melt. Do you know the experience some devotees
have? They say, "I don't love God, but God loves me." And
then you become overwhelmed, just as in very hot weather,
when you move toward the ocean and begin to feel a breeze.
You have not seen the ocean yet, but you begin to get the
breeze, and you feel soothed. It is not that we have aroused
any emotion; it is that we begin to feel his love, his peace.

In this connection I'll quote to you what a Christian mystic, Jan van Ruysbroek, summarized about attaining divine
love. "Whosoever wishes to meet Christ as his beloved bridegroom must now in time go out to meet Christ at these three
points. The first point is that he shall have God in mind in
all things." In other words, constant recollectedness. "The

second point is that there shall be nothing that he needs or loves more than God, or even so much as God. And the third point is that he shall with great zeal seek to rest in God above all creatures and above all God's gifts. Above all the works of virtue and above all feelings that God may infuse into the soul and body." It is a wonderful truth: above all his gifts we have to love him, not because he gives us his blessings. No, it is above those blessings that you have to love him. Not because you find bliss and go into ecstasy do you love him, but you love him for his sake. The supreme experience then comes: you are no longer flesh, and God alone is. That becomes a realized fact. (146)

There are three characteristics of true love. One is that there is no shopkeeping: "I love you. Do you love me?" And there is no rivalry: "My beloved is the beloved of all." And there is no fear: "Love casteth out fear."

We must have this firm conviction that God can be seen, and that as Sri Ramakrishna told his disciple Vivekananda, "He is more real than I see you before me." You can talk to him and realize your union with him. The ultimate truth is to have that union. Then you become silent.

In defining love, Narada uses the words "intense love for this." He doesn't say God, Christ, Krishna, but "this" – which indicates that it is nearer than the nearmost. He does not wish to give any name, because to do so would be sectarian. It is supreme love, which is one with supreme knowledge. But it is only when you have the vision of God in all his aspects, when you reach your union with him, that supreme love arises. You see, supreme love and supreme knowledge are the same.

Of course a beginner needs an anchor, as it were, a personal being. There is the infinite, shoreless ocean and icebergs floating in it: the ocean has taken forms. Are those icebergs different from the ocean? Are they not the same water? And so a divine incarnation is the door through which one peeps into the Infinite.

The question is, "How to love God?" Narada says: "Supreme love is attained by uninterrupted and constant worship of God, by hearing and singing the glory of the Lord even while engaged in the ordinary activities of life." Of course this is a stage to be attained. You may think you can begin today and do that, but it is not possible. It is a stage of development.

Sri Ramakrishna gave the example of keeping your mind in God by the story of a village maiden carrying a jar of water on her head. Her mind is on that jar; otherwise it will fall. Her hands are free; she is balancing the jar and at the same time gossiping. He also gave the illustration of a chaste wife waiting for her husband to come home. Her mind is on the husband, even while she is busy cooking and nursing the baby.

Swamiji said: "Day and night think of God, and as far as possible think of nothing else. The daily necessary thoughts can all be thought through God. Eat to him, drink to him, sleep to him, see him in all. Try to see that same Lord in every being. Talk of God to others, this is most beneficial. When the whole soul pours in a continuous current to God, when there is no time to seek money and name or fame, no time to think of anything but God, then will come into your heart that infinite wonderful bliss of love. All desires are but beads of glass. True love of God increases every moment and is ever new. It is to be known by feeling it. Love is the easiest of disciplines. It waits for no logic. It is natural. We need no demonstrations, no proof. Reasoning is limiting something by our own minds. We throw a net and catch something, and then say that we have demonstrated it. But never, never can we catch God in a net."

Maharaj once told me: "Our love is so deep that we do not let you know that we love you." This is God's love. As you practice disciplines, you begin to feel that love and to realize how this breeze of grace is blowing all the time toward you. As you approach nearer, you begin to feel an overwhelming love of God and your heart goes out. That is ecstasy; you become intoxicated.

As Al Halaj, a Sufi saint, said: "I am the truth. I am he whom I love; and he whom I love is I." And Mohammed said: "Verily I, even I, am God, and there is none else." Dionysius, a Christian mystic, said: "It is the nature of love to change a man into that which he loves." Perhaps you have noticed that if there is real love between a husband and wife, he takes on some of her characteristics, and she takes on some of his. In just the same way, if you love God, you imbibe his nature. As you read in the Bible: "Seek ye first the kingdom of God and everything else shall be added unto you."

When you have realized that, you see the same God everywhere. These are actual experiences in life – not confined to books, or talk, but experience. However, do not talk of your experiences to others. Spiritual experiences must be guarded. (147)

Shankara emphasized the path of knowledge and said that love is a means to attain knowledge. Ramanuja, on the other hand, pointed out that the path of love is the highest, and knowledge is the means. But when Shankara means love as a means, he only refers to the preparatory disciplines of love. And when Ramanuja says knowledge is a means, he means intellectual knowledge. We find in the life of Ramakrishna that he made no distinction whatsoever. He gave equal importance to all paths. And in the Bhagavad Gita we find great emphasis on all paths. In fact, both Sri Ramakrishna and the Gita emphasize that we must follow all four yogas simultaneously.

Now, there are different forms of love that we find expressed in human life, but whatever form love takes, its intrinsic nature is divine, because God is love. It is just that we do not know it, and so we never find fulfillment.

In this connection I'll tell you a story. Mirabai was a great woman saint and devotee of Sri Krishna. At that time there was a disciple of the great teacher, Sri Chaitanya, living in Vrindavan. Mirabai went there to visit this great soul but was told that he did not meet women. Mirabai answered, "I didn't know there was any man other than Sri Krishna in this city of Vrindavan." Immediately the saint ran toward her and bowed down.

We can direct our love towards God only if we have the desire for God. I'll tell you another story. There was a young prince known as Druva. The king threw him and his mother out without any means of support. Druva, still a little boy, asked his mother, "I understand that you are the queen and I am a prince. How can I gain back my kingdom? How can I gain back the love of my father?" The mother said, "Well, my child, there is no other way but to seek that from God. But it is so difficult to devote oneself to God. You have to go away to a deep forest, and live alone and pray." Without letting his mother know, the little boy ran away into the deep forest and began to pray earnestly. Narada, who is said to be the eternal teacher, appeared before him and said, "I have felt your heart's cry for God." He initiated Druva and asked him to practice disciplines, by which he had the vision of God. God said, "Now the kingdom is waiting for you. The king is coming to welcome you and your mother." Druva said, "No, no, I don't want the kingdom. I want only you." You see, once he had found that sweetness in the presence of God, a kingdom meant nothing. But God said, "No, you prayed for it, you have to get it." Don't you know from your own life how many times you have prayed for something and then after you got it, you didn't want it anymore?

Once my master said to me, "Worldly people talk about the joy of life, but what do they know about how to enjoy life? The joy of life is only to be found in the love of God." (149)

PATH OF KNOWLEDGE

Shankara, the great seer-philosopher of India, is said to have expressed the supreme truth in practically one-half of a verse: "Brahman is real, the appearance of this universe is unreal, and the individual soul is none other than Brahman" – none other, none other. This is the truth, the highest reality, to be realized and experienced. Whether you are a dualist, a qualified monist, or a nondualist, you will have to reach this ultimate truth.

The followers of the path of knowledge try to reach it directly. For them, there is no other object of worship than the Self, the Atman. Dualists and qualified monists worship God as an object separate from themselves. But then the Indian or Hindu dualists and qualified monists teach everybody to worship God within the shrine of one's own heart – not as an objective reality somewhere outside, but as the Atman within. There is, then, only a distinction between the ego or individual self and one's true being, the universal Self or Atman.

Meister Eckhart brought this same truth out in a beautiful way. He said: "Some there are so simple as to think of God as if he dwelt there, and of themselves as being here. It is not so: God and I are One." Sufis also realize this same truth, *anul huc*, which means "I am He." Vedantists try to realize, "Thou Art That," or "I am Brahman." That is the highest truth.

Now we must bear in mind that it is not an intellectual understanding. For instance, the appearance of this universe as we perceive with our sense-organs and conceive with our minds – the multiplicity that we experience, the duality of pleasure and pain in everyday life – these cannot simply be nullified by the process of logic and reasoning. True, you can explain through reason and inferential knowledge that this universe as we see it is not real, but that does not help us, because we still have the experience.

A scientist may prove that what I see before me is nothing but vibrations, but I touch it and experience it as solid. How can this experience be nullified? It *has* to be nullified if the appearance is unreal and I am Brahman. And that can only happen by direct experience, by coming face to face with the reality. As a seer of the Upanishads says: "I have known that immortal bliss that is beyond all ignorance and darkness."[Svetasvatara Upanishad] Only one direct knowledge can nullify another direct knowledge.

We are dreaming dreams, and they are so real to us. A tiger is chasing you and you are running. That tiger is real and so is your fear. Nothing can nullify that experience until you wake up. When you wake up and find that it was all a dream, your heart is still palpitating. But the experience of the waking state nullifies the dream experience.

You may be sitting here and suddenly the multiplicity of the universe will disappear from your vision and you will see something else, but not merely a vision. It is the total reality you experience: Brahman, Brahman everywhere, Brahman alone is! This universe has an empirical reality, but it becomes nullified when we see the absolute Reality.

Dr. D. T. Suzuki, the Zen Buddhist, said at a philosopher's conference: "Since ultimate truth cannot be comprehended intellectually, philosophers are not necessarily wise men. Only the person who has known the real Self can discuss philosophy. Make every effort, therefore, to realize the Self, for there can be no joy in the universe for one who is restricted to the empirical ego." What a bold statement! As I wrote in *The Spiritual Heritage of India*: "To become a philosopher is to become transformed in life, or renewed in mind and baptized in Spirit."

This universe is a superimposition upon Brahman. There is a rope lying on the ground and instead of a rope, you see a snake. The snake is superimposed upon the rope; it is not really there. That which has no reality is seen in that which is real. This superimposition is not a theory, but a fact of experience for everyone. Light and darkness are opposed to each other, and there is no way you can mistake one for the other. Similarly, the seer – the subject – and the object are seen opposed to each other like light and darkness. There is no possibility that they can be mixed up. But it has happened through the inscrutable power of maya.

You are not the body, but in every action and behavior, you identify yourself with the body: "I weigh so many pounds, I am so many years old." Every moment you identify with these. Intellectually you might understand that the body is separate from you, but if somebody gives you a pinch, you feel it; it is a direct experience.

Now, concerning Atman-Brahman, the Upanishads say: "Subtler than the subtlest is he, farther than the farthest, nearer than the nearest." [Mundaka Upanishad] He is far away for those who are ignorant of that reality, but those who know him find him within themselves. Not only that: "A knower of Brahman becomes one with Brahman." Christ taught: "Be ye perfect, even as the Father which is in Heaven is perfect." That perfection is complete union. And you are already that. It is not that you are separate from him and then you become united. It is not that you are a sinner and then you become a saint. You are neither a sinner nor a saint! You are actually always Brahman. It is like forgetting a necklace you are wearing. You are already that, only covered by ignorance. Buddha defined it truly when he said: "This waking state is like sleep, and wisdom is to wake up." That is all. It is already there; wake up!

Once this knowledge is attained, you can never lose it. The experience of pleasure or suffering or something most beautiful or very ugly may not affect our character because we forget even though the experience has created an impression in our minds. But the experience of the Reality is something you never lose. It is yours. Holy Mother once said: "It doesn't mean that you get two horns coming out of your forehead!" No, you appear to be the same individual, but a great transformation has come over your whole life: your vision and values have changed. Patanjali, points out this experience as "absolutely infallible and true." Absolutely. The universe disappears altogether. Then again, when the universe reappears, the experiencer has a different vision of it. As my master said: "When you get the eye of the spirit, you see nothing but spirit."

How do we attain that? The Upanishads point out that there are three steps: hearing of the truth of God or Brahman, reflecting upon that truth, and meditating upon that truth. But these three steps are not easy to follow until you are ready. The main point is to desire it. There is a saying in this country, "You can lead a horse to water, but you can't make him drink." You have to thirst for that knowledge.

Longing for God comes with purification of the heart. That is the one condition, the *sine qua non*, of attaining the wisdom of God. To quote the Katha Upanishad: "By learning, a man cannot know him if he desists not from evil, if he controls not his senses, if he quiets not his mind, and practices not meditation." It emphatically points out: "By the purified mind alone, Brahman is to be attained."

And purity means simply this: you come to a stage of development through practice of spiritual disciplines when there is no other desire for anything. When you desire nothing but to have this wisdom, to realize the Infinite, that is the starting point of a spiritual aspirant. And that is also the goal. Understand that it is not a suppression of desires, nor is it something that you feel temporarily. It is that you have come to the clear understanding that in the Infinite alone is there joy.

What is ignorance, what is bondage? To desire or to find satisfaction in the finite. As long as you are satisfied with the finite, desire for the Infinite does not come. But, of course, one does not long for that all at once, or all at once become desireless. It is a gradual unfoldment.

When you go to meditate, you find that many distractions arise in your mind. If you struggle for a few years – whether you are a dualist or a nondualist – and your mind is not concentrated, as you continue, a sweetness comes and you get a glimpse. It first comes in this way: you become convinced that Atman is here, that God is here. You can't see him, don't know him, but you have that conviction. With that conviction comes a thrill in your whole being.

Sri Ramakrishna said that God is the bigger magnet, worldly enjoyments small magnets. The small magnets draw you now because that bigger magnet is not attracting you yet. The point of a needle covered with dust cannot attract, so clean it up. Wash out the impurities with tears for God. People shed jugs full of tears for a husband or a wife or objects, Sri Ramakrishna said, but how many shed tears for God?

As longing comes and a glimpse comes, you feel the magnet drawing you. All those who have experienced anything in spiritual life will tell you that it is grace. The follower of the path of knowledge will call this the grace of the Atman. When you get a glimpse of that, when that large magnet begins to draw you, when you become interested in it, the natural tendency of your mind will be to flow towards Brahman.

To come back to the three steps of hearing the truth, reflecting upon it, and meditating upon it, what truth are we to hear? The truth that "I am Brahman" or "Thou art That." This you hear from the lips of a teacher. Then you have to reflect upon that, because if you consider your empirical self as Brahman, you don't understand. What is the Self? What is it that is one with Brahman? In order to reflect upon this, you must have *shraddha*, faith. Faith in the words of the guru and in the words of the scriptures. Try to understand exactly what the guru says, try to understand what the scriptures say. That is reflection. Try to understand intellectually the simple truth: God is here, within. If you have the faith that he is within, you attain knowledge.

And finally, how to meditate: In the Gita we find: "The light of a lamp does not flicker in a windless place. That is the simile which describes the yogi of one-pointed mind who meditates upon the Atman. When, through the practice of yoga, the mind ceases its restless movement and becomes still, he realizes the Atman. It satisfies him entirely. Then he knows that infinite happiness which can be realized by the purified heart but is beyond the grasp of the senses."

In the Chandogya Upanishad we learn that in the Infinite alone is happiness; and in the Upanishads we also find that when there is purification of food, there is purification of the heart; and when that comes, you have a constant recollectedness of Brahman. Your thought becomes like oil poured from one vessel to another, without any break. When you come to that stage of unfoldment, you have wisdom, you have the illumined knowledge of God.

Now again, purification of food is whatever you sense or perceive. Food is not merely what we eat with our mouths. Sometimes we can eat with our sense of smell. Whatever we gather through the senses must be pure. In other words, our eyes must see what is pure, our ears must hear what is pure.

And, of course, there are certain spiritual disciplines: discrimination between what is eternal and what is noneternal. That is the first step in order to come to the understanding that God alone is the treasure. Then gradually your mind will not run after the pleasures and objects of the finite world.

And then you acquire six treasures of life, such as poise in the midst of the opposites of life, self-control, control of passions, forbearance, contentment within. In other words, you have to establish the interest in God.

Then comes self-surrender.

Of course it is impossible to discriminate and shun the objects of pleasure and devote yourself to God immediately. It takes time. Just consider, if you really love God, is there any room left for anything else? That is what religion is. That is what is meant by spiritual life. It is guaranteed that you will experience a joy that is beyond all expression, beyond all understanding. We shall all reach that ocean because we live in that ocean of blessedness. Ignorance will vanish one day. But do not wait. Try to remove that blindness, from your sight here and now, and make your life blessed. (149)

The followers of the path of devotion ultimately come to the realization and experience that love, the lover, and the beloved are one. One time a disciple of Holy Mother wrote her: "Mother, I follow the path of devotion and I'm living in this ashram which is *advaita*, nondualistic. Am I not a hypocrite?" Mother wrote him back: "Our master was a nondualist; we are all nondualists. That is what we have to attain."

There is only one difference between the followers of other paths and the followers of the path of knowledge. The followers of the path of knowledge make an attempt to reach the ultimate truth directly.

Nondualists do not say that all experiences except the experience of Brahman and Atman are unreal; in fact, they accept the relative reality of every experience. A mirage also has a reality as long as you experience it; but when you come nearer, it vanishes. It has a certain degree of reality. Swami Vivekananda used to say: "You have seen nothing but God all your life." What you are seeing is nothing but Brahman, but your vision is not opened, so you see the appearance, the empirical reality.

There is a beautiful verse in the Upanishads: "The senses have been created outgoing, and so we are looking outward. But there are some who control the outgoing senses and look within. They find the Atman in all its glory!" [Katha Upanishad]

That is not a very simple thing, but once you attain this knowledge, you never lose it. Once you have this experience, it is yours forever. It is not like relative experiences which we can forget. You know the prayer of Chaitanya:

"Ah, how I long for the day
When an instant's separation from Thee, O Govinda,
Will be as a thousand years.
When my heart burns away with its desire,
And the world without Thee is a heartless void."

We have to come to that state in which we cannot do without the thought of God. It is not done in a day or two; you have to practice until you feel: "Ah, I don't want anything, I have no more craving for anything. I only want you, Lord."

When we come to that state, the door opens. That is the grace of Brahman.

You have to have the faith in yourself, that if others have attained God, you can also attain God! If you do not have this faith, you will not struggle.

Even the followers of the path of knowledge have to be dualists, for who is there to meditate upon whom? But their meditation is on the identity of the Atman with Brahman. (150)

The ultimate truth is that there is only Brahman and nothing else. You and I are one with Brahman; there is no you, no I, no universe; there is just Brahman, and I am That.

The Sufis tell an interesting story: A lover comes and knocks on the door. "Who is it?" "It is I." The door does not open. Again, there is the knock at the door: "Who are you?" "I." The door doesn't open. Then a third knock and the question: "Who are you?" "I am Thou." Then the door opens.

"A knower of Brahman becomes Brahman." It is not like I know an object: as long as there is the least demarcation between the subject – the knower – and the object of knowledge, you have not known the truth. It is only when they have become one that the three knots of knower, known, and knowing are untied. When knowledge has become unified knowledge; then it is the supreme knowledge that you are one with Brahman.

Plato said something very interesting: "Its object will not be to generate in the person the power of seeing. On the contrary, it assumes that he possesses it, though he's turned in a wrong direction and does not look to the right quarter. Its aim is to remedy this defect." He gives the analogy of a man chained and looking into a wall, to the finite. Of course the remedy to this defect is not so simple. It is known as the practice of spiritual disciplines. They are very important and necessary.

In the Katha Upanishad we read: "By learning, a man cannot know him, if he desists not from evil, if he controls not his senses, if he quiets not his mind, and practices not meditation." But let me tell you, purity of heart can be achieved by one simple process: longing for him.

It is said that as long as any craving or desire remains, that vision does not open up. Sri Ramakrishna used to give the illustration of a thread and needle. If the thread is not one-pointed, if there is one fiber sticking out, it won't go through the eye of the needle. But to have that deep longing is to be free from all desires. One time a disciple asked our Holy Mother, "Mother what shall I pray for?" She answered: "Pray for desirelessness." This is the point: when you are desireless, you have the fulfillment of all desires.

So I say to you, have your pleasures for now, but at the same time try to devote yourself to God. See what happens. You will find greater happiness, greater joy. Everything else will become a shadow, a reflection. The desire for the Infinite is the very beginning of spiritual life, and it ends in the realization of the Infinite. (151)

YOGA

Yoga has become identified with physical exercises – gymnastics, twisting or torturing the body – and breathing exercises. That is what is known as hatha yoga, but it is not efficacious for spiritual life. Great dangers may arise especially through the practice of breathing exercises. If there is any mistake made, and if chastity and dietary rules are not observed, these breathing exercises may bring disease which is non-diagnosable and for which there is no cure. The brain itself may be damaged without any hope of repair.

The word *yoke* is derived from the Sanskrit word *yoga,* which means "union." The idea is related to the root meaning of the word *religion, religio,* a binding back, a reuniting. It refers to mystic union with God. Patanjali gives the meaning as "to distinguish the reality within you from that which is unreal" – in other words, to realize the truth of God. On the contrary, hatha yoga makes you body-conscious, and that is a great obstacle to spiritual growth. Posture – an easy posture – is only important in making you forget that you have a body so that you can practice mental disciplines.

In the West, psychology is defined as "science of the nature, function, and phenomena of the human soul or mind." Just mark: "human soul *or* mind." In other words, in the West, mind is identified with the soul. In the East, we say that each person is Spirit, the Atman – and *has* a body and mind. The mind is separate from the soul or Atman or Self; the mind is an object of experience. The mind's thoughts we can see and recognize. Just as I can see my body, I can read my mind.

In the Gita Sri Krishna says: "My *prakriti* (that which makes up this universe of mind and matter) is of eight-fold composition: earth, water, fire, air, ether, mind, intellect, ego." These are one category, not distinct. Mind is not distinct from any other object. Behind this, and distinct from it, is the principle of consciousness in all beings, and the source of life in all. This is brought out in the Kena Upanishad: "At whose behest does the mind think? Who bids the body live? Who makes the tongue speak? Who is the effulgent Being that directs the eye to form and color, and the ears to sound? The Self is the ear of the ear, mind of the mind, speech of the speech. He is also breath of the breath, and eye of the eye. Having given up the false identification of the Self with the senses and the mind, and knowing the Self to be Brahman, the wise ... become

Immortal." And that is the objective of yoga – to realize the Atman, pure consciousness.

Many argue, "I can only accept what I can see and perceive and experience with my senses and mind." Very good, but if you could experience God that way, you would not consider him God, because he would be limited and finite like any other object. God cannot be seen with these eyes or experienced with the senses. He is even beyond the thoughts of the mind – but the purified mind realizes him, because he is behind all this. You can see, you can hear, you can experience, because of that presence within you, that pure consciousness within you. And in order to experience that, you have to have your divine sight opened.

According to Western psychology, there are three *areas* of mind – conscious, subconscious, and unconscious – as there are three *states* of consciousness – waking, dreaming, and dreamless sleep. All our experiences are within these three states. We in the East, however, point out that there is a "Fourth." The waking experience contradicts the dream experience, and we accept it as more real because it has greater permanency. But when the awakening of the Fourth comes, the waking experience also appears as dream, because the experience of the Fourth contradicts all other experiences. For instance, in seeing the manifold universe, we are seeing "you" and "I" as different. But this becomes contradicted by the experience of seeing everything as Brahman. We are all one in That. Then our whole view of life changes. It has greater permanency than this waking state because it is eternal, and it is never contradicted by any other experience.

Immanuel Kant thought there was the unknown and the knowable. But Shankara and the sages of the Upanishads and the great mystics in every country and every age, though they speak differently, say that it is not unknown and unknowable

– and it is *more* than known and knowable. True, as long as there is any demarcation between the knower and the object of knowledge, between the subject and the object, so long it is not possible to know the thing in itself. Technically we say there are three knots of knowledge: knower, object of knowledge, and the process of knowing. They can be untied. Then consciousness becomes unified: you realize Brahman, One, "I am That."

When we can live in that, then we can function with harmony and happiness for ourselves and others because we see no difference. As long as there is an ego sticking out in us, we cannot live in harmony; it is impossible. Real harmony is reached only by someone who is established in God.

When Sri Ramakrishna used to go into *samadhi*, his outward consciousness was gone. When a Western-educated young man of India said that Sri Ramakrishna became unconscious, he said, "How can you think I have become unconscious by meditating upon the very source of consciousness? You who keep your heads balanced by thinking of matter and material things think I would lose my balance by thinking of the source of all consciousness and intelligence?"

Now, what is yoga? It is the method by which we can remove ignorance and realize our true nature. It has been defined as "the control of the waves of *chitta* (the mind)." The mind has three functions. Mind (*manas*) sees the object; intellect (*buddhi*) classifies the object and identifies it as such-and-such; and then the ego (*ahamkara*) says, "I know this object."

There are waves in the mind, thought-waves. To control thought-waves does not mean to make your mind blank. In the first place, you cannot, unless you are hit over the head and go unconscious. Control of thought-waves does not mean a superficial control, nor a momentary control, but "a complete overhauling of the mind." As St. Paul said: "Be ye transformed by the renewing of your mind."

There are what we call *samskaras*, impressions, in the subconscious and unconscious mind, created by previous acts and thoughts. To overcome the thought-waves of the mind is to purify the whole mind. (152)

Mind, according to Eastern philosophy, is understood according to its different functions. *Manas* is that which gathers through the senses the objects of experience. *Buddhi* is the intellect, which discriminates between "this" and "that." And then there is the ego-consciousness. For instance, my mind or *manas* sees an object before me. Then my intellect says this object is classified with similar objects but is distinct from them. Then there arises the awareness, I know this. These are the different functions of the mind, but for the sake of our understanding, we will just call the three functions what they are called in the West: thinking, feeling and willing.

There is a story of a student who approached a great sage as a student and said, "Holy sir, I have studied science, drama, etymology, astronomy, philosophy, and scriptures, but I find no peace. Show me the way to peace." The great teacher pointed out: "Know thine own Self." If you know the Self, you know the whole universe, just as by knowing a piece of gold, you know everything that is made of gold. By knowing that Reality, you see how it has become everything. It is the psychology of yoga that teaches how to attain this unified consciousness.

Patanjali points out that "Yoga is the control of the vagaries of the mind." He calls those vagaries "the waves on the lake of the mind." Many ripples and many waves arise and distort the reflection on the lake. The moon is shining, but if there are waves and the water is dirty, that reflection is not correct. And that is how we misread everything.

In the Gita Sri Krishna says: "Patiently, little by little, a man must free himself from all mental distractions with the aid of the intelligent will." And in order to control the waves of the mind, we have to make the mind one-pointed, which means that we have to realize that God is the one treasure in life. As Jesus said: "Where your treasure is, there your heart will be also."

Now, what happens when you try to concentrate your mind upon God? So many distractions, so many waves arise. Just at the moment you are trying to meditate and worship, all the distractions come. They have to be controlled. When they are controlled, the mind becomes crystal clear, and the reflection becomes perfect. As Sri Ramakrishna used to say, "Pure mind and pure Atman are the same; they become identified." Not this mind – but purified heart and mind – realizes the Atman.

How to make the mind one-pointed? In the scriptures we read: "Faith, devotion, and constant union with God or Brahman." Faith is the conviction that what the scriptures say is true and when the guru says, "I have known that Reality," he has known the Reality. My master added this: "You must also have the faith in yourself that others have realized this truth and it is possible for you also to realize it."

Devotion means to have interest in God. Without interest in having that treasure, there will be no striving. It also means there must come a longing for the truth of God, a deep yearning. It comes gradually. If you have even a little desire and you practice, great earnestness and restlessness comes: "I cannot live without God!"

Constant union, or what we call meditation, *dhyana*, is a state to be achieved. The illustration given is oil poured from one vessel to another. There is continuity. You see, the mind, by its very nature, is in flux all the time, so the current of the mind has to be made to flow, unbroken, towards the one reality. That is known as meditation. The Gita states: "Utterly quiet, made clean of passion, the mind of the yogi knows that Brahman." You become absorbed and you attain *samadhi*. "Released from evil, his mind is constant in contemplation." He is performing activities of life, yet is in union with God. "The way is easy." Then the current begins to flow. "Brahman has touched him. That bliss is boundless."

The main thing is to be devoted to God. Shankara said: "Be devoted to Brahman and you will be able to control your senses, and you will gain mastery over your mind. Master your mind and the sense of ego will be dissolved. In this manner the yogi achieves an unbroken realization of the joy of Brahman. Therefore, let the seeker try to give his heart to Brahman." It is a simple thing: fix your mind and heart in God as often as you can. (153)

The gross mind has to be controlled and made subtle or pure. "Then man abides in his real nature," says Patanjali. What is that true nature? *Sat-Chit-Ananda-Brahman* – which is pure consciousness, life eternal, and abiding love and infinite joy. That is your true nature, the Atman, which is one with Brahman. When the mind is kept under complete control, then your true nature becomes revealed to you, and then you have attained the fulfillment of human birth and life.

This Atman, which is within each one of us, is never affected by anything – not by our actions, our thoughts, or our deeds. In other words, you are always Brahman and nothing else. As my master said, he saw Brahman in so many masks – the mask of a thief, of a lustful man, of a saint – but it was all Brahman, one Reality. A great seer or yogi is one who has attained that knowledge – who loves everybody, who loves the Reality, God within, and who sees that same God everywhere.

REALIZING GOD

Patanjali, the great yogi, can also be said to be a great scientist or psychologist. Science is verifiable and demonstrable; in the same way, religion is verifiable and demonstrable to those who are ready to understand. And as in science, you have to go to the laboratory to have a demonstration. As Swamiji said, in order to be a chemist, you must burn your hand in acid from time to time. Just saying, "O chemistry, come to me," doesn't make you a chemist.

In spiritual life the laboratory is our own mind. Patanjali gives us the methods by which to remove the impurities of the mind, and then the individual spirit opens to the light-giving knowledge of the Atman. He gives us eight limbs of yoga through which, if we follow, the Atman becomes revealed.

Yoga has been aptly compared to a tree bearing luscious fruit. The seed of the yoga tree is nourished by *yama* and *niyama*, which I shall explain. As it begins to germinate, it is further fed by *asana* and *pranayama*. And as it matures and becomes a full-grown tree, it bears flowers in the practice of *pratyahara*, and abundant fruit in *dharana*, *dhyana*, and *samadhi*. Now let us try to understand them one by one.

Yama, or restraint, includes *ahimsa*, abstention from harming others in thought, word, or deed. Every other principle of *yama* is to be followed in thought, word, and deed: abstention from falsehood, abstention from stealing, observance of chastity, and abstention from greed. All of these in thought, word, and deed. It is interesting that there are so many limbs and ideals, but if you are perfect in one of these practices, your heart will be purified. Such is their power.

Now abstention from harming others appears to be a negative observance, but in its positive sense the meaning is to do good to all and to learn to live in love and harmony with others. Remember this. This is the first teaching of all great teachers. "Do no harm." Buddha emphasized it especially. One

402

may say another hurts me, hates me, did this to me; I will not forgive and forget. Well, such a person can never be a yogi. Love conquers hatred. Swami Vivekananda gave a wonderful interpretation: "The test of *ahimsa* is absence of jealousy." He points out that the so-called great men of the world may all be seen to become jealous of each other, or for a little name and fame, or for a few bits of gold. Such jealousy exists in the heart, and it is far away from the perfection of *ahimsa*.

Abstention from falsehood means to be truthful in thought, word, and deed. But again, Maharaj often repeated: "Tell the truth, but do not speak a harsh truth that will harm somebody; it is better to keep silent." The Bhagavad Gita says to speak only such truths that are kind and beneficial.

Now abstention from theft. You will all say, "We are not thieves! We don't steal." No – but we *are* all thieves. For instance, if I call this my watch, I am a thief. I cannot possess anything; you cannot possess anything. Does that mean you must not have any possessions, any bank accounts? Oh, have plenty of bank accounts, but do not be possessed by your possessions. In other words, know that everything belongs either to *prakriti* – to nature – or to God; you are only a trustee. Wealth does not belong to you, but to God. The house you live in is the house of God, and the possessions in it are God's possessions. Use them in the right way, as a trustee.

Then chastity in thought, word, and deed. Of course for monks and nuns this is very important, because sexual energy is transmuted into spiritual energy. Through spiritual energy teachers are able to convey the truth to others. For householders, chastity means moderation.

Then greed. Do not covet others' wealth.

These five practices are *yama*, the first limb of yoga.

Now we come to regular habits, *niyama*. First comes cleanliness, physical and mental. There is an English statement,

"Cleanliness is next to Godliness." It is very true. This body is a temple, the body of God. You must keep it clean. It is a very easy task: simply take some soap and water. And the girls can use a little perfume. There is nothing wrong in that if you consider the body as a temple of God. But if you use perfume to attract somebody, that's different. It's the motive that counts.

Mental cleanliness is also very simple, in the sense that the moment you sit to meditate – always think yourself pure – you are bathed in the presence of God. Don't consider yourself a sinner, no matter what you have done or thought in the past. Our Holy Mother said one time, "Suppose a baby gets in the mud. What does the mother do? Does she throw the baby away?" No, she cleans the baby and takes it on her lap. Is not our God more than our mother and father? Do you think that he looks at our sins or cares for our impurities? That doesn't mean that we should sin, but, you see, what you think, you become. Remember that. Think yourself pure, pure, pure – and you become pure. As Sri Ramakrishna said, "The rascal who thinks he's a sinner becomes a sinner."

Now if you clean yourself every day, physically and mentally, what happens? First there comes cheerfulness, a little joy, a sweetness, in your life. You know, this idea of long-faced religion is just nonsense. The other extreme is to be a crank in the heart while smiling. Both are to be avoided. Cheerfulness comes from inside, and with it comes the power of concentration and also the control of passions. You receive results. Not in one day, but as you practice from month to month, there comes a fitness for the vision of God.

The next regular habit is contentment. Be contented with your outward conditions and poised in the midst of the opposites of life. But have divine discontent. Do not think that because you have achieved some spiritual understanding or experience that you have got everything.

The next is austerity. In Sanskrit the word is *tapas*, and it means that which generates heat or energy. It is self-control, directing all our energy towards God. In this connection Sri Krishna says: "You may know those men to be of demonic nature who mortify the body excessively in ways not prescribed by the scriptures. They do this because their lust and attachment to sense objects has filled them with egotism and vanity. In their foolishness they weaken all their sense organs and outrage me, the dweller within this body." At one time I read the life of a so-called Christian saint and I could not proceed after the first few pages: before going to bed, he used to flog himself until he bled so that there would be no lust. God, I'd rather have lust than that!

What is needed is moderation. Buddha himself practiced hard physical austerities and at long last found that moderation is the way, so he emphasized it. Sri Krishna in the Gita points out: "Yoga is not for the man who overeats, or for him who fasts excessively. It is not for him who sleeps too much, or for the keeper of exaggerated vigils. Let a man be moderate in his eating and his recreation, moderately active, moderate in sleep, and in wakefulness."

Now I will quote to you from the Gita what austerity is: "Reverence for the *devas*, the seers, the teachers and the sages, straightforwardness, harmlessness, physical cleanliness, and sexual purity; these are the virtues whose practice is called austerity of the body. To speak without ever causing pain to another, to be truthful, to say always what is kind and beneficial, and to study the scriptures regularly, this practice is called austerity of speech. The practice of serenity, sympathy, meditation upon the Atman, withdrawal of the mind from sense objects, and integrity of motive, is called austerity of the mind. When a man practices this threefold austerity devotedly, with enlightened faith and no desire for reward, he is said to have the nature of *sattva*."

Austerity also means the practice of ritualism. It is a valuable aid, especially for beginners. But it is not to be practiced universally by everybody; it depends upon the temperament of the individual. In this connection what Maharaj said is of vital importance: "A man begins his spiritual journey from where he is. If an average man is instructed to meditate on his union with absolute Brahman, he will not understand, he will neither grasp the truth of it nor be able to follow the instructions. However, if that same man is asked to worship God with flowers, incense, and other accessories of the ritualistic worship, his mind will gradually become concentrated on God and he will feel joy in his worship."

Then study. Study means study of the scriptures, and also the practice of *japam*. You receive a mantra from the guru; study means to practice its repetition. I once met a Vaishnava whom Swami Turiyananda, one of the disciples of Sri Ramakrishna, used to go visit in Vrindavan. To go see him I had to go down a narrow road, on both sides of which there was jungle; suddenly it opened up into a clearing. There was a little hut where this old man lived with one disciple, only one. The disciple brought a blanket for us to sit on, and then the holy man came. I asked him one simple question, because I could feel something in his presence. I asked him, "How did you attain this stage of unfoldment?" His answer was, "nama," the name of God.

The next habit is dedication of the fruits of one's work to God. That is, after you have done your day's work, offer the fruits of your actions to God. This is called karma yoga. To quote the Gita: "Let him who would climb in meditation to heights of the highest union with Brahman take for his path the yoga of action. Then when he nears that height of oneness, his acts will fall from him, his path will be tranquil." (154)

Truth is of two kinds. We have sense perception, we perceive this universe with our five senses, then with the data we get from the senses, we make inferences. This is called empirical or scientific knowledge. But there is another kind of truth or knowledge that can be derived through the yogic process. It is known as transcendental or superconscious vision. Whether you wish it or not today, in some life or other that truth that is within you will become revealed. As the sun remains hidden by clouds but still shines, not affected by them, the truth within us is not affected by our actions and deeds and thoughts. The ideal of human life is to unfold that divinity within.

Now, one thing needed is a regular habit of contentment, which also means mental poise in the midst of the opposites of life. When I first went to the monastery, one of the disciples of Sri Ramakrishna asked me, "Have you held on to the pillar of God?" You see, in India children hold on to a pillar and then spin round it; holding the pillar, they don't fall. So hold on to the pillar of God to keep your mental poise in the midst of the opposites of life. Also be content with your conditions and external circumstances. If you think that by changing these conditions you'll be happier, you sometimes go from the frying pan into the fire. Whenever you are ready, you will find that God will clear your path. But have divine discontent. If you have some vision or a little light or hear some music or sound and you think you have become spiritual, that will not do! My master used to say: "Light. More light. More Light! Is there any end to it?"

The third limb of yoga is posture. There is only one important condition for proper posture: to be seated in a position which is firm but relaxed. In the Gita we find: "His posture must be motionless, with the body, head, and neck erect." In the Vedanta Aphorisms Vyasa points out: "Worship is possible in a sitting posture, because this encourages meditation. The meditating posture is compared to the immovable earth."

The fourth limb is *pranayama*, which is generally translated as breathing exercises. In the Yoga Sutras Patanjali also gives some breathing exercises, but they may be dangerous. Then again he points out that *pranayama* means control of the *prana*. *Prana* cannot be explained in so many words, only expressed as energy in many ways. For instance, my speaking is the power of *prana*; my breathing is the power of *prana*; digesting my food is the power of *prana*. And this *prana* needs to be controlled. The practice of breathing exercises ultimately brings *kumbhaka*, or suspension of breath. It is important so that the spiritual energy may rise and you may become absorbed in the consciousness of God. But Patanjali again points out that stoppage of the breath, which is caused by concentration upon external or internal objects, is involuntary and natural. It is called *sahajapranayama*, the easiest way to attain *kumbhaka*. Sri Ramakrishna gave the example of a housewife cleaning. When somebody comes and informs her that a neighbor has died, she continues her job, saying, "Oh, that is too bad." But if somebody comes and tells her, "Your son died," there is a stoppage of breath; the mind is concentrated.

So when you begin to feel the presence of God within you, there is suspension of breath. You will find that as you are practicing meditation or concentration, it is the breath that sometimes disturbs you, but gradually, as you concentrate, the breathing becomes rhythmical and then stops naturally, and you do not even know when it stopped. Suddenly you find that you have not been breathing for some time.

Next is *pratyahara*, or detachment of the mind from objects of sense by not permitting the mind to join itself to the centers of perception in the sense organs. Before you are ready to concentrate, you have to practice freeing your mind from attachment to any senses or sense organs. Maharaj told us this: "Free your mind when you go to meditate, from all thoughts and anxieties and worries that you have in the world, then begin your meditation."

Swamiji gives a very practical lesson for the practice of *pratyahara*. He says first to sit for some time and let the mind run on; do not try to control it, only keep watch. The mind bubbles up like a monkey jumping about. Let the monkey jump on, jump as much as he can; simply wait and watch. Knowledge is power, says the proverb, and that is true. Until you know what the mind is doing, you cannot control it, so give it rein. Many hideous thoughts may come into it. You will be astonished that it was possible for you to think such thoughts. But you will find that each day its vagaries are becoming fewer and less violent. Each day it becomes calmer. For the first few months you will find it will have a great many thoughts. Later they will have decreased somewhat. In a few more months you will find they are fewer and fewer. At last the mind will be in perfect control. But we must practice patiently every day.

Let us get to the main point. What is concentration? This is the sixth limb of yoga, and Patanjali defines it as "holding the mind within a center of spiritual consciousness in the body, or fixing it there on some divine form. If this is not possible in the beginning, then try fixing the attention on a place outside. That also helps.

Patanjali gives many other ways to concentrate. That is the beauty of his teaching; people have different temperaments, and one method does not apply to everyone. There is no patent medicine. There is a story about a man who was suffering from constipation. When he went to the doctor, he was told to take castor oil. He was cured. Then he became a big doctor in the village; whoever came to him was given castor oil.

In the Kaivalya Upanishad we read: "The Supreme Heaven shines in the lotus of the heart. They enter there who struggle and aspire.... Retire into solitude. Seat yourself on a clean spot and in an erect posture, with the head and neck in a straight line. Control all sense organs. Bow down in devotion to your guru. Then enter the lotus of the heart and meditate there on the presence of Brahman, the pure, the infinite, the blissful."

Patanjali points out also that you can meditate upon the heart of an illumined soul that is free from passion, in other words, on a divine incarnation. Sri Ramakrishna pointed out that you can meditate upon anybody whom you love, but with the consciousness that he or she is God. If you accept a chosen ideal who is a divine incarnation – a Christ or Krishna or Buddha or Ramakrishna – you don't even have to be aware of their being one with God; just by meditating upon them, you attain the highest. Then Patanjali says that one can meditate on any divine form or symbol that appeals to one as good.

Raja yoga means "royal road" or "royal path." You will not find any sectarianism in it. Its practices are common and universal to all religions. (155)

PRANAYAMA

Pranayama is regarded by the great yogi Patanjali as one of the most important processes for the realization of God. But the word *pranayama* has often been misunderstood. It has been associated with breathing exercises, and breathing exercises are only one of the means to practice *pranayam*a.

The word *pranayama* is a compound word. *Prana*, vital energy or the life principle, is one word, and *ayama*, control, is the other. So the word *pranayama* means the control of the vital energy, a most necessary step to the attainment of God.

What *prana* is cannot be exactly defined, just as no scientist can exactly define what the English word electricity is, but electricity can be known by its various expressions. Vital energy, or the vital principle, or the life principle, cannot actually be defined, but its expressions are well known. Any activity in the shape of thought or action is an expression of this life principle – mental thought, physical action, nervous reaction are different expressions of *prana*. And it is of utmost importance to yogis that we gain control over it. Without gaining control of this principle, which guides our life, which controls our mind, which controls our senses, it is not possible to reach the highest truth.

But what does that mean, the attainment of truth? There is a significant passage in the Gita: "Fools pass blindly by the place of my dwelling here in the human form, and of my majesty they know nothing at all, who am the Lord, their soul." Here we find the common denominator of all religious truths, that there is a treasure – called by Christians the kingdom of Heaven, by Hindus Brahman or Atman – that lies hidden within every human soul.

Spiritual life begins when we learn that what we are seeking unconsciously is God. This is not an emotional experience and not an experience of the senses, but in it there is a culmination and fulfillment of all sense-experience and emotional life. We cannot see him with our eyes or smell him with our nose or hug him with our arms: he can only be known by transcendental experience. And in order to transcend our senses, we transcend our physical consciousness. We have to turn our gaze inward, to make the outgoing mind ingoing. That is the whole principle of *sadhana* or spiritual discipline.

You see, the natural inclination of the mind is to go out through the doors of the senses, but what we seek cannot be found in the outside world. At least for a little while we have to be dead to the world so that a new life can be opened, a new vision of the spirit can be achieved by spirit.

Patanjali described religion as a science of transcendental consciousness that can be achieved by anyone who follows the steps one by one with regularity and precision. He pointed out that there is no question of faith or belief, because it is a science; it is experimental. He gave us steps which can be followed without any confusion with regard to personal beliefs. These steps are really the common principles of spiritual disciplines as propounded by all the mystics of all ages and all countries.

The first step is to observe ethical principles of life. The second is to observe regular habits of cleanliness, both in mind as well as body. Purity is within the shrine of your own heart; how can you be impure, how can you be a sinner? You have to be established in this practice with regularity. Whatever you teach your mind, your mind will learn. The mind is obdurate, and we are under its control, but through a careful process of discipline, it can be brought under control; it can learn to follow you. So teach the mind that one thought again and again: God, the embodiment of purity and holiness, the source of light, of love, and of knowledge, is within the shrine of your own heart. Feel that presence, be bathed in that light, feel that you are pure and holy. That is cleanliness of the mind. Now in order to be able to devote yourself to these practices, a posture that is easy and comfortable is important, the only condition being that the spine be kept straight, the neck and chest erect.

In the next step we come to *pranayama*. As life breath is closely related to breathing, if you can gain control over the breath, you gain control over your mind, your nervous energy, and your physical activities. The principle behind this is that with every movement of the mind, there is a change in the breath. For instance, when you are quiet and calm, you breath differently than when you are passionate and angry – or lazy.

Now, it has been found that psychic powers may develop with the practice of breathing exercises. But they are an obstacle to spiritual growth, and if certain conditions are not fulfilled – for instance, perfect chastity – derangement of the brain may result. Patanjali, who knew of these dangers, pointed out that breathing exercises are not the only means to gaining control of the vital principle. If we follow the higher steps without following breathing exercises, we will gain control of breath and control of the vital principle or energy as well. And the results come without danger or difficulty. I am stressing danger and difficulty because in the West, it is so easy to learn breathing exercises. I have seen disastrous results.

The next higher steps give us control of the vital energy when the breath completely stops. We become dead to this world, and a new vista opens up. The next step is *pratyahara*, gathering the forces of the mind from going outward and bringing quietness to your body, remembering that God is within the shrine of your own heart. Withdrawing your mind from the outside world and imagining that you have entered into the shrine of the heart, you shut the doors of the senses.

The next step is concentration upon the chosen ideal of God or the inner light within. What happens is that your mind becomes concentrated for a few moments, and then those moments grow. This is called *dhyana* or meditation, though we don't actually practice meditation, we practice concentration.

But when you can properly and really meditate, you begin to feel the cool breeze of the ocean, as it were, and a joy wells up within. Your faith grows. The feeling becomes intense and gives you ecstasy, and *samadhi*: you come face to face with God, with the Reality. Once you reach that, your whole vision, your whole life, has changed. (156)

MIND AND ITS CONTROL

Most people are driven like leaves before the wind. They live, think, and act subject to the moods and impulses of their own minds. But what is the true nature of the mind? What is the subconscious mind and why do we have to control it? These are not academic problems, but they are vital questions for every spiritual aspirant. When beginning to practice spiritual disciplines, the aspirant realizes the need for the control of the mind, both conscious and subconscious.

By spiritual life I mean the hunger in the heart to see, to know, to experience God. When we come to the understanding that there is no happiness in the finite, we understand that there is only misery if we follow our moods and impulses. Then we know that in God alone are peace and freedom. The fundamental truth of spiritual life, and the purpose of life itself, can be reached only when we are absorbed in God.

Jesus said, "Be of good cheer; I have overcome the world." Each one of us has to overcome this world. How? It is a vast world, but it actually is in our own mind. That is the point. If you analyze, you will find that whatever you see in this world is a mirror of your own mind, your mind's own reading and nothing else. As in darkness we see a rope and mistake it for a snake, so is this whole creation the creation of our mind.

The main principle of spiritual discipline is control of the thought-waves of the mind. The very moment you control the thought, the Atman is revealed. So that control is not superficial. It is not making the mind blank or unconscious. You know, you can't make the mind blank unless you become unconscious. What you have to do is get to the bottom of it. In order to find the treasure at the bottom of the lake, you have to take away all the mud. Then the lake will be crystal clear. Sri Ramakrishna used to say that the pure mind and Atman are identical, because Atman or God becomes reflected perfectly on a pure mind.

The crystal-clear mind is the pure mind. For instance, you try to concentrate or meditate or pray, and you find how your mind is distracted. Those distractions are there because you have not yet gained control of your subconscious mind. The moment you try to calm your mind, the subconscious mind arises.

So what is the subconscious mind? We think and act consciously, and our thoughts and actions are forgotten for the moment when we think another thought. Or we engage in some action, then in some other action. But all these innumerable thoughts and actions are not lost. Each of them creates an impression on the mind. Those impressions remain under the surface. There are three areas of the mind – conscious, subconscious, and unconscious. Some thoughts and impressions go deep into the unconscious where we cannot remember them even if we try.

But then there is a fourth consciousness, *Turiya*, which transcends the conscious, subconscious, and unconscious states of waking, dreaming, and dreamless sleep. That transcending is possible when the mind has been freed from all impressions, subconscious and unconscious – when we have gained control over the whole mind. And that is possible.

What is character? The sum total of all our deeds and thoughts; it is also the subconscious mind. We are good or bad according to our subconscious mind, which we have created for oursevles. Every child is born with a character: the West points out that it is because of inheritance, but Eastern psychology points out that it is because of the individual's pre-existence.

So if we are bad because of our unconscious mind, is there no way out? Yes, because there is free will. Not that there is complete freedom, because you make your will according to your character. In other words, you will work by the constraints of your own character; you will do good or evil according to your character. But the freedom of the Atman within asserts itself all the time. You only have to recognize that voice, that freedom, asserting itself. An alcoholic wishes to be sober, desires self-control, but is helpless. Then somebody points out that there is a higher power through which that control is possible. It can be done. That higher power is the Atman.

In this connection all our prayers are granted. Do you think there is a God way out there to grant them? No. This freedom of the Atman within yourself is the grace of God. And that Atman is Christ, Krishna, Buddha, Ramakrishna, Mother Kali, Brahman, or Allah – one Reality given so many names.

The regular practice of concentration and meditation is necessary. We find in the Gita: "Patiently, little by little, a man must free himself from all mental distractions, with the aid of the intelligent will." You see, the mind will be distracted: bring it back again and again and again. To clean an ink bottle, you pour in clean, clear water and continue to pour until all the ink comes out and the bottle is filled with pure water. Our subconscious mind and unconscious mind are like that ink bottle; pour in clear water, the thought of God. Struggle to keep your mind fixed in God.

Those of you who begin to meditate will think that you're getting worse. That's because until you meditate, you don't realize the nature of your mind. When you learn to meditate, you begin to face yourself and, as it were, the ink begins to ooze out. This is not self-analysis or psychoanalysis, but as you pour the clear water, the ink comes out. If you self-analyze or psychoanalyze, memory comes into play and creates another impression, but meditation regularly practiced clears the mind, which becomes more and more attached to God. And then sweetness comes and you love to think of God. At long last there is constant recollectedness. When that happens, *prajna* arises, the knowledge of Brahman. (157)

The problem of overcoming the world sometimes overwhelms us. How is it possible to overcome the world? Somebody hurts us, and we feel pain and suffering. Somebody is pleasant to us, and we are happy. But where is the happiness? And where is the hurt feeling? In our own mind. We are reacting. All this is in your own mind, not outside of yourself.

How different is this world to each one of us! We live in worlds of our own. A Christ or a Buddha or a Ramakrishna live in joy and bliss, without tribulations. I have seen such people who have overcome the world by conquering their own mind. They declare: "From joy springs this universe, in joy dwells this universe, unto that joy goes back this universe." [Taittiriya Upanishad] God is *ananda* – bliss, joy, pure consciousness, and immortal life. This God, eternal life, is not separate from you, it is abiding in you. Without that presence you cannot think or breathe or live.

In the Gita we read: "Because of ignorance, there are desires, cravings, restlessness of the mind." Each one of us attempts to find God, but we are restless and seek satisfaction in the outside world. How do we pray? To something way above, if we pray at all. Whereas he is the inner guide, he is the soul of our soul. It is not possible to meditate without the understanding that he is within. You may be intellectually convinced of it, but that does not help. This ignorance, this wrong identification, is something that is direct and immediate; in order to free ourselves from it, we have to have another direct and immediate experience.

So what is the way? We have to seek for him sincerely and earnestly. To quote Shankara: "Seek earnestly for liberation, or for the realization of the truth of God, and your lust for sense objects will be rooted out." Whenever anybody would ask Sri Ramakrishna how to realize that truth, his only answer was: "Yearn for him with a longing heart." Such yearning does not come all of a sudden, yet the more we long for God, the more our worldly desires fall away. They become less and less, and eventually you feel that God is the one eternal truth.

At one time Sri Ramakrishna said that very few believe in God. Swamiji, who was young at that time, contradicted him, "What are you saying? Everybody believes in God." Sri Ramakrishna replied, "Suppose a thief knows that there is a treasure just beyond that wall. Will he remain satisfied, keeping himself away from possessing it? He will do everything possible to break through the wall and get hold of the treasure. If there is real belief, real conviction, a great struggle will be made to get hold of that eternal treasure."

Patanjali pointed out: "By practice and exercise of dispassion, you can overcome your mind." The word *dispassion* seems austere and forbidding, but dispassion comes naturally if you long for God. Desires become less and less. As you move toward the light, you are farther from darkness. So the principle is to concentrate your mind upon God patiently. You must force yourself away from all mental distractions with the aid of the intelligent will. You cannot do it all at once, but little by little. Wherever the mind runs, watch it – then bring it back. Through such practice it becomes controlled. (158)

What about this world? Do you have to discard it? No. This world is a misreading; what we see and experience is only a misreading due to our ignorance. There is a saying of Sri Ramakrishna, "If you place zeroes together, you still have only zeroes, but place one before them and there is value." The world as we experience it in our ignorance is not the real world. When the vision opens up, you begin to see behind this appearance.

Shankara says: "By whom is this world conquered? By him who has conquered his own mind." Again Shankara says: "The mind of the experiencer creates all the objects which he experiences while in the waking or dreaming state." We know we create experiences in dream, but Shankara affirms that in our waking state also what we see is our own creation. "It is the mind that deludes man. It binds him with the bonds of the body, the sense organs, and the life-breath. It makes him wander endlessly among the fruits of action it has caused."

You see, it is through the ignorance of the mind that we identify with the body and become subject to the law of karma. Then we go endlessly round and round through birth and death and rebirth, until we wake up. Shankara says: "Therefore, the seeker after liberation must work carefully to purify the mind. When the mind has been made pure, liberation is as easy to grasp as the fruit which lies in the palm of your hand." God is so near! He is the nearmost substance in every one of us. Try to feel that. In every awareness, his presence is there. Without that presence you cannot breathe, live, or think. God is so near – and yet so far away. To quote the Gita: "The uncontrolled mind does not guess that the Atman is present." If the uncontrolled mind does not even guess that God is present within, how can it meditate? And without meditation, where is peace? Without peace, where is happiness?" (159)

I am talking to you; you are listening to me. What power is that? Brahman! He is present in the wink of the eye, in lightning, in air, in and through every nook and corner of the universe.

Please understand this one truth: as long as you feel God is way up in the sky, you have not yet begun your spiritual life. Only when you begin to feel that he is within, that he is the soul of your soul, does spiritual life begin. Because of the restless nature of the mind, we cannot grasp that he is within, so how can we meditate?

Now let us try to understand the nature of the mind. The whole universe of mind and matter is composed of three *gunas*, which can be said to be bundles of energy which express themselves in different ways. When *sattva* predominates, the mind becomes intelligent, keen, pure, and tranquil. Another type of energy, *rajas*, expresses itself as restlessness, passion, activity. This energy may be for higher things, or may lead you downward. It is the same energy. Then again there is *tamas*, which is lethargy, laziness. The mind is made up of these three energies; yet each mind is different according to the predominance of one or other of these energies.

You know, the mind is described as being like a monkey, restless, jumping from one branch to another. But that is not enough: the monkey gets drunk, intoxicated by the vanity of life – by pride, by ego – and then is stung by the bee of attachment. What use is there, then, in talking about control or religion or God?

Why are there different types, why does an individual go through different moods? Who is responsible for what we are? Being good or bad, or a mixture of good and bad, depends on character. What you are – your growth, your evolution, the mind you have – is your own making. You think a thought, any kind of thought – good or bad, pure or impure, holy or passionate – and the next minute that thought has left you. But the thought has created an impression in your mind. You do a certain deed, and the deed creates an impression in your mind. Just consider, in this whole life you have done so many deeds, you have thought so many kinds of thoughts. All the impressions remain in your mind. And the sum total of those impressions is your character.

I have often given you the illustration of a river flowing in two currents. The surface current and the undercurrent flow in opposite directions. In the same way, in us there are two wills. The will to live and enjoy life can be completely wiped out, but nobody can get rid of the will to inner-check, the will to liberation. It may remain in abeyance, but it will assert itself, though perhaps not in this life.

Sri Krishna's teaching to Arjuna on the ideal of controlling the mind is very interesting. The disciple frankly says to the teacher, "Restless man's mind is, so strongly shaken in the grip of the senses, gross and grown hard with stubborn desire for what is worldly. How shall it gain it? Truly, I think the wind is no wilder." Sri Krishna beautifully points out how to do it: "Yes, Arjuna, the mind is restless, no doubt, and hard to subdue, but it can be brought under control by constant practice, and by the exercise of dispassion. Certainly if a man has no control over his ego, he will find this yoga difficult to master. But a self-controlled man can master it if he struggles hard and uses the right means."

People tell us to be good, but you can't suddenly become transformed just by emotions. You have to take the right steps. In other words, you have to follow spiritual disciplines. First you have to have discrimination to find peace; in God alone you find peace. Then you must have the desire to succeed. Discriminate between the real treasure and glass beads. And then long for liberation.

You have to learn to concentrate in order to think of God. He is right within you; turn your gaze inward. Distractions arise – you can't expect your mind to be concentrated and absorbed in God immediately – but patiently try to free yourself from distractions through regular practice. In *Inspired Talks* Swamiji says: "An impatient person can never have religion."

Finally, practice surrendering the fruits of all your actions to God, every day.

These are the regular, universal practices. Everyone must practice these virtues to grow spiritually.

You have to come to the understanding, if I don't find God, what else is there to find? You have to think, I have no other refuge but God. (160)

The nature of this world is dualism: pleasure and pain, life and death, and rebirth. In school I read a story about a king who became old and practiced austerity to regain his youth. He was told that he could have his youth back if one of his sons would take on his age and give up his own youth. One of his sons took on his father's old age and the king became a young man again. He married a hundred wives, and then at long last he understood that by satisfying cravings, desires are not satisfied. In the same way, when you pour butter into the fire, it flares up more and more.

But if we can control the mind, we can control the world. It is the experience of those who have attained any spiritual illumination that this world disappears. It is the mind that deludes and that binds with the bonds of the body, the sense organs, and the life breath. It makes one wander endlessly among the finite actions it has caused.

But does the world really exist? Do we see the same thing that everybody else sees? If you consider a baby's world and a young man's world and an old man's world, you see that the same object can be seen in different ways. A beautiful girl gives pleasure to her husband, but she brings jealousy to the minds of other girls.

When you ask, "What is the way?" Shankara said that we have to do four things: to discriminate between the eternal and non-eternal; to give up desire for pleasures in the world and in heaven; to acquire qualities such as calmness, self-control, forbearance; and to have complete faith in the words of the guru, surrendering to God. When I was studying this ideal of Shankara with a disciple of Sri Ramakrishna, I said, "But when you have these, what need is there for anything more? You have attained everything!" He said, "That's right, and these will come to you as you follow the teachings of your guru."

The Bhagavad Gita is set on the field of battle and the fight is with the senses, sense pleasures. The treasure is hidden within, but you have to give up everything to find that treasure. I will tell you a story. A scholar went to a holy man, because he had all the scholarship but had found no peace. The holy man said, "Renounce!" So the man thought he would renounce the world and live on alms. Afer some time he came back and said, "I find no peace." The holy man said, "Renounce!" The man had only a cloth and his blanket and water-pot, but he gave them away. He came back and said: "I still find no peace." "Renounce!" Then he thought to himself, "This body." So he built a bonfire and was about to sacrifice himself. The holy man came and dragged him by the hair and said, "Whose body is this? This does not belong to you! It belongs to your parents. What have you got to renounce? Your ego!" You see, renunciation does not mean giving up your possessions. Have possessions, but be not possessed by them. (161)

In the Chandogya Upanishad we read: "When the food is purified, the heart is purified. When the heart is purified, there arises constant recollectedness of God. When that arises, the knowledge of Brahman comes." But what is this food that is to be purified? Not merely what we eat; we are taking food through all our senses. Shall we just stop our noses and close our eyes? No. Move amongst the objects of the senses, but without attachment or aversion. Of course it takes time, but practice, practice, practice! Then your heart will be purified. When your heart becomes purified, you have reached the goal.

The nature of the mind is to be always in flux. How then can it be controlled? Take, for instance, an electric light bulb in which the current is flowing steadily. In the same way, if the current of the mind goes to the Atman within and flows continuously, that becomes meditation. As you concentrate your mind, you find it fluctuating, thinking of all kinds of things and objects. Bring it back again and again. Struggle. Then you will succeed. It is said that if you can concentrate for a few minutes, it is meditation. If you meditate for a few minutes, you attain *samadhi*. Think of that! In twenty-five minutes or in half an hour you can attain *samadhi*! (162)

There is an illustration of the stump of a tree in the dark. A little child, or those who are afraid of spooks, see a ghost. A lover expecting his beloved sees his beloved. The same thing appears differently according to the moods of a person's mind. We create our own images. When something goes wrong, we tend to blame externals, but we have created those externals, the environment that we are in. If we want to change the environment, we have to change ourselves. If we reform ourselves, the whole world becomes reformed. When divine vision opens up, this very universe becomes a mart of joy.

But with an uncontrolled mind the conviction does not come that the one truth we must learn and convince ourselves of again and again is that God is here, that we have to find him within ourselves, that we must feel that presence within. Controlling the thought-waves of the mind is not a superficial control; it is a complete overhauling of the mind. Patanjali says that when you have gained that control over your mind, then you dwell, you exist, in your own true nature, which is divine. (163)

You cannot find God by just going through rituals. Does this mean that rituals are not important? They are, because they prepare us; but they do not give us a direct vision of God. As long as we feel we can find our security and happiness and freedom in the objective world, so long that great longing for God does not arise.

Take the life of Sri Ramakrishna. He showed, in this age, how much you have to yearn for God. A day would not pass in which he'd not pray, meditate, worship, and in the evening he would rub his head on the ground and say: "Mother, another day is gone and I have not seen you!" Life is vain, life is futile, until you can see God. He said he had done one hundred percent to give us the example, that if we do even ten percent of that, we shall reach that ultimate Reality, here while living on earth. We have to come to that understanding.

We come to understanding through discrimination. And then feel the need for God. The crux of the whole problem is in controlling the mind, and before we can control the mind, we must have the longing for liberation.

When you follow the spiritual disciplines taught by your guru, your heart becomes purified, and yearning for God arises. When this longing becomes such that you feel you cannot live without God, that your life is in vain if you cannot love God, then longing arises in the heart such that control comes automatically.

Kant and Herbert Spencer point out that the Infinite is unknown and unknowable. But a Christ or a Buddha or a Krishna or a Ramakrishna, or any spiritual aspirant would tell you no, when the mind has become purified, overhauled and completely transformed, you go into a transcendental state called the Fourth, and you realize the Atman.

You may write down New Years' resolutions and act on them for three or four days, but then you forget everything. If you take refuge in God and get a little grace, you become completely transformed. My master used to say that sins are like heaps of cotton: one match stick can burn the whole mountain. If you can take your refuge in God, which means refuge within your own Self, you submit yourself to this higher Self. You submit your little ego to God, and then a continuous transformation comes.

But it takes a long time to surrender yourself to him. One minute you say, "Lord, you are my refuge," and the next moment you are asserting your ego. But try again and again. You may fail hundreds of times but – and this is the beauty in spiritual struggle – you are bound to succeed. There is no such thing as failure in spiritual life, as long as you keep up the struggle. My master used to say, "Watch a little calf. As soon as it is born, it tries to get up. It falls down. It tries to get up again. Again it falls down. Hundreds of times it falls down, but it doesn't give up the struggle. Then suddenly the calf begins to run."

Just so with our spiritual life. We have to learn to love God. We have to surrender ourselves to God. We have to take our refuge in him. We pray, we meditate, but we have distractions and we forget. You sit for an hour to meditate, but perhaps for five seconds you have the thought of him. It doesn't matter. That five seconds were blessed moments of your life. And then when you really feel that he is your refuge, you begin to walk, and finally you can run. (164)

MYSTICISM AND MYSTIC VISIONS OR SUPERCONSCIOUS VISION

Let us first try to understand what is meant by mysticism. A mystic has the firm conviction that God or the ultimate Reality or Brahman – whatever name you give it – can be experienced in this very life, and that Brahman is the indwelling Self within each one of us. It is when that vision opens up that we become true mystics and see then that this whole universe is filled with the presence of Brahman. There is the same Self, I – the true I, the Being that I am – dwelling within everyone in the universe. There is no distinction between man and man, man and woman, race and race, nation and nation. My own Self, my own Being, the same Reality, dwells, exists, everywhere in the universe.

In the words of Swami Vivekananda, religion "is the unfoldment of the divinity that is already within man." We see that divinity everywhere. And in the words of the Greek mystic Plotinus, "I shall restore the Divine in me to the Divine that is all." That is the purpose and one supreme goal of every human life. Our human life will be wasted if we fail to realize that truth in this very existence. That – the highest goal – must be the one goal.

Swamiji said, "We must have this highest ideal. Unfortunately, the vast majority of persons are now groping in the dark without any ideal at all. If a man with an ideal makes a thousand mistakes, I am sure that the man without an ideal will make fifty thousand. Therefore, it is better to have an ideal. And this ideal we must hear about, as often as we can, till it enters into our hearts, into our brains, into our very veins; until it tingles in every drop of our blood and permeates every pore in our body. We must meditate upon it. Out of the fullness of the heart, the mouth speaks; and out of the fullness of the heart, the hand works, too. It is thought which is the compelling force in us. Fill the mind with the highest thoughts, hear them day after day, think them month after month, and never mind failures. They are quite natural. They are the beauty of life, these failures. What would life be without them? It would not be worth having if it were not for the struggle. Where would be the poetry of life? Never mind the struggle, the mistakes. I never heard a cow tell a lie, but it is only a cow, not a man. Hold the ideal a thousand times, and if you fail a thousand times, make the attempt once more."

Of course everyone has some goal in life. A person wants to become a politician, another a lawyer, a doctor, or something else. I do not object to such things. We need politicians, lawyers, doctors, and businessmen. But they must learn to spiritualize their lives and move toward the supreme goal: to experience God within themselves.

Why is there such chaos in this world? Why is there violence and youth rebellion? Because we have forgotten the ideal! That ideal is not even taught in churches. Yes, there are scriptures, there are gospels, the truth, the revealed words of God – but what good are they if there is no living example of those truths? In the words of Vivekananda, "Until you have that experience for yourself, you have not yet drunk of that fountain which makes reason unreason, mortals immortal, the world a zero, and of man a God."

To quote the words of Shankara: "Those who echo borrowed teachings are not free from worldliness, but those who have attained the transcendental consciousness, *samadhi*, by merging the external universe, the sense organs, the mind, the ego, into that pure consciousness of the Atman, they alone are free from the bondages of life and death."

Why should I have to see God and realize him? What is the effect? The effect is this: the knot of ignorance in the heart becomes loosened, all doubts cease to exist, all effects of deeds of the past, present and future are wiped out.

In the Upanishads it is called *Turiya*, the Fourth – transcending the waking, dreaming, and dreamless sleep states. Is it then that we just know God as I know you? In fact, I do not know you, I do not know anything at all. I only read what my senses bring to my mind. Immanuel Kant, pointed out that the-thing-in-itself remains unknown and unknowable. Whereas the seers point out that It is more than known and knowable; it is being and becoming, the untying of the three knots of knowledge – subject, object and the process of knowledge. The knot of distinction between subject and object has to be untied to reach unitary consciousness.

How is it possible? When the heart is purified, there is constant recollectedness of God. Now reverse the process: practice thinking of God, hearing about the ideal, until it gets into your blood, as it were. And then naturally the heart becomes purified. My master used to say again and again: "Practice, practice, practice." There is a line in Sanskrit: "Adopt any means by which you can keep your mind in the Lord." That is the secret.

When we realize the Supreme Truth, can we express what it is? Has anybody been able to express that? Sri Ramakrishna used to say, "Even the scriptures have been defiled because they have been uttered by the lips of man." But the ultimate truth of God has never been uttered by the lips of man. It is not possible. That is why you find in the same scripture one seer says something, another seer says something else – because they are relative expressions of the same truth.

Though it is not communicable, the truth can be transmitted. Not by words, but I have known how my master, with a touch, could transmit that power. A mystic can describe some of these experiences, and they are true spiritual experiences and visions, but they are not the supreme truth. If we stop and do not move onward, we miss the ultimate reality. That often happens: mystics having some visions or experiences think they have seen God, have realized the ultimate reality, and they do not study anymore. But my Master told me this truth: "Light, more light, more light, more light! Is there any end to it?"

Let me point out the difference between hallucinations, delirium, and spiritual visions. There is a saying in the Bible, "Ye shall know a tree by its fruits." Hallucinations weaken the brain, and the character is not transformed. Delirium is from a diseased brain. But when spiritual visions come, the effect is a stamp on the character; it is transformed. Love, compassion, sympathy, devotion arise in the heart – as does self-control.

I have often heard that mysticism is escapism, but suppose the house is on fire. Won't you try to escape? This is the escape from suffering and misery, to reach that domain where there is no night, but only light and bliss.

Psychologically speaking, a human being is Spirit encased in sheaths: physical, subtle, and causal. Fundamentally, therefore, each one of us is a spiritual being, because our true nature is the indwelling God. Now, just as we consist of sheaths, similarly Brahman is encased in sheaths – physical, subtle and causal. A seer experiences this physical universe as Brahman everywhere. When you see clay dolls of many different kinds and forms, you know it is all clay, only the names and forms are different.

There is another kind of experience brought out in the Mundaka Upanishad: "Heaven is his head, the sun and moon his eyes, the four quarters his ears, the revealed scriptures his voice, the air his breath." Try to feel that, that you are breathing the breath of God. "The universe his heart. From his feet came the earth. He is the innermost Self of all."

Now again, we experience the physical universe with our ordinary five senses – hearing, touch, smell, taste, sight. Similarly, when we rise to the psychic plane, there is sound, smell, sight, and so on. You can hear a sound, taste something, see some light. Not only that, powers may come to you – for instance, clairvoyance or clairaudience, or reading the thoughts of others. Patanjali says: "The psychic powers may be obtained either by birth, or by means of drugs, or by power of words (special mantras), or by the practice of austerities, or by concentration." Drugs can give psychic power or vision momentarily, but the effect, if continued, is that the brain becomes completely deranged. Beware!

A spiritual aspirant tries to avoid psychic powers. My master taught me that even if you are not seeking psychic powers, if you are simply meditating and counting your beads and trying to pray to God for love, devotion, and knowledge, you may suddenly feel a power in you. Try it once to test its validity, but never try a second time. If you do not try anymore, you lose that power.

Patanjali also points out that these are powers in the worldly sense, but obstacles on the spiritual path. They are temptations. Do not trust anyone who shows such occult powers. Both Patanjali and Swami Vivekananda point out that the spiritual progress of those who show such powers is completely blocked.

In some spiritual aspirants, visions may come – but not in all. If they do not, it does not mean there is no growth. The main thing is character: love, devotion, purity. These are the things we have to achieve.

There is a kind of vision called the lower *samadhi*, in which you have the vision of what I may call a personal God, form-less or with form. Of course great joy and bliss come, but there is still a feeling of separation, because you are having the vision and experience. Do not stop there. The highest, what we call *nirvikalpa samadhi,* unitary consciousness, we must struggle and struggle for until we realize, "I am Brahman. I am He. Everything that I see before me is my own Self, is the one Lord in so many forms." Just consider! If only a few of you realize that, you can bring a complete change in the whole world! (165)

The knowledge which is gained from inference and the study of scriptures is knowledge of one kind; the knowledge which is gained from *samadhi* or transcendental experience is of a much higher order; it goes beyond inference and scriptures.

Thus we find that our five senses give us the experience of this world – we cannot deny these experiences as long as we are experiencing them – and also we gather certain data out of which we can come to an inference, and this is called infer-ential or empirical or scientific knowledge. It is also true.

There are philosophers in the West who try to prove the existence of God through inferential knowledge, and there are others who, through reason, can disprove the existence of God. The point is: suppose we prove the existence of God. What does it mean? What have we proved? For instance, Hegel proved through his dialectic process the existence of an abso-lute reality, but he proved only an idea of the Absolute. Is there any guarantee that his idea of the Absolute and the Absolute itself are identical? In other words, until you have directly experienced that Absolute, it does not mean anything.

Now take the revealed scriptures. We come to some understanding because they are experiences of the great sages and seers. And so we believe in the existence of God. Does that give us any satisfaction? It is just like somebody being sick and another taking medicine for him. Scriptural knowledge gives us no ultimate satisfaction because the absolute truth is indefinable and inexpressible. It is a matter of experience. You have to reach a stage of unfoldment when, it is said, "scriptures are no longer scriptures, the Vedas become no Vedas." How bold this statement is! To quote Swami Vivekananda, "Realization is real religion; all the rest is only preparation. Hearing lectures or reading books or reasoning is merely preparing the ground. Intellectual assent or dissent are not religion."

Now, in the presence of my master who was filled with God, you didn't have to ask whether God is or is not. You could feel the presence tangibly. Not only that, he would make us feel that God is so near that he is just like a fruit in the palm of our hand. And he would always insist that others have realized their union with God and it is possible for you also.

In the Mahabharata we read that King Yudhisthira was asked, "What is the greatest wonder in the world?" He replied, "The greatest wonder is this: that we see people dying, but still we do not believe that we shall die." We think that we shall live forever, because there is eternal life. But we seek to find that eternal life in this surface life of the body.

Concentration, meditation, and absorption are the direct means to realization. Shankara puts it a little differently. He says: "Faith, devotion, and constant union with God, through prayer, these are declared by sacred scriptures to be the seeker's direct means of liberation. To him who abides by them comes liberation from the bondage of physical consciousness, which has been forged by ignorance." Faith is the faith in the words of the guru and the scriptures – what we call *shraddha*. We must have faith that what the scriptures say is true: that God can be attained. And faith in the guru who has attained and says, "Yes, it is possible for you, for everyone, to realize That." And then also to have that confidence in yourself that, yes, I can realize him. This is the first thing.

There are seven centers of spiritual consciousness. Generally the minds of all people dwell within the three lower centers – the anus, the sex organ, the navel. The mind begins to dwell in the fourth center, in the heart, when you begin to meditate upon God. Then love grows in your heart. During that time you can see a light or something – or you may not. When the mind goes to the next higher center at the throat, you have become purified. When the mind goes there, you cannot bear – at least for some time – to talk or think of anything but God. If somebody talks about other things, it jars you.

Then when the mind comes to the center between the eyebrows, you enter into *samadhi*. There you see either God with form or God without form, and you enjoy such bliss, such happiness, as you have never felt in your life. That is known as the lower *samadhi*. When the mind comes to the thousand-petaled lotus, in the center of the brain, there is what is known as *nirvikalpa samadhi*, union with Brahman. In the lower, or *savikalpa samadhi*, though you see Reality, there is still a distinction between you and God. You are, as it were, a part of God, you are experiencing God. But when you go to the very highest, the ego is wiped out completely. As Patanjali points out: "When the impression made by that *samadhi* is also wiped out, so that there are no more thought waves at all in the mind, then one enters the *samadhi* which is called 'seedless.'" That is *nirvikalpa*.

In this connection let me quote to you Sri Ramakrishna's experience. He first had the experience of Divine Mother in *savikalpa samadhi*. He said, "Every time I gathered my mind together, I came face to face with the blissful form of Divine Mother. However much I tried to free my mind from consciousness of Mother, I did not have the will to go beyond. But at last, collecting all the strength of my will, I cut Mother's form to pieces with the sword of discrimination, and at once my mind became seedless and I reached *nirvikalpa samadhi*. It was beyond all expression."

Philosophically, it is called *tripurti veda*, the untying of the three knots of knowledge: subject, object, and the process of knowledge. You see, in all our knowledge, there is "I," ego, experiencing something, and there is the process of knowledge. But when these three knots are untied, there is the unitary consciousness in which the consciousness of subject and object is dissolved away. Then infinite, unitary consciousness alone remains. Then one knows the bliss of *nirvana* while still living on earth.

Nirvikalpa samadhi has been described by Shankara as follows: "There is a continuous consciousness of the unity of Atman and Brahman. There is no longer any identification of the Atman with its coverings. All sense of duality is obliterated. There is pure, unified consciousness. The man who is well established in this consciousness is said to be illumined. ... Even though his mind is dissolved in Brahman, he is fully awake, but free from the ignorance of the waking life. He is fully conscious, but free from any craving. Such a man is said to be free even in this life. For him, the sorrows of this world are over. Though he possesses a finite body, he remains united with the Infinite. His heart knows no anxiety. Such a man is said to be free even in this life."

Sri Ramakrishna would go into this *nirvikalpa samadhi* many times every day. Think of that! This I heard from my master. Generally if you go into that, you are through. And then again, when he returned to normal consciousness, he would speak of God the Mother; his chosen aspect of God did not lose its reality because he had known Brahman. Thus Sri Ramakrishna showed how the divine aspects of the chosen ideal are also real. All the *avataras* kept a certain amount of separation in order to teach mankind. My master told me one time, "At times I see God playing, wearing so many masks. Then how can I teach? Then again I come down to the normal plane and see your weaknesses and defects, and I try to correct them." (166)

To be a true mystic three conditions are necessary. The first is human birth. The next is the longing for God, for liberation. The third is the grace of a guru, a holy man.

How does a teacher teach? Not by words merely, because the truth of God is transmitted in silence. In the Upanishads we read: "To many it is not given to hear of the Atman. Many, though they hear of it, do not understand it. Wonderful is he who speaks of it, intelligent is he who learns of it, blessed is he who, taught by a good teacher, is able to understand."

In the West a distinction is made between religion and mysticism, that religion is a faith, a belief in certain dogmas or creeds and doctrines, certain rites and ceremonies, while mysticism is the belief that God can be known and realized. In India we make no distinction. Religion means not faith or belief in dogmas or doctrines, even in God, but to realize God. Sri Ramakrishna used to say that in the Hindu almanac there is the forecast of how many inches of rain will fall in the year. You can squeeze that almanac, but not a drop falls. Lectures and religious talks do not give you religion, but they can give you the urge to experience.

You can describe your experiences in life because you have something to compare them with, but the truth of God has never been expressed by the lips of man. It is indescribable, inexpressible, beyond feeling. Mystic visions and experiences have been described, and they are true, they are wonderful, but they are not experiences of the ultimate Reality. They are milestones on the path of progress. We must understand that. They show that we are progressing, but not that we have attained the highest and ultimate Reality. One also must not despair at not having visions; not everyone needs them, or needs ecstasy. The main thing on the path of progress is to gain greater self-mastery, to find sweetness in the thought of God, and to broaden our outlook.

There are two conditions to test supreme experiences. First, if you see or experience something which can be known and experienced through other means, then that is not a true revelation. For instance, the power of clairvoyance. You see something at a distance, but if you go there, you can see it. Or you can be psychic and know how much money is in my pocket, or what I am thinking. That has nothing to do with spiritual life, because it is not the experience of God.

Another test is that spiritual knowledge is not opposed to reason. Though it transcends reason, it does not contradict it. You do not become irrational. In the Vedas we read that there are three steps: to hear about this truth from one who has experienced it – but not to believe him; to reason it out – otherwise you won't understand what he is saying; and then to meditate upon that in order to have the personal experience.

The fundamental truth is that your experience is what matters. You cannot enjoy the beauty of the moon by looking at a painting. You are the measure of all truths. Try to understand that your nature contains and reflects every level of reality from matter to God. (167)

In the Upanishads we read: "With mind illumined by the power of meditation, the wise know him, the blissful, the immortal." [Mundaka Upanishad] This is mysticism, that God can be known and realized and experienced within our own souls. This is religion.

In all our experiences, whether we are wise or dull, all our visions and experiences of this world are in duality or in the manifold. There is pleasure, there is pain. Sometimes we have wonderful feelings of divine presence; again we lose that feeling. Mystic vision is beyond intellectual understanding or mere feeling of the heart. It is an experience of unalloyed bliss: no more dual throngs of life. In short, there is the empirical universe before us, which is perceived by our senses, and then we reason out with what you may call inferential knowledge. But the Atman can be perceived, not with these eyes or these ears; and that power is in every one of us, and can be developed by the power of meditation. This is a subtle superconscious power that is not given only to a few, but is in every human being. In that experience is the fulfillment.

In a Christ or a Buddha, a Krishna or a Ramakrishna, that power was evolved, and there have been great mystics and saints and sages, some still living, in whom this power is also evolved. And it can be evolved by every one of us. My master often pointed out to us, "Spiritual life begins after you attain the vision of God in *samadhi*." Before that, we only play with words, quote scriptures, talk about God. It is merely talk until this vision opens up.

It is beyond self-consciousness, but you are fully conscious. You see, in the unconscious state there is no ego, and in this transcendental state there is no ego – but there is full consciousness. Swami Vivekananda explained the difference be-tween deep sleep, when you go unconscious, and *samadhi*, in which you *appear* to be unconscious. He said that if you go to sleep a fool, you wake up a fool; but if you go into the transcendental state once, you come out wise, completely transformed. And you become a blessing to all. Then you live in love and service for all mankind.

The great Shankara said, "In the matter of inquiry into Brah-man, scriptures are not the only authority; but your personal experience is the only proof, the only authority." In the Maha-bharata we read: "He who has no personal knowledge but has heard many things cannot really understand the scriptures, even as a spoon has no idea of the taste of the soup." And Mo-hammed said that one who does not have personal knowledge but is full of scriptural knowledge is like an ass carrying a load of books.

Shankara also pointed out that if worldliness persists, one has not attained to the knowledge of Brahman. Worldliness means, in one short word, selfishness – attachment to the little self, to "me" and "mine." The heart of one who has attained the know-ledge of Brahman becomes big. A disciple of Sri Ramakrishna who was in California was asked by Swami Vivekananda if he had had any visions or experiences. He said, "Brother, I don't know anything about your vision and experience, but this much I can tell you: my heart has grown big. When I was eighteen, I would not walk the same path where there were prostitutes, but today I could live in the same house with them and there would be no condemnation in my heart." My master one day told me: "Go, practice *japam*, repeat the name of the Lord, meditate, and then your heart will grow in compassion and sympathy for the sufferings of others." That's what happens.

Spiritual aspirants try to avoid the psychic plane and get into the causal plane, as it were. The causal plane is God as the creator, the cause, of this universe, realized as a personal being. Here the attraction is so great that you want to break through all barriers and become one with him. And when you do, you attain *nirvikalpa samadhi*, the supreme experience of unitary consciousness.

Samadhi is known by its fruits. Your life becomes transformed. Purity, compassion, love, sympathy, self-mastery, freedom from passions, all these characteristics come to you. (168)

Infinite knowledge is not intellectual knowledge, nor is it a feeling of the heart. Intellect and heart both play an important part in attaining it, and it is not that we have to give up either our reasoning power or the feeling of our hearts. But these are only the means and methods. Infinite knowledge transcends the intellect and all feeling. You see, a realized soul lives in the body with an apparent consciousness of the body, apparently subject to heat and cold and so-called experiences of the world, but in a moment can withdraw and be free from body-consciousness or identification with the moods of the mind.

Sri Ramakrishna used to give this illustration: "Take a green coconut with the meat and shell together; if you hurt the shell, it hurts the meat. But when this coconut becomes dry, the meat and the shell become separated. Then you can drive a nail into the shell and it won't affect the meat." A disciple of Sri Ramakrishna once told me, "Now I see the Atman as completely separate and detached from the body."

A surgeon once operated on Swami Turiyananda, another disciple of Ramakrishna. He was not under anesthesia and spoke to the disciples joyfully while the surgeon operated. After that the surgeon thought the swami was always detached from his body, so when Swami Turiyananda had a spot on his big toe, the surgeon came and prostrated and, without the knowledge of the swami, took the knife and cut the toe. Swami Turiyananda shuddered and said, "You should have told me. I could have prepared myself."

You have to be holy to recognize holiness. Outwardly holy people behave like everybody else, but if you live with them, you will find something different. The illustration given is of a burnt rope. There is the appearance of a rope, but it cannot bind. Shankara says, "In him who attains this unitive knowledge, the worldliness that affected him previously is completely gone. If you find that worldliness attached to him, then know that he has not attained that wisdom." Sri Ramakrishna defined this worldliness as lust and greed. One who has attained the knowledge of God is freed from lust and greed. That is the effect that comes. (169)

Why must there be mystics? Is it not enough just to be good, moral, ethical, and to do good to the world? Why should we have to see God? Matthew Arnold defined religion as "ethical life with a touch of emotionalism." But what is ethical life? To be completely selfless, to be completely egoless. Can you really practice what is called humanism without love for God? It is not possible. You become egotistic if all you do is to do good.

Mysticism is beyond all feelings, emotions, ecstasies. My master said at one time, "Bliss, yes, but you have to go beyond that also." What that is, of course, is indefinable, inexpressible. And coming back after that highest *samadhi*, one may continue to live, but then considers the world a mirage. The appearance is there, but the eye has changed: it is the eye of Spirit only. Shankara says: "With physical eyes what would you see but matter; and with the eye of Spirit, what would you see but Spirit, Brahman?" In other words, you either see

everything as matter – when you are in ignorance – or you
see nothing but God.

Swami Vivekananda said, "All is not; God is." The world
disappears completely. Then you realize that Brahman is
above, Brahman is below, Brahman is to the right, Brahman
is to the left, Brahman is within, and Brahman is without. All
is Brahman. (170)

SILENCE

The whole truth of religion and spiritual life is in the one
word *silence*. Only in silence can the truth of God be known.
And only in silence can the teacher teach. We may be silent,
but how to still the noises inside is the whole of religion.

It is an experience that transforms your whole life and
brings complete fulfillment inside. You may experience this
thing or that thing and perhaps gain knowledge, but the experience of God is something that transforms your whole life
and being.

In the Upanishads we read: "I have known that which is
beyond all darkness." Then the seer says that you also have to
experience that in order to reach immortal bliss. Sri Ramakrishna said, "You hear about God, then you see God, then
you talk to him, you become intimate with him. And you
realize your union with him." This union has to be achieved
in this life.

What is the way? The light, God, is within each one of us,
but how do you find it? In the Gita we read: "When the mind
is under perfect control and freed from desires, he becomes
absorbed in the Atman and nothing else." *You have to be completely absorbed in God.* Or, as Meister Eckhart said: "There
must be perfect stillness in the soul before God can whisper
his words into it, before the Light of God can shine in the

soul and transform the soul into God. When the passions are stilled and worldly desires silenced, then the word of God can be heard in the soul."

If we struggle and practice, it becomes easy. You see, the mind is like a lake. If the lake is waving and rippling, a reflection is not perfect. You must somehow quiet the lake. We must calm the mind, have complete control over it. And this is possible only by controlling our passions and cravings. Only then is the glory of God, who is within, becomes revealed.

This is a psychological principle: the consciousness of the Atman is there; that consciousness is God, blissful, immortal, eternal, and unchangeable by its very nature. When you are awake or asleep or dreaming, the background is that consciousness – God – always, always. *You are never separate, never apart from God, not for one moment.* But the consciousness is reflecting on the mind which rises in waves of craving and desiring all the time, so that the reflection is not complete or perfect.

Now, how to gain control over the mind, how to achieve silence? It is not something passive. When you go to sleep, your mind is blank, unconscious, but the mind freed from the contents of consciousness is very different. When you free yourself from the contents of consciousness, there is full consciousness. It is not unconscious; it is full consciousness. In the same way, the waking state is also partial consciousness; it is not full consciousness.

So the way is not to make the mind blank, but to raise one huge wave to the exclusion of the rest, and that huge wave must be the thought of God. No matter how you conceive of him, whatever you consider God to be, that will ultimately lead you to the Reality.

Nobody can really define God, but each one of us can have a conception of God. A conception is the reading with our human minds of the great Truth. The illustration can be given of the ocean with containers of different shapes and sizes. You go and dip your vessel into the ocean and what have you got? Water – but it has taken the shape of your vessel. So think of God in any way that appeals to you. Eventually, the vessel will break, and the water will return to the ocean; that is the experience of Reality.

The moment you try to think of God, to raise that one wave to the exclusion of others, all the other cravings and desires and thoughts and distractions pour in. You feel you were better off before you began. That's what happens and that is why Arjuna said in the Gita: "I think the wind is no wilder!" To which Sri Krishna responded: "Yes, Arjuna, the mind is restless no doubt, and hard to subdue, but it can be brought under control by constant practice, and by the exercise of dispassion."

For that we have to create a new character, we have to be transformed. You see, religion is transformation of life and character, not for the moment, but permanently. For that we must try to have a conception of God and concentrate upon that with regularity. But not only that, we have to keep recollectedness – while we are walking, while we are sitting, running, cooking, while we are doing anything. You may say you are too busy with your work and distracting thoughts associated with your work, but just analyze yourself and you will find that you are not really concentrated fully on any kind of work. Your mind is on other things. Keep your mind busy with God and do those other things too. My master used to say: "If you keep twenty percent of your mind on duties and business and work, you can do wonderfully well. Keep eighty percent of your mind on God." This comes through practice.

When you reach that stage, your mind flows towards God without any break or distraction. You become completely absorbed, and through such absorption, revelation comes. You see, it all depends on where your consciousness is.

Aim at the highest; then you achieve something. All the great ones urge us to be up and doing, to struggle and realize that complete absorption in God. That is the one common goal of all religions. If we have that one goal, then we shall find all religions are true and we shall come to the ideal of harmony and universality. (171)

What is God? Everything that we sense and perceive and experience today is and tomorrow is not. But behind this surface experience where everything is transitory – happiness and misery, life, death, and birth – there is a changeless Reality. To quote the Upanishads: "The eternal amongst the noneternals of life, the pure consciousness amongst everything that is conscious, the highest abiding joy in the midst of the fleeting pleasures of life." That is the reality, that is Brahman, that is God, it doesn't matter what you call it.

You are free, perfect, divine – that is your very nature. And that is what you are seeking to unfold. Only you are trying to unfold it, as Swami Vivekananda said, in little mud puddles. What is religion? It is to seek consciously what you are seeking unknowingly in the shadows of life.

To quote the words of a Christian mystic, Meister Eckhart: "The word of God can be heard in the soul; the light of God can shine in the soul and transform the soul into God."

Try to meditate upon the truth that we are living in the city of Brahman: we live, move, and have our being in God. Swami Vivekananda once said: "Seek not God, see Him." He is right with you. He is your very Self. You are never apart from him. See him, see him, see him.

When the sense of ego arises, we feel limited, finite, dry, lacking. We want love, so we go outside. We want happiness, so we go outside. We form attachment to things and objects and persons that give us pleasure, and we consider them as separate from us. And also we feel aversion to things that give us suffering or pain. Our ignorance is so thick that we cling to life, thinking that it is Reality. You know, ignorance is so sticky! If somebody this moment tried to give you ultimate knowledge, you'd shrink back, "No, no, no! I don't want it!" Our ignorance is not our real nature but is just something that has covered the reality, like clouds covering the sun. The clouds are not permanent; a gust of wind removes them, and the sun is shining.

Stilling the mind does not mean going to sleep, being unconscious, or not thinking anything. There is a difference between being unconscious, making the mind blank, and attaining *samadhi* or the illumined knowledge of God. When you are asleep, you are unconscious; but in *samadhi*, there is full consciousness. The principle is, in the waking state raise one wave of thought to the exclusion of everything else. In other words, *think of God*, no matter how you think of Him. We cannot truly conceive of what God is, yet we all conceive in some way or another. Recollectedness or meditation upon God doesn't mean just imagining things, but trying to see him, to feel the presence. That is the most important part of meditation, to feel that presence. He is here. I can't see him, but he is here. And he knows, he listens. That is a fact. Practice, practice, practice. Give your whole life to him and you are bound to succeed! (172)

It sounds very strange that I am going to speak on silence. I wish we could go into silence, for only then could we really understand what it means. I am reminded of a pen-picture as given by the great seer philosopher, Shankara. He describes a teacher who is young, seated with his disciples who are old.

They are seated under a tree in silence. All the doubts and superstitions in these old disciples are being removed by the silence of this great teacher. The disciples are said to be old because superstitions, traditions, and doubts are ancient. It is not that only a few individuals are subject to doubt and superstition and tradition: all mankind is subject to them. Only when the truth becomes revealed in the heart do all doubts cease to exist.

There was a disciple of Sri Ramakrishna who would talk about nothing but God. If any other topic came up, within a few minutes he would say, "We are wasting our time." On the other hand, Maharaj would hardly talk of God, yet in his presence you would feel you were in the presence of God, and that, to experience God, was simple.

I have often told you the story of how a father sent a son to learn of God. After twelve years, the son came back and the father asked him, "Tell me what you have learned about God." He gave a wonderful discourse, quoting scriptures, and his father said, "Go back. You have not yet learned what is to be learned." So he went back, and came home after another twelve years. When the father asked him this time, he remained silent. Then the father said, "Why, my boy, your face shines like a knower of Brahman! You have known him. His name is Silence."

The search for God begins as soon as a man or a woman or a child becomes self-conscious. There is that urge in every one of us to unfold divinity. As soon as self-consciousness arises, the urge is to be happy and to know. Why is this? What is this? I feel certain limitations and I want to be free from such limitations. There is the urge in every one of us to seek knowledge, happiness, and freedom – to unfold divinity – and we want to love and be loved. And what is God? *Sat-Chit-Ananda*: absolute existence, absolute knowledge, absolute love and bliss. In ignorance we do not know consciously what this urge is, but through experience, we ultimately come to understand that it is only by finding God within ourselves that we can find fulfillment.

In the Lord's Prayer we find: "Lead us not into temptation." Temptation is the outside world, the senses outgoing. And there is the prayer Sri Ramakrishna taught: "Lord, do not delude me by your bewitching *maya*." It is difficult to explain why there is *maya*, ignorance, but it is there. Swamiji explained that you cannot ask the question logically because, as long as you are in *maya* or ignorance, you hear from another about the supersensuous state, but really you don't know anything about it. You don't realize that you are in darkness; you think it is light. And then when you realize the truth, you see there was no ignorance at any time.

Somehow you have to still the waves of your mind, all the thoughts and distractions that are there. If they can be stilled, then the truth of God becomes revealed immediately. But this stilling of the mind is not simple or easy. For that you need spiritual disciplines. The mind has to be made pure like crystal. Subconscious impressions have to be replaced with impressions of divinity – thinking of God all the time. Purity is thinking without any distraction and concentrating on God. When the passions are stilled, and worldly desires silenced, then the word of God can be heard in the soul.

We have to change our whole mode of living, not by giving up duties, but by changing our whole attitude. Think of God, feel the presence of God. If you feel that presence, you are bathed in his light. This is one of the first vows we take: "I will not brood over my past mistakes when I go to meditate; when I go to think of God, I'll think myself pure, free, divine." (173)

What sincere seeking means, in a word, is to go into silence where there is cessation of all desires. When the mind is eager, waiting for God, grace comes immediately. It is in silence that the truth of God is imparted through the grace of a guru or teacher.

Sri Ramakrishna was asked once, "Where is God?" He put his cloth in front of his face and said, "You see, God is there, but you can't see him because of this veil. That is the veil of ignorance." Just try to understand this simple truth. Even though there is the veil of ignorance and we do not see him, still try to feel that he is nearer than hands and feet. He is the very consciousness of our being conscious. With spiritual growth, as you practice spiritual disciplines, the first understanding that comes is the "Is-ness" of God. He is! I don't see him, I don't know him yet, but he is! This conviction comes, but only when we rend asunder this veil of ignorance.

Now consider that individuality is the first-begotten child of ignorance. Has it any reality? Often the question arises that we shall have to lose our individuality, because our whole universe, as it were, is centered around this little ego. I want this, I want that; I seek this, I seek that. What remains if I give that up? What happens to my individuality? If you analyze, you find that there is no such thing as individuality. You can't find that illusion centered around the ego. You seek everywhere, and yet what the ego is, you don't inquire about. Behind the appearance of ego is the real Self, the Atman, which is the Self in every being, and which is one with God. By this shadow of an ego, we are bound down. Sri Ramakrishna gave the illustration that it's like trying to find what is inside an onion. You peel off layer after layer after layer and come to nothing. What we think as our individuality, we are losing every moment. You are not the same person from moment to moment: your character changes, your mind grows, your body changes. Everything that you have that distinguishes you from others is always changing; yet you have the consciousness that "I am I." Seek to know that "I." That is the Atman, that is Brahman, that is God.

Our Holy Mother used to say: "Pray that you may be desireless." Of course this truth discourages people, but you don't have to struggle to give up desire: if you move toward the light, you will be farther from the darkness. As you get something that is greater than anything else, naturally lesser things fall away.

In plain words, practice! Also discriminate and be dispassionate. If you have too much attachment to the world and you do not discriminate, it is like trying to water a dry field with rat holes that carry the water away. Sri Ramakrishna gave the illustration that some drunkards got into a boat one evening and rowed all night, thinking they were crossing the river. When the daylight came, they saw they were in the same place. They had forgotten to lift the anchor. (174)

I never tire of repeating this one truth: religion is experience. Not belief, not an acceptance of any creed or dogma, not the authority of any scripture, but a matter of experience. A spiritual aspirant in India does not ask you, "What is your belief?" but asks, "What is your experience?"

Experience of what? We are experiencing this universe; we gather knowledge and experience of things and ideas – but what is the experience that religion claims? It is the experience of the ultimate Reality – call that Godhead or whatever name you wish. Whatever we experience in this universe and in our consciousness is fleeting, changing, but Reality is that which is unchangeable, beyond time and space and relativity. The only way this Reality or God can be described, if there is any possibility of description, is "the eternal amongst the noneternals of life, the highest abiding joy in the midst of the fleeting pleasures of life." But even that does not convey any inkling of God-consciousness until we see and experience it for ourselves.

You find those who have attained to that silence, reached that ultimate Reality, again speaking about God. Otherwise, how could anybody know? They give us some idea, a thread, as it were, to hold onto so that we can proceed into that depth of silence. Sri Ramakrishna gave this illustration to explain why these God-men speak: The bee, before it sits on a flower, makes a buzzing noise. Then, as it sits on the flower and begins to suck the honey, it remains silent. Then, drinking deep of that honey and becoming intoxicated, it makes a sweet humming sound. Similarly, before knowing God, one speaks abundantly of God, sometimes saying that God is this, and not that. Then, after going into that silence and drinking deep, one who has become God-intoxicated, speaks differently of God, sometimes saying he is this or that, but not limiting him, not trying to define him. That person points out that God is beyond all conception, thought, and expression.

When you seek pleasure, aren't you seeking pleasure that will last forever? Subconsciously you are seeking that highest abiding joy, but in a wrong way, ignorantly. The same with knowledge. None of us remains satisfied with knowledge of the finite. I often tell this story of a professor who used to walk the beach every day. He found a young boy with a little vessel, ladling out the water of the ocean. He watched him for some days, then he says to the boy, "What are you doing?" "Oh, I wish to ladle out all the water of the ocean." Aren't you also a child like that? You are trying to gain infinite knowledge by knowing the finite. But infinite knowledge is in the Infinite! Seek God! Know the Self!

In the Upanishads it is asked, what is that truth knowing which everything is known, just as by knowing a piece of gold, we know everything that is made of gold, or just by knowing clay, we know everything that is made of clay? The answer was: "Know thy Self. Give up all vain talk."

St. John of the Cross, a Christian mystic, wrote: "The more the soul leads to created things, relying on its own strength by habit and inclination, the less it is disposed for this union, because it does not completely resign itself into the hands of God that he may transform it supernaturally." Does that mean that we just renounce everything and have nothing to do with this world? No. But this world has no reality. It is a dream, an illusion, like zeroes added without a one in front to give value. Similarly, this whole universe, this whole life, has meaning only if we center our life in that One that is God.

The plain truth is that we have to go into silence. All the thought-waves of the mind have to be stilled. The sun of pure consciousness is reflected in our mind – that is why there is consciousness in the mind and body – but the reflection is not perfect. With that imperfect reflection, we experience the world in waves and ripples of thought, restlessness of the mind. If we can calm the mind, overhaul it, clear up all the dirt, then the truth of the indwelling God becomes revealed to us.

Going into silence is explained beautifully by Swami Vivekananda: "Suppose a carriage is drawn down the hill by four powerful horses and you are the rider in that carriage. It is so easy to go down the hill, but suppose you restrain the horses, hold back, and with such strength that the horses want to gallop, and there is the hill rolling down, but the carriage is standing still. Consider that as silence, consider that as meditation." In other words, mental control is the highest form of activity. The senses are the horses and want to drag you down the slippery slope of the world, but you are holding the reins, and if your mind is absorbed in God and no other thought, that is silence. (175)

"Going into silence" conveys two ideas: silence is the method and also the goal. But the idea of silence is often misunderstood. I have known some so-called holy men carrying a slate with them, taking a vow of silence, and writing on the slate. Another misunderstanding is that silence is to make the mind blank, not to think of anything. Is that possible? Only in two extremes: one who has become like a jellyfish, and one who lives in blissful consciousness.

One time Sri Ramakrishna's disciples asked him, "Tell us about that experience." He said, "I will try." The moment he tried, he would go into *samadhi*; there would be silence. So, as it is said in the Upanishads: "His name is Silence."

Sri Ramakrishna used to give the illustration of a salt doll trying to find the depth of the ocean. It melted away. Narada gave the illustration of a dumb man trying to express the taste of delicious food. Shankara, pointed out, "This state of silence is a state of complete peace in which the intellect ceases to occupy itself with the unreal. In this silence, the great soul who knows and is one with Brahman enjoys unmingled bliss forever." (176)

The method is to still the passions of the mind and become one with God. Meister Eckhart realized his oneness with Godhead. He said, "Ordinary people think God is over there, and I am here, but God and I are one."

The Upanishads teach that God is to be realized here and now – not after the death of the body. There is a saying in our country that when a husking machine goes to heaven, what does it do? Husk! So in this very life we have to attain freedom from the shackles of karma and reincarnation, which is possible only by realizing the ultimate truth.

You see, we are all running after pleasures – joy and happiness – and we do not know that there is unmingled joy that knows no end only in God and nowhere else. That God is your very nature. You are That! You only have to be aware of it. (177)

From an ancient source quoted by Shankara we hear: "Silence is his name. In silence alone, he can be known, he can be realized."[14] We learned from the disciples of Ramakrishna that by merely looking at a disciple in silence, he would awaken spiritual consciousness in the disciple.

Anyone who has reached superconscious vision, or any ecstasy, will tell you that you go into a deep silence. The whole universe disappears. Often it seems, in the beginning, like we are going to be drowned in that lonely ocean, and we resist it. Then, of course, we don't go into that silence. But try again: when you go into complete silence, your whole vision changes, and you come face to face with the Reality. That is the stillness. And it is an actual experience.

Our *samskaras*, our impressions of the past, force us to go through worldly experiences, but if we keep the ideal in view, gradually we overcome them and gain self-mastery. Never, never compromise the ideal. Self-mastery, purity of heart, complete absorption in God are the ideals you must not compromise. Yes, we all have weaknesses and human desires, but if you keep the ideal in view, you will gain mastery. It will come to you suddenly one day if you try, day by day, to love God, to concentrate on him.

Never cover your weaknesses with gold leaf. Know them and you will overcome them. Gradually you will find yourself free from them and will reach that state when your mind becomes absorbed in the Atman and nothing else. According to yoga psychology, union with God is defined as control of

14. Shankara quotes this verse in his Brahma-Sutra Bhasya (III.ii.19).

the waves of the mind. The mind is lashed into waves, and purity of heart is to make it calm and clear. That is all there is to it. Not in temples and churches, not in books, can you find religion and God, but in yourself, in your own consciousness. *There* is that presence of God: this truth becomes revealed. (178)

AFTERWORD

Swami Prabhavananda contributed a great deal to the understanding of Vedanta in the West. He was a teacher with an extraordinary ability to make even the most subtle or enigmatic ideas exciting and comprehensible. He himself said, "If I truly understand, I have been given the ability to express the most abstruse philosophy in a way that others can understand." Not only did he contribute substantially to the Ramakrishna Vedanta movement itself, but he also facilitated better understanding of all the religions of the world. His intellectual scope was grand and his influence extended to the intellectual, artistic, and religious circles of his time. Among others, he had close contact with such luminaries as Aldous Huxley, Christopher Isherwood, Gerald Heard, D. T. Suzuki, Rabbi Asher Block, and even Greta Garbo and Jennifer Jones. What attracted them to him?

Swami Yogeshananda has commented: "Sometimes in attempts to explain how Vedanta has flourished in California we credit the coastal location or the physical and mental climates, or the cosmopolitan origins of the populace; more than these, surely, was the personal determination of Swami Prabhavananda and Swami Ashokananda, head of the Vedanta Society of Northern California, to put India behind them in a sense; to try to *feel* themselves Western and American, in order better to identify with us. They saw through our eyes. They accepted the students as Westerners, rooted in American values, customs and culture, destined to remain Western, and so encouraged them to feed their spiritual life from these nutritive capillaries. Their own self-adaptation replaced, through their

surpassing humility, attempts to Indianize the students."[15]
It is interesting to note that Swami Prabhavananda never
allowed anyone to call him Swamiji or Maharaj, saying that
there is only *one* Swamiji [Swami Vivekananda] and *one* Maharaj [Swami Brahmananda]. Swami Yogeshananda goes on
to say that Swami Prabhavananda favored using the English
language for chants and songs, though he retained the traditional Sanskrit vesper service.

Nancy Mayorga wrote: "For twenty-eight years I was priv-
ileged to sit at the feet of a great soul. For the first ten years I
listened, watched, argued within myself, pondered, weighed
evidence. And it was borne in upon me, little by little, inexo-
rably and inescapably, like water dripping on a stone, that
here at last was somebody absolutely consistent, absolutely
truthful, absolutely sure."[16]

Swami Yogeshananda again writes: "Sometimes one won-
dered if Swami Prabhavananda were even of this world. His
immersion in Elsewhere was of longer duration and more
evident than in most persons of spiritual eminence. It was
simply that he had practiced being absorbed in God until it
had become natural, spontaneous."[17] But again, "On most oc-
casions his clothes were quite informal. He preferred sweaters
and jackets and wore casual slacks. When I think of him at
[the Ramakrishna Monastery at] Trabuco I always picture him
this way. ... He seemed just ready to pitch in and help us with
the manual work at any moment and sometimes did."[18]

15. Swami Yogeshananda, *Six Lighted Windows: Memories of Swamis in the
West* (Atlanta: Private Imprint, 1995), p. 59.
16. Nancy Pope Mayorga, *The Hunger of the Soul: A Spiritual Diary* (Los
Angeles: Whitmarsh and Co., 1981), p. 143.
17. Yogeshananda, p. 45.
18. Yogeshananda, p. 60.

Swami Prabhavananda was charismatic, he was loving, and he had a great sense of humor. He also was a stern teacher. Perhaps, however, his authority lay in his great practicality. Once when asked if there was a Ramakrishna *loka*, or heaven, he answered, "I don't know. I'm an existentialist. I only talk about things I have experienced."

He was a man of tremendous learning, and he was a man of mystical wisdom. Most important for his students was his lion's will that encouraged and insisted on the very highest ideal, no matter what the student's level of understanding happened to be. "Never lower the ideal!" he would thunder. "Have the unswerving faith that others have known that Truth, and you also can know it!" No matter what the subject, his goal was to take the listener to the highest pinnacle of understanding and then, from that perspective, to drop him lovingly onto the updraft of spiritual aspiration. But he was tough. "Practice, practice, practice! Rome was not built in a day! This much I can say: If one struggles to find God, it is not difficult to find him – *if* one *desires* to find him. The difficulty lies in desiring." Or: "Struggle, struggle, I would say, is all the method I can give."

That authority was hard learned. Swami Prabhavananda arrived in the United States in 1923 at the age of twenty-nine, looking nineteen, to assist Swami Prakashananda in San Francisco. When first told of the assignment, he had exclaimed, "You are sending me, but what do I know that I can teach or preach?" Swami Saradananda, a direct disciple of Ramakrishna, had answered him, "That is none of your business. We shall see to that!" In later years Swami Prabhavananda would affirm, "And they have seen to it."

He felt that Swami Shivananda, another direct disciple, gave him an important lesson through the following incident: A young disciple bowed down to him, but the Swami treated him like a stranger. The boy's feelings were very hurt. "Don't you remember me?" he cried. "I am your disciple!" Swami Shivananda answered, "Whoever comes to me, I throw at the feet of the Lord and let the Lord take care of him." Swami Prabhavananda would later say to his own disciples, "I know nothing. I have only put you at the feet of Maharaj." He felt that whatever success he enjoyed in his work was all Maharaj's; that if he desired to put something forward himself, it would come to naught.

To illustrate his being only a tool, he used to relate a dream he had when he first came to America. Swami Vivekananda had put his hands on his shoulders and pressed down hard, saying, "I want to see if you can carry my weight." Earlier in Madras Maharaj had told him, "Sri Ramakrishna does his own preaching. Be the witness." Swami Prabhavananda was to say many times, "I really feel that I have done nothing. And I could not have done anything. The Lord is doing everything. Remember that the Lord does his own work, you can only be an instrument." He would also say that humility is not slavishness because you know you are nobody, but because you know that you are a child of God: when you become intimate with God, you become humble.

Looking back, the swami felt that in several instances he had been trained specifically for work in the Christian West. While he was still a brahmachari at Belur Math, the swami in San Francisco, Swami Trigunatitananda, had died and the American devotees wanted Swami Premananda, another direct disciple of Ramakrishna, to replace him. Swami Premananda instructed the future Swami Prabhavananda and another brahmachari to read the Bible and prepare to go with him. As it happened, they did not go to America, but the two young men did read the Bible. It is interesting that another connection with San Francisco dated from a still earlier time in Swami Prabhavananda's life. In his parents' home in Vishnupur, along with pictures of Ramakrishna, Maharaj, and Swamiji, there was one of the Hindu Temple of San Francisco; it had been given free to subscribers of the Ramakrishna Order's journal, *Udbodhan.*

Concerning Swami Prabhavananda's connection with Christianity, Swami Yogeshananda has written: "Swami's knowledge of Christianity was exceeded only by his sympathy for it or empathy with it. This was one of the potent factors, throughout the years, in his obtaining and retaining the attraction of his Western listeners. It contributed much to the success of Vedanta in Southern California."[19]

Swami Prabhavananda was fond of quoting what his guru, Maharaj, had said on one of the last days they spent together in Madras. He knew that Maharaj never read the Bible, yet he would quote Christ to him almost word for word. That day in Madras, as he was arranging flowers in Maharaj's room, the latter had stolen in silently and whispered in the young swami's ear, "Lovest thou me?" Only much later did he read the words of Christ in the Bible (John 21:15-17). He was also particularly struck by a comment of Maharaj on his deathbed: "Don't grieve. I shall be with you always." Those words were very reminiscent of Christ's and, to Swami Prabhavananda, Maharaj *was* Christ in his being a son of god, the spiritual son of Ramakrishna.

When he was fourteen or fifteen years old, the future Swami Prabhavananda used to visit Swami Sadananda, a disciple of Swami Vivekananda, after school. The swami told him, "Abani, you will go to America to do my Swamiji's work." One day he asked the boy to look up the words "constructive" and "destructive," and then he repeated to him three times,

---

19. Yogeshananda, p. 70.

"Be constructive, be constructive, be constructive." He would talk to Abani for hours and afterwards say, "I know you don't understand what I'm saying to you now, but I'm talking to your subconscious mind. Some day it will all bear fruit."

Before the young swami departed for America, Swami Shivananda, then President of the Order, wanted him to get used to being in the presence of women. Accordingly, he sent him to teach near Kalighat in Calcutta, where educated women of all ages would come to study the Gita and Upanishads. Because they approached the young swami all day long to ask questions about the scriptures, he became used to being in the company of women. Perhaps this, too, was training for eventually heading a Western center.

So who was this young Swami sent so young to the West? He was born Abani Ghosh on December 26, 1893 in Surmanagar, a village three miles from Vishnupur, in West Bengal. His parents were very devoted, his father, Kumud Behari Ghosh, so tenderhearted and charitable that, although he made a very good living as a lawyer, he gave to the poor what was not needed immediately for his family. There was nothing left when he died. He was extraordinarily ethical and would not represent anyone involved in falsehood. Perhaps he took his lead from his wife's father, Ishwar Sarkar, who had taken him into his home in Vishnupur as a young child after his parents had died of cholera. It was Ishwar who was the attorney representing a client in a case in which Ramakrishna was to be called as witness. Ramakrishna had come to Vishnupur and told Ishwar that if he were called, he would tell the truth. Ishwar arranged for settlement out of court.

Ishwar Sarkar's family deity was Shiva and as a child, Abani was a devotee of Shiva. He was later to think that he had been a worshiper of Lord Shiva in a past birth as well because when Maharaj sent him to Madras, he was told to offer worship at the Kapaleeshwara Shiva temple every Monday for a year, and to chant certain verses from a book which he had marked for him. The swami kept that book always.

At Calcutta City College, Abani studied general philosophy, mathematics, psychology, ethics, and theology, all from the Western perspective. In 1914, when he was twenty years old, he received his B.A. degree. He then studied at Calcutta University toward an M.A. in philosophy. During his college years he had become interested in India's independence movement, feeling that to free India was Swamiji's work. For the cause of independence he wrote leaflets, urging young men to revolt against British rule. He never carried a gun, but he did hide them in his hostel room. In December of 1914, six months into his M.A. study, his college education came to an end when he joined Belur Math. About a month later Maharaj gave him first monastic vows and named him Bhakti Chaitanya, and in 1921 he gave him sannyas, naming him Prabhavananda. The name means "he whose bliss is in the source" or "in the creator of the universe."

It was only two years later that the young swami joined Swami Prakashananda in San Francisco. After six months he was assigned to give a class on the Bhagavad Gita, which he found an easy task, but the following year he began to deliver Sunday lectures, which he laboriously wrote down in longhand. At his first lecture he was so nervous that he read it in record speed, and then his mind went blank. He said to those who had gathered, "That's all for tonight," and then walked out. Some ten minutes later, finding the temple empty, Swami Prakashananda went in search of the young swami. He comforted him, and said, "Why didn't you ask for questions?" It was perhaps this embarrassing incident that later prompted Swami Prabhavananda to advise a young swami just learning to lecture: "Decide exactly what you want to say. You have to be absorbed in the thought. An architect makes a plan of a building first. Then he begins to work. Systematically develop the subject point by point. One idea must lead to another. Your conclusion should be a logical development of the subject." He advised another: "Speak as few words as possible – and speak slowly." As for himself, by the following year he complained, "Oh! I am already tired of speaking. Week after week to speak on religion to the same audience – what a task!" But he continued to speak – for another fifty-two years.

Swami Prabhavananda spent two years in San Francisco before going to Portland. He set out with train fare and forty dollars, and he spent that for advertising and renting a lecture hall. It took ten days to make the money back. He was young and on his own and he had to be creative: he was known as "the Militant Swami." Whenever attendance dropped off, he would announce an enticing topic, such as "On Becoming Rich Through Psychology." A large crowd attended that particular lecture, and he scolded them: "You have come to hear me, who has no bank account, tell you how to get rich through psychology!" And then he spoke on Christ who did not have a place to lay his head.

In the twenties and thirties many people associated yoga and swamis with acquiring wealth, beauty and psychic powers. It was also during the time of the Great Depression and it was difficult to gain financial support from the small number of interested people. One day, quite discouraged, Swami Prabhavananda stood in front of a painting of Swamiji and asked him, "Do you want me to go back?" The next day a letter arrived from Mrs. Carrie Mead Wyckoff (known as Sister) who, with her sisters Helen Mead and Mrs. Alice Mead Hansbrough, had hosted Swami Vivekananda in their home in South Pasadena in 1899-1900 and Swami Turiyananda in July of 1900. Carrie had become Swami Turiyananda's disciple, and had been told by him, "You will have work to do, but it will be quiet work." In 1928, nearly thirty years after that remark, she met Swami Prabhavananda in San Francisco and invited him to go to Los Angeles to give three lectures. Later she joined him in Portland, and then invited him to move into her home in Hollywood. Receiving permission from Swami Shivananda to open a center in Los Angeles, he took up residence in her house in December of 1929.

But life was very difficult during the Depression, even to afford cream for their coffee. Some suppers consisted of only popcorn and milk. An English seamstress moved in and supplied what she could earn, both by sewing and by coaching actors for English accents. At the time a ten dollar lecture collection was considered doing well. For six months a black maid appeared with food and cooked meals for them, but she vanished as mysteriously as she had come. Just as mysterious, basic funds also arrived. Just before five hundred dollars was due in taxes, the swami interviewed a person who handed him some money. He didn't count it, but put it in his pocket. It was five hundred dollars exactly. Another time a tax of one hundred fifty dollars was due on a Monday, and on the day before, fifty dollars appeared in the collection plate. Then on Monday morning when the swami picked up Josephine MacLeod (Tantine) at the railway station, the first thing she said was, "Give me a pen." She wrote a check for one hundred dollars. In similar fashion, the needs of the Vedanta Society were often met and the properties acquired.

In 1938 Swami Prabhavananda decided that for the work to grow, the Vedanta Society needed a temple. As inheritance from her brother, Carrie Wyckoff had received ten thousand dollars as well as the Hollywood property. Swami thought the money would be sufficient to build a temple, but it was not. He was encouraged to borrow the remaining sum needed; however, Swami Prakashananda's words rang in his ears: "Abani, never take out a mortgage and leave it for someone else to pay off." It had taken Swami Prakashananda the remainder of his life to pay Swami Trigunatitananda's ten thousand dollar mortgage in San Francisco. So Swami Prabhavananda ordered the temple windows boarded up. Just then a new devotee, a Dr. Kolisch, came forward to supply the two thousand dollars needed to finish.

The work in Southern California continued to grow. In 1942 Spencer Kellogg deeded the original property in Santa Barbara, which has now been added to by donations from other devotees; in 1949 Gerald Heard deeded the Trabuco Monastery to the Vedanta Society; and in 1955 the house in Pasadena which Swami Vivekananda had visited was given to the society. By 1949 the work had so expanded that an assistant swami was needed, and by 1967 two assistants were necessary to keep up to the demand. Maharaj had given a teaching on service to Swami Prabhavananda in Madras: "Wherever you go, stay patiently, 'bite the earth,' and build something for me." "To bite the earth" is a Bengali expression meaning to stay at all costs; "to build something for me" meant that Maharaj wanted his disciple to establish a house for the Lord. Swami Prabhavananda observed: "You cannot establish anything unless you give your whole life to a place. It is not an easy task."

That sense of dedication was his instruction and his goal – one he practiced diligently. Not only did he adopt Western clothing and learn to move freely in Western society; he also became an American citizen in order to feel absolutely no separation from his adopted country. He was the only one of the Indian swamis to do so.

Swami Prabhavananda died on July 4th, America's Independence Day and the date of Swami Vivekananda's passing.

He had suffered a heart attack the day before. On that evening of July 3rd, he asked his nurse what time it was. When she said that it was 11:15, he responded, "No, too soon, too soon. It must be midnight." Earlier in the day monks and nuns from Santa Barbara and Trabuco had joined the rest of the monastic family in Hollywood. At 11:55 p.m. they gathered at his bedside. His shining eyes gazed far into the distance as his lips silently repeated the Lord's name. At 12:03 on the morning of July 4, 1976 he quietly slipped away.

Swami Prabhavananda (1893–1976)

So long as we feel we can do it, so long God remains hidden.

As you proceed further, you will say, I don't understand anything — until the darkness goes away and there is the light of Brahman.

I know it's hard to hear but, as I have repeated many times over the years, there is absolutely no one who is your own but the Lord.

People have a right to their pain and suffering. Don't try to remove it. Sustain and comfort.

The secret of meditation is fourfold: 1) The chosen ideal is you, yourself, no different; learn to feel that living presence, 2) patience, 3) perseverance, and 4) expectation.

If each one of us would see ourselves as the Atman, the true Self, and look at things of the world objectively, everything would pass by, and be all right.

At the moment we become completely freed from cravings and we are overpowered by the one desire for God, that very moment God becomes revealed to us.

SOURCES

1. "Renaissance of the Vedanta," Hollywood 19/06/1960, Santa Barbara 26/06/1960
2. "Sri Ramakrishna and the Religion of Tomorrow," Hollywood 23/04/1967
3. "Perennial Philosophy," Hollywood 15/06/1947
4. "Sri Ramakrishna and the Harmony of Religions," Hollywood 09/03/1969
5. "Sri Ramakrishna and the Harmony of Religions," Santa Barbara 23/03/1969
6. "God the Mother," Santa Barbara 31/10/1965
7. "God, Soul, Universe," Hollywood 31/05/1964
8. "God, Soul, Universe," Santa Barbara 07/06/1964
9. "God, Soul, Universe," Hollywood 01/02/1970
10. "Om," Hollywood 13/06/1971
11. "God the Mother," Santa Barbara 31/10/1965
12. "Divine Grace," Hollywood 21/11/1965
13. "God the Mother," Hollywood 24/10/1965
14. "God the Mother," Santa Barbara 16/11/1969
15. "The Awakening of the Kundalini," Hollywood 30/05/1943
16. "The Illumined Life and Work in the World," Hollywood 23/04/1944
17. "Supreme Goal of Life," Santa Barbara 14/09/1969
18. "The Practice of Religion," Hollywood 25/02/1962
19. "Active and Contemplative Life," Hollywood 25/03/1945
20. "The Self," Hollywood 25/02/1968
21. "The Impersonal Life," Santa Barbara 28/01/1965
22. "Thou Art That," Hollywood 18/10/1964
23. "Thou Art That," Santa Barbara 20/02/1966
24. "Thou Art That," Trabuco 20/03/1966
25. "Thou Art That," Hollywood 17/06/1972
26. "Thou Art That," Hollywood 09/10/1960
27. "The Impersonal Life," Hollywood 05/02/1961
28. "The Problem of Evil," Hollywood 19/03/1961
29. "Reincarnation," Hollywood 02/04/1961
30. "Reincarnation and Immortality," Hollywood 18/04/1965
31. "Reincarnation and Immortality," Hollywood 26/03/1967

32. "Reincarnation and Immortality," Santa Barbara 02/04/1967
33. "Reincarnation and Immortality," Santa Barbara 11/04/1971
34. "Reincarnation and Immortality," Santa Barbara 10/04/1966
35. "Reincarnation and Immortality," Hollywood 22/03/1970
36. "Reincarnation, Resurrection and Immortality," Santa Barbara 02/04/1972
37. "Peace and Holiness," Santa Barbara 28/01/1968
38. "Peace and Holiness," Hollywood 21/01/1968
39. "Peace," Hollywood 22/02/1970
40. "Peace," Santa Barbara 01/03/1970
41. "Peace," Hollywood 05/11/1961
42. "Peace," Santa Barbara 13/11/1961
43. "Saints and Miracles," Hollywood 19/05/1963
44. "What Makes a Saint," Santa Barbara 14/11/1968
45. "What Makes a Saint," Trabuco 07/11/1965
46. "Cast Out Fear," Hollywood 19/11/1944
47. "Divine Incarnation," Santa Barbara 21/06/1970
48. "What Christ Means to Me," Hollywood 26/12/1965
49. "Buddha and Buddhism," Hollywood 02/05/1965
50. "Buddha and Buddhism," Santa Barbara 09/05/1965
51. "Buddha and Buddhism," Santa Barbara 08/05/1966
52. "Buddha and His Message," Hollywood 11/05/1969
53. "Buddha and Buddhism," Hollywood 02/05/1971
54. "Buddha and Buddhism," Santa Barbara 24/05/1964
55. "Buddha and Buddhism," Hollywood 17/05/1964
56. "Buddha and Buddhism," Hollywood 28/05/1972
57. "The Eight-Fold Path of Buddhism," Santa Barbara 08/05/1960
58. "Buddha and Buddhism," Hollywood 20/05/1962
59. "Buddha and Buddhism," Hollywood 05/05/1963
60. "Buddha and Buddhism," Santa Barbara 12/05/1963
61. "Buddha and His Sermon," Santa Barbara 09/05/1971
62. "Hindu View of Christ," Hollywood 21/12/1969 and "What Christ Means to Me," Hollywood 25/12/1960, 17/12/1961
63. "What Christ Means to Me," Hollywood 27/12/1970
64. "Shankara and His Teachings," Hollywood 03/05/1970, Santa Barbara 10/05/1970
65. "Ramanuja: His Life and Teachings," Hollywood 28/11/1943
66. "Sri Chaitanya: His Life and Teachings," Hollywood 05/12/1943
67. "Totapuri: the Teacher of Sri Ramakrishna," Hollywood 12/12/1943
68. "Sri Ramakrishna," Hollywood 28/03/1965
69. "Sri Ramakrishna and His Message," Hollywood 06/03/1966

70. "Ramakrishna and His Message," Santa Barbara 06/06/1971
71. "Sri Ramakrishna and His Message," Hollywood 19/04/1970
72. "Sri Ramakrishna and His Message," Santa Barbara 21/02/1960
73. "Sri Ramakrishna," Hollywood 28/02/1960
74. "Sri Ramakrishna," Santa Barbara 12/03/1962
75. "Vivekananda and His Message," Hollywood 24/01/1965
76. "Holy Mother," Santa Barbara 12/12/1965
77. "Holy Mother," Santa Barbara 07/10/1973
78. "Holy Mother," Santa Barbara 27/10/1974
79. "Holy Mother," Hollywood 04/12/1960
80. "Vivekananda and the West," Hollywood 18/01/1970
81. "Vivekananda and His Message," Hollywood 24/01/1965
82. "Vivekananda and His Message," Santa Barbara 31/01/1965
83. "Vivekananda and His Message," Hollywood 09/01/1966
84. "The Universal Message of Vivekananda," Santa Barbara 16/01/1966
85. "Vivekananda and the West," Hollywood 10/01/1971
86. "My Master," Santa Barbara 14/02/1965
87. "My Master," Trabuco 30/01/1966
88. "My Master," Hollywood 23/01/1966
89. "My Master," Hollywood 08/02/1970
90. "My Master," Santa Barbara 15/02/1970
91. "Self-Effort and Divine Grace," Hollywood 16/11/1975
92. "My Master," Hollywood 24/01/1971
93. "My Master," Hollywood 22/01/1961
94. "My Master," Hollywood 01/02/1962
95. "Philosophy of the Upanishads," Hollywood 20/06/1965
96. "Philosophy of the Upanishads," Trabuco 12/09/1965
97. "Philosophy of the Upanishads," Santa Barbara 27/06/1965
98. "Philosophy of the Gita," Hollywood 31/10/1943
99. "Tantra," Hollywood 02/01/1955
100. "The Beatitudes," Hollywood 11/11/1962
101. "I am the Way, the Truth, and the Life," Santa Barbara 23/05/1971
102. "I am the Way, the Truth, and the Life," Hollywood 01/10/1961
103. "The Lord's Prayer," Hollywood 16/09/1962
104. "Peace I Give Unto You," Hollywood 02/01/1943
105. "Not Peace, But a Sword," Hollywood 26/03/1944
106. "Be Still and Know That I am God," Hollywood 20/09/1970
107. "A Well of Water Springing Up into Everlasting Life," Hollywood 07/04/1963
108. "Know Ye Not that Ye Are the Temples of God?" Hollywood, 09/11/1947

109. "Except a Man be Born Again," Santa Barbara 15/04/1956
110. "Vedanta in Practice," Santa Barbara 17/10/1965
111. "Householder and Monastic Life," Hollywood 13/04/1969
112. "Contemplation and Happiness," Trabuco 04/10/1964, Santa Barbara 11/10/1964
113. "Contemplation and Happiness," Hollywood 31/05/1970
114. "How to Gain Poise," Hollywood 27/05/1945
115. "How to Pray," Hollywood 17/03/1946
116. "Yoga of Meditation," Santa Barbara 23/05/1965
117. "Faith," Santa Barbara 01/01/1961
118. "Faith and Realization," Hollywood 18/04/1971
119. "Stages of Spiritual Unfoldment," Hollywood 08/12/1968
120. "Meditation," Hollywood 10/11/1968
121. "Stages of Spiritual Unfoldment," Hollywood 08/12/1968, Santa Barbara 10/11/1963
122. "Stages of Spiritual Unfoldment," Hollywood 05/06/1950
123. "Divine Grace," Hollywood 08/03/1970
124. "Self-Effort and Divine Grace," Santa Barbara 11/10/1970
125. "Divine Grace," Santa Barbara 15/03/1970
126. "Self-Effort and Divine Grace," Hollywood 11/03/1973
127. "Self-Effort and Divine Grace," Hollywood 16/04/1961
128. "Karma and Grace," Santa Barbara 12/04/1964
129. "Karma and Freedom," Hollywood 12/10/1969
130. "Karma and Freedom," Hollywood 18/10/1970
131. "The Meaning of Ritualism," Hollywood 22/10/1967
132. "The Meaning of Ritualism," Santa Barbara 29/10/1967
133. "The Meaning of Ritualism," Hollywood 23/11/1969
134. "Overcoming Obstacles in Spiritual Life," Santa Barbara 22/05/1966
135. "Overcoming Obstacles in Spiritual Life," Hollywood 28/06/1964
136. "Overcoming Obstacles in Spiritual Life," Santa Barbara 05/07/1964
137. "Overcoming Obstacles in Spiritual Life," Hollywood 17/04/1966
138. "Yoga of Meditation," Santa Barbara 23/05/1965, Hollywood 30/05/1965
139. "Yoga of Meditation," Trabuco 06/06/1965
140. "Meditation," Hollywood 10/11/1968
141. "Meditation – Why and How," Hollywood 06/09/1970
142. "Yoga of Action," Santa Barbara 13/06/1965
143. "Path of Devotion," Santa Barbara 17/01/1965
144. "Path of Devotion," Hollywood 03/1/1965
145. "Path of Devotion," Trabuco 21/03/1965
146. "Devotion," Santa Barbara 26/02/1961

147. "What is Divine Love?" Hollywood 21/09/1969
148. "The Path of Divine Love," Hollywood 01/11/1970
149. "The Path of Knowledge," Hollywood 07/03/1965
150. "The Path of Knowledge," Santa Barbara 14/03/1965
151. "The Path of Knowledge," Trabuco 04/04/1965
152. "Psychology of Yoga," Hollywood 05/06/1966
153. "Psychology of Yoga," Santa Barbara 05/10/1969
154. "Limbs of Yoga," Hollywood 07/02/1971
155. "Limbs of Yoga," Santa Barbara 14/02/1971, Hollywood 21/02/1971
156. "Pranayama," Hollywood 07/03/1948
157. "Subconscious Mind and Its Control," Hollywood 01/11/1964
158. "Mind, Its Power and Uses," Hollywood 29/11/1970
159. "Mind and Its Control," Santa Barbara 24/11/1963
160. "Mind and Its Control," Hollywood 17/11/1963
161. "Mind, Its Power and Uses," Hollywood 13/05/1973
162. "Mind, Its Power and Uses," Santa Barbara 11/06/1973
163. "Subconscious Mind and Its Control," Santa Barbara 08/11/1964
164. "Subconscious Mind and Its Control," Trabuco 27/12/1964
165. "Mysticism and Mystic Visions," Hollywood 07/12/1969
166. "Mysticism and Mystic Experiences," Hollywood 07/03/1971
167. "Mysticism and Mystic Vision," Hollywood 03/05/1964
168. "Mysticism and Mystic Visions," Santa Barbara 13/03/1966
169. "Mysticism and Mystic Visions," Hollywood 27/03/1966
170. "Mysticism – True and False," Hollywood 19/11/1967
171. "Silence," Hollywood 19/04/1964
172. "Silence," Santa Barbara 26/04/1964
173. "Silence," Hollywood 05/12/1965
174. "Silence," Santa Barbara 02/01/1966
175. "Silence," Hollywood 27/06/1971
176. "Silence," Santa Barbara 26/06/1966
177. "Silence," Santa Barbara 29/08/1971
178. "Silence," Hollywood 22/05/1960

INDEX

A

abhyasa 326

Abraham Lincoln 30

Absolute 367; unable to conceive 341

absorbed 367, 414

absorption 61, 80, 318, 347, 363, 380, 401, 433, 442, 445, 454

abstention from falsehood 403

abstention from harming others 402

abstention from theft 403

ache; together with joy 338

act 69, 414

action 63, 79, 105, 107, 326, 344, 372, 375, 423; and purity of heart 372; and worship 349; fruit of 406; giving up 347; not lost 374; reflex 345; renunciation of 351; secret of 348; selfless 67

actions 415

active; temperament 367

activity 73, 411, 420, 452

Adbhutananda 99

Advaita Vedanta 18

agnostic 90

Aham Brahmasmi 10

ahimsa 402

ajna 61

Alexander the Great; and holy man 136

Al Halaj 384

Allah; and Atman 416

ambition 168

Amriteswarananda 222

anahata 60

analysis 92

ananda 126; definition 125

anandamayakosha 87

Angelus Silesius 118

anguish 137

animal kingdom 72

animals 125

an inner light 368

annamayakosha 87

anxious; for truth 161

aphorisms 18

appearance 102, 320

Arjuna 282

artha 67, 319

Atharva Veda 47

asana 402

Ashtavakra Samhita 242

association; with holy 69

atheist 90

Atman 33, 95, 101, 334, 401, 416, 449; and Brahman 10, 11, 33, 388; and Holy Ghost 166; as Brahman 84; attributes of 347; knowledge of 81; the way and the truth 299

attachment 105, 124, 169, 309, 338, 359, 446, 450; freeing mind from 409; one of five obstacles 357; to results 374

attainment 152

attitude 448; of impersonal life 96; of religion 212; of spiritual aspirant 296

attraction 376, 379

austerity 405

authority 43, 126, 148, 155, 450; to speak with 165

avatara 89, 143, 213; according to Christian viewpoint 165; and Holy Mother 220

aversion 124, 169, 338, 359, 446; one of five obstacles 357

awaken/awakened/awakening 149, 160

awareness 312

initiation 315; two kinds 290
inner light 413
inner vision 336
instrument 307
Intellect 31
intellect 95, 125; and mind 399
intellectual; temperament 367
interest 83, 366, 392, 400; and
    prayer 332
ishvarakoti 213
ishvarakotis 264, 266
Islam 25; and Ramakrishna 204

J

jagat 135
Jan van Ruysbroek 381
japam 343, 352, 406; and path of
    action 373
jealousy; overcoming 71
Jesus 30, 37, 45, 66, 72, 108, 114, 118,
    119, 127, 132, 133, 141, 144, 159, 165,
    166, 167, 215, 244, 303, 312, 315,
    323, 324, 355, 379, 400, 414; and
    path of devotion 303; and renun-
    ciation 316
jiva 11, 85, 90
jivanmukta 14, 236
jnana 82
jnanakanda 10
jnana yoga 17, 285
Jonah and the whale 36
joy 92, 322, 390, 451, 453; acc. to
    Brahmananda 267; together with
    ache 338
Judaism 27, 107

K

Kabir 25
Kali 53, 381; and Atman 416
Kalidas 34
kama 319
Kant, Immanuel 94, 106, 397, 426,
    429
Kapila 98, 125, 321
karma 69, 100, 105, 142, 306, 338,
    373; definition 344; free from 369

karmakanda 10
karmas 317
karma yoga 17, 284, 406
Karttika 64
Kedarnath 174
Keshab Sen 207
Keshab Sharata; Chaitanya's guru
    189
king and holy man 114
kingdom of God 300
kingdom of heaven 89, 103
king who lost his memory 117
knot of ignorance 429
knots of knowledge 324, 394, 398,
    429; untying of 435
knower of Brahman 16
knowledge 85, 90, 93, 137, 156, 278,
    312, 324, 333, 337, 389, 451; acc. to
    Ramanuja 185; and love 380, 382;
    empirical or scientific 407; higher
    15; inferential 438; infinite 440;
    in path of action 373; kinds of 86;
    knots of 94, 324; lower 15; path
    of 17; spiritual 57; that nullifies
    another knowledge 387; two kinds
    of 432; unified 394
knowledge of Brahman 69, 417
knowledge of God 72
Koran 333
Krishna 25, 37, 55, 56, 104, 107, 110,
    141, 147, 166, 215, 300, 331, 347,
    350, 379, 385, 396, 400, 405, 410,
    421, 438, 444; acc. to Chaitanya
    191; and Atman 416; and Holy
    Mother 221; as myself 381; on
    himself 36
kumbhaka 408
kundalini 58, 338; in ritualistic wor-
    ship 356
kundalini yoga; in Tantra 288

L

Laotze; quote 294
law of karma 68, 81, 94, 321, 419
laziness 420
lazy/laziness 150
learning 84

S

BOOKS BY
SWAMI PRABHAVANANDA

Vedic Religion and Philosophy

Narada's Way of Divine Love

Bhagavad Gita: Song of God

Spiritual Heritage of India

The Eternal Companion

Patanjali Yoga Sutras

Srimad Bhagavatam

The Upanishads